Lecture Notes in Computer Science   7897

Commenced Publication in 1973
Founding and Former Series Editors:
Gerhard Goos, Juris Hartmanis, and Jan van Leet

Yvonne Dittrich   Margaret Burnett
Anders Mørch   David Redmiles (Eds.)

End-User Development

4th International Symposium, IS-EUD 2013
Copenhagen, Denmark, June 10-13, 2013
Proceedings

 Springer

Volume Editors

Yvonne Dittrich
IT University of Copenhagen
2300 Copenhagen, Denmark
E-mail: ydi@itu.dk

Margaret Burnett
Oregon State University
Corvallis, OR 97331-5501, USA
E-mail: burnett@eecs.oregonstate.edu

Anders Mørch
University of Oslo, InterMedia
0318 Oslo, Norway
E-mail: anders.morch@intermedia.uio.no

David Redmiles
University of California
Irvine, CA 92697-3440, USA
E-mail: redmiles@ics.uci.edu

ISSN 0302-9743   e-ISSN 1611-3349
ISBN 978-3-642-38705-0   e-ISBN 978-3-642-38706-7
DOI 10.1007/978-3-642-38706-7
Springer Heidelberg Dordrecht London New York

Library of Congress Control Number: 2013939110

CR Subject Classification (1998): D.2, H.5, K.4, D.1, K.6, K.3

LNCS Sublibrary: SL 2 – Programming and Software Engineering

Typesetting: Camera-ready by author, data conversion by Scientific Publishing Services, Chennai, India

Printed on acid-free paper

Springer is part of Springer Science+Business Media (www.springer.com)

Preface

Taking the International Symposium of End User Development to Copenhagen and Scandinavia brought it to the origin of the participatory design community. Participatory design explores techniques and methods to facilitate users to contribute toward shaping the technology they use in the contexts of use, for example, work processes. In Copenhagen and in Malmö, situated across the Øresund Strait, linked by the 8-km Øresund Bridge, Scandinavian architecture and design traditions meet with participatory design. This connection has brought forward a (sub-) community of design combining esthetic with utilitarian design. The emphasis of the co development of the social and the technical has resulted in a broadening of design beyond the workplace to embrace community-based design, which in turn leads to an opening toward heterogeneous design constituencies and users not only as participating but also developing their own technology.

At the same time, Copenhagen is a hub of programming language research and technology. Since Peter Naur's Algol 60 compiler, Copenhagen researchers have continued to improve upon the development of programming languages, domain-specific languages and tools supporting the programmers who deploy them. Naur's concept of "Programming as Theory Building" that emphasizes the need to relate the technical design to the use context opens up for rethinking the relation between development and use.

End user development relates to both traditions: The idea that users can be part of configuring, customizing, and assembling their software tools and environments is seen by many of the end user development researchers as a natural extension to participatory design. From a programming language point of view, this requires the development of languages and programming environments that can be used by non-IT professionals.

The ambition on the one side, to make programming language technologies useful for non-IT professionals and, on the other side, explore the shaping of technology by users and user communities, requires relating these two traditions. Both traditions met in the 2013 End User Development International Symposium. Whereas some contributions focus on the development of domain-specific languages, e.g., for the insurance domain, others explore community collaboration in the shaping of technology. This gives a chance to explore the complementarity and interdependency of the two perspectives on and in end user development.

Program Chairs David Redmiles and Anders Mørch were responsible for developing the program. Based on a rigorous review process, 13 full papers (45% acceptance rate) and 11 short papers (50% acceptance rate) were selected. The resulting program provided a broad overview of the current state of end user development research with interesting presentations and discussions. We would like to take this opportunity to thank the members of the Program Committee. Their high-quality reviews have provided us with a sound base for the selection of the articles.

Two keynote speakers brought their expertise to the program: Pelle Ehn and Mary Beth Rosson. Mary Beth Rosson, professor at the College of Information Sciences and Technology at the Pennsylvania State University, is well known for her research in human–computer interaction, including participatory and scenario-based design and evaluation methods, and end user development. She has been a founding member of the end user development community. Pelle Ehn is professor at the School of Arts and Communication, Malmö University, Sweden. He has for four decades shaped and contributed to the research field of participatory design and in bridging design and information technology.

Laura Beckwith and Mike Twidale arranged the doctoral consortium, introducing a number of young and promising EUD scholars to the community. It was the second time that the award in memory of Prof. Piero Mussio (University of Milan, Italy) was awarded to the PhD student presenting the most interesting and innovative research.

Barbara Baricelli and Gunnar Stevenson took care of the workshop program. Brief descriptions of the two workshops, held in parallel with the Doctoral Consortium on June 10, are included in the final part of these proceedings.

Thanks also to all those others who contributed to the success of IS-EUD 2013, including the authors, the International Program Committee, and the Steering Committee. Boris de Ruyter, Phillips Research, The Netherlands, and Andrew Begel, Microsoft Research, acted as Industrial Liaison Chairs. Special thanks to the other members of the Organizing Committee: Benjamin Koehne did a great job with handling the electronic submission system and supporting the authors when assembling the proceedings. Johan Bolmsten, World Maritime University, Malmö, and IT University of Copenhagen, and Scott Fleming, University of Memphis, did a great job as publicity co-chairs and designed and managed the website; Jeanette Eriksson, Malmö University, served as a Student Volunteer Chair and helped with the local organization; Nhi Quyen Le and Emilia Wasik of the IT University of Copenhagen, served as local chairs and took care of offering an enjoyable stay to the participants of the conference. Last but not least, we thank the IT University of Copenhagen for the resources provided to support the organization of the 4th International Symposium on EUD.

March 2013   Yvonne Dittrich
                                                    Margaret Burnett
                                                      Anders Mørch
                                                     David Redmiles

Organization

Program Committee

Michael Atwood	Drexel University, USA
Barbara Rita Barricelli	University of West London, UK
Andrew Begel	Microsoft Research, USA
Tone Bratteteig	University of Oslo, Norway
Susanne Bødker	University of Aarhus, Denmark
Maria Francesca Costabile	University of Bari, Italy
Antonella De Angeli	University of Trento, Italy
Rogerio de Paula	IBM Research, Brazil
Boris de Ruyter	Philips Research Eindhoven, The Netherlands
Clarisse de Souza	PUC-Rio, Brazil
Cleidson de Souza	Vale Institute of Technology and Federal University of Pará, Brazil
Robert Deline	Microsoft Research, USA
Paloma Díaz	Universidad Carlos III de Madrid, Spain
Daniela Fogli	Università di Brescia, Italy
Sean Goggins	Drexel University, USA
Thomas Herrmann	Ruhr-University Bochum, Germany
Letizia Jaccheri	Norwegian University of Science and Technology, Norway
Caitlin Kelleher	Washington University, USA
Thomas Latoza	University of California, Irvine, USA
Catherine Letondal	ENAC, France
Monica Maceli	Drexel University, USA
Nikolay Mehandjiev	University of Manchester, UK
Kumiyo Nakakoji	Software Research Associates Inc., Japan
Jeffrey Nichols	IBM Almaden Research Center, USA
Samuli Pekkola	Tampere University of Technology, Finland
Marian Petre	The Open University, UK
Antonio Piccinno	University of Bari, Italy
Volkmar Pipek	University of Siegen, Germany
Alexander Repenning	University of Colorado Boulder, USA
Mary Beth Rosson	Pennsylvania State University, USA
Anita Sarma	University of Nebraska, Lincoln, USA
Christopher Scaffidi	Oregon State University, USA
Gunnar Stevens	University of Siegen, Germany
Simone Stumpf	City University London, UK

Erik Trainer	University of California, Irvine, USA
Michael Twidale	University of Illinois, USA
Stefano Valtolina	Università degli Studi di Milano, Italy
Steve Voida	Cornell University, USA
Jacob Winther	Microsoft Development Center Copenhagen, Denmark
Volker Wulf	University of Siegen, Germany
Li Zhu	Early Morning, Italy

Additional Reviewers

Bortzmeyer, Stephane
Kuttal, Sandeep
Namoun, Abdallah
Neufeldt, Cornelius
Schönau, Niko
von Rekowski, Thomas

Table of Contents

Collaboration in End User Development

Part III: Short Papers

End User Development in Theory and Practice

End User Development Technology

End User Development in Technology and Society

Part IV: Doctoral Consortium

Part V: Workshops

Evolutionary Design
of a Developmental Learning Community

Mary Beth Rosson

Center for Human-Computer Interaction/College of Information Sciences and Technology,
The Pennsylvania State University,
University Park, Pennsylvania 16802 USA
mrosson@psu.edu

Abstract. In the United States, young women continue to turn away from education that would prepare them for careers in the information technology (IT) workforce. Researchers studying this phenomenon have identified a wide range of contributing factors, including the career attitudes and guidance of family members, friends and mentors; curricular approaches to teaching software development skills; and well-entrenched stereotypes of IT professionals as anti-social "geeks." I describe a research project that explored a community-oriented approach to attracting and retaining women in our own College's IT education program. Our design goal was to seed and support the evolution of a multi-leveled emergent community pursuing its own developmental trajectory, with a focus on the online community for wConnect – a system that hosts a variety of online activities and communication options. In this talk, I will chronicle the system's development as an instance of action design research, showing how a sequence of four design phases were motivated by evolving design goals that led to systems with differing design rationales. I conclude with a synthesis and discussion of lessons learned, including design implications for online tools aimed at building and supporting developmental learning communities.

Keywords: women in computing, developmental learning community, evolutionary design.

1   Introduction

In the United States, many girls entering their teenage years lose interest in computer and information sciences (CIS); in the past ten years, the number of women graduating with CIS degrees has dropped by almost 25% [4]. This trend is a challenge for university educators who are working hard to prepare a diverse and competent workforce of computing professionals. As a result, universities have been exploring a variety of curricular initiatives to attract and retain women and other under-represented minorities in their CIS programs and courses [3,5,6]. In this paper I describe a complementary approach, namely a project that initiated and studied a *developmental learning community* aimed at attracting and retaining women in CIS. In particular, I reflect on the design and evolution of a series of online spaces that were designed and built for and by the community to support its activities.

Y. Dittrich et al. (Eds.): IS-EUD 2013, LNCS 7897, pp. 1–7, 2013.

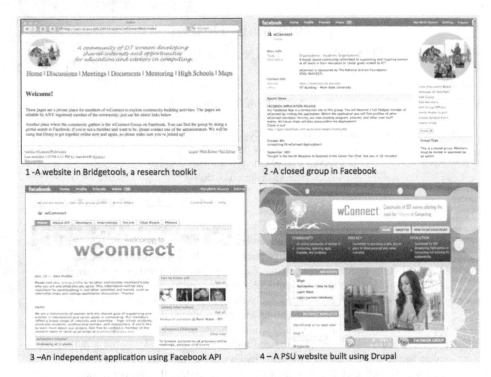

1 -A website in Bridgetools, a research toolkit

2 -A closed group in Facebook

3 –An independent application using Facebook API

4 – A PSU website built using Drupal

Fig. 1. Four different phases in the evolution of wConnect's online community system

This brief paper summarizes and integrates a number of earlier publications reporting on the *wConnect* action research project at varying points in its development (Figure 1). Some of these reports have emphasized the activities that the emerging community organized and conducted to meet their developmental goals [11]; others discussed the design and use of one or more online tools created by the community for outreach [12] or community building [9]. In this summary paper I draw from all of these, including the recent exposition of the design rationale for successive phases in wConnect's online community system [7].

2   Evolution of the wConnect Online Community System

The target audience for the wConnect community is women who vary in age, computer expertise, and level of interest and commitment to education and careers in CIS. Even before joining wConnect, they are connected implicitly through an affiliation (whether current, past or future) with our college's education programs, and one of our goals was to leverage these implicit social connections.

The core members of the community are current undergraduate students who may already be taking courses together, participating in extra-curricular and social activities, and engaging in other real world community building activities. However because the percentage of women in our programs is quite small (around 13% at the initiation of wConnect), there is no guarantee that any specific female undergraduate will enjoy face-to-face social interactions with another. Further, there are other target members of wConnect who are not co-present. These include younger females (e.g., high school students who are not even considering (yet) university education programs); alumnae who have recently completed one of our programs and are now working in a professional position; and mentors in residence or elsewhere in the workforce. Thus we assumed from the beginning that the online "space" for wConnect would be an essential defining element of the community.

With this assumption in place, we began to consider the design features of an online community space that would help us to attract and build community amongst the diverse stakeholders, but at the same time that could have a *developmental* impact on those individuals. By developmental, I mean that members regularly interact with one another to pursue the shared goal of developing their own or other members' skills, understandings and interests in CIS education or careers. With respect to the online system, this meant that that members should be able to initiate activities that would have this developmental character; secondarily, we hoped that by making the design and construction of the online system a participatory design effort, we could cause the system building activities themselves to have a developmental impact.

The first wConnect community system was a skeleton website created with an existing toolkit already in use for a variety of projects in our research lab. The website was not built by members, but was intentionally simplistic and "empty" so as to encourage and accept their contributions (see #1 in Figure 1). The supporting toolkit is quite rich and can support many different styles of collaboration, privacy management, content objects, and so on [10]. However, we soon learned that the core members of wConnect (female undergraduates) found the toolkit to be too unfamiliar and challenging to use even for simple tasks like web content creation.

The undergraduate members suggested instead that the community use Facebook, at that point an emerging but already very popular social networking site. On their own, they created a closed Facebook group and started recruiting members (#2 in the figure). This strategy led to a rapid growth in membership, but the group found themselves frustrated with the dearth of community features in Facebook; as a social networking site Facebook is focused primarily on person-to-person links and exchanges, not community relationships or interactions.

The group next explored a compromise solution – still leveraging the popularity of Facebook but through an independent application that operated in parallel with the main social networking site (#3 in the figure). In this way they hoped to leverage members' familiarity with the popular networking site, but still design their own community-centered activities (e.g., member profiles, job boards, group chats and blogs). The Facebook application was received well but ultimately did not sustain much activity – when we probed the reasons for this, we found that Facebook is experienced as a personal and highly social site, not a place for planning or discussing more "serious" topics of education or professional preparation. In fact, we noted that some advanced undergraduate members who were preparing to interview and launch their own careers had a tendency to withdraw from the community, at least partly because it was associated with Facebook.

In the fourth phase, a small group of community members used the Drupal CMS to built a site that combined features that we had observed to be important for online interaction by wConnect members. First, the site is attractive and familiar, with a look and feel that is not the same as but similar to other online spaces. Second, it is open, with relatively few constraints imposed by the API (e.g., compared to Facebook), enabling and encouraging innovation and appropriation. Third, Drupal programming can take place at multiple levels of abstraction; even members who have modest skill levels can contribute "code". Fourth, it has a rich infrastructure for role differentiation and management, so that members can operate at levels and in roles that are consonant with their technical sophistication and associated community identities. Finally, Drupal works seamlessly with our institutional authentication system, simplifying the creation of accounts and credentials, while at the same conveying that the privacy protection mechanisms of the university are in place to ensure a safe and comfortable context for interaction.

3   Design Implications for Developmental Community Systems

We positioned wConnect as an action research project, in that a primary goal was to work with a specific group of young women to support community building and developmental activities. However, the concept of developmental learning community is a general one and should hold whenever 1) a group of individuals relate to a skill or knowledge domain at different levels of expertise; and 2) they come together to develop their own and each others' expertise. Thus one question is whether and how the lessons we draw from the wConnect project have more general implications for the design of developmental learning community systems.

3.1   Open Tool Sets That Are Rich, but Extensible on Multiple Levels of Abstraction

Many designers have argued for the importance of open software infrastructures in situations where communities are emerging and growing [2]; importantly, an open system enables tool customization and appropriation [13]. The wConnect experience reinforces this general characteristic as a goal for developmental learning communities. However, for a learning community whose domain skills can be enhanced by EUD, our experience emphasizes the importance of software development at multiple levels of abstraction. The toolset should provide simple "hooks" for the most junior members that guide them gradually to more complex activities and contributions.

For example, in a Drupal-based community, a novice member can begin by creating and uploading content, move to a role as a page editor (using basic HTML), to website maintenance (understanding user tables, roles, etc.), to theme installation (open source investigation and installation), to module editing or even module creation (Php or SQL programming). When different members operate in parallel at these varying levels, there can be a fluid give-and-take that promotes personal development.

3.2   Member Profiles That Encode and Mediate Developmental Roles

In a developmental learning community, junior members receive guidance and support from their more advanced peers. In physical settings, members have many
options for expressing developmental roles and expectations (e.g., a badge at a professional meeting, an elected position in a student club), but in an online community the
tools mediate the expression of one's developmental identity and trajectory. For example, the Facebook group had no distinctions among members; middle school girls
were "equals" to university students or educators. In the third and fourth phases,
members created community profiles that included their current roles, and these were
a constant reminder of why members had joined, and how they might behave toward
others. Although we used these roles primarily to convey who might be looking for
help and who might be offering it, once the distinctions are in the system they can
also be used to manage access to different services and functionalities.

Note that one consequence of encoded developmental roles is that the roles should
evolve as members develop and acquire more expertise. In our community system we
were unable to develop automated methods for accomplishing this; role shifts were
possible only through the initiative and profile editing of individual members. Machine learning techniques for "observing" a member's online activities and interactions and drawing inferences could be very useful in this regard.

3.3   Emulation of Familiar User Interaction Styles

Finding an effective user interaction style was a constant challenge when building the
wConnect community system. On the one hand, our early experiences with Bridgetools emphasized that an interaction style that is distant from everyday activities is a
deterrent, even if the system is not "difficult" to use per se. When attraction and engagement is a critical first step in building community, the perceived cost of using a
novel system must be very low, and members must immediately feel comfortable and
rewarded. On the other hand, we also observed that moving too far toward what is
familiar and comfortable has its own costs – members felt awkward building and
interacting within a separate "professional" community that was part of a comfortable
Facebook world. In the end, we suggest that an interaction style designed primarily to
attract the most junior members might be a good general solution, with the understanding that more advanced members might choose to customize their experience.

3.4   Authenticated Access to a Private Space for Developmental Interactions

Developmental learning communities form and operate to support the personal
growth of their members; joining such a community may be a significant investment,
in that members transit through different roles and consequently behave in different
ways over time. Depending on the domain of development, some of these behaviors
and exchanges might be sensitive, perhaps seen as appropriate only within the context

of the community. For instance, wConnect members discussed strategies for negotiating salaries or managing work-life balance – these are topics that they would not choose to discuss in a public setting but that were natural and expected in their private space. For all these reasons, it is important to protect member's community identities by a robust authentication practice. This creates the corresponding cost of maintaining yet another online identity; however this cost can be reduced by using existing identities (e.g., an institution or a generic social networking service like Facebook).

3.5   Activities That Invite Relaxation and Recreation in Parallel with Development

When we began the wConnect project, we focused on activities that might help girls develop their understandings and skills in CIS – for example, video blogs with more accomplished women, forums discussing career options, or blogs from members who were adjusting to an internship or new job. As the project grew however, the team recognized that community building was not *only* about development; we found that it was important to have activities where members could just "hang out", participating in simple and familiar social behaviors like sharing photos or playing games that had nothing to do with CIS education and careers. More generally, a developmental learning community must offer a variety of options for attracting new members. Interactions aimed specifically at development are one possibility, in that some members will join simply because they want to help or be helped. But others may join simply to check out the community, and the system should always offer activities that are relatively undemanding yet rewarding for these more casual members.

4   Final Words

In this brief paper, I have outlined the exploration of a design space for an online system created to support the wConnect developmental community. I described our efforts to meet the developmental goals of this community while also attracting and engaging members at multiple levels of sophistication. In the course of balancing our multiple design goals, we evolved toward a community system that was familiar – but not too familiar – and that was open and extensible at multiple levels of abstraction. I have proposed that some characteristics we explored in wConnect might also be useful to others who are seeking to initiate and promote personal development within an online group. I hope that in the future, other researchers will join me in to applying, validating and extending these concepts.

Acknowledgements. This research was supported by the U.S. National Science Foundation (CNS-0634337). I thank my collaborators John Carroll, Elizabeth Thiry, Dejin Zhao, Hansa Sinha, Craig Ganoe, Heather Fawcett, Nicole Harshbarger, and Anastasia Ioujanina as well as many other contributing members of the wConnect community.

References

1. Carroll, J.M., Rosson, M.B., VanMetre, C.A., Kengeri, R., Kelso, J., Darshani, M.: Blacksburg Nostalgia: A Community History Archive. In: Sasse, M.A., Johnson, C. (eds.) Proceedings of Seventh IFIP Conference on Human-Computer Interaction, INTERACT 1999, Edinburgh, August 30-September 3, pp. 637–647. IOS Press/IFIP, Amsterdam (1999)
2. Fischer, G., Ostwald, J.: Seeding, Evolutionary Growth, and Reseeding: Enriching Participatory Design with Informed Participation. In: Binder, T., Gregory, J., Wagner, I. (eds.) Proceedings of the 7th Biennial Participatory Design Conference 2002, Malmo, Sweden, June 23-25, pp. 135–143. CPSR, Palo Alto (2002)
3. Guzdial, M., Tew, A.: Imagineering Inauthentic Legitimate Peripheral Participation: An Instructional Design Approach for Motivating Computing Education. In: Anderson, R., Fincher, S., Guzdial, M. (eds.) Proceedings of the 2nd International Workshop on Computing Education Research, ICER 2006, Canterbury, UK, September 9-10, pp. 51–58. ACM Press, New York (2006)
4. Leonard, E.B.: Women, Technology, and the Myth of Progress. Prentice Hall, New York (2003)
5. Margolis, J., Fisher, A.: Unlocking the Clubhouse: Women in Computing. MIT Press, Cambridge (2002)
6. McDowell, C., Werner, L., Bullock, H., Fernald, J.: The Impact of Pair Programming on Student Performance, Perception, and Persistence. In: Clarke, L., Dillon, L., Tichy, W. (eds.) Proceedings of ICSE 2003: The 25th International Conference on Software Engineering, Portland, OR, May 3-10, pp. 602–607. IEEE Computer Society, Washington, D.C. (2003)
7. Rosson, M.B., Carroll, J.M.: Developing an online community for women in computer and information sciences: A design rationale analysis. Transactions on Human-Computer Interaction (in press, 2013)
8. Rosson, M.B., Carroll, J.M., Sinha, H.: Orientation of Undergraduates Toward Careers in the Computer and Information Sciences: Gender, Self-efficacy and Social Support. ACM Transactions on Computing Education 11(3), Art. 14 (2011)
9. Rosson, M.B., Carroll, J.M., Zhao, D., Paone, T.: wConnect: A Facebook-based Developmental Learning Community to Support Women in Information Technology. In: Proceedings of Communities and Technology 2009, State College, PA, June 25-27, pp. 125–134. ACM, New York (2009)
10. Rosson, M.B., Dunlap, D., Isenhour, P., Carroll, J.M.: Teacher Bridge: Building a Community of Teacher Developers. In: Sprague, R. (ed.) Proceedings of HICSS 40: Hawaii International Conference on System Sciences, CD-ROM, Waikoloa, Big Island, HI, January 3-7, 10 pages. IEEE Computer Society, Washington, D.C. (2007)
11. Rosson, M.B., Ioujanina, A., Paone, T., Sheasley, G., Sinha, H., Ganoe, G., Carroll, J.M., Mahar, J.: A Scaffolded Introduction to Dynamic Website Development for Female High School Students. In: Fitzgerald, S., Guzdial, M., Lewandowski, G., Wolfman, S. (eds.) Proceedings of the 40th Technical Symposium on Computer Science Education, Chattanooga, TN, March 4-7, pp. 226–230. ACM Press, New York (2009)
12. Rosson, M.B., Sinha, H., Zhao, D., Carroll, J.M., Ganoe, C., Mahar, J.: wConnect: Cultivating a Landscape of Online Places for a Developmental Learning Community. Educational Technology & Society 12(4), 87–97 (2009)
13. Wulf, V., Pipek, V., Won, M.: Component-based Tailorability: Enabling Highly Flexible Software Applications. International Journal of Human-Computer Studies 66(1), 1–22 (2008)

The End of the User – The Computer as a Thing

Pelle Ehn

School of Arts and Communication, Malmö University, Sweden
pelle.ehn@mah.se

We may all agree on the importance of end users, as in end user programming, human centred design or user driven innovation. But are there theoretical limits with political implications to this anthropocentric understanding of our engagement with users, technology and the artifacts we call computers? Has the end user been patronised by contemporary progressive design and taken hostage by neo-liberal capitalism? In sociology it is becoming clear that society is not just social, but also material. The neglected objects strike back. Just think of global environmental crises. With design research it might be just the same. We know design cannot be reduced to the shaping of dead objects, as in object oriented programming, but humans are neither users living external to objects. Where sociology have had to acknowledge that society is a collective of humans and non-humans, design might have to do away with both users and objects to remain socially and politically relevant. This talk explores the consequences of replacing the object and the user with the *thing*. Etymologically the thing was originally not an objective matter, but a political assembly dealing with matters of concern. Which humans and non-humans should be invited to participate in contemporary design things? Who invites? Who is marginalised or excluded? What issues should be dealt with? Which designarly and parliamentary technologies should be invoked in prototyping futures? If the computer is to become a controversial thing, is that a well-grounded end of the user?

Y. Dittrich et al. (Eds.): IS-EUD 2013, LNCS 7897, p. 8, 2013.

"Human Crafters" Once again: Supporting Users as Designers in Continuous Co-design

Monica Maceli and Michael E. Atwood

Drexel University, College of Information Science and Technology
3141 Chestnut St, Philadelphia, Pa 19104 USA
{Monica.Maceli,Atwood}@drexel.edu

Abstract. Designers can never anticipate all future uses of their system. Meta-design theory emphasizes that systems should therefore be designed to adapt to future conditions in the hands of end users. As our technological environments increase in complexity, designers must provide the flexibility for users to shape their technologies. This paper describes a series of experiments, from a laboratory study to a digital library design exercise, exploring the use of meta-design inspired guidelines as design heuristics in an iterative, participatory design process. The meta-design inspired guidelines were found to help designers and end users shift the types of design ideas generated towards building features supporting end-user customization and modification in use. While true meta-design systems are highly complex, we intend to demonstrate that "discount" methods at design-time can help to shift design thinking towards future modifications in the hands of end users and that such methods have application in real-world contexts.

Keywords: design methods, co-design, meta-design, context, heuristics.

1 Introduction

In the past, design and use were closely entwined activities: human crafters designed tools through use and there was no distinctly separate design process [21]. People designed to meet their needs and as their needs changes, so did their designs [24]. As technology advanced, industrialization introduced a divide between the setting of design (design time) and the setting of use (use time). Design time focused on experts creating a completed design artifact, while use time was oriented towards gradual user-driven evolution and change, responsive to environment and context. This tension between what could be accomplished at design time and what unpredictable situations the system would encounter during use has been an ongoing challenge to the evolving field of HCI.

This divide, between design time and use time, has driven our approach to design and our resulting design methods and paradigms. As detailed in previous assessments of the field of HCI [e.g. 4, 6, 25] this progression has happened in waves, moving us away from the earliest days of design when we were all human crafters. These early human crafters were followed post-industrialization by a human factors approach, which eventually yielded to a human actors focus. This human actors approach, in

Y. Dittrich et al. (Eds.): IS-EUD 2013, LNCS 7897, pp. 9–24, 2013.

which users contribute to design activities at design time, continues to dominate our current design theories and methodologies. However, as will be discussed further in this section, our technologies and our attitudes towards technologies have come full circle, taking us back to the days of human crafters. We will briefly discuss each of these phases next.

When environments of use were constrained to the workplace, our early HCI methodologies could strive to match known work tasks with suitable interfaces; this human factors approach focused on the line between man and machine and the interfaces that afford interactions between the two. In the 1990s, when technology moved into the home and into more complex environments of use and practice, HCI methodologies began to take a broader view of interaction, supporting human actors who controlled the technologies used in their daily lives and participated in design-time activities [4]. Our current HCI methodologies and theories are largely oriented towards this "human actors" relationship between technology, users, and use.

However, recently developed technologies have allowed for complex and shifting contexts of use [6] as well as empowered users to design their own technological environments. Novel means of information and technology production (e.g. open source software development, mash-ups, commons-based peer production [5]) have radically changed the technological landscape. Users are again behaving as human crafters – controlling, designing, and developing not only their relationships with technology, but the very form and function of this technology.

As a result, our traditional HCI design time activities have become increasingly ill-suited to the unpredictability of real life use. As users become more empowered to design their own technology environments, HCI theory and methodology must shift as well to better support and shape these activities. In order to address these challenges, the conceptual framework of meta-design [13] suggests redirecting our attention towards bridging the differences between design time and use time through systems and techniques allowing for real-time co-design of systems. Users function as both consumers and designers of their environment and the boundaries of system design are extended from one original system to an ongoing co-design process between users and designers [e.g. 20].

1.1   The Challenge to Today's Designers

In order to fully realize the vision of meta-design which is increasingly becoming a reality, we must take our participatory design practices further. Instead of focusing on the known present, we must shift our focus to the unknown future, one in which the users of the system will drive design. Our current technologies, while supporting some end-user customization, are not true meta-design systems. Further evolution in technology tools and design methods is required to reach a future state in which end users can take on greater levels of responsibility for system modification; this future is coming, but it is not here yet.

In the present, however, there is an opportunity to shift our design methods towards the vision of meta-design, in orienting design time conversations towards future use time and beginning to have these conversations over time. As meta-design theory reinforces, future use can never be entirely anticipated, yet some work must happen at design time.

This raises the key questions: what techniques in the present can help anticipate some use time possibilities at design time? And how can designers and users communicate around the inevitable future changes that will arise over the life of the system?

In this research study, a series of guidelines aimed at orienting design time activities towards future use, as well as providing a frame for users and designers to communicate changes across the entire life of the system are explored. These guidelines are based primarily on literature and recent technological trends and were validated with real world designers and users through studies in both the laboratory and real-world contexts. In this study, we begin to address the challenge of continuous co-design and explore how such guidelines can help anticipate future changes in the hands of end users. This is a complex problem with no easy solution. However, this study begins to fill in the gap between design time and use time, moving design towards use time and towards end users designing-in-use. Design power is shifting towards the end user; as designers and as researchers we must design for such a world, one in which designing-in-use becomes increasingly commonplace.

2   Perspectives on Designing-in-Use

The challenge and necessity of designing-in-use is not new; the problem of designing for unpredictable futures has existed since design time and use time diverged. These ideas were highlighted in earlier influential works: notably Christopher Alexander's vision of an "unselfconscious culture of design" [2] where users had the skills and confidence to tailor their environment, Ivan Illich's concept of convivial technology tools [19] that would empower people to conduct creative and autonomous actions, and Henderson and Kyng's [17] vision of "designing in use" such that end users could tailor their environments to fit their emergent needs. These largely theoretical works described a fundamentally different culture of design, one which introduced complex questions around the goal of allowing and encouraging users to act as (and with) designers.

However, many open questions exist around how to practically support users during the process of designing in use. Anticipatory techniques explored what could be done at design time (often by designers alone) to endow the system with the properties to be flexible in use. Architect Stewart Brand's process of scenario-buffered design [7] encouraged users and designers to strategize around potential future uses for the building and space, yielding a final design that could respond well to multiple futures, not just the "official future" that was initially envisioned. In the field of information systems, Fischer's research has explored how systems can be user modifiable such that they might be designed in use [e.g. 15]. Early work focused on building knowledge-based design environments [10] (or DODEs) which provide a constantly evolving space in which users can create, reflect, and shape the system. Fischer's Seeding, Evolutionary Growth, and Reseeding (SER) Model [12, 16] attempted to address the changing nature of use as the system evolved. In this model, a participatory design (or co-design) process between environment developers and domain designers yielded a "seed" within which as much information as possible is designed. This seeded environment is then used by domain designers on real projects. Fischer, in more recent work [e.g. 11, 13, 15], addresses these issues and endeavors to take HCI beyond the limitations of participatory design methods and towards a future of meta-design systems. Meta-design describes a future state of co-design consisting of open systems that evolve during use, with design activities redistributed across time and levels of interaction with the environment.

The idea of co-design has gained momentum in participatory design practices wherein users and designers work together to envision future environments of use, in a variety of contexts (e.g. designing for children, people with disabilities, workers in companies, etc. [23]). Indeed, co-design has become increasingly desirable as the role of "user" and "designer" and use time and design time become blurred. However, a future of continuous co-design necessitates a change in "how we design, what we design, and who designs" [26]. Although participatory design methods and practices have existed for decades and their contributions have been critically assessed over time [e.g. 26, 27], practical co-design techniques that can be applied continuously throughout the life of the system remain a complex challenge. One approach to this problem, explored by Costabile et al. [9], are software environments called Software Shaping Workshops (SSWs); these environments allow end-user domain experts to design their environments using a high-level visual language [e.g. 9]. The SSW methodology has yielded the Hive-Mind Space (HMS) model which describes multiple levels of participation and design activities [30]. The HMS model has been applied in systems such as MikiWiki which empowers end users to customize the system during use [e.g. 30].

In further exploration of these challenges, recent work by Fischer and Hermann [15] has identified the following key guidelines for the meta-design of socio-technical systems: provide building blocks, under-design for emergent behavior, establish cultures of participation, share control, promote mutual learning and the support of knowledge exchange, and structure communication to support reflection on practice. A key principle for the meta-design of socio-technical systems, included in this series of guidelines, is to provide building blocks for the eventual end users of the system to "freely combine, customize, and improve these components or ask others to do so" [15]. This principle offers a natural connection to practical meta-design methods that can bridge the gap between theory and practice in this area.

2.1   Guidelines for Designing-in-Use

As discussed earlier, the concept of designing-in-use is not new – in both theoretical and practical work, researchers have noted these ideas over time [e.g. 4, 6] and they are increasingly emerging in the technological behaviors and expectations of our end users [e.g. 5]. New products and technologies are showing these trends as well (e.g. open source systems, mobile app development, customizable tools, personalization, etc.) In the following guidelines, we seek to consolidate and build on these ideas such that they can be applied to practical design activities. Our highly complex environments of use, consisting of rapidly evolving technologies and new means of information production, require a new focus for design activities.

Designing-in-use supports users acting as designers, as well as systems that must continuously evolve to conform to future, unpredictable needs. It requires design time thought to be focused away from immediate needs and towards common emergent behaviors that users engage in over time. These behaviors center around: connecting – to people with similar interests or needs, having conversations – in real-time across space and time, combining – the system with other tools and systems they use, getting up to speed quickly – so undue time is not spent learning the system, and tailoring and adapting – such that the system is molded to their personal needs. These behaviors originate from our growing understanding of real world environments of use, informed both by theory and practice, and the many perspectives and complexities of this use time. Looking at how interactive systems are currently used suggests that these behaviors are already beginning to emerge. We suggest the series of guidelines that follow (summarized in Table 1, below) – aimed at orienting design time activities towards future use, as well as providing a frame for users and designers to communicate changes across the entire life of the system.

Table 1. Guidelines for Designing in Use

People like to use systems where they can:

1. **Connect** with other people with similar needs and interests, both nearby and far away.
2. **Reach out** and converse with other people in real-time, while they are using the system.
3. **Combine** it with other tools and systems they use regularly.
4. **Begin using it quickly**, without a lot of help or instruction.
5. **Adapt** it to their personalized needs.

These guidelines are derived from consolidating the broad literature on participatory co-design and technological and social trends. The rationale behind the inclusion of each guideline is described briefly below:

Guideline 1. *Connect with other people with similar needs and interests, both nearby and far away.*

John Thackara's [29] series of design frameworks for complex worlds emphasizes the increasing importance of systems that allow people to connect and communicate both locally and across the boundaries of time and space. This guideline intends to encourage these possibilities by focusing designers on how users can use the system to connect to similar people, and how they might attempt to extend the system.

Guideline 2. *Reach out and converse with other people in real-time, while they are using the system.*

Research prior to meta-design has explored modifiable systems that allow for reflective use-time conversations to occur, between designers and users [e.g. 10]. This guideline seeks to emphasize how users can have live experiences and conversation with other people within, or around, the system. This may be with other users, with designers, or with knowledgeable users acting as designers. And, more generally, people use their social networks to accomplish their goals and answer questions, even if it means ignoring "formal" channels [e.g. 28].

Guideline 3. *Combine it with other tools and systems they use regularly.*

The new (or redesigned) system may be only one of several tools and systems they use on a daily basis or even at the same time. Designing for these complex environments is a challenge facing HCI today and many theoretical frameworks (e.g. distributed cognition [18], situated action [28]) describe the intensely combinatory and situated nature of real life use. While designers can never anticipate exactly how their system might be used, they can view it as only one piece of a larger, evolving puzzle and not assume it to be a discrete system with 100% of the user's focus. This focus, to the surrounding edge and combinatory effects, may spark new ideas [29].

Guideline 4. *Begin using it quickly, without a lot of help or instruction.*

Alexander's unselfconscious culture of design [2] requires systems users can understand relatively quickly and then contribute to confidently. This breaks down mental and physical barriers that prevent users from understanding the space or system well enough to have opinions and take actions to modify it. The goal of this design exercise is not to overload users with a multitude of features; this guideline is oriented towards envisioning ways in which novice users could begin using systems quickly and confidently, potentially becoming empowered to act as designers.

Guideline 5. *Adapt it to their personalized needs.*

Henderson and Kyng's [17] early writings on designing in use identified tailorability as essential to systems supporting users acting as designers. There are many ways in which systems can be tailorable or adaptable: the system may tailor itself to the particular individual's needs automatically or through the user's tailoring actions. Successful systems, at this stage of technological development and users expectations, will likely all require some level of personalization and tailoring. It is the intent of this guideline to bring these needs to the forefront of design discussions and decisions.

3   Research Study Design

The guidelines (Table 1) are based on literature and recent technological trends and require further validation with real world designers and users. A laboratory study was first conducted to assess the usefulness and understandability of the guidelines to both designers and end users. A subsequent design exercise was undertaken in which the guidelines were used with an existing website's design team working with end users.

3.1   Laboratory Study

In a laboratory setting, 32 participants were used in a two-factor between subjects design, exploring the main effects of participation (including end users or designers only) and the guidelines (working with or without guidelines). The participants were graduate and undergraduate students from a variety of majors, with roughly equal numbers of male and female participants. The mean age of participants was 25 years (SD = 5.5 years). Individual participants were first asked to rate their systems development and design skills on a five-point scale. Participants categorized as "users" had not taken any courses in design or had any formal training in design methodology. Participants categorized as "designers" were enrolled in information technology programs and had completed at least one design course. Participants, working in pairs of either two designers or one designer and one user, were asked to conduct ideation using the meta-design inspired guidelines. Participants were asked to design a "textbook trading website" for college students. This particular design challenge was chosen as participants could easily generate ideas for potential features but had little experience using a site with that exact functionality. They were first asked to brainstorm and identify key issues and trend that may affect their website in the future (e.g. – "The price of textbooks keeps going up and students want cheaper options"). Participants were then given the guidelines to review individually, and asked to work together to write down any design ideas for the website that were sparked by the various guidelines, as well as any ideas they felt fell outside them.

3.2   Design Exercise – The ipl2

In order to explore the use of the guidelines in a real world context a design exercise was then undertaken involving the ipl2. The ipl2 is a digital public library, hosted by the iSchool at Drexel University, and continuously developed by faculty and students at a consortium of colleges and universities with information science programs [1]. The participants in the design exercise consisted of two ipl2 designers, one ipl2 designer/developer, and two end users. All participants had worked on the ipl2 for a minimum of 6 months. The design exercise participants met in two iterative sessions to conduct ideation using the meta-design inspired guidelines, in a similar design process as in the laboratory study. Additionally, the end user participants maintained diaries recording their design suggestions while they used the website in the context of their daily lives. The diaries were kept over the course of the several weeks spanning the two design sessions.

4   Results

4.1   Laboratory Study

In the laboratory study, working with 16 groups (32 participants in total, as detailed in section 3.1 above), the dependent variables collected included the number of ideas generated, the time spent talking by each participant, and the quality of the ideas generated, as assessed by design experts after the session on a 7-point scale. Quality rating means were slightly higher in the groups without guidelines, however, neither factor (guidelines or participation) was found to be statistically significantly different in a univariate analysis of variance for any of the dependent variables collected ($p >$ .05). There was a strong positive correlation between the overall quality rating of design ideas and the number of words written by participants (r=.856, n=16, p < .001). The ideas were then explored in more depth, using inductive qualitative analysis to code text and identify themes from the idea data [22], in order to understand the semantic differences between the treatment groups. Although many ideas were common to all treatments (e.g. user profiles, book reviews), several themes emerged as being more common to one or another treatment group. The emerging themes were rated by the researcher across a the key principle of customizable building blocks for meta-design as described by Fischer and Hermann [15].

Table 2. Themes and frequencies of design ideas, grouped by level of customization

	Theme	Guidelines	No-Guidelines
High Customization	Finding/searching	19	7
(Functional Changes)	Localization	5	7
	Personalization	21	12
	Real-time communication	6	6
	Recommendations	8	5
	Social networking	10	7
	Total	*69*	*44*
Medium	Course content	0	6
Customization	Digital materials	8	5
(Display Changes)	Helping users	6	0
	Layout & design	11	1
	Mobile access	5	4
	Personal cataloging	1	0
	Reputation/trust	10	8
	Total	*41*	*24*
Low Customization	Accessing site	2	0
(Fixed Features)	Book metadata	16	27
	Marketplace rules	1	17
	Purchasing tools & options	7	16
	Technical details	2	4
	Total	*28*	*64*

In general, ideas characterized as low customization referred to fixed features with *little to no user contribution or customization*. Medium customization ideas typically allowed for users to *contribute content or customize on a content or display basis*. High customization ideas were oriented towards ways of allowing users to *customize or extend the website in order to make it functionally different* or improved in some way. The design ideas were then grouped according to their ability to support end-user customization; each theme was ranked high (e.g. *"Personalization"*), medium (e.g. *"Mobile access"*), or low customization (e.g. *"Book metadata"*). Table 2, above, shows the grouping of themes into high, medium, and low customization.

Table 3. Ability of idea to facilitate "combination, customization, and improvement of system components" [15]

Treatment Group	Low Ability	Medium Ability	High Ability	Total Ideas
With Guidelines	28 (20%)	41 (29%)	69 (50%)	138
W/o Guidelines	64 (48%)	24 (18%)	44 (33%)	132

The overall distribution of ideas across the treatments working with and without guidelines was found to be statistically significantly different ($X^2(2, N=270) = 23.94$, p <.001), with a higher than expected number of ideas relating to high/medium customization in the groups working with the guidelines (Table 3 above). Furthermore, the groups working without guidelines showed a higher than expected number of low-customization ideas. The implications of these significant differences will be explored further in the discussion section of this paper.

The different treatment groups attributed ideas across guidelines similarly with the exception of guideline #4 ("begin using it quickly"), which was more often used in the groups that included end users (Figure 2). Participants were given the option to identify ideas that did not relate to any of the guidelines (i.e. fell into an "other" category) but this was not used for any of the ideas, indicating that each idea generated related in some way to one of the guidelines.

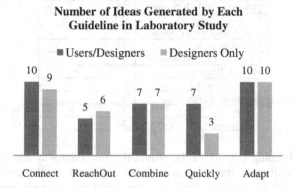

Fig. 1. Ideas attributed to each guideline by laboratory participants

4.2   ipl2 Design Exercise

After the initial laboratory to explore the usefulness and understandability of the meta-design inspired guidelines, an ipl2 design exercise was conducted. In the ipl2 design exercise, the group of designers and end-users generated 25 ideas in the first session and 21 design ideas in the second session, for a total of 46 ideas. The number of ideas generated individually in the design exercise appeared to be related to the amount of design experience of each participant. More HCI design experience generally meant more ideas generated. The raw data consisting of the text of ideas generated in the ipl2 design exercise was analyzed qualitatively in order to build an understanding of the themes addressed by participants in their proposed design ideas. Similar to the preceding laboratory study, a process of data reduction was first undertaken to code the concepts addressed in each idea, then a thematic analysis explored the patterns that emerged from the data. The thematic analysis revealed that the design ideas generated were oriented around several themes, some of which related to current features and functionality and others oriented towards future improvements or new features. The below table (Table 4) summarized the findings in the thematic analysis of the ipl2 design exercise idea data.

The themes were then evaluated against Fischer and Hermann's principle of customization in meta-design, as in the laboratory experiment. Due to the design exercise approach, there were not multiple treatments to be compared; however a few general observations were made: the majority of the themes focused on communication (e.g. asking questions, real-time communication, social networking), adapting to personal needs (e.g. finding and searching, personalization, new apps and platforms), and contributing (e.g. user-contributed content). These themes are largely dedicated to allowing opportunities for end-user modification and contribution in use. Relatively few ideas focused on fixed features, such as the layout and design of the website.

Table 4. Themes in ipl2 design exercise ideas generated

Theme	Number of Times Theme Observed
Asking Questions	15
New Apps and Platforms	15
Finding & Searching	9
User-Contributed Content	7
Personalization	7
Real-time Communication	6
News & History	6
Social Networking	4
Layout & Design	4
Games	3
Collections	3

For the diary keeping portion of the study, the raw data was analyzed in order to build an understanding of the general themes addressed by the end users in their design suggestions. In general, the ideas generated by end user participants were oriented towards more efficient, immediate use of the system in the present. The bulk of the participant suggestions involved functional changes to the system. The majority of the ideas suggested changes to features (or brand new features) that the end users would not have the technical knowledge to implement. Therefore, the ideas were presented on a high level, without including any implementation details. The ideas were all existing concepts, either improvements to existing features or common features on other websites, with no novel concepts suggested.

5   Discussion

The initial laboratory study yielded some unexpected findings. Although the different treatment groups came up with roughly the same number of ideas and spent roughly the same amount of time talking, the qualitative analysis revealed that the concepts covered in the design ideas differed. Of the design ideas generated by participants, low-customization ideas (fixed features) were the majority for the groups working without the guidelines (Table 3, above). In the treatment groups with the guidelines, more ideas fell into the medium and high-customization categories than for groups working without the guidelines. These mid-level customization ideas focus on ways to modify the system on a content or display basis, with high-level customization ideas suggesting functional changes made by end users.

As the thematic analysis revealed there were significantly more ideas involving finding/searching (e.g. *"list of school's required books per term"*) and personalization (e.g. *"connection to school library"*, *"personal profiles"*) in the groups that used the guidelines; these themes are inherently related to end user modification and adaptation of the system to fit their needs in use. The non-guidelines groups had a higher number of ideas related to the specifics of the domain and purchasing (ie – book metadata and ways of purchasing, such as payment methods) and fewer around customization. As the chi-square test revealed these differences were significant, indicating the guidelines were effective in shifting design-time thought towards future opportunities for user customization.

However, it remains an open question in meta-design systems as to how to create (and maintain) the right balance between highly modifiable and fixed elements of the system (examples in Table 5, below). A healthy and usable system must no doubt contain features from both ends of the spectrum, but too fixed may become overly rigid and highly modifiable may become unusable. As the ratio of ideas generated indicates, a system may require a great number of low-modifiable and mid-level content modifiable ideas, with only a few features allowing for higher modifiability.

Table 5. Levels of Customization in Ideas Generated by Participants

Customization Level	Description	Example
Low	Fixed features	"Book metadata"
Medium	Display or content changes	"Mobile access"
High	Functional changes	"Personalization"

These levels of end-user customization in the technology used in the experimental design activities are interesting and relevant to meta-design on several dimensions. Most importantly, this indicates that the vision of meta-design systems is beginning to be realized in common systems used on a daily basis. All groups were able to brainstorm design ideas falling into each category, this includes the groups of designers-only and also the groups of designers-and-users. This indicates that not only is end-user customization becoming commonplace, but it is also expected and desirable by users with a varying level of design and development experience. Even those with little technical knowledge can envision ways in which technology systems might be modifiable by future end-users.

Building on these findings from the laboratory study, the goal of the ipl2 design exercise was to explore the use of the meta-design inspired guidelines in an environment closer to real-world design, through using actual designers and end users of a digital library system (ipl2). The intention was to assess whether such a process might be suited to real-world design ideation. In general, the meta-design inspired guidelines seem well-suited to the ipl2 design team's ideation process. Key measures of success in this phase of the study related to the understandability of the guidelines (i.e. was the wording and intention of the guideline clear to all participants?) as well as usefulness (i.e. did participants reference each guideline and employ it in generating design ideas?). Participants were not asked to directly assess the guidelines; rather they were provided as a general framework to spark idea generation. The guidelines seemed to be generally well-understood by both designers and end-users engaged in the design activity. At no point during the two design

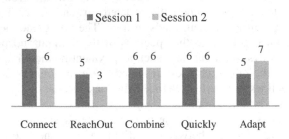

Fig. 2. ipl2 design exercise ideas assigned to guidelines

sessions or the previous laboratory experiment did any participant appear to struggle with the meaning or wording of any of the guidelines.

Both end users and designers were observed to reference the guidelines during design discussion and relate them to the ideas generated. Each guideline was used to generate between 3 and 9 design ideas in each session, with a generally equal distribution across each guideline and across the two design sessions. All of the design ideas generated were reported to relate to one or more of the five guidelines, by the participants (Figure 2, above). This indicates that the concepts embodied by the guidelines were relevant to all the design ideas generated by all the participants across all of the phases of the study.

The guidelines mapped well to design ideas both in the context of the laboratory study exercise and in a real-world design problem, in redesign of the ipl2. Furthermore, the guidelines appeared to be sufficiently flexible to frame design discussion without being explicitly grounded in specific, current technologies. Throughout the series of experiments, both in the laboratory and real-world contexts, design ideas were suggested that covered a range of technologies, both old (e.g. desktop applications) and new (e.g. cell phone barcode scanning). These promising findings indicate that the guidelines likely have the necessary flexibility and generalizability to support and encourage design ideation in a variety of real-world design domains.

In addition to the design sessions with the guidelines, the end users that participated in this ipl2 design exercise also kept diaries recording changes they would like to make to the system while they were using it in real-world design activities. The findings indicated that these design ideas from the end users tended to focus on immediate improvements to the system that would provide features to increase the efficiency of use of the ipl2; these ideas generated by end-users did not focus on extensive customization features or future possibilities.

Overall, the ipl2 design exercise with the group of designers and end users generated more ideas oriented towards customization, than did the end user diaries. The diary-keeping exercise was conducted with end users working alone, in the context of their daily work. The end users were asked to provide general suggestions and ideas for future changes to the system. These findings suggest that future-focused ideation may be most productive when working in pairs or larger groups, and when participants are asked to focus on the guidelines instead of on the system in its current state. These findings suggest that the guidelines are best employed in environments where they can frame thought and spark ideas between multiple designers and end users, and where the guidelines, and not the existing system, can be the focus of discussion. Furthermore, the ipl2 design exercise incorporated designers with significant design experience; in this context, a high percentage of the ideas generated covered themes oriented towards customization (Table 3, above). This indicates that they value of the guidelines may increase with the experience of the designer.

Finally, systems that are continuously co-designed must have end users willing and able to be active contributors. As discussed in the review of literature, this shift requires a cultural change towards Alexander's vision of an "unselfconscious culture of design" [2] in which end users feel confident and knowledgeable enough to contribute changes to their designed environments. This familiarity with the system may, in reality, already be commonplace with our current technologies, as end users acting as potential designers are likely already building a deep familiarity with the system through using it in their daily activities. In both the diary keeping study and the ipl2 design exercise including end users, lack of end user motivation was a non-issue. The participants were confident, willing contributors to their technological environments. However, it bears noting that the conversational channels between end users and designers were not open during real world use. The system, as it stands, was not able to be modified to support their needs that emerged during use. A traditional participatory design process may have explored some of these needs and built them into the system. But undoubtedly many of these needs would not be known until use time. As meta-designers, we must become better not at predicting future contexts of use, but of predicting tools that may be of use to future modifiers of the system. These tools, combined with opening channels for continuous, participatory co-design between designers and users, can empower end users to modify systems in use.

All design work is necessarily bounded by multiple real-world constraints. The role of a meta-designer cannot simply be to give future end-users the potential to design all possible environments; the environments designed by future end-users are bounded both by practical concerns and by the imaginations of the meta-designers. As a fluid and ongoing co-design process, this system evolution can become a conversation over time, and over multiple designers and users. With such a model of meta-design, the design ideas generated by meta-designers are of upmost importance in facilitating future modifications by end-users. This requires an understanding of what functions such customization tools should support and how they should be represented proportionally to the more fixed features of the system. This empirical work begins to explore a practical approach to endowing meta-design systems with features supporting future end-user customization.

5.1   Summary of Findings

Guidelines Shifted Themes in Design Ideas towards Those Facilitating End User Customization: The guidelines yield a qualitative difference in ideas in all treatment groups, including those with skilled designers. Even skilled designers may not be accustomed to thinking about future opportunities for end-user customization; the guidelines are a simple and effective approach.

No Statistically Significant Difference in Number of Ideas, Time Talking, or Quality of Design Ideas: The output of the design activities (number of ideas generated, amount of design conversation) were not better or worse, but the ideas were *qualitatively different* in the groups working with the guidelines. This indicates that even unskilled designers are good at envisioning solutions in today's technologies. There is an *expectation* of customization; successful systems must provide these tools.

End-Users Focused on Practical, Immediate Improvements: On their own, in the diary keeping exercise, end users suggested small-scale, practical improvements to the system that were beyond their technical capabilities. When working with designers and the guidelines, end users were effective contributors to design discussion and idea generation.

Meta-design Most Effective as Continuous, Co-design: The research study suggests that meta-design is not something best done with designers working alone or with end-users working alone, but rather, through a process of continuous co-design.

6   Conclusion

The framework of meta-design [13] provides a powerful vision of a future in which we are all designers of our technology; however, empirical work is needed to build a practical understanding of how meta-design might be conducted in real-world contexts and to further research agendas in the area. The series of research studies discussed in this paper have begun to explore some "discount" methods of focusing design-time thought on future, unpredictable contexts of use through meta-design inspired guidelines used in design ideation. The meta-design inspired guidelines were found to be well-understood by experimental participants, in both a laboratory and real-world context, and used to spark customization-focused design ideas oriented towards future end-user crafters. The experiments begin to suggest the appropriate techniques for meta-design activities as those including both end users and designers, engaged in guideline-framed design discussions across time.

As discussed earlier, true meta-design systems are complex and require highly modifiable technologies. While our current technologies widely in use today do not support extensive customization by end users, this future is coming. In 1991, Brown envisioned a future in which information technology is rendered invisible, becoming "a kind of generic entity, almost like clay" [8] that can be molded to fit the customer's needs. Looking forward to the immediate future, a great deal of our design will still happen at "design time", with end user participants. In our exploration of meta-design inspired guidelines, we hope to contribute a way of design-time thinking to inspire ideas oriented around future system modification in the hands of end users. A few simple heuristics, such as the series we have generated and begun to validate, can help designers and users communicate and brainstorm around future functional changes to the system. None of the guidelines are novel concepts – rather, they seek to once again ground our relationship with technology in the same fundamental needs and motivations that drive all our design actions. As Christopher Alexander claims, every person has the inherent ability to design their environment; "each one of us has, somewhere in his heart, the dream to make a living world, a universe" [3]. This vision of design can only be realized if users are acting fully as designers. As discussed earlier, we are not quite at this point with our computer-based systems. However, the findings from this research study point us in a promising direction that can move us closer to facilitating users designing in use.

From the long history of conducting participatory design, we've learned that designers, on their own, can't anticipate all the changes that might occur during use time. They do not have the users' "lived in" experiences and knowledge. Participatory design practices involve users such that this gap can be bridged and designers can have a window into the user's perspective. Designers are necessarily in the business of predicting the future in framing and exploring design problems. In this study, they did a better job than users at utilizing the future-focused guidelines to generate design ideas. The users, on their own, concentrated on the immediate modifications to the current technology, without a broader, future-focused vision. Stewart Brand noted this tendency towards end users narrowly addressing problems with "good enough" solutions – "The solutions are inelegant, incomplete, impermanent, inexpensive, just barely good enough to work…It is precisely how evolution and adaption operate in nature" [7]. As designers, we must provide the tools for users to make these small, continuous changes to the system in use.

To that end, the goal of meta-design is to make systems that are malleable enough that users can make their own customizations during user time. To move closer to this goal, we need co-design activities to encourage input from users and build an understanding of their needs. But we need guidelines, such as the ones explored in this study, to keep design activities future-focused. This was shown to be a simple but effective addition to current co-design practices. As this research study emphasizes, our technologies have evolved to begin to support the creation of personalized environments. Our co-design methodologies must evolve as well, to support today's designers and end users to work together in creating tools for future end-user crafters. The guidelines explored in this research study take us one step closer to designing information technology that performs as "clay", to be molded in use by the emergent needs of users.

References

1. About ipl2, http://www.ipl.org/div/about/
2. Alexander, C.: Notes on the synthesis of form. Harvard University Press, Cambridge (1964)
3. Alexander, C.: The Timeless Way of Building. Oxford University Press, New York (1979)
4. Bannon, L.J.: From human factors to human actors: the role of psychology and human-computer interaction studies in system design. In: Greenbaum, J., Kyng, M. (eds.) Design At Work: Cooperative Design of Computer Systems, pp. 25–44. L. Erlbaum Associates, Hillsdale (1991)
5. Benkler, Y.: The Wealth of Networks. Yale University Press, New Haven (2006)
6. Bødker, S.: When second wave HCI meets third wave challenges. In: Proceedings of the 4th Nordic Conference on Human-Computer Interaction: Changing Roles. ACM, Oslo (2006)
7. Brand, S.: How Buildings Learn. Viking, New York (1994)

8. Brown, J.S.: Research That Reinvents the Corporation. Harvard Business Review 68(1), 102 (1991)
9. Costabile, M.F., Fogli, D., Mussio, P., Piccinno, A.: End-User Development: the Software Shaping Workshop Approach. In: Lieberman, H., Paternò, F., Wulf, V. (eds.) End-User Development, pp. 183–205. Springer, Dordrecht (2006)
10. Fischer, G.: Domain-Oriented Design Environments. Automated Software Engineering 1, 177–203 (1994)
11. Fischer, G.: Meta-Design: Expanding Boundaries and Redistributing Control in Design. In: Baranauskas, C., Abascal, J., Barbosa, S.D.J. (eds.) INTERACT 2007. LNCS, vol. 4662, pp. 193–206. Springer, Heidelberg (2007)
12. Fischer, G.: Seeding, Evolutionary Growth and Reseeding: Constructing, Capturing and Evolving Knowledge in Domain-Oriented Design Environments. Automated Software Engineering 5(4), 447–464 (1998)
13. Fischer, G., Giaccardi, E.: Meta-Design: A Framework for the Future of End User Development. In: Lieberman, H., Paternò, F., Wulf, V. (eds.) End User Development, pp. 427–457. Kluwer Academic Publishers, Dordrecht (2006)
14. Fischer, G., Girgensohn, A.: End-user modifiability in design environments. In: Proc. of CHI 1990, pp. 183–192. ACM, New York (1990)
15. Fischer, G., Hermann, T.: Socio-Technical Systems - A Meta-Design Perspective. International Journal for Sociotechnology and Knowledge Development 3(1), 1–33 (2011)
16. Fischer, G., McCall, R., Ostwald, J., Reeves, B., Shipman, F.: Seeding, evolutionary growth and reseeding: supporting the incremental development of design environments. In: Olson, G.M., Malone, T.W., Smith, J.B. (eds.) Coordination Theory and Collaboration Technology, pp. 447–472. Lawrence Erlbaum Associates, Mahwah (2001)
17. Henderson, A., Kyng, M.: There's No Place Like Home: Continuing Design in Use. In: Greenbaum, J., Kyng, M. (eds.) Design At Work: Cooperative Design of Computer Systems, pp. 219–240. L. Erlbaum Associates, Hillsdale (1991)
18. Hutchins, E.: Cognition in the Wild. MIT Press, Cambridge (1995)
19. Illich, I.: Tools for Conviviality. Harper & Row Publishers, New York (1973)
20. Maceli, M., Atwood, M.E.: From Human Crafters to Human Factors to Human Actors and Back Again: Bridging the Design Time – Use Time Divide. In: Costabile, M.F., Dittrich, Y., Fischer, G., Piccinno, A. (eds.) IS-EUD 2011. LNCS, vol. 6654, pp. 76–91. Springer, Heidelberg (2011)
21. Mayall, W.H.: Principles in Design. Design Council, London (1979)
22. Miles, M.B., Huberman, A.M.: Qualitative analysis: An expanded sourcebook. Sage, Thousand Oaks (1994)
23. Muller, M.J.: Participatory design: the third space in HCI. In: Jacko, J.A., Sears, A. (eds.) The Human-Computer Interaction Handbook, pp. 1051–1086. L. Erlbaum Associates Inc., Hillsdale (2002)
24. Petroski, H.: The Evolution of Useful Things. Knopf, New York (1992)
25. Rogers, Y.: New Theoretical Approaches for Human-Computer Interaction. Annual Review of Information Science and Technology 38, 87–143 (2004)
26. Sanders, E., Stappers, P.J.: Co-creation and the new landscapes of design. CoDesign 4(1), 5–18 (2008)
27. Spinuzzi, C.: The Methodology of Participatory Design. Technical Communication 52(2), 163–174 (2005)
28. Suchman, L.: Plans and Situated Actions: The Problem of Human-Machine Communication. Cambridge University Press, Cambridge (1987)
29. Thackara, J.: In the Bubble: Designing in a Complex World. MIT Press, Cambridge (2005)
30. Zhu, L., Vaghi, I., Barricelli, B.R.: MikiWiki: A Meta Wiki Architecture and Prototype Based on the Hive-Mind Space Model. In: Costabile, M.F., Dittrich, Y., Fischer, G., Piccinno, A. (eds.) IS-EUD 2011. LNCS, vol. 6654, pp. 343–348. Springer, Heidelberg (2011)

End-User Experiences of Visual and Textual Programming Environments for Arduino

Tracey Booth and Simone Stumpf

City University London
{tracey.booth.2,simone.stumpf.1}@city.ac.uk

Abstract. Arduino is an open source electronics platform aimed at hobbyists, artists, and other people who want to make things but do not necessarily have a background in electronics or programming. We report the results of an exploratory empirical study that investigated the potential for a visual programming environment to provide benefits with respect to efficacy and user experience to end-user programmers of Arduino as an alternative to traditional text-based coding. We also investigated learning barriers that participants encountered in order to inform future programming environment design. Our study provides a first step in exploring end-user programming environments for open source electronics platforms.

Keywords: End-user programmers, Arduino, Visual Programming.

1 Introduction

Open source hardware platforms such as Arduino [23] and Raspberry Pi [32] have reinvigorated interest in hacking and tinkering to create interactive electronics-based projects. These platforms present an opportunity for end users to move beyond being mere consumers of technology to being producers of it. Arduino is based on a simple microcontroller board (Figure 1) that was designed for use in personal projects, even by people with little electronics or programming experience – artists, hobbyists, or children.

However, although easier to learn than many other programming languages, the Arduino programming language still requires some skill to master and for potential end-user programmers of Arduino this means getting to grips with coding. Recently, visual programming languages (VPLs) for Arduino have been developed and we wondered whether a visual representation might provide an easier route of entry into programming. This fits with the rise of other visual programming environments aimed, for example, at children to engage them and facilitate the learning process. Would a VPL have similar benefits for *adult* users beginning to learn to program an *electronics platform*? Similarly, some work has started to emerge to investigate learning barriers for specific end-user programming environments [5, 11, 12]. Consequently, we wondered what barriers end users encounter when programming electronics platforms.

Y. Dittrich et al. (Eds.): IS-EUD 2013, LNCS 7897, pp. 25–39, 2013.

In this paper we describe and discuss findings from an empirical study with adult novice end-user programmers of Arduino, using textual and visual programming environments. The overall aim of our research was to investigate whether a visual programming language for Arduino offers benefits over a traditional, text-based language for adult end-user programmers, specifically in terms of efficacy and user experience. We were also interested in what barriers end users currently face with a view to improving these environments.

Our study is the first of its kind (as far as we know) to investigate a VPL for Arduino. We contribute novel insights into understanding how end users interact with these programming environments in the growing area involving physical prototyping and study their benefits, costs and learning barriers. Our findings can provide the basis for improving the design of visual programming environments for the Arduino, and potentially also programming environments suitable for other related domains.

Fig. 1. Example of a prototype using an Arduino microcontroller board

2   Related Work

A visual programming language (VPL) uses a visual representation instead of, or in addition to, more traditional textual representations of program source code. Examples of VPLs are Forms/3 [4] in the spreadsheet paradigm, LabVIEW [31] for instrument control and industrial automation, as well as Scratch [18] for teaching children how to program using animations.

There have been numerous investigations to substantiate the benefits of VPLs, both generally and in certain application areas. Whitley [20] found that visual notations have potential for making information explicit and providing better organisation, which may help with program design, problem-solving and performance, even more so as the size of problems increases. However, there is still a lack of evidence that they are generally easier to learn, understand, use and share [2] and in addition it appears that the benefits of a notation are relative to a particular application area (task [8]).

One area where visual notations have been used with great success is in teaching children and young people to program. Scratch uses a building-block metaphor; programs are created by snapping graphical blocks of different colours and shapes together to form "stacks" (procedures). These blocks represent commands, datatypes, etc. and users can choose them from a palette of available blocks. The shape of the blocks determines what they can connect with. In this way syntactically correct statements and programs are encouraged: the shapes of the blocks hint as to what is expected and thus provide a guide to the user as to what is possible. There is a growing body of research into the efficacy of Scratch as a tool for learning to program. Several studies report that children and young people - both boys and girls - find Scratch engaging and fun to use, while successfully familiarising them with fundamental programming concepts without the distraction of syntax [7, 13, 14, 16].There is also evidence of continued engagement with computer science. A positive first experience with programming in an environment with a low barrier to entry, like Scratch, can sustain enthusiasm and ease transition to more sophisticated languages, such as Java and C [13, 21]. The visual programming environment used in our study, Modkit [27], was heavily influenced by Scratch and uses a similar building-block metaphor. Modkit has been used in workshops teaching children how to program Arduino [17]. Yet while Scratch has been studied to some extent, so far there are no similar studies to investigate the benefits of ModKit or other VPLs for the Arduino.

There are also some concerns about the habits Scratch engenders [15]. Following a constructivist philosophy of learning-by-making, Scratch both supports and encourages a bottom-up approach to program construction – programming by bricolage [19], rather than design. This can lead to a trial and error approach of programming with extreme decomposition and, in turn, this can make the code highly concurrent and difficult to debug. However, this type of opportunistic construction – tinkering and experimenting – is often characteristic of prototyping that involves electronic components [3, 10], so an environment explicitly designed to support this style of program creation may provide a good route into programming Arduino. Our work is the first step to investigate barriers that end users encounter in the area of programming of physical prototypes.

3   Study Design

We recruited participants for our empirical study through the MzTEK [30] and London Hackspace [25] mailing lists. We used a within-subject, think-aloud design, comprising eleven participants (8 female, 3 male, mean age 36.18), exposing each participant to both a visual and textual environment. None of the participants had previous experience of programming an Arduino or were professional programmers but they were required to have some previous programming experience (declaring and using variables and 'if statements' in at least one procedural programming language).

Participants used both a textual and visual environment for Arduino programming in our study. The textual environment was the default Arduino programming environment v1.0.1 [24] (Figure 2), which contains a text editor, a message area (for compiler messages), a text console (for text input and output during runtime), a toolbar containing frequently used commands and various menus for operation.

Fig. 2. Arduino IDE (textual programming environment)

The visual environment used was Modkit Alpha Editor (preview version) [28]. It supports multiple code representations, with both a Blocks view (Figure 3), where users manipulate coloured, graphical blocks representing code, and a Source view, which provides a textual representation of the current program(s), also editable. The Hardware view allows users to configure hardware setup visually. While there are a number of other visual programming environments for Arduino, we chose to use Modkit for this study because in terms of terminology, commands available, feature set and code constructs it matches the Arduino language and IDE most closely, thus facilitating isolation of the visual component to the programming experience.

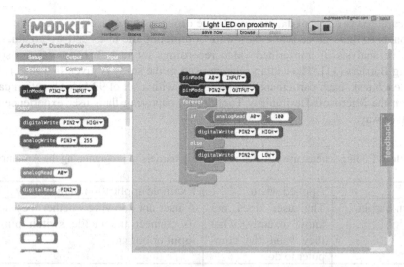

Fig. 3. Modkit Alpha Editor IDE - Blocks view (visual programming environment)

Study sessions took place in the Interaction Lab at City University London, lasting approximately 2 hours per participant. Each session was video-recorded using Morae [29], capturing all on-screen activity, verbal comments and non-verbal behaviour. Mouse-clicks, keystrokes and mouse movements (in pixels) were also logged automatically. Participants were asked to 'think aloud', to provide us with insight into their thought processes.

At the start of the session participants completed a background questionnaire and semi-structured interview regarding their previous programming experience. We then familiarized the participants with the Arduino platform and key Arduino programming concepts and constructs. The tutorial also included a printed hardcopy of a list of key commands, which the participant was able to refer to during the whole session.

For the main part of the study, participants completed two tasks (counterbalancing was used to counter any order effects of environment). In task 1 they were asked to modify an existing program, extending it to meet new requirements. The original prototype contained a single LED and a proximity sensor. The goal of the original program was to light the single LED when an object reached a specific 'closeness' to the proximity sensor. The second prototype extended upon this with the addition of four more LEDs. Each LED was associated with a specific proximity threshold and only when that threshold was reached must the LED be lit. When an object reached the 'closest' threshold, all of the LEDs must be lit. In task 2 they were asked to create a new program from the ground up. The participant was shown a prototype that contained a single LED and a tactile switch. The program must light the LED when the switch is pushed down. Hardware prototypes of the circuits required for each task were prepared in advance; participants therefore did not have to understand and construct electronic circuits. The facilitator demonstrated the desired results using the hardware prototype so that the participants were able to view the working prototype and desired result. Participants were given twenty minutes to complete each task.

We captured two sets of data to investigate efficacy and user experience. We asked participants to think-aloud while they were completing the tasks and we conducted a qualitative analysis of transcribed video recordings for task 2, based on the set of Learning Barriers [11]. The coding scheme used in the study is given in Table 1. Following each task, each participant was presented with a set of 92 word reaction cards, based on the Microsoft Desirability Toolkit [1], capturing their user experience in a qualitative way.

Table 1. Coding scheme used to identify learning barriers in programming the Arduino

Code	Applied when...	Example application in this study
Design barrier	The user does not know exactly what they want the computer to do.	A user not knowing whether they need to connect the tactile switch pin as input or output.
Selection barrier	The user knows what they want to do, but does not know which tool to use.	A user not knowing which block to use to achieve a particular goal, which operator to use in a conditional statement, or which command to use to read the value of a digital pin.
Coordination barrier	The user knows what tools to use, but not how to make them work together.	A user not knowing how to use blocks or functions in conjunction with one another. The user may know that they need to declare variables and read pins, but not how to get them to work together.
Use barrier	The user knows what tools to use, but does not know how to use them properly.	A user not knowing how to use pin-Mode to set input or output for a digital pin, or how to use the digital-Write command to write a value to one; also not knowing how to declare variables or use an if-else statement.
Understanding barrier	The user thought they know how to use something but it did not do what they expected.	A user unable to correctly interpret a compiler error or understand why something did not happen when it was supposed it, e.g. an LED does not light up when a switch is pushed.
Information barrier	The user has an idea or hypothesis about why their program did not do what they expected, but they do not know how to check.	A user not knowing how to use the serial monitor for debugging, or whether there is a code verification tool they can use.

We used two quantitative measures to evaluate potential benefits and costs. First, we used a self-efficacy questionnaire [6] which gathered participants' levels of confidence with regards to completing programming tasks in programming environments. Participants filled in this questionnaire at the start of the session prior to the participant undertaking any task and then following each of the two tasks. The initial self-efficacy questionnaire provided a baseline score against which post-task self-efficacy could be compared. Further, the NASA-TLX questionnaire [9] was completed by each participant following each task, which measured the perceived load of a task in terms of mental, physical and temporal demand, performance, effort and frustration.

4   Results

4.1   Effects on End-User Programming Efficacy

We wondered if using the Arduino VPL would have any benefits in helping end-users to program compared to the textual programming environment. We found that task completion rates were low in both environments. Only two participants out of eleven completed both tasks that were set in the study, two completed one task and seven did not complete any task. However, the four participants who completed tasks were more successful using the visual programming environment: only two tasks were completed using the textual environment whereas four tasks were completed using the visual environment (Figure 4, left).

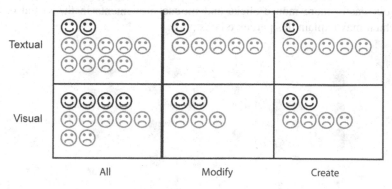

Fig. 4. Participant completion using programming environments for all tasks (left) and for create/modify task types (right)

Most of the problems, which we explore more fully in section 4.3 Learning Barriers, that seemed to prevent completion, were due to difficulties with syntax in the textual environment:

"I just can't remember what all the little coding mean [sic], you know, whether it's an exclamation mark or an equals and then the curly brackets".

One explanation for the low task completion scores in the textual environment may therefore be that participants were focusing more on syntax rather than on program design. As participant 1 reflected: *"I was too busy worrying about where it should go and not what was actually in it"*.

We also noticed that the kinds of tasks mattered: visual programming helped slightly more in the modification task than the creation task (Figure 4, right) Again, this difficulty may have been compounded by the visual programming environment, which may encourage less focus on overall design and only encourage a trial and error approach [19].

This suggests visual programming environments may provide a slight edge for successful programming over textual programming environments, if users have relatively little programming experience. However, visual programming may be most helpful if users do not have to write the program from scratch.

4.2   Effects on User Experience

In addition to contributing to actual programming efficacy, the type of programming environment may lead to *perceived* benefits which in turn can determine preference and encourage continued use. We measured the effects on participants' experience through three aspects: their perceived workload and success, their self-efficacy ratings and their reactions to the two programming environments.

Participants in our study generally rated their perceived workload as higher in the textual environment, although they rated the visual environment as more physically demanding (Figure 5; a higher score indicates either higher workload or decreased performance). Although this may seem initially perplexing we found that participants carried out vastly more mouse clicks and mouse movements in the visual environment, which may explain this perceived cost.

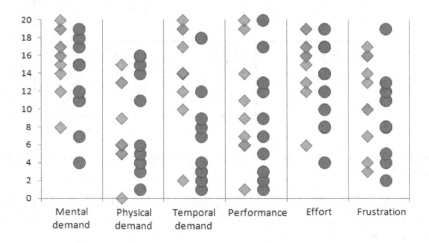

Fig. 5. Participants' TLX scores for textual (diamonds) and visual (circles) environments. The mean score was always higher for the textual environment, except relating to Physical demand.

Furthermore, as the performance scores show, in addition to being slightly more successful in actual programming efficacy, participants also perceived themselves to perform better using the visual programming environment. This effect on perceived efficacy was also reflected to some extent by participants' self-efficacy scores, which suggest that these benefits may carry over to future tasks. We observed that while self-efficacy scores improved from their initial self-assessments (mean 7.26) in both environments (mean textual 7.38, mean visual 7.90), participants rated themselves as slightly more capable of completing similar tasks after encountering the visual environment. This is summarized well by the following comment from participant 1:

"I think I would quite happily play with that one [visual] and see if I could get something going and if I got stuck...but I'm really confident I could make something work without getting stuck, and, you know, be able to build from there."

Task type mattered in participants' self-efficacy rating (Figure 6) and echoes our findings for observed efficacy. Participants felt more confident modifying a program using the visual environment than creating one. In contrast, when they employed the textual environment the reverse tended to be true; creating programs made them feel more confident than modifying existing ones. As program reuse is a common strategy for novice programmers, visual programming environments may therefore provide an initial boost to learning by increasing an individual's confidence in their ability to successfully modify existing programs.

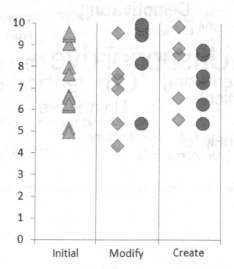

Fig. 6. Participants' self-efficacy scores initially (triangles) and after completing a task using the textual environment (diamonds) and visual environment (circles). Mean score for visual environment is higher than textual environment in the modify task but lower in the create task.

We also noted differences in the type of reactions to the environments. From the set of word reaction cards, to describe the textual environment, participants chose 62 positive words and 69 negative words. This means that they had a fairly balanced experience. Contrast this to the visual environment which received 101 positive word descriptions and only 37 negative words – participants viewed the visual programming environment much more favourably.

Looking at the meaning of the words that participants chose provides further insight about qualitative differences in user experience. Figures 7 and 8 show a visual representation of the words participants selected, their frequency (size) and type (positive vs negative). On the positive side, participants found the visual environment 'fun', 'attractive' and 'easy to learn', whereas they found the textual environment 'clean', 'familiar' and 'understandable'. This suggests that the visual environment is much more emotive, particularly for someone beginning to program, whereas the textual environment is seen as more practical, as this comment from participant 1 suggests:

"It looks the same as every other blank bit of paper programming environment. But I know that that's efficient."

On the negative side, the main complaint in the textual environment was that it was 'unsupportive'; the visual programming environment was seen as 'confusing'. Part of the challenge in the visual environment may have been due to the "puzzle-like" nature of the screen elements which lock together, mentioned by both participant 9 and 4:

"At the same time, for me, it's like a puzzle on top of a puzzle."

"You feel like you're solving a puzzle here, but yeah, I'm not sure what the solution to the puzzle is."

Fig. 7. Textual environment reactions, positive (in grey) and negative (in black)

Fig. 8. Visual environment reactions, positive (in grey) and negative (in black)

When asked in the post-session debriefing interview which of the environments they would choose to use for learning to program Arduino, the participants were overwhelmingly in favour of the visual environment, with seven of the eleven choosing it. However several participants commented that graphical and textual representations of the same program – like the Blocks view and the Source view in Modkit - might prove useful for different activities or stages of a programming project.

4.3 Learning Barriers

We wanted to explore the reasons for some of the negative user experiences reported and also how to facilitate improvements to these programming environments. We therefore looked at what learning barriers our participants faced in the creation task (recall that this was the more "difficult" task to complete). Recall that we randomised the order of programming environments over tasks; this means that six participants encountered the visual environment whereas only five used the textual environment in the creation task. On average, participants encountered 16.82 learning barriers (15.4 textual, 18 visual). Figure 9 shows the percentage of occurrences of each learning barrier in the respective environments; in the remainder of the paper we show raw counts of barriers encountered. In our analysis we will focus on four learning barriers – Use, Understanding, Coordination, and Selection – because this is where the main differences between the environments occurred.

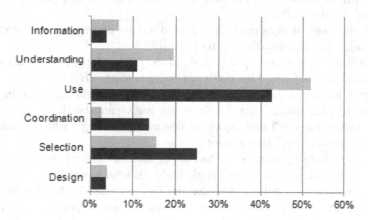

Fig. 9. Percentage of learning barriers observed during the create task for texual (grey) and visual (black) environment

Use barriers proved to be a big challenge for participants but more so in the textual environment (40/77 textual, 46/108 visual). As already mentioned in section 4.1, a lot of instances for this type of barriers were caused by a lack of familiarity with the syntax of the textual notation, for example:

"If, then, else... It's a standard, conditional thing which you use in every single programming language, but it's always different. It always appears to come with some extra thing which you don't know about." (Participant 2)

This barrier is somewhat lessened by the visual environment but still, both environments could provide users with better instructions for correct usage, possibly through context-sensitive instructions which some other IDEs already provide. (The most recent version of Modkit - Modkit Micro - now provides tooltips).

Similarly, understanding barriers encountered in the textual environment outnumbered those found in the visual environment (15/77 textual, 12/108 visual), as this quote from participant 3 demonstrates:

"So it's doing output of zero and one. Oh, ok. So now it's obvious that the problem is that [squints at the screen and shakes her head slightly] it needs some sort of delay. But that still doesn't make sense, because it shouldn't be doing anything; it should just be in an off state. So why is it flashing on and off?"

This suggests that the textual environment could provide more support to users in understanding information received at runtime or on compile, and making them aware how to check any hypothesis they may have about the reason for a compiler or runtime error, including the facilities available for testing.

Coordination barriers proved to be a more challenging aspect for participants in the visual environment than the textual environment (2/77 textual, 15/108 visual). Several of these related to the unsuccessful docking together of blocks, which some participants struggled with, suggesting that this interaction could perhaps be improved. In some cases participants were not sure whether blocks had connected, for example participant 5 remarked:

"Did it fit? Yes...No... I'm not sure if it's fitting in the loop, in the If case. It doesn't look like it does."

Some participants, such as participant 2, also did not understand why some blocks did not fit together when they thought they should:

"What I really want to do is put it there, in the forever loop, [tries to dock digitalRead again unsuccessfully...] but that's not going to happen is it?"

A frequent barrier for participants in the visual environment proved to be a selection barrier (12/77 textual, 27/108 visual), as this participant stated:

"It's a shame you can't find anywhere like a help or thingy what's... what those [the operator blocks] are." (participant 4)

This is somewhat surprising, as we had anticipated that making the blocks explicitly available might make it easier for people to decide what to use. However, it may be that in fact people felt confused because the tool provided both a proliferation of choices yet no clue as which one was the right one – again, a "puzzle on top of a puzzle". Future work could concentrate how to guide users in selecting the right blocks to use.

5   Discussion and Future Work

Our study suggests that task type, such as creation and modification, play a role in the success of using a programming environment. Participants in our study also felt more confident using the visual programming environment in the modification task. This may explain the effectiveness of using VPLs for teaching: often novices start out by reusing existing solutions and modifying them – a task for which a visual environment may be better suited. Consequently, there may be an additional "boost" to learners to continue using VPLs for this and similar tasks. Arduino draws in adults with little programming experience and how best to teach these individuals to develop physical prototypes, possibly through 'prototype repositories' which they can reuse, would be an interesting area for further study.

We have started to identify the barriers end users may encounter when programming an electronics platform, however, this work could benefit from comparative studies both between application areas (e.g. intelligent agents, spreadsheets, etc.), as well as other visual programming environments for Arduino, such as S4A (Scratch for Arduino) [33], Minibloq [26], ArduBlock [22] and Modkit. The Blocks view in Modkit, while graphical, uses similar terminology to the default Arduino IDE. Other visual environments, such as Minibloq, differ more radically in their presentation of programming constructs and their approaches to program construction. It would be useful to evaluate these empirically for learning barriers, usability and user experience.

Finally, our participants hinted at the effect of visual and textual environments on programming *activities*, stating that visual may be good to get them started but that they may want to switch. It could be that debugging in particular is hampered in VPLs: our findings show that Coordination barriers were especially more frequent in the visual environment. One possible solution is to provide *both* representations at the same time, to provide information to the end user in combination in order to overcome this learning barrier. Future work may be able to explore this solution on programming effectiveness, or how certain programming activities could be better supported in visual programming environments.

6   Conclusion

The overall objective of this project was to investigate whether a visual programming language for Arduino offers benefits over a traditional, text-based language for adult end-user programmers. We learned that:

- Visual environments seemed to help but possible more to modify programs than create them. Further studies are necessary to look into this in more detail.
- Visual environments provided a more positive user experience, alongside a reduced perceived workload and higher perceived success, both for the tasks in the study as well as future tasks. This may entice beginners to continue using these environments even in the absence of actual benefits.
- Both environments are not perfect, and may be perceived as unsupportive or confusing. We showed that this may be due to Use, Understanding, Selection and Coordination barriers. Addressing these may help to improve support for end-user programmers.

Taken together, visual programming languages appear to hold promise for adult novice end-user Arduino programmers but further work is needed to fully understand how best to support end users to achieve both actual and perceived benefits. Our study is a first step in this direction.

Acknowledgements. We thank Ed Baafi and the Modkit team, who kindly gave us access to the Modkit Alpha Editor for use in our study. Thank you also to our study participants.

References

1. Benedek, J., Miner, T.: Measuring Desirability: New methods for evaluating desirability in a usability lab setting. Presented at the Usability Professionals' Association Conference 2002, Orlando, Florida, USA (July 8, 2002)
2. Blackwell, A.F.: Metacognitive Theories of Visual Programming: What do we think we are doing? In: Proceedings of the IEEE Symposium on Visual Languages, pp. 240–246 (1996)
3. Brandt, J., et al.: Opportunistic Programming: How Rapid Ideation and Prototyping Occur in Practice. In: Proceedings of the 4th International Workshop on End-user Software Engineering, pp. 1–5. ACM, New York (2008)
4. Burnett, M., et al.: Forms/3: A First-Order Visual Language to Explore the Boundaries of the Spreadsheet Paradigm. Journal of Functional Programming 11(02), 155–206 (2001)
5. Cao, J., et al.: End-User Mashup Programming: Through the Design Lens. In: Proceedings of the 28th International Conference on Human Factors in Computing Systems, pp. 1009–1018. ACM, New York (2010)
6. Compeau, D.R., Higgins, C.A.: Computer Self-Efficacy: Development of a Measure and Initial Test. MIS Quarterly 19(2), 189–211 (1995)
7. Franklin, D., et al.: Assessment of Computer Science Learning in a Scratch-Based Outreach Program. In: Proceeding of the 44th ACM Technical Symposium on Computer Science Education, pp. 371–376. ACM, New York (2013)
8. Gilmore, D.J., Green, T.R.G.: Comprehension and Recall of Miniature Programs. International Journal of Man-Machine Studies 21(1), 31–48 (1984)
9. Hart, S.G., Staveland, L.E.: Development of NASA-TLX (Task Load Index): Results of empirical and theoretical research. In: Hancock, P.A., Meshkati, N. (eds.) Human Mental Workload, pp. 239–250. North Holland, Amsterdam (1988)
10. Hartmann, B., et al.: Hacking, Mashing, Gluing: Understanding Opportunistic Design. IEEE Pervasive Computing 7(3), 46–54 (2008)
11. Ko, A.J., et al.: Six Learning Barriers in End-User Programming Systems. In: Proceedings of the 2004 IEEE Symposium on Visual Languages - Human Centric Computing, pp. 199–206. IEEE Computer Society, Washington, DC (2004)
12. Kulesza, T., et al.: Fixing the Program My Computer Learned: Barriers for End Users, Challenges for the Machine. In: Proceedings of the 14th International Conference on Intelligent User Interfaces, pp. 187–196. ACM, New York (2009)
13. Malan, D.J., Leitner, H.H.: Scratch for Budding Computer Scientists. In: Proceedings of the 38th SIGCSE Technical Symposium on Computer Science Education, pp. 223–227. ACM, New York (2007)
14. Maloney, J.H., et al.: Programming by Choice: Urban Youth Learning Programming with Scratch. In: Proceedings of the 39th SIGCSE Technical Symposium on Computer Science Education, pp. 367–371. ACM, New York (2008)

15. Meerbaum-Salant, O., et al.: Habits of Programming in Scratch. In: Proceedings of the 16th Annual Joint Conference on Innovation and Technology in Computer Science Education, pp. 168–172. ACM, New York (2011)
16. Meerbaum-Salant, O., et al.: Learning Computer Science Concepts with Scratch. In: Proceedings of the Sixth International Workshop on Computing Education Research, pp. 69–76. ACM, New York (2010)
17. Millner, A., Baafi, E.: Modkit: Blending and Extending Approachable Platforms for Creating Computer Programs and Interactive Objects. In: Proceedings of the 10th International Conference on Interaction Design and Children, pp. 250–253. ACM, New York (2011)
18. Resnick, M., et al.: Scratch: Programming for All. Commun. ACM 52(11), 60–67 (2009)
19. Turkle, S., Papert, S.: Epistemological Pluralism and the Revaluation of the Concrete. Journal of Mathematical Behavior 11(1), 3–33 (1992)
20. Whitley, K.N.: Visual Programming Languages and the Empirical Evidence for and Against. Journal of Visual Languages & Computing 8(1), 109–142 (1997)
21. Wolz, U., et al.: Starting with Scratch in CS 1. In: Proceedings of the 40th ACM Technical Symposium on Computer Science Education, pp. 2–3. ACM, New York (2009)
22. ArduBlock, http://blog.ardublock.com/
23. Arduino, http://www.arduino.cc/
24. Download the Arduino Software, http://arduino.cc/en/Main/Software
25. London Hackspace, https://london.hackspace.org.uk/
26. Minibloq, http://blog.minibloq.org/
27. Modkit, http://www.modk.it/
28. Modkit Alpha Club, http://www.modk.it/alpha
29. Morae usability testing software, http://www.techsmith.com/morae.html
30. MzTEK: A learning community in technology and arts for women, http://www.mztek.org/
31. National Instruments LabVIEW, http://www.ni.com/labview/
32. Raspberry Pi, http://www.raspberrypi.org/
33. S4A: Scratch for Arduino, http://seaside.citilab.eu/scratch/arduino

Enabling End Users to Create, Annotate and Share Personal Information Spaces

Carmelo Ardito[1], Paolo Bottoni[2], Maria Francesca Costabile[1], Giuseppe Desolda[1], Maristella Matera[3], Antonio Piccinno[1], and Matteo Picozzi[3]

[1] Dipartimento di Informatica, Università degli Studi di Bari Aldo Moro
Via Orabona, 4 – 70125 – Bari, Italy
{carmelo.ardito,maria.costabile,giuseppe.desolda,
antonio.piccinno}@uniba.it
[2] Dipartimento di Informatica, Sapienza Università di Roma
Viale Regina Elena, 295 – 00161 – Roma
bottoni@di.uniroma1.it
[3] Dipartimento di Elettronica, Informazione e Bioingegneria, Politecnico di Milano
Piazza Leonardo da Vinci, 32 – 20134 – Milano, Italy
{matera,picozzi}@elet.polimi.it

Abstract. The revolutionary advances of Information and Communication Technology push towards the evolution of end users from passive information consumers to information producers. In many contexts, end users are increasingly willing to manipulate content they get from various resources in the Web, move it across the boundaries of their original applications, and integrate it in Personal Information Spaces (PISs), where they can tailor it to their personal needs, use it, and possibly share it with other people. This paper extends our previous work on the definition of paradigms and tools for lightweight construction of PISs, and shows how to address the need for communicating and sharing information with other stakeholders, which emerged during a field study performed in November 2012 with the previous version of our platform.

Keywords: End-User Development, Personal Information Spaces, Annotation.

1   Introduction

Recent research and technology advances are pushing end users toward a more active role in their interaction with systems, evolving from passive information consumers to information producers. Supporting this evolution requires changes in the way systems are designed and developed, and primarily demands for a new interaction paradigm that should enable end users to access content from various resources in the Web, move it across the boundaries of their original applications, and integrate it in Personal Information Spaces (PISs), where they can manipulate it to create new content, tailor it to their own personal needs, use it, and possibly share it with others [1, 2]. In this way, content becomes accessible independently of a particular application, and can be integrated in different applications depending on the specific situational needs.

Y. Dittrich et al. (Eds.): IS-EUD 2013, LNCS 7897, pp. 40–55, 2013.

This vision requires new mechanisms to let data objects (content) interact with their contexts and to leverage this flexibility to enable end users to compose and transform content as required from task situations [3]. It also demands new models and techniques for content extraction, integration and reuse, due to the content and functionality dynamics, differing from their fixed nature in traditional applications.

We are currently working on the definition of new paradigms for lightweight construction of Personal Information Spaces (PISs) by end users, i.e., integrated workspaces able to satisfy situational needs, which can be accessed through different devices. The main concepts and some preliminary results of this on-going, long-term research have been published in [4], where specific requirements in the construction of PISs have been addressed and a first prototype of a software platform has been described: it implements a new composition paradigm to allow end users, not necessarily experts of technologies, to retrieve contents from heterogeneous sources and use them to compose their PISs. According to the culture of participation [5, 6] and to End-User Development approaches [7-10], the developed platform can provide people with the means to integrate data, services and tools, playing an active role in solving their every-day problems. The platform is general and may be relevant in several application domains. In our current research, it is used in some case studies in the Cultural Heritage domain, with the aim of bringing practical value to different stakeholders in the context of visits to archaeological parks and other sites of cultural interest. We have implemented different software solutions that allow professional guides to create and use PISs in the archaeological context through different devices. While working at home or at the office, each guide can retrieve and compose, via a desktop application, the material for his/her PIS to be shown to a group of visitors during a visit of an archeological park [4]. As a further step, we have recently implemented two new solutions to support the access to and the interaction with the created PIS on large multi-touch displays and tablets. This required the development of an execution engine to deploy and run the PIS on each specific device.

A field study has been performed last November in order to evaluate the different prototypes (desktop, multi-touch display, tablet) with guides and visitors of the archeological park of Egnathia, in Southern Italy. The detailed analysis of the results will be reported in a forthcoming paper. Here, we discuss some new requirements that emerged during the study, related to the cooperative composition of the PIS and to the use of annotations on the content of the PIS, on some of its services, or on some parts of the user interface. Finally, we describe our proposal to meet these requirements.

The paper is organized as follows. Section 2 illustrates our composition paradigm and the platform for composing and using PISs. Section 3 describes the use of PISs in the cultural heritage domain and briefly illustrates the field study recently performed with real users. Section 4 discusses PIS annotation and sharing, and describes how such possibilities have been implemented in high-fidelity prototypes. Section 5 reports related work. Finally, Section 6 concludes the paper also outlining future work.

2   Composition of Personal Information Spaces by End Users

We have been working on the development of a platform implementing a new composition paradigm to allow end users, who may not be technology experts, to retrieve contents from heterogeneous sources and use them to compose PISs that satisfy their information needs in specific situations and can be ubiquitously executed on different devices. We started from a generic composition platform, which is flexible enough to be adopted in different contexts of use [11, 12], and we adapted it with respect to the requirements identified within the specific communities of users. The resulting platform allows users to access services offering heterogeneous contents, to compose such services creating their own PISs to support specific activities (e.g., to support the guide's work during the visit of an archaeological park), to store remotely the created PISs and to share PISs with others, who may access them from multiple devices.

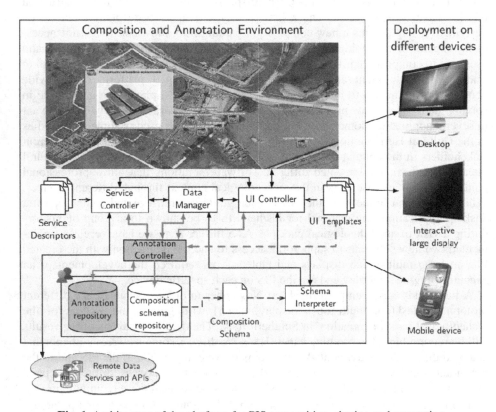

Fig. 1. Architecture of the platform for PIS composition, sharing and annotation

Fig. 1 shows the platform architecture. For the sake of brevity, we do not illustrate here all the architectural components, and focus especially on those elements for PIS execution which are involved in PIS sharing and annotation. More details on the overall architecture, and in particular on the modules supporting the creation of composition schemas, can be found in [4]. Architectural elements colored in green (in grey if printed in black and white) relate to annotation features, recently introduced and presented in this paper, which will be described in Section 4. The platform is based on a general-purpose Web mashup environment [7, 11], in which the composition of interactive spaces exploits a "lightweight" paradigm for the integration of heterogeneous resources, mainly adopting visual mechanisms through which end users, without any need to program or adopt complicated design notations, can express desiderata about the orchestration of different services. The accessible services have to be registered and described into the platform by means of *Service Descriptors*. Each descriptor specifies properties, such as the service URI and the values of parameters that the platform has to know for querying that service. Service registration is needed to prevent end users from dealing with technical properties when accessing a service. Service description is however kept very simple and is created by inputting data in visual forms. Therefore, the addition of a new resource in the platform could be performed even by non-technical users.

Based on the registered services, end users easily compose, by means of a Web composition environment and through visual mechanisms, contents, functions and visualizations, thus creating composition schemas, stored in the *Composition Schema Repository*. An execution engine, which can run on different client devices, interprets the created schema and dynamically generates the corresponding PIS. In particular, a *Model Interpreter* parses the composition schema. It then invokes the *UI Controller* that, based on the *Visual Template* selected by the user during the PIS composition, dynamically generates the PIS user interface. The UI controller also invokes the *Data Manager* module, which in turn, based on the specification in the composition schema, queries the involved remote services through the *Service Controller*. The Data Manager is also in charge of storing (and managing the access to) possible user personal data stored in local repositories. The UI controller finally manages the rendering of the retrieved data through the visual elements of the adopted Visual Template.

A relevant characteristic of our approach is the interleaving of the design and execution phases: users can define their compositions, immediately experience the effect of their composition actions (i.e., the composition schema is immediately interpreted and executed), and iteratively and interactively refine the resulting applications [7].

3   PISs in the Cultural Heritage Domain

The flexibility offered by the proposed approach for PIS construction is beneficial in several application domains. To validate our choices with respect to both their technological feasibility and their compliance with the user requirements, we developed prototypes for archaeological park guides, to allow them to flexibly create and use their PISs. In particular, we implemented different software solutions that allow professional archaeological guides to create and use PISs in the archaeological context via a desktop application and interact with their PISs during visits to an archaeological park using multi-touch displays and tablets. The multi-touch display enables a briefing phase during which the guide can explain the history of the park to visitors and show them media contents, such as photos, videos and wiki pages, associated with artifacts and areas that will be seen during the guided tour. The tablet is used by guides during the walk through the ruins to show media contents, in order to "augment" and enhance their explanation. Each media content is represented by an icon and a title placed on a Google map centered on the archeological park of

Egnathia. By tapping on the icon, a pop-up window visualizes the corresponding media in the middle of the display (this effect is shown in Fig. 1).

A field study was conducted in two different phases to assess composition and use of PISs in real conditions. The first phase aimed at assessing the effects of PIS composition with two professional tourist guides (Achille and Conny), who composed their PISs relative to the archaeological park of Egnathia using the desktop application, accessible through a PC placed in their office (Fig. 2).

Fig. 2. Achille is composing a PIS for visiting the archaeological park of Egnathia

A few days later, we experimented use and update of PISs with a large multi-touch display (46-inch) and a tablet device (7-inch) in a real context at the archaeological park of Egnathia during two guided visits, involving 28 visitors randomly divided into two groups of 14 persons. The groups were heterogeneous with respect to age (from 21 to 50 year-old, plus an 8-year old child), gender and cultural background.

Each guide first interacted with his/her PIS on the multi-touch display during a briefing phase carried out at the entrance of museum associated to the park to introduce the history of Egnathia and the ruins that they would see later in the park (Fig. 3a). During the tour of the park, the guides used tablet devices to show visitors the contents of their PISs regarding what they were looking at. The guides could also seek for new contents, if and when the opportunity arose (Fig. 3b), by dynamically formulating new queries to the services integrated in their PISs.

Six HCI experts followed every phase of the field study, taking notes of the most important episodes. At the end of the visit, three experts conducted a focus group with each group of visitors; the discussion addressed the overall visit experience. A third focus group was conducted with the two guides to discuss in more details their experience in using the systems, highlighting pros and cons.

a)   b)

Fig. 3. a) Achille using the multi-touch display during briefing to visitors; b) Conny interacting with the tablet while walking through the ruins

The detailed analysis of the field study results is still going on and will be reported in a forthcoming paper. However, during the field study, the need emerged to add annotations of various nature within the PIS, through which the user would communicate and share information with other stakeholders. For example, users expressed the need to communicate with software engineers managing the platform, to ask for modifications of the user interface structure or the introduction of new visual templates for information visualization. Users would also like to communicate with their peers (e.g., other guides), for example to ask advice about new services that can provide material they are not able to find through the services they have access to.

Another important requirement that the field study revealed concerned the sharing of PISs and annotations: guides would appreciate collaborating with their colleagues during PIS composition. They would also like to share their PISs with visitors to allow them to view and possibly add contents.

In the rest of the paper we specifically concentrate on this last requirement and describe the platform extensions we have designed to address it.

4   PIS Annotation

The availability of annotations at different levels has been identified as a key feature in the interaction with the PIS, as well as in PIS composition and update. Annotations can be used as personal memos, e.g.: *remembering* – by highlighting the most significant parts of a PIS; *thinking* – by adding one's own ideas, critical remarks, questions; and *clarifying* – by reshaping the information contained in the PIS into one's own verbal representations. Annotations are also useful for sharing information, by supporting discussions among users having access to a same information space, as well as communications among PIS stakeholders.

We now contextualize annotations within the interaction with a PIS. A PIS document is here considered as an online resource identified by a URI. A document is made up of several objects with different types of content: online services (APIs), text, hyperlinks, images, audio and video files. A digital annotation consists of two main components: *metadata* and *content* [13]. Metadata are a set of attributes: *author*, *title*, *creation date*, *modification date*, *location* (a reference to the position of the annotated object in the document, typically an XPath expression), *URL* (of the original document), *sharing level* (private, group, public), *type* of the annotation, which describes its intent, e.g. comment, clarification, query.

In this view, we consider the annotation process as the construction of an additional structure, parallel to that of an original document, on top of which personalised contents can be added with reference to the original ones. Hence, the annotation of a digital document D results in a set A of digital documents. Each document a_i in A is typically formed by textual comments on some content c_i in D, possibly associated with external references to links, services, or multimedia files. Moreover, each a_i is associated with c_i. By considering that the structure of D conforms to some Document Object Model, expressed through an XML Schema, the connection between a_i and c_i is maintained via the *location* attribute. Each a_i is then identified by a URI and becomes an annotatable document in its turn. An initial formal treatment of the notion of annotation is in [14]. Users can perform annotations at each of these three levels:

- **Service**: the online services available in the platform, for example Flickr, YouTube and Wikipedia, that the users access to retrieve content, can be annotated with comments giving suggestions to help other users to choose the most appropriate services. In this case, the location for the annotation can be a <service> tag in the PIS composition schema, specifying the way the PIS is structured, if the annotated service is already included in the annotated PIS; otherwise, it can be a <service> tag in the service registry including pointers to the descriptors of the different services registered into the platform. The content of a service annotation could also be a request to the software engineers to modify some service properties, e.g., setting new query parameters to access further content.
- **Content**: the PIS content can be annotated freely. Users can indicate fragments of texts, images or videos as objects of their annotations. The location of such annotation will be an XPath expression to navigate within the result set returned by the PIS services and identify the corresponding content fragment, or a reference to a "materialized" data item in case of annotations addressing objects managed or stored by the users in personal repositories. The content of the annotation can then be additional text as well as links to web pages or multimedia documents.
- **User interface** (UI): users can annotate parts of the PIS user interface to ask for modifications of structure, widgets, and functionalities. In this case, a special modality has to be entered, in which a glass is superimposed on the PIS UI and sketches are drawn on top of it. In this case, the value of the location attribute refers to the whole PIS document – not to a specific element composing it, but also includes cross-references to elements of the visual template adopted for the PIS rendering on a given template (e.g., a map-based template for Android tablets), which will have to be adapted in accordance with the annotated request, every time the annotated PIS is executed. The annotation content, besides the user request in textual form, incorporates an SVG description of the drawn sketch.

To manage these different levels of annotation, an attribute *level* has been added to the original model introduced in [13], and used to drive the interpretation of which object has been annotated, namely to specify if the annotation is performed on service, content or user interface. New elements to allow users to share PISs and to facilitate the management and storage of annotations have also been introduced in the system architecture for PIS composition and execution presented in [4]. Such modules, colored in green in Fig. 1, are described in the following.

The *Annotation Controller* is in charge of interpreting the user annotation actions, identifying the annotation location and establishing whether it is related to services internal to the PIS composition, to services generally available in the platform -- and not necessarily included in a specific PIS -- or to specific content items or UI elements. The Annotation Controller communicates with the different modules managing the different levels the annotations can refer to. For example, when a user annotates a photo, the Annotation Controller retrieves the photo URI from the result set managed by the Data Manager (e.g., a Flickr result set with photos and their metadata), associates with this URI the note inserted by the user, and stores the created annotation to the *Annotation Repository*. The latter is used to store all the produced annotations and their associations with the original annotated PIS documents. In order to contextualize the annotation within the specific situation of use where it is created, the Annotation Controller receives a *state representation* from the different modules. The state representation makes it possible to present the annotations during later executions of the PIS, by reconstructing the original context where the annotation was created. For example, when a UI annotation is created, a set of properties of the template the UI is based on are also stored, such as the type of the template (e.g., a map), and the notable visualization elements that characterize the template (i.e., markers showing points on a map) that can be objects of annotations. Also when the annotation refers to a service or to the service result set, the service settings and the specific query executed at the time when the annotation is created are stored.

4.1   Sharing PISs and Annotations

Besides PIS annotation, another important feature is the sharing of annotations among guides, to allow the collaboration during the PISs composition, and between guides and visitors to allow them to view and possibly add contents.

For these reasons, as highlighted by the share symbol in the architecture of Fig. 1, the Annotation Repository and the Composition Schema Repository are shareable among users. In fact, when a user creates a PIS s/he can decide whether to share it, part of it, and its annotations according to three different level:

- *Public*: PIS and annotations are shared with every users registered in the platform.
- *Specified users or user groups*: PIS and annotations are shared with specific users indicating their email or, if they are already registered in the platform, their username. Sharing can also occur within groups the PIS owner belongs to.
- *Private*: PIS and annotations are private to the owner.

A user can decide to share the PIS, but not annotations. Moreover, when a user shares a PIS or some annotations, s/he can specify the actions other users can perform: with the *view* option, invited users can view only the shared PIS or the shared annotations; with *comment*, invited users can view and put comments; with *edit*, users can view, put comments, and modify PIS contents and annotations.

4.2 Scenarios for PIS Annotation and Sharing

To demonstrate the use of the platform for composing and using PISs in the Cultural Heritage domain, in [4] a usage scenario was proposed, in which Tony, a professional guide working in several archaeological parks in Apulia, used the Web platform to create a PIS to be shown, through a large multi-touch display and a tablet, to a group of tourists during a guided visit to the Egnathia archeological park. The PIS consisted of contents (photos, videos, web pages) collected from public sources (Flickr, YouTube, Wikipedia) and linked to various points of the virtual map of the park. As discussed in the previous sections, the field study highlighted new needs in PIS management, illustrated in the following through three further scenarios extracted from the requirement analysis phase, to better understand the use of annotations for service, content and UI in the cultural heritage domain.

Service annotation. Tony is not totally satisfied with the PIS he has just composed. In fact, he would need other contents, but these cannot be retrieved through the services currently included in his composition environment. Tony, however, does not know which services, among all those offered by the platform, might respond to his need. He issues a call for help to his colleague Conny, who is more experienced in the use of the platform. Conny accesses the platform and visits the section showing the list of the services already registered in the platform. Each service in the list has associated a name, an icon and a short description. In addition, annotations (e.g., opinions, comments) provided by the whole community of platform users could be associated with it. According to Tony's requests, Conny chooses some services, specifies the reason for the choice, and gives some suggestions. She can decide to redirect the annotation exclusively to Tony, to the group of colleagues working at the same place, or to make it publicly available to any platform user. When Tony accesses the service section, he focuses his attention on the services annotated by Conny and adds some of them to his composition environment. Now Tony has new sources from which to extract contents for his PISs.

Content annotation. A group of visitors arrives at an important location in the park, namely the Trajan Way, a paved road that, at Roman times, connected the two cities of Benevento and Brindisi. A visitor, Mary, who has visited many archaeological parks, reports to Tony that in Portugal she visited the park of an ancient Roman city whose streets are paved with mosaics of very high quality. Tony is curious and would like to know more, but Mary does not remember the name of the park. The next day,

Mary is back home; she finds the brochure of the archaeological park of Conimbriga, an ancient city about 17 km south of Coimbra, Portugal. She accesses Tony's PIS, which the guide had previously shared with her, and annotates the Trajan Way by entering the name of the park of Conimbriga, the link to the Wikipedia page about Conimbriga and some pictures from her Flickr account she took during the visit to that park. Now Tony can include the new content in his PIS.

UI annotation. During the visit, Tony wants to make comparisons with other Italian archaeological parks. For example, the walls of Egnathia were impressive and inside there were routes organized on several levels. Instead, those of Monte Sannace, another archaeological park of Apulia, were much simpler. Tony searches and finds an image of the walls of Monte Sannace, but does not know where to place it on the PIS. In fact, if he put the photo on the map at the park of Monte Sannace, he would be forced to reduce the scale of the map, find Monte Sannace, centre the map on it and then zoom in again. Instead, if he puts the image of the walls of Monte Sannace on the map of Egnathia this could be confusing. He would need a PIS that shows on the screen, in addition to the map, a list of optional contents, such as contents relating to other parks, or to objects displayed in the museum. Tony draws a circle to highlight an area at the bottom right of the information space and writes a message in a text box to specify the problem to the software engineer. The software engineer will get the message and change the structure of the information space.

4.3   The Prototypes

With reference to the scenarios in the previous section, we describe how annotation and sharing functionalities have been implemented in high-fidelity prototypes of PIS user interface.

At the top of the interface a menu bar is displayed. It contains the items for interacting with the PIS (*new*, *open*, *close*, *share*, etc.), managing annotations and using other tools. Fig. 4 shows an example of service annotation. The first level of the Annotation menu allows the user to select the object to be annotated (i.e., *Service*, *Content*, *User Interface*). The second level presents the actions that can be performed on the selected object, namely *Highlight* to draw a freehand sketch, *Comment* to add a text, *Save* or *Delete* an annotation, and *Undo* the last action. The same actions can be performed on service, content and user interface objects. In Fig. 4, the user (a male) has previously performed a search using "Fornace" (Italian for "kiln") as a keyword, but he is not satisfied with the results. He would refine the search by specifying further query parameters for filtering by upload date, duration, and resolution the results returned by the video sources. Thus, he highlights the video icon on top of the search widget and writes a note for the software engineers managing the platform, asking them to improve the search features by adding further filters for querying video sources. The annotation can be saved via the icon on the top right of the comment text box.

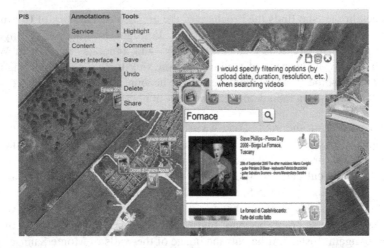

Fig. 4. Service annotation: the user asks for more flexibility in querying services

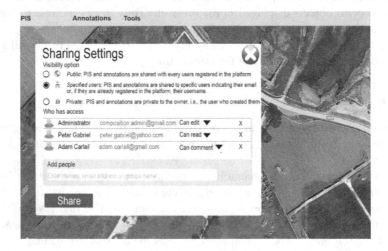

Fig. 5. User interface for defining sharing policies

Another possibility is that the user needs to modify and/or annotate the set of services currently registered into the platform, which can be displayed by selecting the "Services" item in the PIS menu. The services already available in the PIS of the user can be removed by means of the trash icon, while those registered in the platform, but not yet in the PIS, can be added using the "+" icon (see Fig. 6). The user can search for new services not available in the platform by typing keywords in the text box and, when found, possibly register them. The service annotation modality allows the user to highlight a service in the list, annotate it and share the annotation as in the previous example. For example, in Fig. 6 the user has received a note from Conny, who suggests him to add the Vimeo video service to his PIS.

Fig. 6. Service annotation: Conny, another user, suggests including the Vimeo video service

Fig. 7 shows an example of content annotation. The user, Maria, has been previously invited to join the displayed PIS with "edit" permission by its owner; she has highlighted the Wikipedia page about the Trajan Way ("Via Traiana" in Italian) and is adding a text comment suggesting the PIS owner to visit the Wikipedia page about the archaeological park of Conimbriga. She also included some pictures of that park.

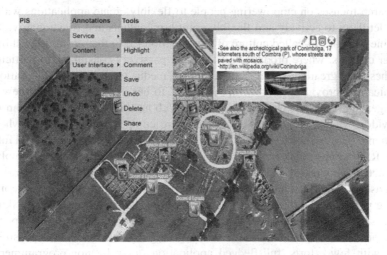

Fig. 7. Content annotation: the user is annotating the Wikipedia page about Via Traiana

Fig. 8 shows how a user can annotate an area of the interface to request possible changes to the software engineers who administer the platform. In particular, it refers to the UI annotation scenario, where Tony uses an annotation to ask the software engineers a window to show a list of contents that he does not want to show on the map.

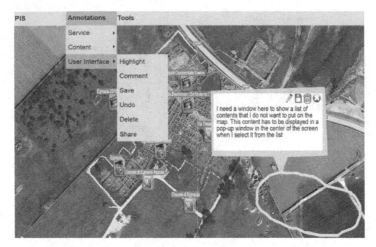

Fig. 8. Example of PIS User Interface annotation

The three scenarios were validated with representative of guides and tourist users in order to perform a formative evaluation of the prototypes being implemented.

5   Related Work

Our research focuses on empowering people to flexibly create applications with tools that can let them to actively and flexibly compose contents and functionality. This is also in line with the so-called culture of participation [5, 6] that promotes a shift from consumer cultures, where produced artifacts are passively consumed, to participatory approaches that greatly exploit computational media to support collaboration and communication, providing users with the means to become co-creators of new ideas, knowledge, and products [1]. In this scenario, Web mashup methods and technologies can provide a viable solution. Web mashups are composite applications, where the "components" are as heterogeneous as SOAP/WSDL Web services, RESTful Web services, RSS/Atom feeds, user interface widgets, JavaScript libraries, or simply content extracted (wrapped) from common HTML Web pages (and many more). What makes mashup composition different from the more traditional Web service composition is the potential as a paradigm through which end users, not necessarily skilled in computer science, are empowered to develop their own applications. Mashups indeed specially promote integration at the UI level, giving to the end users the possibility to achieve, with few efforts, full-fledged applications even by non-programmer users [15]. However, this potential is rarely exploited. So far the research on mashups has focused on enabling technologies and standards, with little attention to easing the mashup development process – in many cases mashup creation still involves the manual programming of the service integration. Some recent user-centric studies also found that, although the most prominent platforms (e.g., Yahoo!Pipes) simplify the mashup development, they are still difficult to use by non-technical users [16].

Our work tries to combine EUD principles with the potential of mashup models and technologies, to create paradigms and tools, based on intuitive visual composition mechanisms. A visual composition paradigm strongly characterizes our approach [17], especially with respect to others requiring the adoption of specific design notations (as for example in [18]) or scripting languages (as for example in [19]). Also, to our knowledge, the aspect of sharing and annotating mashup applications has been scarcely investigated.

The use of annotation in the context of Web services has been typically introduced to integrate quality criteria in the service composition process [20], e.g., specifying quality attributes to guide service selection, or to add semantic information on what a service does and functional information on how it behaves [21]. The use of annotations for the automatic generation of user interfaces for Web services has been one of the topics of the ServFace project[1], as documented for example in [22]. In all these cases, annotations are intended for use by automatic systems generating specific configurations of a service, based on the features described via the annotations, which need then to be expressed with formal languages, e.g., OWL.

An approach to the creation of personalised versions of a service, based on some information on the results it can give, is presented in [23]. The approach is supported by the adaptation of a planning algorithm able to gather information during the service composition phase [24].

The approach presented here moves from previous work on annotation of content as a way to focus the production of user-generated content with reference to generally available documents, rather than specific web-sites [13] and on annotation of parts of the user interface as a way to foster co-evolution of software implementation and user requirements [25]. In the integration presented in this paper, the user can exploit annotations for several purposes: for annotating existing content and adding new one, for reasoning about the current composition and interaction of a personalised information space, for communicating with other people providing or requesting information on contents, services and interface features.

6 Conclusion and Future Work

This paper has reported recent work on the construction by end users of Personal Information Spaces, which are integrated work-spaces that satisfy end users' situational needs and that can be accessed through different devices. Specifically, we have shown how to address the need for communicating and sharing information with other stakeholders, which emerged during a field study performed in November 2012. Thus, our platform for PIS composition has been extended with features that allow users to make annotations on services, content and user interfaces.

The prototypes implementing the annotation features described in this paper have been created by a participatory design team, involving the two professional guides and eight visitors who had previously participated in the field study. In the meetings

---

[1] http://www.servface.org/

they contributed to elaborate new ideas and to sketch paper mock-ups. Finally, some of them have been involved in formative evaluations of such prototypes.

We are interested in investigating about the appropriation of the system we propose. We have planned to provide a tablet device to the two guides and to allow them to use the platform for a period of two months. During this period, they will be asked to write a diary, they will be regularly interviewed and observed in some occasions in order to detect possible problems and analyze the evolution of their work habits.

Moreover, we will investigate the possibility to integrate the facilities for *multi-selection* proposed in [26], allowing users to select arbitrary groups of objects, even of different nature, and provide a single annotation for the resulting *multi-structure*. Awareness mechanisms will be also investigated, for example to notify the users about the availability of new annotations, and of PIS modifications responding to previous annotation-based requests.

References

1. Latzina, M., Beringer, J.: Transformative user experience: beyond packaged design. Interactions 19(2), 30–33 (2012)
2. Tapscott, D., Williams, A.D.: Wikinomics: How Mass Collaboration Changes Everything. Portofolio, Penguin Group, New York (2006)
3. Daniel, F., Matera, M., Weiss, M.: Next in Mashup Development: User-Created Apps on the Web. IT Professional 13(5), 22–29 (2011)
4. Ardito, C., Costabile, M.F., Desolda, G., Matera, M., Piccinno, A., Picozzi, M.: Composition of situational interactive spaces by end users: a case for cultural heritage. In: 7th Nordic Conference on Human-Computer Interaction: Making Sense Through Design (NordiCHI 2012), Copenhagen, Denmark, pp. 79–88. ACM Press, New York (2012)
5. Fischer, G.: End User Development and Meta-Design: Foundations for Cultures of Participation. Journal of Organizational and End User Computing 22(1), 52–82 (2010)
6. Jenkins, H.: Confronting the Challenges of Participatory Culture: Media Education for the 21st Century. MIT Press, Cambridge (2009)
7. Cappiello, C., Daniel, F., Matera, M., Picozzi, M., Weiss, M.: Enabling end user development through mashups: Requirements, abstractions and innovation toolkits. In: Costabile, M.F., Dittrich, Y., Fischer, G., Piccinno, A. (eds.) IS-EUD 2011. LNCS, vol. 6654, pp. 9–24. Springer, Heidelberg (2011)
8. Costabile, M.F., Fogli, D., Mussio, P., Piccinno, A.: Visual Interactive Systems for End-User Development: A Model-Based Design Methodology. IEEE Transactions on Systems, Man, and Cybernetics - Part A: Systems and Humans 37(6), 1029–1046 (2007)
9. Costabile, M.F., Dittrich, Y., Fischer, G., Piccinno, A. (eds.): IS-EUD 2011. LNCS, vol. 6654. Springer, Heidelberg (2011)
10. Lieberman, H., Paternò, F., Wulf, V. (eds.): End User Development, vol. 9. Springer, Dordrecht (2006)
11. Cappiello, C., Matera, M., Picozzi, M., Sprega, G., Barbagallo, D., Francalanci, C.: DashMash: A Mashup Environment for End User Development. In: Auer, S., Díaz, O., Papadopoulos, G.A. (eds.) ICWE 2011. LNCS, vol. 6757, pp. 152–166. Springer, Heidelberg (2011)
12. Cappiello, C., Matera, M., Picozzi, M., Caio, A., Guevara, M.T.: MobiMash: end user development for mobile mashups. In: 21st International Conference Companion on World Wide Web, Lyon, France, pp. 473–474. ACM, New York (2012)

13. Bottoni, P., Civica, R., Levialdi, S., Orso, L., Panizzi, E., Trinchese, R.: MADCOW: a multimedia digital annotation system. In: Advanced Visual Interfaces (AVI 2004), Gallipoli, Italy, pp. 55–62. ACM, New York (2004)

14. Bottoni, P., Levialdi, S., Rizzo, P.: An Analysis and Case Study of Digital Annotation. In: Bianchi-Berthouze, N. (ed.) DNIS 2003. LNCS, vol. 2822, pp. 216–230. Springer, Heidelberg (2003)

15. Daniel, F., Yu, J., Benatallah, B., Casati, F., Matera, M., Saint-Paul, R.: Understanding UI Integration: A Survey of Problems, Technologies, and Opportunities. IEEE Internet Computing 11(3), 59–66 (2007)

16. Namoun, A., Nestler, T., De Angeli, A.: Conceptual and Usability Issues in the Composable Web of Software Services. In: Daniel, F., Facca, F.M. (eds.) ICWE 2010. LNCS, vol. 6385, pp. 396–407. Springer, Heidelberg (2010)

17. Aghaee, S., Nowak, M., Pautasso, C.: Reusable decision space for mashup tool design. In: 4th ACM SIGCHI Symposium on Engineering Iteractive Computing Systems (EICS 2012), Copenhagen, Denmark, pp. 211–220. ACM, New York (2012)

18. Daniel, F., Casati, F., Benatallah, B., Shan, M.-C.: Hosted Universal Composition: Models, Languages and Infrastructure in mashArt. In: Laender, A.H.F., Castano, S., Dayal, U., Casati, F., de Oliveira, J.P.M. (eds.) ER 2009. LNCS, vol. 5829, pp. 428–443. Springer, Heidelberg (2009)

19. Maximilien, E.M., Wilkinson, H., Desai, N., Tai, S.: A Domain-Specific Language for Web APIs and Services Mashups. In: Krämer, B., Lin, K.-J., Narasimhan, P. (eds.) ICSOC 2007. LNCS, vol. 4749, pp. 13–26. Springer, Heidelberg (2007)

20. Nagarajan, M.: Semantic Annotations in Web Services. In: Jorge, C., Amit, P.S. (eds.) Semantic Web Services, Processes and Applications, New York, NY, vol. 3 (2006)

21. Srivastava, B., Koehler, J.: Web Service Composition - Current Solutions and Open Problems. In: ICAPS 2003 Workshop on Planning for Web Services, pp. 28–35 (2003)

22. Feldmann, M., Janeiro, J., Nestler, T., Hübsch, G., Jugel, U., Preussner, A., Schill, A.: An Integrated Approach for Creating Service-Based Interactive Applications. In: Gross, T., Gulliksen, J., Kotzé, P., Oestreicher, L., Palanque, P., Prates, R.O., Winckler, M. (eds.) INTERACT 2009, Part II. LNCS, vol. 5727, pp. 896–899. Springer, Heidelberg (2009)

23. Sirin, E., Parsia, B., Hendler, J.: Filtering and Selecting Semantic Web Services with Interactive Composition Techniques. IEEE Intelligent Systems 19(4), 42–49 (2004)

24. Kuter, U., Sirin, E., Parsia, B., Nau, D., Hendler, J.: Information gathering during planning for Web Service composition. Web Semant. 3(2-3), 183–205 (2005)

25. Costabile, M.F., Fogli, D., Mussio, P., Piccinno, A.: End-User Development: the Software Shaping Workshop Approach. In: Lieberman, H., Paternò, F., Wulf, V. (eds.) End User Development, pp. 183–205. Springer, Dordrecht (2006)

26. Addisu, M., Avola, D., Bianchi, P., Bottoni, P., Levialdi, S., Panizzi, E.: Annotating Significant Relations on Multimedia Web Documents. In: Multimedia Information Extraction, pp. 401–417. John Wiley & Sons, Inc. (2012)

Identity Design in Virtual Worlds

Benjamin Koehne, Matthew J. Bietz, and David Redmiles

Department of Informatics
University of California, Irvine
Irvine, CA 92697-3425 USA
{bkoehne,mbietz,dfredmil}@uci.edu

Abstract. Designers in HCI and end user development require a good understanding of actors in virtual interaction spaces. Persistent virtual worlds represent a rather new but growing class of complex design and interaction platforms. Online identities form the basis for interaction of individuals in virtual environments. We present results from an ethnographic study of a popular online game, and develop a socio-technical model of identity formation that illuminates the processes of identity design in online environments. This framework demonstrates how virtual worlds provide social and technological structures that shape self-presentation and interaction. This allows us to explore the relationship between the real-world identity of the game player and the virtual-world identity of their avatar.

Keywords: Virtual worlds, design theory, end user design, user-centered design, identity.

1   Introduction

Electronically mediated environments challenge our notions of identity and the self. Today, end user development and collaboration increasingly takes place in virtual collaboration contexts and across geographical distances [4, 5]. When collaborators are not present in the same physical context, they assume a virtual identity that is mediated through communication technology. While the end user development community increasingly designs for distributed collaboration, relatively little is known about how a virtual identity is assumed or perceived by end users in virtual spaces.

Sociological and psychological understandings of identity cannot be assumed to transfer seamlessly into online contexts. What is required is a socio-technical framework that helps us understand issues of identity development and design. We use an online role-playing game set in a graphical virtual world (VW) as a case study to examine how social, psychological, and technological influences affect online identity creation.

Virtual environments range from text-based communication spaces to complex persistent graphical 3D environments supported by rich media applications. These environments represent a specific class of technology-mediated spaces that allow for particularly immersive virtual experiences and interactions with others.

Y. Dittrich et al. (Eds.): IS-EUD 2013, LNCS 7897, pp. 56–71, 2013.
© Springer-Verlag Berlin Heidelberg 2013

Virtual identities have been discussed in the VW literature since the introduction of text-based multi-user dungeons (MUDs) [29]. VWs were often regarded as opportunities to experiment with alternate identities. At the same time, constraints of VWs limit the possibilities of users to design an online identity. In modern VWs, such as game-oriented systems like Lord of the Rings Online (LOTRO), a player's online identity is not only carefully designed but, as importantly, enacted in the VW.

This paper makes two key contributions to our understanding of identity in virtual worlds. First, using Côté & Levine's [3] model of identity formation, we explore the relationship between the real-world identity of the game player and the virtual world identity of the avatar. We extend their model to include not only the influence of social structure, but also the influence of the technological constraints designed into the VW. Second, by exploring a particular virtual world where identity design is an explicit part of game play, we are able to better illuminate the mechanisms of identity formation, self-presentation, and interpersonal interaction in virtual worlds.

To illustrate our argument, we present the results of a qualitative investigation of the massively multiplayer online role-playing game (MMORPG) LOTRO. LOTRO is popular game set in a mythic virtual world, similar to other games like World of Warcraft or Everquest. LOTRO is based on the fictional world created by J.R.R. Tolkien in his Lord of the Rings books. Players of the game use avatars to navigate through the world, interact with other players, and complete various challenges (which frequently involve killing computer-controlled monsters). In our investigation of LOTRO, the theme of identity design serves as an analytic lens to unpack individual activities and develop a model of identity formation in VWs.

The next section of the paper provides background on the concept of identity and the theory of online identity in VWs. Following that, we describe our study and present findings about identity in the LOTRO virtual world. The last sections of the paper critically analyze the findings in relation to our extended model of online identity and discuss some implications of this work.

2   Towards Online Identity

In this paper, we use identity design to refer to those practices that contribute to the development of a particular identity. We draw on social-psychological theories of identity that suggest that identity can be understood as a complex aggregation of an individual's place in a social structure, aspects of individual experience and interactions, and personality [3]. We are specifically not focusing on the engineering problems surrounding establishing that one is who one claims to be as talked about in contexts of security or access. Instead, we use identity as it might be discussed in the sociology or psychology literature.

In this section, we first discuss Côté and Levine's [3] framework for understanding the multiple levels of identity formation and the interactions among them. We then use Lanzara's [15] concept of "remediation" to understand how identity development and design practices might move into the new context of virtual worlds. We then survey the existing literature on identity design in virtual worlds.

2.1 Sociological and Psychological Identity

A great variety of sociological and psychological perspectives on identity have been developed in social science, but here we draw on Côté and Levine [3], who develop a multi-level model that helps to integrate these perspectives. The framework (Figure 1) presents a three-level taxonomy of identity. Social identity is defined by the individual's position in the social structure. Existing cultures and social roles affect this position. Still under the influence of social structure, the personal identity develops based on an individual's interaction in the world. Individuals act with the goal to fit in societal structures and roles. Ego identity refers to the psychological structures related to individual personality.

The power of this model lies in understanding the ongoing and iterative paths of influence among the layers. Social structures influence everyday interactions through processes of socialization and social control (Arrow 1). Interaction in the everyday world, over time, leads to the internalization of social norms and values (2). Influence simultaneously moves outward from the individual to the world. The personal ego produces a self-presentation that influences interactions with others (3). Ultimately, social structure is changed or maintained through active performance in the everyday world (4).

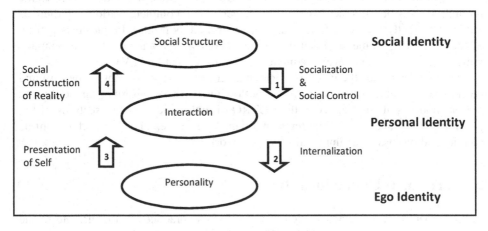

Fig. 1. Identity formation (adapted from Côté & Levine [3], p.7)

Self-identity is increasingly a product of critical reflexivity [8]. Humans living in modernity are increasingly faced with making choices concerning who they eventually want to be. More choices may give individuals more liberties, but they also contribute to an increasingly complex identity formation process. Information systems that connect people over large distances and make vast amounts of information readily accessible have contributed to this development. We believe that this reflexivity can be observed and theorized in VWs where players carefully design an online character's identity. Players need to make important choices and plan their characters' performances in the game. They actively reflect on their appearance and standing in the social system created by the VW, and how that VW identity relates to their real-world selves.

2.2   Mediation of Identity

The formation of identity can be understood as a mediated activity in the real world, just like any other human practice. Human practices are mediated through physical objects and systems of conventions that determine the use of these objects [12]. The growing availability of novel online media has led to the migration of many everyday practices to virtual environments. Use of online systems frequently requires actors to establish a technologically-mediated online identity. The introduction of new media to established practices can lead to a process that Lanzara defines as the 'remediation of practice':

"Switching medium produces a discontinuity in the smooth flow of familiar routines and a displacement in the practitioners' perceptions and understandings of what they do and how they do it. [...] The new medium opens up a window for novel things to happen in a new space of possibilities, revealing features of the domain that were not visible, or not easily accessible, or rather not paid attention to, in the traditional medium." [15]

We draw from this remediation perspective to analyze the formation processes of identity in LOTRO. Even though VWs, such as LOTRO and Second Life, simulate a realistic environment with human-like characters, real-world identities do not move effortlessly into virtual worlds. Players must "remediate" their identities through active redesign of identity presentation and interactions.

The relationship that develops between the individual playing the game and the controlled character is an important part of the remediation process. Players form a long-term relationship with the virtual characters and are highly immersed in the VW. The rich VW medium offers the tools and social context within which identity is created. The individual's goals and actions are mediated through the interface software. Players project their individual intentions and values onto the online character to create the desired online identity.

2.3   Identity in Virtual Worlds

Identity has been an important concern throughout the literature on virtual worlds. In her book, Life on the Screen, Sherry Turkle examines the creation of identity in text-based MUDs:

On MUDs, one's body is represented by one's own textual description, so the obese can be slender, the beautiful plain, the "nerdy" sophisticated [...]. MUDs make possible the creation of an identity so fluid and multiple that it strains the limits of the notion. Identity, after all, refers to the sameness between two qualities, in this case between a person and his or her persona. But in MUDs, one can be many. [29]

Whether produced through text description or through social interaction [13], this ability to experiment with alternate identities intrigued many early writers on the subject, who debated the degree to which one's on-line identities could be separated from real-life identity [26, 27].

As a consequence, scholars began to focus on how virtual environments constrain the kinds of identity choices that users can make. For example, McDonough explores how "virtual environment designers wield a certain degree of power over users' ability to represent themselves and interact within virtual worlds" [19].

Avatar design choices are also influenced by the social environment of the virtual world. Neustaedter and Fedorovskaya [22] found that users of Second Life felt stigma about using the default avatar design, and felt pressure from other players to change their appearance. They created a typology of appearance and identity around four types of players: realistics, ideals, fantasies, and roleplayers. Realistics worked to match their online identity to their real-life identity—the virtual was an extension of the real. Ideals had a similar outlook, but designed their avatars to make up for perceived inadequacies in their real identities. Fantasies saw their online identity as distinct from their real identity, but worked to maintain a consistent avatar identity over time. Roleplayers also see their online identities as distinct from real-life, but frequently change their online identities to explore new situations. This typology is useful for highlighting the difference between a VW like Second Life and a game-based VW like LOTRO. Where Second Life provides the breadth of choices to allow all of these types, LOTRO constrains users mostly to the Fantasy role by making it difficult to have realistic avatars or to make major identity changes to an avatar after it has been created.

Kolko [14] is also interested in how design choices constrain users, especially around the ways that they are able to communicate through their avatars.

"Designing an avatar is never solely the act of an end user [...]. In text-based MOOs, for example, end users can set an @gender category because the designers of the database decided that having knowledge of specific gender was important to discursive interaction [...]. Those same designers (as multiple and dispersed as they were) decided that an @race characteristic was not essential to discursive social interaction [...]. This is exactly the kind of control that designers of [virtual worlds] hold. " (p.184)

This control carries over to graphical virtual environments, where the degrees of freedom given to users over their avatar's identity, how they look or the ways they can move affects what and how they can communicate. The design space for users to create their online identity is thus often limited by the structure of the VW.

A key aspect of identity presentation involves the degree to which it is intentional. In his dramaturgical approach to identity presentation, Goffman [9] refers to cues that are "given" and those that are "given off." The given cues include those that are intentionally controlled by the "performer." An example in the virtual world is the chosen appearance of an avatar that reflects a character class or other specialization of the player. Cues given off are those that are "inaccessible" to our control, including not only physical appearance, but also many non-verbal cues like gestures and vocal timbre. In the virtual world, given off cues become noticeable during group play and over longer periods of interactions in the game when players learn to read other players based on their behavioral patterns and communication styles.

Technically mediated communication environments shift the balance in communication away from "cues given off" to "cues given". Geser [7] claims that in virtual worlds like Second Life, all self-presentation is intentional: "While my physical body is shaped by exogenous biological factors, my avatar is completely the product of my explicit decisions." While we agree that many virtual worlds can offer greater and different kinds of freedom of self-presentation than real life, we side with earlier authors who find that VWs do enforce certain choices that are inaccessible to the user. How these constraints are enacted shapes the ways that self-presentation takes place in these virtual worlds.

Tayler begins to explore virtual identity creation process in virtual worlds and notes that technological structures can limit design choices, a concept that we also find reflected in our research [29]. In this paper we contribute to this literature by exploring the relationship between the real-world identity of the game player and the VW identity of the avatar. We develop a model of identity development that includes the influence of both social structure and technological constraints imposed by the VW system. We investigate how the design of virtual worlds affects the possibilities for identity design and how self-presentation and interaction in virtual worlds can inform our thinking about user engagement and its limitations in virtual contexts.

3   Method

Our study draws on methods used in previous ethnographic explorations of virtual words. Virtual ethnography [11] provides us with a method to analyze activities in the digital, virtual spaces. Multi-sited ethnography [17] allows for the inclusion of the virtual field site LOTRO, online forums and interviews in the physical world.

In his investigation of the culture of Second Life, Boellstorff [1] provides thick description [6] of everyday encounters in Second Life based on his own participation. Nardi has also conducted extensive ethnographic studies of virtual worlds (e.g. [20, 21]). In her account of the MMORPG World of Warcraft, a game related to LOTRO but set in a different fantasy narrative, Nardi also investigates the relationship between player and virtual representation in the game [17].

For our study, one author actively immersed himself in LOTRO and joined a community of players, conducting more than 80 hours of participant observation over a four-month period. The goal was to develop an understanding of the culture of the game and the activities that defined the players' identities.

Additionally, we conducted 6 semi-structured interviews with players of the game. Interviews lasted from 40 minutes to 1 hour. Informants were recruited through snowball-sampling in the player community. The interviews focused on topics that we related to the character's appearance and capabilities. Additionally, we asked about personal motivations of the players to conduct certain design-related activities. We used open-coding techniques [16] to discover patterns and themes in our observations. Observations in the VW helped us to contextualize the interview data.

Our research site was the "Lord of the Rings Online", a popular massively multiplayer online role-playing game produced by Turbine, Inc. The concept of the game can be compared to other MMORGs such as the current market leader World of Warcraft and Dungeons & Dragons Online. LOTRO is aimed at the online gaming market at large and more specifically at the online role playing game market.

4   Identity Design in LOTRO

In this section we investigate the process of identity formation in virtual worlds by examining occasions for identity design work. These occasions are periods in the game when the player is faced with choices about who his or her avatar will be. Some of these occasions occur at precise moments and with a great deal of predictability. Others occur at various points in the game and may extend over many cycles of play.

4.1   Initial Character Creation

The first occasion for identity design occurs immediately when players begin playing the game. As part of the setup process, a player must create an avatar and make choices about who that avatar will be. The choices made here at the very outset of the game can irreversibly affect the future experience and the development possibilities of the envisioned online identity.

At this stage, LOTRO structures identity around two key concepts. First, the player must choose a "race." Because the VW is based on Tolkien's novels, the possible races are man, dwarf, hobbit and elf. The player must also choose gender (although all dwarves are male). Each race has defining characteristics which are summarized for the player. For example, man is described, "Not as long-lived as Elves, sturdy as Dwarves, or resilient as Hobbits, Men are renowned for their courage and resourcefulness."

The player must also choose a "class" for the avatar. Character classes define the basic characteristics of the avatar. Champions, for instance, master warfare in the game, whereas minstrels specialize on supportive healing activities instead of fighting in the front line of the battle. After choosing race and class, the avatar can be further customized with a specific area of origin (e.g. Gondor or Rohan), skin color, hair style, and other physical features. Race, character class, and most basic physical properties of the avatar cannot be changed later in the game.

Design requires making choices. The decision making process in LOTRO is prompted by the structure of the game. Choices about identity at a very early stage during the creation of the character define future roles and development possibilities. These choices can also profoundly affect the players' experience of the virtual world itself. For example, the choice of race determines where the avatar is initially placed in the VW (based on the story line of Tolkien's novels). One player described how after choosing the Hobbit race, his avatar was placed into a part of the world called the Shire:

"You don't know what's out there. I started a Hobbit. And I thought the Shire [an area mostly inhabited by the Hobbit race] was a really huge world. But then I found out it's not the end of it."(player_1)

Here, the player confronts the boundaries of the virtual environment from the perspective of the character. Players were drawn in to the story lines and felt an identification between their avatars and the home areas in the game. Interestingly, these aspects of identity were chosen and locked in before players had a sense of what the ramifications of their choices might be.

LOTRO allows players to create up to 7 avatars per subscription account. Many advanced players have at least 2 avatars and in many cases even more. Most players maintain one 'main' avatar and several other 'toons'. Usually, the main avatar is best equipped and at a high level. Players have varying motivations to create toon avatars. One player in our kinship switched between his avatars almost every 5 minutes. It turned out that he maintained 7 avatars. Each of them specialized on certain skills. By switching between classes he was able to become completely self-sufficient in terms of resources for his different professions. Avatars are not visibly linked to the account of the player. It is thus possible that a player maintains multiple completely isolated virtual identities.

Creating a new avatar requires considerable effort, since it means starting over with the character development from the very beginning. One player explained to us why he chose to play more than one avatar. He wanted to understand the playability and specifics of all different classes in LOTRO:

"The reason I play the classes is, when you are playing in groups, you would understand what everybody had to do. You just understand the game more by playing the classes." (player_5)

Players recognize the complexity of the game. Playing together with other players not only requires knowledge about your own skills and abilities, but also about the identity and capacity of other players in your team.

4.2   Kinships and Social Identity

Like many other recent MMORPGs, the design of LOTRO encourages not only social interaction, but coordinated and collaborative behavior. The primary social groupings in LOTRO are fellowships and kinships. Fellowships are temporary groups, formed to compete as a team and master a challenging undertaking. Kinships can also perform in-game challenges as a group, but have a more permanent character.

One of the authors played in a kinship from the day it was initially founded. Over time, members became familiar with each other. Players support each other by providing resources for game play or by giving advice related to the game content. Different social roles develop in these communities. The game structure prescribes the role of the kinship leader. The kinship leader has control over the administrative functions. He can promote kinship members to officers and manage the members. Officers can also recruit other players into the kinship. Taking on leadership roles can be a demanding task and not everyone is willing or capable to take on the responsibility. A kinship leader reflects on his experiences:

"Everybody wants to be on the winning team but nobody wants to build it. [...] It's the nature of people." (player_1)

Creating kinships takes work, and not everyone is cut out for the task. We can see in this comment that the player is thinking about identity—who would and would not be a good leader? Identity does not reside in just the avatar or the real-world player. At times the in-world character has an identity that is clearly distinct from the real-world player (e.g. a hobbit in the Shire vs. a grandmother in Hoboken). But at the same time, the search for a good leader has as much to do with the player's identity as the avatar's.

The complexity of the social identity, avatar identity, and real-world personal identity can be seen when one player describes switching characters to serve the needs of the kinship:

"I started with one [avatar] and leveled it right to the top. And then I started on another because I saw the need for the kin to have a Loremaster. [...] So I developed a Loremaster. And now I see the kin needs a Runekeeper. So that will be my next character." (player_2)

The kinship is both a social and functional structure. It brings people together in interaction, but frequently the grouping is goal directed (accomplishing group challenges in the game) and requires having the right mix of characters skills. This player is willing to give up a well-developed character identity in the world to start new characters that meet his kinship's needs. However, this type of character switching only works if membership in the kinship inheres in the real-world player more than the in-game character.

4.3   Identity Presentation

The appearance of the character in the VW is an important concern for the players of LOTRO. However, appearance is not a static feature. The appearance of a character is tied to the performative action of characters in the VW. Basic character elements, such as height and facial details, remain unchanged throughout the lifetime of a character. However, the clothing of an avatar can be changed by the player at any time. Avatars can also wear their weaponry and battle gear that they have accumulated. More powerful items with higher value usually appear more visually appealing to observers in the VW. For instance, a powerful sword glows when wielded and worn by the avatar.

An impressive appearance of the character signals an experienced player. The game has some popular gathering places that serve as travel hubs and meeting points. Here, players can easily catch a glimpse of others. Many players strive for unique gear that they can wear to stand out:

"I wear the armor for my burglar because nobody else does." (player_1)

LOTRO allows players not only to observe others visually but to inspect other characters in detail. This inspection reveals details about the worn gear and its properties.

"It's pretty cool to inspect some players. And you think: Wow, this person has been playing a lot - they have fricking all blue [powerful and rare] items. You get inspired to get that one day. It keeps the drive in it." (player_3)

As this example shows, players tend to compare themselves to other characters in the game which in turn can motivate them to reach higher goals.

Avatars can also choose (usually in "safer" environments) to wear cosmetic wardrobe items that do not have functional properties (e.g. armor) but only serve to provide a different visual appearance in the world. But clothing and visual appearance is not the only way that a character's identity is presented to the world.

Regularly, groups of players team up to face powerful enemies in various adventures. In these groups, players take on different roles based on their character class. For instance, playing a minstrel means that the character takes a supportive role in the group and is generally assigned tasks that aim at keeping the other group members alive. However, this role, as it is prescribed by the game mechanics, can be performed in multiple ways. Players communicate over voice chat; they use different tactics and show their emotions during battle via the voice chat system. The way the game is played and the vocal communication present not only the intentional identity cues, but also the unintentional "cues given off." Players can learn about who the character is by the way they act and speak in the world.

The character's identity is a complex amalgam of avatar and player. Identity in LOTRO is expressed in the avatar's clothing, how players perform actions with their avatars, and the voice of the player during battle. In terms of identity, self, character, etc., trying to cleanly separate what is in the game from what is real-life is counterproductive. Our observations also suggest that these distinctions are fluid for players, and that they move easily between different and sometimes multiple identity orientations.

We could see this clearly when real-life concerns intruded into the world of LOTRO. When playing in larger groups it is common to run into situations where players need to arrange for time in their real life to play LOTRO. Some group challenges in the game require many hours of concentrated commitment to the game. In one of the author's kinships the personal life of the players was often openly discussed. Well-known kinship members were rarely reduced to his or her online character alone.

During long challenges, the group would take breaks to wait for another kinship member when he had to attend to his newly born son at night. Another particular member, a truck driver in real life, could only play during breaks on the road with his internet-enabled laptop computer. In our experience, players were very much aware of other players' real life circumstances despite the immersive character of the game.

Players held varying attitudes about the relationship between real world and virtual world experiences. Reflecting on the experience of the game, a player told us:

"To me it is just a game. This is really about having fun. We all have personal lives that we might need to get away from and kind of get into the game as an escape from the real life." (player_04)

From this perspective, the game becomes an escape from real life and an opportunity to engage in an exciting and enjoyable environment. But in other ways, the virtual world was part of or an extension of the real world. One player reflected on what motivates her to help out other players.

"I'm a big believer in spreading around more goodness than everything else. A lot of people don't have many friends in the game. So I'm just kind of trying to - not that I am into karma or anything - but it's more that I'm trying to be nice because many people are not very nice." (player_4)

This player strives to project her personal values on her character's actions in the game.

5   Discussion

Our findings demonstrate the complexity of identity formation in the LOTRO virtual world. Character identity design sometimes takes the form of atomistic choices of skin color or character class, but it also occurs over longer time scales as players work to develop their characters' capabilities, reputations, and social relationships. In this section we provide a more general discussion of facets of identity design in virtual worlds and draw some implications for end user development and design.

5.1   A Socio-technical Model of Identity Formation

The identity formation model introduced in Figure 1 is a purely social model, drawing on understandings from sociology and psychology. However, the analysis of VWs requires a slightly different model with a more socio-technical understanding. Figure 2 shows our conceptual model of identity information in virtual worlds that extends Côté & Levine's [3] model.

This new model captures several aspects of identity formation specific to virtual worlds. First, the model recognizes the distinction between the player and the in-world character. This makes the relationship between the player's identity and the possibly numerous virtual identities more complex. Online characters interact in the virtual world on behalf of the player. In our model, we recognize that the relationship between the personality and interaction levels of identity is mediated through the avatar.

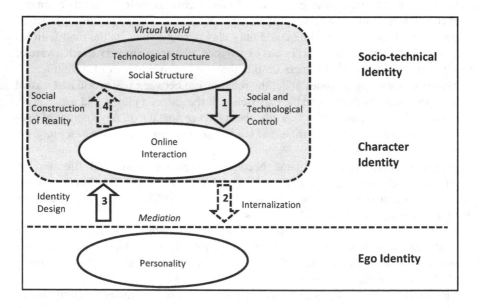

Fig. 2. Formation of Online Identity

The second addition to the model is that the high-level structures that influence identity formation are both social and technological. Explicit technological constraints on identity design are obvious in the first interactions a player has with the LOTRO VW. Similar to the way that social structures in the real world influence what kinds of identities are acceptable for men and women, the technological rules of the virtual world do not allow Dwarves to be female, or a Man to be a rune-keeper. However, we feel that it is important to recognize the distinction in the model between social and technological structures. Whereas social structures affect interaction through various processes of social influence (e.g. validations and challenges of identities), technological structures control identity possibilities through more absolute means. Whereas a character can decide not to join a kinship, a player cannot decide to have a race-less avatar. Additionally, while social structures emerge, are reinforced, and change through social interaction, the technological structures are much more rigid. While it may be possible to change the technological structures of identity (perhaps by petitioning the game's designers or hacking the interface), these changes must be affected outside the virtual world.

What was a social model of identity has become socio-technical by recognizing the high-level technological constraints on identity and the mediation of the avatar. While the mechanisms of identity control represented in arrows 1 and 3 have become more explicit, the feedback mechanisms in arrows 2 and 4 have been problematized. Côté & Levine claim that the personal identity influences ego identity through "ego synthesis of self-presentations and others' appraisals" [3] (p.135), but it is not clear to what extent multiple online identities will have the same effect on the player's ego. And as we discussed above, the rigidity of the virtual world's programming makes it difficult if not impossible for new socio-technical identities to emerge.

5.2   Designing Identity in Virtual Worlds and EUD Contexts

Discussions of identity in the social sciences have typically not invoked the word "design." Sociologists tend to discuss identity as endowed from outside, a set of categorical bins in which the individual is placed. Psychologists focus on the ways that identity develops/is developed in the individual. Côté and Levine provide a model that allows us to understand the relationships between the top-down sociological and the bottom-up psychological views.

However, virtual worlds provide a unique set of tensions that are not revealed by these earlier approaches. The avatar is simultaneously one with the player and a separable persona. The identities in the world are multiple (avatars) and one (player). The avatar is both a product of the player's ambition, and preconfigured by the constraints of the world. The avatar is both identity and artifact. Seeing identity formation as a process of design helps us understand how these tensions play out.

The field of socio-technical design in HCI advocates the direct participation of end users in information system design process [25]. The focus lies on the socio-technical system that needs to co-evolve with the user base [24]. In LOTRO, we see the development of a socio-technical identity design circle. However, the technological constraints do not necessarily co-evolve with the social dynamics of the game. Social and technological structures form a unity that can only function in a dual mode: social structure evolves dynamically around technological constraints. We can see this socio-technical model underlying much work in the field of end-user development (EUD). EUD Tool developers require an understanding of how users can be constrained and at the same time liberated by technology. At the same time, the social structures that we saw evolve around groups of players in the virtual world, also need to be considered when designers aim to engage users in virtual EUD collaboration contexts.

At first glance, the constraints imposed by the LOTRO environment on the design possibilities in the virtual world might appear to limit sophisticated identity design. However, the constraints create a design space that makes choices in the VW meaningful. Specific choices, such as choosing a rare or difficult profession, can create strong identity cues. A high-level character in the game, that is not equipped with at least some clothes representing its high standing can signal a lack of commitment or disinterest in a 'serious' approach to the game.

The technological and social structure of LOTRO imposes a complex rules system on its players. For instance, regulations limit character design, and group activities. Characters in the VW cannot attack other non-hostile characters. Some zones on the virtual map cannot be accessed without successfully completing a series of quests that unlocks the area. Nardi describes rules in digital environment as "resources preserving good design" ([21], p. 74). The designers of LOTRO have defined rules to preserve a carefully designed system which provides a balanced and exciting game experience to the players. From this perspective, the structure of LOTRO provides coded rules that, when executed, recreate the imagined multi-facetted VW experience. Through performative action in LOTRO, players preserve the design and maintain the structure for identity design.

For EUD environments, rules can provide an interesting metaphor describing the tension between open-ended meta-design systems and systems that provide sufficient seeds and structures for enabling end-users to become designers. The challenge is to preserve a good design that allows for EUD activities with the right rules and technological structures.

The constraints and rules of the game also shape how players understand identity and make it meaningful. LOTRO constrains identity choices such as race and physical appearance to such a degree that players seemed to find them relatively meaningless as opportunities for self-presentation. Instead, players felt that they came to know who characters really were when they saw how they acted in quests and how they interacted in kinships.

Avatar design in LOTRO is a sophisticated activity that requires knowledge about the mechanics of the game and the context of planned future activities with the created character. Players learn that certain visual elements, such as glowing equipment, represent the cue for a more powerful artifact. In LOTRO, activity contexts can change rapidly. Confronted with the new situation, players need to make conscious choices how to adapt their online identity to the new design space. Remediation processes are occurring frequently and become part of the game. An online character represents a complex identity that undergoes constant changes and inherits properties that are only partially visible to observers. In agreement with Newman [23] we found that, for the most part, the capabilities and activities of the online character define the player's identification with the avatar. A strong connection develops between the player and the performances in the VW. By performing skillful activities in the virtual world, players create live identities for the given context that brings the desired identity cues to the foreground of the avatar presentation.

While the avatar identity can never equal the player identity, it is quite possible for players to project personal beliefs on the performance of their online characters. Our investigation showed that players do look beyond the avatar and recognize a real person behind the virtual figure. For instance, the long-term absence of a character from the kinship caused concern because many of his friends knew that in real life he was only recently deployed to Iraq. Playing the game represents a highly immersive experience but most players are very much aware of the person behind the virtual identity. Other cues, such as difficult to obtain sets of equipment, can signal observers the commitment of individuals to the game and the potential skills of the person playing the game. The boundaries between avatar and player become blurry and the real person controlling the avatar is recognized as acting through the avatar while still maintaining a real-world identity [10].

For Boellstorff, this kind of virtuality is part of human nature. Virtual worlds represent an opportunity to express selfhood and identity in enhanced, virtual dimensions. This perspective reaffirms our finding that even in the fantasy word of LOTRO, the real person behind the avatar is still consciously present for most players we encountered.

"The relationship between the virtual and the human is not a "post" relationship where one term displaces another; it is a relationship of coconstitution. Far from it being the case that virtual worlds herald the emergence of the posthuman, [...] it is in being virtual that we are human. Virtual worlds reconfigure selfhood and sociality, but this is only possible because they rework the virtuality that characterizes human being in the actual world." [1]

With more and more interactions moving to virtual spaces this virtuality aspect of human life is moved to the forefront in order to understand human behavior. Designing technology for humans increasingly requires an understanding of identity formation in virtual spaces.

Thinking about EUD practices in mediated contexts requires designers to think about the consequences of virtual spaces for end-users. Providing users with multiple virtual identities to exercise different levels of participation in system design processes can be seen as a way to democratize the end-user development process, while maintaining the overall flexibility of the system.

5.3   Limitations and Open Questions

We have proposed a model that we believe can serve as a useful framework for understanding identity development in a number of different mediated contexts. However, the current study focused on a single gaming-oriented VW, and the robustness of the model remains to be seen. While we found advantages in looking at this more controlled environment, an undirected VW, such as Second Life, may provide different insights about identity.

Our approach to identity in this paper has focused on the mechanisms of identity construction without significant attention to the social and psychological effects of particular identity choices. We do not analyze specific identities such as gender, race, etc., and we have not considered important processes such as stigma and discrimination. There is much work that remains to be done on understanding how socio-technical identities are constructed, interpreted, and used in virtual worlds.

6   Conclusions

Virtual worlds allow us to see identity formation not as a process of passive development but as an active process of design. Designers create artifacts to meet particular goals given a set of resources and constraints. This study helps us understand the ways that identities take shape in virtual environments, where resources and constraints are frequently explicit and rigid.

This approach gives us deeper understanding into issues of online identity and end user development. Identity is particularly salient in LOTRO and similar VW games, but the question of how users design their identities and how systems constrain those design choices are equally (if not more) important in other kinds of systems. Consider, for example, the ways that social-networking sites like Facebook enforce particular identity choices on user profile pages [2], or how Wikipedia editors manage their identities to establish their authority [18]. The relationship between the real person and the online identity can be understood as one of remediation. This context change—from "real life" to the virtual environment—opens a new design space for identity exploration.

References

1. Boellstorff, T.: Coming of age in Second Life: an anthropologist explores the virtually human. Princeton University Press, Princeton (2008)
2. Brubaker, J.R., Hayes, G.R.: SELECT * FROM USER: infrastructure and socio-technical representation. In: Proceedings of the ACM 2011 Conference on Computer Supported Cooperative Work, pp. 369–378. ACM (2011)
3. Côté, J.E., Levine, C.: Identity formation, agency, and culture: a social psychological synthesis. L. Erlbaum Associates, Mahwah (2002)
4. Díez, D., Díaz, P., Aedo, I.: Meta-design Blueprints: Principles and Guidelines for Co-design in Virtual Environments. In: Costabile, M.F., Dittrich, Y., Fischer, G., Piccinno, A. (eds.) IS-EUD 2011. LNCS, vol. 6654, pp. 276–281. Springer, Heidelberg (2011)
5. Fogli, D., Parasiliti Provenza, L.: End-User Development of e-Government Services through Meta-modeling. In: Costabile, M.F., Dittrich, Y., Fischer, G., Piccinno, A. (eds.) IS-EUD 2011. LNCS, vol. 6654, pp. 107–122. Springer, Heidelberg (2011)
6. Geertz, C.: Thick Description: Towards an Interpretive Theory of Culture. In: The Interpretation of Cultures. Basic Books (1973)
7. Geser, H.: Me, myself and my avatar: Some microsociological reflections on Second Life. In: Sociology in Switzerland: Towards Cybersociety and Vireal Social Relations (2007)

8. Giddens, A.: Modernity and self-identity: self and society in the late modern age. Stanford University Press, Stanford (1991)
9. Goffman, E.: The presentation of self in everyday life. Anchor Doubleday, Garden City (1959)
10. Haraway, J.: Manifesto for cyborgs: Science technology and socialist feminism in the 1980s. Socialist Review 80, 65–108 (1985)
11. Hine, C.: Virtual ethnography. SAGE, London (2000)
12. Kallinikos, J.: Mediated action and representation on the vicissitudes of human signification. Homo Oeconomicus 19(4), 607–622 (2003)
13. Kauppinen, K., Kivimäki, A., Era, T., Robinson, M.: Producing identity in collaborative virtual environments. In: Proceedings of the ACM Symposium on Virtual Reality Software and Technology. ACM, Taipei (1998)
14. Kolko, B.E.: Representing Bodies in Virtual Space: The Rhetoric of Avatar Design. The Information Society: An International Journal 15(3), 177–186 (1999)
15. Lanzara, G.F.: Remediation of practices: How new media change the ways we see and do things in practical domains (2010)
16. Lofland, J.: Analyzing social settings: a guide to qualitative observation and analysis, 4th edn. Wadsworth/Thomson Learning, Belmont (2006)
17. Marcus, G.E.: Ethnography in/of the World System: The Emergence of Multi-Sited Ethnography. Annual Review of Anthropology 24, 95–117 (1995)
18. O'Neil, M.: Wikipedia and authority. In: Lovink, G., Tkacz, N. (eds.) Critical Point of View Reader, pp. 309–324. Institute of Network Cultures, Amsterdam (2010)
19. McDonough, J.P.: Designer selves: Construction of technologically mediated identity within graphical, multiuser virtual environments. Journal of the American Society for Information Science 50(1), 855–869 (1999)
20. Nardi, B.A., Harris, J.: Strangers and friends: collaborative play in world of warcraft. In: Proceedings of the 2006 20th Anniversary Conference on Computer Supported Cooperative Work. ACM, Banff (2006)
21. Nardi, B.A.: My life as a night elf priest: an anthropological account of world of warcraft. The University of Michigan Press, Ann Arbor (2010)
22. Neustaedter, C., Fedorovskaya, E.: Capturing and sharing memories in a virtual world. In: Proceedings of the 27th International Conference on Human Factors in Computing Systems. ACM, Boston (2009)
23. Newman, J.: The Myth of the Ergodic Videogame. The International Journal of Computer Game Research 2(1) (2002)
24. O'Day, V.L., Bobrow, D.G., Shirley, M.: The social-technical design circle. In: Proceedings of the 1996 ACM Conference on Computer Supported Cooperative Work. ACM, Boston (1996)
25. Scacchi, W.: Socio-Technical Design. In: Bainbridge, W.S. (ed.) The Encyclopedia of Human-Computer Interaction, p. 659. Berkshire Publishing Group (2004)
26. Stone, A.R.: Will the real body please stand up? Boundary stories about virtual cultures. In: Trend, D. (ed.) Reading Digital Culture, pp. 185–198. Blackwell, Malden (1991)
27. Takayoshi, P.: Building new networks from the old: Women's experiences with electronic communications. Computers and Composition 11(1), 21–35 (1994)
28. Taylor, T.L.: Living Digitally: Embodiment in Virtual Worlds. In: Schroeder, R. (ed.) The Social Life of Avatars Presence and Interaction in Shared Virtual Environments, pp. 40–62. Springer (2002)
29. Turkle, S.: Life on the screen: Identity in the age of the Internet. Simon & Schuster, New York (1995)

Using Meta-modelling for Construction of an End-User Development Framework

Erlend Stav[1], Jacqueline Floch[1], Mohammad Ullah Khan[2], and Rune Sætre[2]

[1] SINTEF ICT, NO-7465 Trondheim, Norway
{Erlend.Stav,Jacqueline.Floch}@sintef.no
[2] NTNU, NO-7491 Trondheim, Norway
mukhan@item.ntnu.no, satre@idi.ntnu.no

Abstract. A main activity in meta-design is the creation of design spaces allowing problem owners to act as system developers. Meta-design is a conceptual framework; it does not provide concrete design space solutions or engineering guidelines for constructing tools that support design spaces. This paper discusses the applicability of a model-driven engineering approach for the realization of an end-user service composition framework, in line with the conceptual meta-design framework. We report our experience of using meta-modelling techniques as supported by the Eclipse Modelling Framework (EMF) family of tools. In our work we found that meta-models are well-suited to formalize the composition language, and the core parts of the EMF framework are useful to represent the language elements and user-made compositions both at design and runtime. Although EMF-based tools exist for creating visual editors, we found that in our case these did not map well to the visual notation we selected for our end-users.

Keywords: End-User Development, Meta-Design, Meta-Modelling, Model driven Engineering, Eclipse Modeling Framework.

1 Introduction

Our research starts with the vision of mobile pervasive computing, i.e. environments where objects are becoming increasingly intelligent and provide information and services to the user when and where needed. Tailoring the user environment to exactly what the user wants is challenging and requires a good understanding of individual needs. While several ambient intelligence approaches combine gathering of context and user activities with reasoning techniques to adapt environments to users, the vision where computers act as intelligent assistant "agents" is still an unrealistic promise [1] . We propose instead to empower the users so that they themselves can develop or adapt applications to their own needs and tasks in mobile pervasive environments. More specifically, we seek to develop a framework for end-user service composition. We see two main reasons for selecting services as a basis for end-user development. One is technical: the principles of the Service Oriented Architecture (SOA) are widely applied

Y. Dittrich et al. (Eds.): IS-EUD 2013, LNCS 7897, pp. 72–87, 2013.

in the construction of software systems in mobile pervasive environments. SOA supports the dynamic composition of systems from loosely coupled functional entities (specified as services), which fits the needs of pervasive computing where resources can be represented as discoverable services and dynamically added to a system as they appear. The other reason relates to user understanding. SOA provides a paradigm shift in the way we think of software systems. Services are decoupled from the system realization and rather represent activities or results (i.e. a kind of consumables). Thus services are close to a human way of thinking in the real world, and SOA has the potential to reduce the gap between idea and system construction also for people without IT expertise.

In order to provide support for end-user composition, we adopt a meta-design approach [2]. *Meta-design is a conceptual framework that extends the traditional notion of system development to include users as co-designers, not only at design time, but throughout the entire life-cycle of the system* [3]. An important concern is that the user needs are not static. The users learn while using a system, and their needs evolve. It is therefore important to involve the users not only during system design, but also after system deployment. Meta-design describes an ecosystem for the collaboration between developers and users, with the *seeding, evolutionary growth and reseeding* (SER) process model as a central element. Seeds are initial system entities designed through participatory design activities involving developers and users. Seeds can grow, i.e. evolve, following the tailoring of the system by users. Finally, reseeding is about the enhancement of the initial system to integrate changes. The concepts of meta-design fit well in the context of end-user service composition: services map to the concept of seeds, user extensions through service composition map to evolutionary growth, and finally the creation of new services based on user compositions and new needs emerging during composition map to re-seeding.

A main activity in meta-design is the creation of a design space that supports the ecosystem for collaborative design. Meta-design is a conceptual framework. It does not provide concrete design space solutions or engineering guidelines for constructing tools that support design spaces. This paper discusses the applicability of a model-based approach for the realisation of an engineering framework for end-user service composition, in line with the conceptual meta-design framework. We describe our approach to the development of the model-based framework UbiSys and illustrate the usage of UbiSys for the end-user extension of a case application. Finally we discuss our experience of using meta-modelling techniques as well as the EMF technology.

2   Related Work

Various technical approaches have been exploited for the creation of End-User Development (EUD) frameworks [4]. Task specific Programming Languages, TSPLs, were advocated by Nardi [1] for two main reasons: 1) The concepts of the language relate to the task domain and thus are easy to understand by users familiar with the domain; 2) The language supports high-level operations related to the task domain and thus the user can express the desired system functionality without using low-level operations. Nardi also points out two main drawbacks of TSPLs: 1) It is expensive to build different TSPLs for different needs and computer usages; 2) The definition of multiple languages may require the users to learn different interfaces. In our work, we define a Domain-Specific Language (DSL) to support the development of applications adapted to the user tasks in mobile pervasive environments. The proposed DSL is therefore close to a TPSL. We may benefit from the advantages of using TSPLs, but have to face similar drawbacks. The complexity of realising a DSL-based end-user framework is one of the main issues in our work: we investigate the application of model-driven software engineering approaches and technologies for that purpose. Related to the second drawback, we differentiate between the composition concepts common across several domains, e.g. sequential service execution, and the service concepts of the application domain. In other words, we provide a single composition interface to the end users. The variation lies in the service abstractions (we call them building blocks) that need to be parameterized during composition.

Several approaches can be applied to develop a DSL [5]. We exploit existing techniques. A first issue is the identification of the domain concepts. Our work has addressed three application domains: city exploration [6], mobile telecom services [7] and mobile asset management. The separation between the composition concepts and the application domain services is a bit similar to that introduced in AgentSheets [8]. Although the agent-based approach of AgentSheets differs from ours, it also supports two programming levels: a domain-oriented language for defining the behaviour of agents, and domain-oriented agents to be used in domain-construction kits. The former corresponds to our composition, the latter to the building blocks.

A second issue in the development of a DSL is the design of the language itself. Since the composition model is to be transformed to an executable program that orchestrates the composed services, precise language semantics are important. Precise semantics are also needed for the construction of advanced end-user engineering tools, such as simulation and validation tools. We exploit meta-modelling that was found to be a good tool for the specification of DSLs in terms of expressive power, flexibility, constraints and clarity of the semantics [9]. We thereby avoid building a notation upon any existing software engineering modelling language, e.g. UML, because their focus on software professionals is likely to not suit non-IT experts.

Finally, a third issue is the construction of tools. To that end, we explore model-driven engineering (MDE) frameworks. MDE is an approach to software development where models are given a central role in the development process, and where the models are used directly to derive implementation artefacts [10]. Meta-modelling is usually used to define the modelling language in MDE approaches. Transformations, both model-to-model and model-to-text, are used to generate implementation artefacts. Recently, using models directly at runtime has also received some attention from the research community [11]. While MDE has principally been used in a professional software engineering context, [12, 13] are examples of work closer to our own, where MDE is applied for to the creation of an end-user development framework.

Also related to our work, a number of end-user frameworks have newly been launched empowering mobile users to develop mobile applications themselves, for instance Google's App Inventor framework[1], Microsoft's TouchDevelop[2], NFC Task Launcher[3] or atooma[4]. As mobile devices are becoming more powerful in terms of computing and memory resources, and touchscreen technologies facilitate the construction of user-friendly interfaces, we expect that mobile software development will also get more accessible for all. Similar to the end-user frameworks for desktop environments, the mobile frameworks currently proposed adopt different language abstraction levels, i.e. programming vs. composition, and different development platforms, i.e. desktop vs. mobile tools. None of them explicitly support the extension of the framework by domain developers (i.e. the re-seeding step in the SER model).

3   Research Approach

Our research follows the design science paradigm [14]. While behavioural-science approaches focus mainly on the use and benefits of a system implemented in an organization, design science approaches develop and evaluate IT artefacts intended to solve identified organizational problems. Developing such artefacts requires domain knowledge and justification in form of proper evaluations. Design-science suggests an iterative work process allowing a gradual understanding of the problem to be solved and improvement of the solutions. It does not impose any concrete research and evaluation method since choice of method depends on the nature of the research problem and the type of the artefact being created.

The first step in our work was the specification of a set of scenarios that illustrate the concept of end-user service composition in mobile ubiquitous environments, and their evaluation and improvement through focus groups. The scenarios were used to: 1) elaborate the idea of end-user service composition and understand how it is perceived by the users; 2) identify an initial set of functionalities that users wish to create and a set of reusable services needed to create these functionalities. The scenarios were developed for three application domains related to the business areas of the research partners (see Section 2).

Following the specification of scenarios, our work has investigated alternative end-user notations. The notation for UbiComposer was selected to support both mobile-based and web-based scenarios. After the initial testing of a more complex notation through paper-prototyping, we decided to use a simple trigger-action sequence notation for the composition and a form-based presentation for the parameterisation of the services in a composition (see Section 5.4 for more

---

[1] The Site for Learning and Teaching App Inventor: http://www.appinventor.org

[2] TouchDevelop (Microsoft Research): https://www.touchdevelop.com

[3] NFC Task Launcher available on GooglePlay: https://play.google.com

[4] atooma: http://atooma.com

details). While the concepts of the proposed notation are inspired from the underlying concepts of visual flow languages that have proven to be successful in a number of end-users development environments, e.g. Lego MindStorm[5], the form-based approach is widely used for the parameterisation of online services and mobile applications. We have avoided a pure visual notation since it does not fit the pocket-size screens of mobile environments. As we will discuss later in this paper, the proposed UbiSys framework supports the realization of different end-user editors, and thus different notations may be provided in the future.

The focus of this paper, though, is on the development of engineering tools for end-user service composition. The main research problem is to find out what tools and technologies are well suited to building service composition environments for end users. This paper addresses the following questions:

1. How applicable is meta-modelling in the design of an engineering framework for end-user service composition?
2. Is it feasible to realize composition environments with existing model-driven engineering technologies, as exemplified by the Eclipse Modelling Framework (EMF) family of tools?
3. What are the architectural implications of meta-modelling and model-driven engineering technologies?

To answer these questions, we have prototyped and applied the service composition environment UbiSys. This paper discusses the experience we gained.

4   Overall Architecture

Figure 1 gives an overview of the UbiSys architecture, with the stakeholders in end-user service composition that we have identified, and with the tools and artefacts they use and create. We distinguish between two roles for meta-designers:

1. The *environment developers* create the service composition framework and the runtime environment for a specific composition approach, e.g. UbiSys. They are meta-designers that create tools for the composition design space.
2. The *domain developers* create reusable software services adapted to the needs of a particular domain, e.g. by adaptation of generic solutions. The services are created to fit the service composition framework. For instance, generic calendar services may be adapted to the needs of elderly people and to UbiSys. The domain developers are meta-designers that create seeds for composition in the design space, either as part of seeding or re-seeding steps.

These roles are motivated by the fact that creating tools for a design space requires different skills from creating services for composition by end-users. According to this separation, the developers in our own research activities were also organized in two teams: one on UbiSys and one on the City Explorer application example (see Section 6). In that way, we were able to identify initial difficulties that domain developers may face when taking the tools in use. Beyond developers, we also define two roles for the users:

---

[5] LEGO MINDSTORMS: http://mindstorms.lego.com

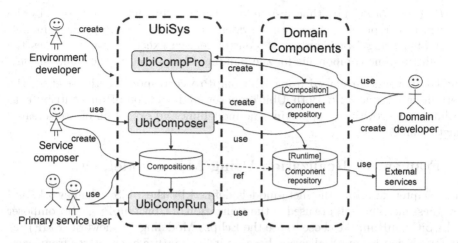

Fig. 1. System model

1. The *service composers* compose and tailor services into applications for service users. They test the service composition and eventually deploy it (or part of it) to one or several devices or servers.
2. The *primary service users* install, configure and use the services and applications created by service composers.

Similarly to [15], we consider end-user service composition to be an activity related to the development of software for personal use - unlike professional development targeting public use. It is, however, useful to differentiate between service composers and service users in several application domains. For instance, a caregiver may play the former role to create a service adapted to the needs of an assisted person, or a teacher to create a game for pupils. A user may play both the composer and user roles, e.g. a caregiver may participate in a service composed for assisted persons.

Our approach explores the application of a meta-modelling framework for the creation of a service composition framework by environment developers. The service composition framework itself, depicted as UbiSys in Figure 1, consists of three components:

1. *UbiCompPro* is a tool for domain developers allowing the creation of reusable components for composition. The domain developers implement components compliant with the runtime system in the framework, invoking domain services as needed. In addition they provide component descriptors that appear as building blocks for service composers to specify compositions from.
2. *UbiComposer* is a composition editor used by the service composers to select among the set of components defined using UbiCompPro and combine them into user-defined services and applications.

3. *UbiCompRun* is a runtime system for executing the services composed by the service composers. The runtime system interprets the composition models created using UbiComposer to control service execution, and invokes the right runtime components for the building blocks used in the composition.

The components developed using UbiCompPro correspond to the seeds of the meta-design framework. Both UbiComposer and UbiCompRun contribute to evolutionary growth by supporting the modelling and execution of user-created functionalities.

5 Framework Realization Using Meta-modelling

This chapter describes the meta-models defined by the UbiSys framework, and how these meta-models are used in the realization of UbiCompPro, UbiComposer and UbiCompRun. We chose to use the Eclipse Modeling Framework (EMF)[6] as the foundation for our realization because it is a mature open source framework with a whole family of tools built on top of it (e.g., it is the foundation of several commercial Eclipse based UML tools, including IBM's Rational Software Architect). In the first sub-section we give as background a short description of the EMF family of tools. We then describe the meta-models, before we give further details about our framework realisation based on these meta-models and EMF. The UbiSys framework and the City Explorer example application (See Section 6) are available as open source and documented on github[7].

5.1   EMF at a Glance

The Eclipse Modeling Project[8] is a top-level project in the Eclipse community that organizes the model-based development activities in the community. The foundation for most of tools that are sub-projects within Modeling is the Eclipse Modeling Framework (EMF). The core of EMF consists of three parts:

- eCore [16], the meta-meta-model of EMF, with supporting Java runtime libraries. The libraries contain APIs for managing model elements, and support for XMI-based persistence. EMF supports instantiation of meta-models based on generated Java classes, but also dynamic instantiation of non-generated classes using a generic, reflective API. This foundation provides interoperability between the tools based on EMF.
- EMF.Edit, a framework foundation for creating editors and views on top of the EMF models. This framework includes a command framework with a set of pre-defined commands that can be used to provide undoable operations on the model, like adding, deleting or moving model entities. Also, it provides facilities for defining the viewable structure and textual labels for model elements, giving a generic foundation for creating model views and editors.
- tools for the generation of runtime parts and a default model editor.

---

[6] Eclipse Modeling Framework (EMF): http://www.eclipse.org/modeling/emf/
[7] UbiSys and City Explorer source code: https://github.com/UbiCompForAll
[8] Eclipse Modeling Project: http://www.eclipse.org/modeling/

The runtime libraries and EMF.Edit were designed for use within the OSGi and Eclipse frameworks, but can also be used in stand-alone Java applications. From an EMF model, the generator tools of EMF enable the generation of:

- a Java representation of the model, including Java interfaces representing the model entity, implementation classes for these interfaces, and support classes including factories for creating instances.
- adapters based on EMF.Edit for presentation of the model elements.
- a fully functioning tree-based model editor that can be used from within Eclipse or in a stand-alone application using Eclipse Rich Client Platform.

While EMF can be considered to be a technology for developing abstract syntax, the Eclipse Modeling Project contains several tools for developing concrete syntaxes using EMF as their foundation. Among these are the Graphical Modeling Framework (GMF)[9] and Graphiti[10] for developing graphical modelling tools, and xText and EMF Text for developing tools using textual syntaxes.

5.2   The UbiSys Meta-models

The meta-models shown in this section were developed using EMF (using the standard EMF editors), but are conceptually independent of EMF and could be realized using other meta-modelling frameworks with a meta-meta-model similar to EMF's eCore. For the UbiSys tools, two meta-models were developed:

- The component descriptor meta-model (Figure 2) is used to model libraries of building block descriptors using the UbiCompPro tool. These libraries are used for providing the palette of building blocks in the UbiComposer tools.
- The user service meta-model (Figure 3) defines the abstract syntax for composing user services. The UbiComposer tool uses this to edit compositions, and the compositions are further used by UbiCompRun during runtime.

As shown in Figure 2, a descriptor library for components consists of a set of elements, which are building blocks, data types, or descriptors for domain objects (i.e. objects from the application domain). The main types of building blocks are triggers and steps, and each building block defines a set of properties. Elements and properties have user-friendly names that will be shown in UbiComposer.

The meta-model of the end-user's language is shown in Figure 3. It is used to represent the user services composed by the service composer. As shown in the figure, a user service is composed of one or more tasks, where each task has a trigger and a sequence of steps (actions). This corresponds to the trigger-action sequence used in the notations (see Section 5.4 for more details). Each building block (including trigger and step) has a number of property assignments, which can either be constant values, references to other properties, or references to domain objects. As shown in the figure, some concepts from the component descriptor meta-model are referenced to from this meta-model – e.g. each building block refers to its corresponding building block descriptor.

---

[9] Graphical Modeling Framework (GMF): http://wiki.eclipse.org/GMF

[10] Graphiti - a Graphical Tooling Infrastructure: http://www.eclipse.org/graphiti/

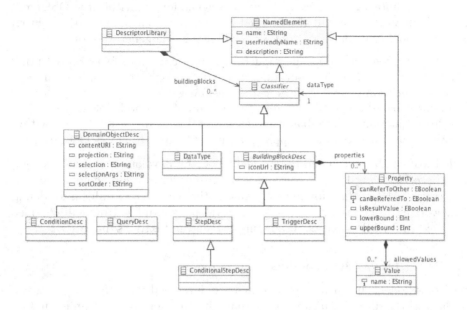

Fig. 2. Component descriptor meta-model

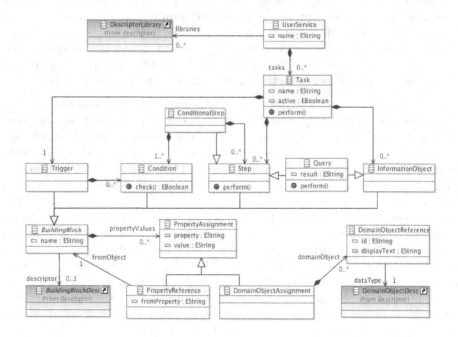

Fig. 3. User service meta-model

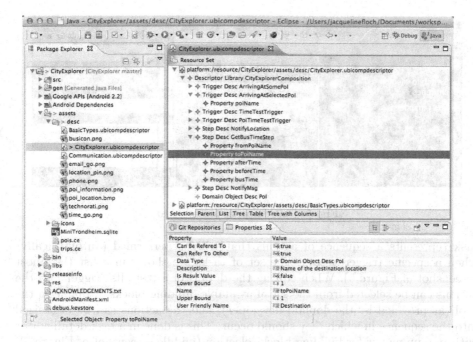

Fig. 4. UbiCompPro editor

5.3   UbiCompPro Implementation

UbiCompPro (Figure 4) is fully generated from the component descriptor meta-model. The tool is an example of the standard tree-based editor generated by EMF. As the target users of UbiCompPro are software developers, our assumption is that the generated tree-based editor is suitable for the task of creating component descriptors. The descriptor files created using the tool are used directly in UbiComposer for displaying the palette of building blocks that are available to create compositions from.

Figure 4 shows a screenshot for the UbiCompPro editor where the developer can create entries for each building block in the library. The editor as shown in the figure is running in the Eclipse environment, with the current project expanded in the view at the left. In the figure, the descriptor library developed for the City Explorer example application case is selected and the property "toPoiName" of the building block "GetBusTimeStep" is being edited. The data type for that descriptor is a domain descriptor "PoI" that supports access to data shared by the City Explorer application.

5.4   UbiComposer Implementation

UbiComposer is implemented in a mobile version for the Android platform (Figure 5) and in a web version (not depicted in this paper). At the top level of the composition, the service composer can define one or more tasks, where each

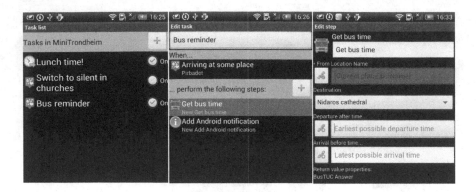

Fig. 5. UbiComposer for Android

task represents a sequence of actions that will be performed (automatically) when a specific trigger occurs. The set of tasks are shown in a list (left-most screenshot of Figure 5). When editing the details of a task, its trigger and the actions can be selected from the set of available building blocks available in the tool (as provided by the domain developer), and the actions can be organized into the sequence in which they should occur. This is done in a task detail editor with pop-up menus for building block selection (middle screenshot of Figure 5). Form-based editing is used for setting the parameters of each building block. Parameter values can be typed in, selected among constants, or linked to properties of other building blocks or domain objects from applications. This is done in a detail editor for each building block. The right most screenshot of Figure 5 illustrates different cases: while "Current place.poiName" is a reference to another building block, "Nidaros cathedral" is a value from the City Explorer application (see Section 6). The editors perform some validation, e.g. actions with missing values for required parameters are highlighted in red in the Android version.

The Android implementation of UbiComposer is partially generated and uses the core EMF libraries without EMF.edit. The in-memory representation of the composition directly uses the Java classes generated from the EMF metamodel, and the default EMF persistence mechanism is used to load and save the compositions to a file-based storage. Also, UbiComposer uses the EMF-generated classes for the component descriptors to provide the palette of building blocks, and for setting up the detail editors for each component. The rest of the editor, including the user interface providing the concrete notation is hand-coded using standard Android libraries.

The implementation of the web version uses the Google Web Toolkit (GWT)[11]. A main criterion for the selection of GWT is the availability of end-user friendly widgets such as text boxes, selection boxes, forms, Google Maps, calendars etc. In addition to GWT, third party widgets from SmartGWT and the Google Map library were also integrated on the client side. GWT RPC was used for the communication with the server. Tools exist that generate tree-based editors

---

[11] Google Web Toolkit (GWT): https://developers.google.com/web-toolkit/

(like UbiCompPro) for GWT from EMF meta-models[12]. However, the generated editor is far from our selected end-user notation, and we found it difficult to adapt the generated code for our purpose. The current implementation of the web-based version of UbiComposer was therefore hand-coded based on the concepts of the meta-models. It can directly use component descriptor libraries created using UbiCompPro.

GMF was initially considered for implementing UbiComposer, but we found that its strength primarily lies in the development of notations such as UML class-diagrams that are different from the form-based notation we wanted for UbiComposer. Graphiti was not yet available at the time of our choice, and textual syntax tools such as XText were not an option for our notation.

5.5 UbiCompRun Implementation

Two runtime approaches are supported: interpretation of compositions and transformation to code. The former was realised on Android as UbiCompRun for Android. The latter was realised as a transformation (currently manual) to Drools rules since the Drools engine is used by one of our industry partners. This paper does not provide further details on the transformation to Drools because this is a proprietary solution of our industry partner.

Although the implementation of UbiCompRun on Android is mostly hand-coded, it also exploits the core EMF libraries. More specifically, it also uses the same Java classes generated from the user service meta-model as UbiComposer.

The hand-coded parts include the definition of the Java interfaces and abstract classes of the runtime framework that the domain developers use to implement their runtime components. Also, they include the classes performing the interpretation of the service compositions and the invocation calls to the runtime components. As part of the implementation of runtime components, the domain developer must also provide a simple map between component descriptors and component implementation classes.

6 Application Example: City Explorer

City Explorer is a mobile Android application that was developed in order to assess the UbiSys composition framework. City Explorer supports the management and sharing of contents for city exploration, e.g. places and itineraries, and the navigation to places. In addition, it supports the creation of new functionalities by the user. For example, the user may add tasks for sharing information through social media, getting bus information to a place defined by City Explorer, or setting up a lunch meeting place with friends. To support such creation, a number of components (and building blocks) that the user can compose together were defined. Respective to the meta-design framework, both City Explorer and the set of building blocks map to seeds. New building blocks, i.e. new seeds, may be

---

[12] EMF SDK for GWT: http://wiki.eclipse.org/EMF/GWT

gradually added depending on the emergence of new ideas and needs. Support for end-user extension of City Explorer is realised using UbiSys:

- UbiCompPro is used to create building blocks. In our experimentation, we have created event triggers, e.g. "at a specific time", "at a specific place" or "at any place in a specific itinerary", and steps, e.g. "send SMS", "add post on Facebook" or "get bus time".
- The UbiComposer Android library is integrated in the mobile application code. Thus, UbiComposer can be invoked from the application.
- The UbiCompRun Android library is also integrated in the mobile application code. Thus the composed services can be activated from the application.

An important requirement in the extension of City Explorer was the ability to access to application data both during composition and runtime:

- The service composer may wish to specify an extension for a particular entity or set of entities defined by City Explorer, e.g. "when arriving at a church, switch my phone to the silent mode." To do so, the service composer needs access to the place classifications defined by the application during service composition.
- The executing code extension may also need to access application data, e.g. "when arriving close to one of my favourite places, give me a notification and display information about that place." The executing code needs to retrieve the set of favourite places (and possibly listens to changes made to that set). It also needs to retrieve information about a place when getting close to it.

UbiSys introduces the concept of "domain descriptor" that supports the creation of building blocks that access application data. Access to data requires the application to expose its data in compliance to the rules defined by UbiSys. Currently, UbiSys supports the Android Content Provider mechanism. In that way, Android application developers do need to learn any new mechanism to expose application data.

7   Discussion

The discussion provided in this chapter is based on our own experiences in applying meta-modelling and EMF to the development of the UbiSys framework and example applications. While the team working on UbiSys have obviously had a personal interest in succeeding with development, we do not have any bias regarding the use of meta-modelling or the EMF family of tools.

Most of the attention of the MDE research community has been on simplifying development for different groups of software developers. In our work, we found that MDE is also useful for the realization of end-user development tools:

- Meta-models were found useful for discussing the realization of the composition language for the selected end-user notation. The development of meta-models requires a precise definition of notation concepts. In addition it is a tool for seeking simplification of the models.

- MDE simplifies the task of environments developers, i.e. the realisation of the end-user composition framework.
- When meta-models are used all the way from design of building blocks, via composition, to runtime, consistency is enforced. This contributes to a smooth transition between the activities of domain developers and the activities of service composers in the design space.

On the other hand, we found meta-modelling inadequate for the rapid exploration of alternative notation concepts. Instead, visual prototypes (paper and quick SW mock-ups) are in our experience better suited for discussing and agreeing on the end-user composition language because they also provide the concrete syntax elements of the language. The different application domains addressed in our research gradually raised new requirements on the structural concepts needed for service composition. For instance the telco case added a requirement for if-then-else structures (not needed by other cases), while the mobile asset management case added a requirement related to the use of conditions in association with triggers. We were able to extend the initial meta-models to support these concepts, but have completed implementation of them. We have no experience so far on supporting extensions that would require more complex adjustments of the meta-model.

The basic EMF technology selected in our work to realize the model-driven engineering approach was found to be suitable for the "invisible" parts of the composition and runtime tools (i.e. the parts not exposed to end users):

- EMF supports the instantiations of meta-models (i.e. the creation of models) and persistent storage. We use EMF libraries and generated Java classes to support the specification of compositions based on the composition notation, and to implement import and use of component descriptor libraries in UbiComposer.
- Based the specification of a meta-model, EMF supports the generation of a tree-base editor for the creation of models. UbiCompPro is such an editor. The domain developers can easily install UbiCompPro as a plug-in in their development environment and create descriptors for the building blocks descriptors the service composer will choose among during composition.
- The EMF cross-platform support worked between Eclipse-based / Desktop Java, and Android. In the case of Android some repackaging of the EMF libraries was required, and also the full potential of EMF was not used. Although there is also support for automatic generation of GWT projects from EMF meta-models, we found it too difficult to integrate this with the end user-friendly widgets that we needed, and thus EMF libraries were not used in the web-based UbiComposer.

When starting the development of UbiComposer, we also looked for tools based on EMF that could assist in developing the visual parts of our notation. The main candidate we found at that time was GMF, but it was not selected because it did not match well to our selected notation. Also, it does not support the Android and web-based platforms, and thus would only have been useful on the desktop.

The different industry partners involved in our work had different requirements on composition and runtime. Using a MDE approach, the proposed notation models remain platform-independent and we were able to integrate the tools with other applications and middleware. The adoption of a meta-modelling approach and the EMF technology has provided us the flexibility to fulfil various architectural needs:

- Composition editors were developed both in native code for Android and as a web-based solution. The former enables integration of the editor with any Android app. The latter enables access to the editor on any platform.
- The compositions were both interpreted at runtime on Android and transformed to Drools rules. In the former case, as the editor is also available on Android compositions can be modified at runtime.

8 Conclusion and Further Work

The EUD community have mostly focused on the end-user perspective of EUD, and not so much on technical realization of the required tools. This paper describes a MDE approach to the realisation of such tools. It positions the approach with respect to the meta-design framework and reports our experience, mostly positive, in adopting MDE and the EMF technology. Our work is a first step in the realisation of end-user tools. Relevant future areas of work include:

- *Validation support.* End-users lack knowledge in software engineering practices. Support for creating correct compositions and avoiding errors is therefore a critical concern. We intend to investigate how the EMF validation framework can be exploited to check the models.
- *Simulation support.* Most service compositions created for mobile pervasive computing do not occur at once, but are triggered in a specific context. Thus, differently from spread-sheet applications or EUD game environments, the end user cannot observe the effect of a composition at once. We intend to build simulation and debugging tools allowing end users to test the compositions and search for the causes of eventual errors.
- *Guidance to domain developers.* The proposed framework does not provide any guidelines for the specification of building blocks adapted to the level of expertise of non-IT experts. Few software developers are familiar with the discipline of end-user development. We intend to enhance the tools with guidelines based on earlier experience such as found in [17, 18]
- *Adaptation to emerging technologies.* Another relevant work is the exploration of new tools to realize visual notations, such as the recent additions to the EMF family of tools, including Graphiti and Extended Editing Framework.
- *End-user evaluation.* The tools were improved based on feedback from project participants. A more extensive evaluation including both external developers and end-users is required.

Acknowledgement. Our research has been performed in the Norwegian Research Council (NFR) project UbiCompForAll in cooperation with the EU IST project SOCIETIES (contract 257493).

References

1. Nardi, B.A.: A small Matter of Programming. The MIT Press (1993) ISBN: 9780262140539
2. Fischer, G.: End-User Development and Meta-Design: Foundations for Cultures of Participation. Journal of Organizational and End User Computing 22(1), 52–82 (2010)
3. Fischer, G., et al.: Meta-design: a manifesto for end-user development. Communication of ACM 47(9), 33–37 (2004)
4. Sutcliffe, A., Mehandjiev, N.: Special issue on End-User Development. Communications of the ACM 47(9) (2004)
5. Mernik, M.: When and How to Develop Domain-Specific Languages. ACM Computing Surveys 37(4) (2005)
6. Floch, J.: A Framework for User-Tailored City Exploration. In: Costabile, M.F., Dittrich, Y., Fischer, G., Piccinno, A. (eds.) IS-EUD 2011. LNCS, vol. 6654, pp. 239–244. Springer, Heidelberg (2011)
7. Sanders, R.T., Mbaabu, F., Shiaa, M.M.: End-user Configuration of Telco Services. In: Proc. of 16th Int. Conf. Intelligence in Next Generation Networks: Realising the Power of the Network (ICIN 2012). IEEE (2012) (10.1109/ICIN.2012.6376036)
8. Repenning, A., Ioannidou, A.: Agent-based End User Development. Communications of the ACM 47(9) (1994)
9. Weisemöller, I., Schürr, A.: A Comparison of Standard Compliant Ways to Define Domain Specific Languages. In: Giese, H. (ed.) MoDELS 2007 Workshops. LNCS, vol. 5002, pp. 47–58. Springer, Heidelberg (2008)
10. Stahl, T., Völter, M.: Model-driven software development: technology, engineering, management. Wiley, Chichester (2006)
11. Blair, G., Bencomo, N., France, R.B.: Models@ run.time. IEEE Computer 42(10) (2009)
12. De Silva, B., Ginige, A.: Meta-model to support end-user development of web based business information systems. In: Baresi, L., Fraternali, P., Houben, G.-J. (eds.) ICWE 2007. LNCS, vol. 4607, pp. 248–253. Springer, Heidelberg (2007)
13. Fogli, D., Parasiliti Provenza, L.: End-user development of e-government services through meta-modeling. In: Costabile, M.F., Dittrich, Y., Fischer, G., Piccinno, A. (eds.) IS-EUD 2011. LNCS, vol. 6654, pp. 107–122. Springer, Heidelberg (2011)
14. Hevner, A.R., March, S.T., Jinsoo, P.: Design Science in Information Systems Research. MIS Quarterly 28, 75–105 (2004)
15. Ko, A.J., et al.: The State of the Art in End-User Software Engineering. ACM Computing Surveys 43(3) (2011)
16. Steinberg, D., Budinsky, F., Paternostro, M., Merks, E.: EMF: Eclipse Modeling Framework, 2nd edn. Addison-Wesley Professional (2008)
17. Myers, B.A., Pane, J.F.: Natural Programming Languages and Environments. Communication of ACM 47(9), 47–52 (2004)
18. Repenning, A., Ioannidou, A.: What makes end-user development tick? 13 design guidelines. In: Lieberman, H., Paterno, F., Wulf, V. (eds.) End-User Development. Springer (2006) ISBN 1-4020-4220-5

Sheet-Defined Functions: Implementation and Initial Evaluation

Peter Sestoft and Jens Zeilund Sørensen

IT University of Copenhagen
Rued Langgaards Vej 7, DK-2300 Copenhagen S, Denmark

Abstract. Spreadsheets are ubiquitous end-user programming tools, but lack even the simplest abstraction mechanism: The ability to encapsulate a computation as a function. This was observed by Peyton-Jones and others [14], who proposed a mechanism to define such functions using only standard spreadsheet cells, formulas and references.

This paper extends their work by increasing expressiveness and emphasizing execution speed of the functions thus defined. First, we support recursive and higher-order functions, while still using only standard spreadsheet notation. Secondly, we obtain fast execution by a careful choice of data representation and compiler technology.

The result is a concept of *sheet-defined functions* that should be understandable to most spreadsheet users, yet offer sufficient programming power and performance to make end-user development of function libraries practical and attractive.

We outline a prototype implementation Funcalc of sheet-defined functions, and provide a case study with some evidence that it can express many important functions while maintaining good performance.

1 Introduction

Spreadsheet programs such as Microsoft Excel, OpenOffice Calc, Gnumeric and Google Docs provide a simple, powerful and easily mastered end-user programming platform for mostly-numeric computation. Yet as observed by several authors [12,14], spreadsheets lack even the most basic abstraction mechanism: The creation of a named function directly from spreadsheet formulas.

Many spreadsheet programs allow function definitions in external languages such as VBA, Java or Python, but those languages present a completely different programming model that many competent spreadsheet users do not master.

Here we present a prototype implementation, called Funcalc, of *sheet-defined functions* that (1) uses only standard spreadsheet concepts and notations, as proposed by Peyton-Jones et al. [14], so it should be understandable to competent spreadsheet users, and (2) is very efficient, so that user-defined functions can be as fast as built-in ones. Furthermore, the ability to define functions directly from spreadsheet formulas should (3) permit gradual untangling of data and algorithms in spreadsheet models and (4) encourage the development of shared function libraries; both of these in turn should (5) improve reuse, reliability and upgradability of spreadsheet models.

Y. Dittrich et al. (Eds.): IS-EUD 2013, LNCS 7897, pp. 88–103, 2013.

Our implementation is written in C# and achieves high performance thanks to portable runtime code generation on the Common Language Infrastructure (CLI) [6], as implemented by Microsoft .NET and the Mono project.

Our ultimate motivation is pragmatic. A sizable minority of spreadsheet users, including biologists, physicists and financial analysts, build very complex spreadsheet models. This is because spreadsheets make it convenient to experiment with both computations and data, and because the resulting models are easy to share and distribute. We believe that one can advance the state of the art by giving spreadsheet users better tools, rather than telling them that they should have used Matlab, Java, Python or Haskell instead.

We *do not* think that spreadsheets will make programming languages redundant, but we do believe that they provide a computation platform with many useful features that can be considerably improved by fairly simple technical means.

2 Sheet-Defined Functions

2.1 A Small Example

Consider the problem of calculating the area of each of a large number of triangles whose side lengths a, b and c are given in columns E, F and G of a spreadsheet, as in Fig. 1. The area is given by the formula $\sqrt{s(s-a)(s-b)(s-c)}$ where $s = (a+b+c)/2$ is half the perimeter. Now, either one must allocate column H to hold the value s and compute the area in column I, or one must inline s four times in the area formula. The former pollutes the spreadsheet with intermediate results, whereas the latter would create a long expression that is nearly impossible to enter without mistakes. It is clear that most realistic problems would require even more space for intermediate results and even more unwieldy formulas.

	D	E	F	G	H	I
1		a	b	c	s	area
2		3	4	5	6	6
3		30	40	50	60	600
4		100	100	100	150	4330.127019
5		6	8	10	12	24

Fig. 1. Triangle side lengths and computed areas; intermediate results in column H

Here we propose instead to define a function, TRIAREA say, using standard spreadsheet cells and formulas, but on a separate *function sheet*, and then call this function as needed from the sheet containing the triangle data.

Fig. 2 shows a function sheet containing a definition of function TRIAREA, with inputs a, b and c in cells A3, B3 and C3, the intermediate result s in cell D3, and the output in cell E3.

A6	A	B	C	D	E	F
1	'Area ...					
2	'a	'b	'c	's	'area	
3	3	4	5	=(A3+B3+C3)/2	=SQRT(D3*(D3-A3)*(D3-B3)*(D3-C3))	
4					=DEFINE("triarea", E3, A3, B3, C3)	
5						

Fig. 2. Function sheet, where DEFINE in E4 creates function TRIAREA with input cells A3, B3 and C3, output cell E3, and intermediate cell D3

Fig. 3 shows an ordinary sheet with triangle side lengths in columns E, F and G, function calls =TRIAREA(E2,F2,G2) in column H to compute the triangles' areas, and no intermediate results; the latter exist only on the function sheet. As usual in spreadsheets, it suffices to enter the function call once in cell H2 and then copy it down column H with automatic adjustment of cell references.

H2	E	F	G	H	I
1	a	b	c	area	
▶ 2	3	4	5	=TRIAREA(E2, F2, G2)	
3	30	40	50	600	
4	100	100	100	4330.12701892219	
5	6	8	10	24	
6	1	1	1	0.433012701892219	

Fig. 3. Ordinary sheet calling TRIAREA, defined in Fig. 2, from cells H2:H5

2.2   Expected Mode of Use

A user may develop formulas on a function sheet and interactively experiment with input values and formulas until satisfied that the results are correct. Subsequently the user may turn these formulas into a sheet-defined function by calling the DEFINE built-in (see Sect. 2.3); the function is immediately ready to use from ordinary sheets and from other functions.

Within a project, company or scientific discipline, groups of frequently used functions can be turned into function libraries, distributed on function sheets. This makes for a smooth transition from experiments and *ad hoc* models to more stable and reliable libraries of functions, without barring end-users from adapting library functions to new scientific or business requirements, as may be the case with libraries created by external "professional" developers.

Moreover, improving the separation between "mostly data" ordinary sheets and "mostly model" function sheets provides a way to mitigate the upgrade and consistency problems sometimes caused by the strong intermixing of model and data found in many spreadsheets.

2.3 New Built-In Functions

Our Funcalc prototype implementation uses the standard notions of sheet, cell, formula and built-in function. It adds just three new built-in functions to support the definition and use of sheet-defined functions. As illustrated by cell E4 in Fig. 2, there is a function to create a new function:

- DEFINE("name", out, in1..inN) creates a function with the given name, result cell out, and input cells in1..inN, where N >= 0.

Two other functions are used to create a function value (closure) and to apply it, respectively:

- CLOSURE("name", e1..eM) evaluates e1..eM to values a1..aM and returns a closure for the sheet-defined function "name". An argument ai that is an ordinary value gets stored in the closure, whereas an argument that is NA() signifies that this argument will be provided later when calling the closure.
- APPLY(fv, e1..eN) evaluates fv to a closure, evaluates e1..eN to values b1..bN, and applies the closure by using the bj values for those arguments in the closure that were NA() at closure creation.

The NA() mechanism provides a very flexible way to create closures (partially applied functions), which is rather unusual from a programming language perspective, but fits well with the standard spreadsheet usage of NA() to signify a value that is not (yet) available.

3 Interpretive Implementation

Our prototype implementation is written in C# and consists of a rather straight-forward *interpretive implementation* combined with a novel *compiled implementation* of sheet-defined functions, described in Sects. 4 and 5.

As in most spreadsheet programs, a workbook contains worksheets, each worksheet contains a grid of cells, and each cell may contain a constant or a formula or nothing. A formula contains an expression and a value cache. A worksheet is represented as a "lumpy" sparse array data structure that is space-efficient, highly scalable, and performs very well on modern CPUs.

Since spreadsheet formulas are dynamically typed, runtime values are represented by concrete subclasses Number, Text, Error, Array, and Function with a common of abstract superclass Value.

A formula expression e in a given cell on a given worksheet is evaluated interpretively by calling e.Eval(sheet,col,row), which returns a Value object. Such interpretive evaluation involves repeated wrapping and unwrapping of values, where the most costly in terms of runtime overhead is the wrapping of IEEE 64-bit floating-point numbers (C# type double) as Number objects, and testing and unwrapping of Number objects as IEEE floating-point numbers. One goal of the compiled implementation presented in Sect. 4 is to avoid this overhead.

4 Compiled Implementation

Our prototype is written in C# and compiles a sheet-defined function to CLI bytecode [6] at runtime, so that functions can be created and edited interactively, like everything else in the spreadsheet.

This section outlines the compilation process and some of the steps taken to ensure good performance.

4.1 Compilation Process Outline

1. Build a dependency graph whose nodes are the cells transitively reachable, by cell references, from the sheet-defined function's output cell.
2. Perform a topological sort of the dependency graph, so a cell is preceded by all cells that it references. It is illegal for a sheet-defined function to have static cyclic dependencies.
3. If a cell in the graph is referred only once (statically), inline its formula at its unique occurrence. This saves a local variable at no cost in code size.
4. Using the dependency graph, determine the evaluation condition (see Sect. 5) for each remaining cell; build a new dependency graph that takes evaluation conditions into account; and redo the topological sort.
5. Generate CLI bytecode for the cells in forward topological order. For each cell c with associated variable v_c, generate code corresponding to this assignment: v_c = <code for c's formula>;

4.2 No Value Wrapping

The simplest compilation scheme generates code to emulate interpretive evaluation. The code for an expression e leaves the value of e on the (CLI virtual machine) stack top as a Value object.

However, wrapping every intermediate result as an object of a subclass of Value would be inefficient, in particular for numeric operations. In an expression such as A1*B1+C1, the intermediate result A1*B1 would be wrapped as a Number, only to be immediately unwrapped. The creation of that useless Number object is slow: it requires allocation in the heap and causes work for the garbage collector.

Therefore, when the result of an expression e will definitely be used as a number, we use a second compilation method. It generates code that, when executed, leaves the value of e on the stack as a 64-bit floating-point value, avoiding costly allocation in the heap. If the result of e is an error (or a non-number such as a text or array), the resulting number will be a NaN [8].

4.3 Efficient Error Propagation

When computing with naked 64-bit floating-point values, we represent an error value as a NaN and use the 51 bit "payload" of the NaN to distinguish error values, as per the IEEE standard [8, section 6.2], which is supported by all modern hardware. Since arithmetic operations and mathematical functions preserve

NaN operands, we get error propagation for free. For instance, if d is a NaN, then Math.Sqrt(6.1*d+7.5) will be a NaN with the same payload, thus representing the same error. As an alternative to error propagation via NaNs, one could use CLI/.NET exceptions, but that would be vastly slower.

4.4   Compilation of Comparisons

According to spreadsheet principles, a comparison such as B8>37 must propagate errors: If B8 evaluates to an error, then the entire comparison evaluates to the same error. When compiling a comparison we cannot rely on NaN propagation; a comparison involving one or more NaNs is either true or false, never undefined, in CLI [6, section III.3].

Therefore we introduce a third compilation method. It takes an expression e and two code generators ifProper and ifBad. It generates code that evaluates e; and if the value is a non-NaN number, leaves that value on the stack top as a 64-bit floating-point value and continues with the code generated by ifProper; otherwise, continues with the code generated by ifBad.

The code generators ifProper and ifBad generate the success continuation and the failure continuation [20] for the evaluation of e.

4.5   Compilation of Conditions

Like other expressions, a conditional IF(e0,e1,e2) must propagate errors from the condition e0, so if e0 gives an error value, then the entire conditional expression must give the same error value.

To achieve this we introduce a fourth compilation method, for expressions that are used as conditions. The method takes an expression e0 and three code generators ifT, ifF and ifBad, and generates code that evaluates e0; and if the value is a non-NaN number different from zero, it continues with the code generated by ifT; if it is non-NaN and equal to zero, continues with the code generated by ifF; otherwise, continues with the code generated by ifBad.

For instance, to compile IF(e0,e1,e2), we compile e0 as a condition whose ifT and ifF continuations generate code for e1 and e2.

5   Evaluation Conditions

Whereas most of the compilation machinery described in Sect. 4 would be applicable to any dynamically typed language in which numerical computations and error propagation play a prominent role, this section addresses a problem that seems unique to recursive sheet-defined functions.

5.1   Motivation and Outline

Consider computing s^n, the string consisting of $n \geq 0$ concatenated copies of string s, corresponding to Excel's built-in REPT(s,n). The sheet-defined function

B83	A	B	C
65	=DEFINE("re…	'REPT4(s,n), fast recursive implementation, relies on eval…	
66	's =	'abc	
67	'n =	5	
68	'rept4(s,n/2) =	=REPT4(B66, FLOOR(B67/2, 1))	
69	'result =	=IF(B67=0, "", IF(MOD(B67, 2), B66&B68&B68, B68&B68))	
70			

Fig. 4. Recursive function REPT4(s,n) illustrates the need for evaluation conditions

REPT4(s,n) in Fig. 4 is optimal, using $O(\log n)$ string concatenation operations (written &) for a total running time of $O(n \cdot |s|)$, where $|s|$ is the length of s.

If $n = 0$, that is B67=0, then the result is the empty string and there is no need to evaluate cell B68. In fact, it would be horribly wrong to unconditionally evaluate B68 because it performs a recursive call to the function itself, so this would cause an infinite loop. It would be equally wrong to inline B68's formula in the B69 formula, since that would duplicate the recursive call and make the total execution time $O(n^2 \cdot |s|)$ rather than $O(n \cdot |s|)$, thwarting the programmer's intentions.

A cell such as B68 must be evaluated only when actually needed by further computations. That is the reason for step 4 in the compilation process outline in Sect. 4.1, which we flesh out as follows:

4.1 For each cell in the sheet-defined function, compute its *evaluation condition*, a logical expression that says when the cell must be evaluated; see Sect. 5.2.

4.2 While building the evaluation conditions, perform logical simplifications; see Sect. 5.3.

4.3 If the cell's formula is *trivial*, for instance a constant or a cell reference, then set its evaluation condition to constant true, indicating unconditional evaluation.

4.4 Rebuild the cell dependency graph and redo the topological sort of cells, taking also the cell references in the cell's evaluation condition into account.

4.5 Generate code in topological order, as in step 5 of Sect. 4.1, modified as follows: If the cell's evaluation condition is not constant true, generate code to evaluate and cache (Sect. 5.4) and test the evaluation condition, and to evaluate the cell's formula only if true:

```
if (<evaluation condition for c>)
  v_c = <code for c's formula>;
```

5.2   Finding the Evaluation Conditions

A cell needs to be evaluated if the output cell depends on the cell, given the actual values of the input cells. Hence evaluation conditions can be computed from a *conditional dependency graph*, which is a labelled multigraph.

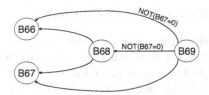

Fig. 5. Evaluation dependencies in REPT4. Output cell B69 depends on B66 and on B68 if NOT(B67=0), and depends unconditionally on B67.

Fig. 5 shows the conditional dependency graph for function REPT4 from Fig. 4. A node represents a cell, and an edge represents a dependency of one cell on another, arising from a particular cell-to-cell reference. An edge label is the condition under which the cell reference will be evaluated.

Now the *evaluation condition* of a non-input cell c is the disjunction, over all reference paths π from the output cell to c, of the conjunction of all labels ℓ_p along path π. More precisely, if P_c is the set of labelled paths from the output cell to c, then the evaluation condition b_c of c is

$$b_c = \bigvee_{\pi \in P_c} \bigwedge_{p \in \pi} \ell_p$$

Note that when c is the output cell itself, there is a single empty path in $P_c = \{\langle\rangle\}$, so the evaluation condition is true (must evaluate). Also, if there is no path from the output to c, then the evaluation condition is false (need not evaluate).

The labels, or cell-cell reference conditions, on the conditional dependency graph arise from the non-strict functions IF(p,e1,e2) and CHOOSE(n,e1..en). For instance:

- If a cell contains the formula IF(q,A1,A2+A3), then it has an edge to A1 with label q, and edges to A2 and A3 both with label $\neg q$. Also, if q is e.g. B8>37, then the cell has an edge to B8 with label true, because the condition must always be evaluated.
- If a cell contains CHOOSE(n,A1,A2,A3), then it has an edge to A1 labelled with the assertion n=1, an edge to A2 labelled n=2, and an edge to A3 labelled n=3.
- In general, if a cell contains the formula IF(q,e_1,e_2), then edges arising from references inside e_1 will have labels of form $q \wedge r$, and edges arising from references inside e_2 will have labels of form $\neg q \wedge r$.

We can compute the evaluation conditions of all cells in backwards topological order. We start with the output cell, whose evaluation condition is constant true, and initially set the evaluation condition of all other non-input cells to false. To process a cell whose evaluation condition p has already been found, we traverse the abstract syntax tree of the cell's formula and accumulate (conjoin) conditions q when we process the operands of non-strict functions. Whenever we encounter a reference to cell c, we update that cell's evaluation condition b_c with $b_c := b_c \vee (p \wedge q)$.

5.3   Simplification of Evaluation Conditions

Since an evaluation condition must be evaluated to control the evaluation of a formula, efficiency could suffer dramatically unless the evaluation condition is reduced to the simplest logically equivalent form.

A subexpression of an evaluation condition itself may involve a recursive call or effectful external call, and therefore should be evaluated only if needed, so any logical simplifications must preserve order of evaluation. Hence we use order-preserving simplification rules, rather than reduction to disjunctive or conjunctive normal form.

The approach outlined above finds the evaluation condition NOT(B67=0) for B68 in REPT4 from Fig. 4, which is exactly as desired.

5.4   Caching Atomic Conditions

An evaluation condition is built from logical connectives and from the conditions in non-strict functions such as IF(B67=0,...); we call such a condition an *atom*. An atom may appear in the evaluation condition of multiple cells, but for correctness it must be evaluated at most once, because it may involve a call to a volatile function such as RAND() that would produce different results on each evaluation.

Hence each occurrence of an atom is compiled to a *cache* that tests whether the atom has already been evaluated, and if so just returns the cached value; and if not, evaluates the atom and saves the value. In the cache, an evaluated atom is represented by its value, and an unevaluated one is represented by a special NaN.

5.5   Reflection on Evaluation Conditions

Why don't we simply use the caching mechanism for all cell values (instead of bothering with evaluation conditions), as in lazy functional languages [13]? One reason is that unlike atom caching, general expression caching may lead to an exponential code size increase: one lazily evaluated cell may contain multiple references to another lazily evaluated cell, and the code for that cell's formula will be duplicated at each possible use. Moreover, this exponential code size blowup is likely to happen in practice.

6   Some Example Functions

Distribution Function of the Normal Distribution. Sheet-defined functions may be used to define statistical functions, such as Excel's NORMSDIST(z), the cumulative distribution function $F(z)$ of the normal distribution. A widely used approximation due to Hart [7] can be implemented as shown in Fig. 6. Depending on z, it either computes a quotient between two polynomials (in A14:B20 and C14:D21) or a continued fraction (in B11). Our implementation

6	'z =	-5		
7	'p =	=IF(B6<0, B11, 1-B11)		
8	'zabs =	=ABS(B6)		
9	'expntl =	=EXP(-1*B8*B8/2)		
10	'pdf =	=B9/SQRT(2*PI())		
11	'p' =	=IF(B8>37, 0, IF(B8<7.071, B9*B14/D14, B10/(B8+1/(B8+2/(B8+3/(B8+4/(B8+0.65)))))))		
12				
13	'pi		'qi	
14	220.206867912376	=A14+$B$8*B15	440.413735824752	=C14+$B$8*D15
15	221.213596169931	=A15+$B$8*B16	793.826512519948	=C15+$B$8*D16
16	112.07929149787	=A16+$B$8*B17	637.333633378931	=C16+$B$8*D17
17	33.912866078383	=A17+$B$8*B18	296.564248779673	=C17+$B$8*D18
18	6.37396220353165	=A18+$B$8*B19	86.780732202946	=C18+$B$8*D19
19	0.700383064443688	=A19+$B$8*B20	16.0641775792069	=C19+$B$8*D20
20	0.035262496599891	=A20	1.75566716318264	=C20+$B$8*D21
21			0.0883883476483184	=C21

Fig. 6. Sheet-defined function NORMDISTCDF(z), with input cell B6 and output cell B7, computes the cumulative distribution function of the normal distribution $N(0,1)$

compiles this sheet-defined function to fast bytecode that is faster than Excel's built-in one.

Sheet-Defined Functions as Predicates. The ability to create a (sheet-defined) function and treat it as a value gives much expressive power as is known from functional programming, with operations such as a map, fold/reduce, filter and tabulate. Here we focus on the added value for more common spreadsheet operations.

For instance, Excel's COUNTIF function takes as argument a cell area and a criterion, which may be a string that encodes a comparison such as ">= 18.5". However, one cannot express composite criteria such as "18.5 <= x < 25". Passing the criterion as a string imposes arbitrary restrictions and also raises questions about the meaning of cell references in the criterion.

Passing the criterion as a sheet-defined function makes COUNTIF more powerful and avoids these unclarities. For instance, assume we want to count the number of peoples' weights in range C1:C100 whose body mass index (BMI) is between 18.5 and 25, that is, "normal". Then we can create a sheet-defined function NORMALBMI with some input cell A1 and output cell containing =AND(18.5<=A1, A1<25), and then use COUNTIF(C1:C100, CLOSURE("NORMALBMI",NA())) to obtain that count.

Numerical Equation Solving. Perhaps more surprisingly, we can implement Excel's Goal Seek feature as a sheet-defined function. Goal Seek is a dialog-based mechanism for numerical equation solving, such as "set cell C1 to 100 by changing cell B1", which really means to find a solution B1 to the equation $f(B1) = 100$ where f expresses the contents of cell C1 as a function of B1. Clearly, this f can be expressed as a sheet-defined function, just because C1 depends on B1 through standard spreadsheet functions and so on.

A sheet-defined function GOALSEEK(f,r,a) that returns an x so that $f(x) = r$, if one exists, can be defined as follows. The input is a function f, a target value r, and an initial guess a at the value of x. Function GOALSEEK first calls an auxiliary function to find a value b so that $f(a)$ and $f(b)$ have different signs, if possible. Then it uses a finite number of explicit bisection steps, expressed in the usual spreadsheet style of copying a row of formulas.

Once GOALSEEK has been encapsulated as a function, we can numerically solve multiple equations by ordinary copying of formulas, whereas Excel's dialog-based Goal Seek would have to be manually invoked for each equation.

Adaptive Integration. To compute the integral of a function $f(x)$ on an interval $[a, b]$, we can use a combination of higher-order functions and recursion. Compute $m = (a + b)/2$ and two approximations to the integral, for instance by Simpson's rule $(b - a)(f(a) + 4f(m) + f(b))/6$ and the midpoint formula $(b - a)f(m)$. If the approximations are nearly equal, return one of them; otherwise recursively compute the integral on $[a, m]$ and the integral on $[b, m]$ and add the results. Such higher-order adaptive integration can be implemented by a user-defined function using just seven formula cells; it cannot be implemented using only standard spreadsheet functions or VBA.

Correct and Comprehensive Calendar Functions. The calendar functions in many spreadsheet programs do not handle ISO week numbers, calculation of holidays (such as Easter), finding the first Monday of a given month, and so on. Such computations are easily and efficiently implementable as sheet-defined functions, starting from a source such as [5].

7   Case Study: Financial Functions

The second author [21] evaluated the feasibility of using sheet-defined functions instead of built-in ones, by implementing many of the financial functions that are built into Microsoft Excel 2010. This case study was chosen because (1) finance is an important application domain for spreadsheets, and (2) a faithful implementation of Excel financial functions is available in the functional language F#, complete with source code and thousands of test cases [2].

This evaluation was carried out by a software development student, and we do not claim that it says much about the ease of programming with sheet-defined functions. However, we do claim that it demonstrates that sheet-defined functions can be expressive and fast enough to replace built-in ones.

7.1   Performance of Sheet-Defined Financial Functions

Fig. 7 lists some of the implemented financial functions. In most cases the sheet-defined functions are faster than the corresponding Excel built-ins, or comparable to them. Two notable exceptions are functions RATE and IRR, marked by an asterisk (*) in the figure. The reason for their poor performance probably is that they use the rather simplistic general binary search procedure GOALSEEK mentioned in Sect. 6, instead of a faster Newton-Raphson root-finding algorithm, for instance. This is a question of choice of algorithm, not a problem of the sheet-defined function implementation itself.

Function	Excel	Funcalc	Note
PV	1461	804	
FV	1445	1138	
NPER	1055	472	
RATE	2297	44864	*
PMT	1523	664	
FVSCHEDULE	2960	928	
IMPT	1593	1732	
PPMT	1805	1292	
CUMIPMT	3117	3400	
CUMPRINC	2742	4072	
ISPMT	468	170	
IRR	4750	79804	*
NPV	2156	2060	
MIRR	3515	8328	
SLN	125	158	
SYD	453	212	
AMORLINC	14921	2054	
AMORDEGRC	16343	4444	

Fig. 7. Execution time for Excel 2010 built-in functions and Funcalc sheet-defined functions (ns/call). For the *-marked cases, see text.

7.2 Ideas for Improvement Arising from Case Study

The process of implementing the financial functions generated several ideas for improving our prototype Funcalc (none of which have yet been implemented), including these:

- Proposal: Add a simple scope mechanism.
  Problem: Funcalc, like other spreadsheet programs, has a single scope, so all names are visible anywhere in a workbook. This pollutes the global namespace with auxiliary functions and may lead to name clashes.
  Possible solutions: (1) Name-based scope. A function _FOO whose name begins with a single underscore is a *global auxiliary* and can be called only from function sheets, not from an ordinary sheet; a function __FOO whose name begins with two underscores is *sheet-local* and can be called only from the function sheet in which it is defined; a function _BAR_FOO is *function-local* and can be called only from public function BAR and from other function-local auxiliaries such as _BAR_BAZ. (2) Visual scope. A global function and all its auxiliaries are surrounded by a graphical "fence", restricting the scope of the auxiliaries.
- Proposal: Avoid infinite recursion, especially when loading workbooks.
  Problem: A recursive function may fail to terminate (go into an infinite loop), a mistake that is especially nasty during the loading of a workbook from file.
  Possible solutions: (1) Allow manual interruption of computations, for instance by pressing ESC or Ctrl-C. Such interruption may leave a computation (a recursive call) unfinished; in this case its result might be a special

kind of error such as #BREAK or #LOOP, which would propagate as usual to any cell depending on it. (2) Set a function call limit for each recalculation, and make it low when recalculating a workbook upon reloading. The same error mechanism could be used as for manual interruption. It would be more useful to limit the call depth rather than the total number of calls, but the latter may be simpler to implement, and faster.

- Proposal: Error messages should be made more informative.
  Problem: According to spreadsheet semantics, an error value propagates from operand to result. In an ordinary spreadsheet where all cells are manifest, it is fairly easy to trace an error back to the cell containing the original offending formula. With sheet-defined functions, the error may have originated in a deeply nested auxiliary function, and tracing this can be very cumbersome. Possible solutions: (1) Make error values carry the address of the cell containing the original offending computation, for instance, as #NUM!#Sheet1!A1, instead of just #NUM!. (2) For errors originating from within a sheet-defined function, make the error value carry the entire argument vector of the (innermost) function call that caused the function to return an error value. This would enable "replaying" that call and hence enable debugging.

8   Evaluation

8.1   Simplicity

We believe we have obtained a dramatic extension of the expressiveness and user-programmability of spreadsheet models, despite using no new syntax, only two new concepts, namely *sheet-defined function* and *function value*, and only three new built-in functions DEFINE, CLOSURE and APPLY, described in Sect. 2.3.

The prototype implementation is relatively compact, comprising less than 13,000 lines of C# code.

8.2   Expressiveness

Sects. 6 and 7 show that many useful functions can be implemented efficiently as sheet-defined functions, including functions that must be built-in black boxes in Excel and other spreadsheet programs. Also, by writing predicates as higher-order functions, Excel built-ins such as COUNTIF and SUMIF can be both much more powerful and have a less obscure (less text-based) semantics.

Although not illustrated here, sheet-defined functions can take array (range) values as arguments and return them as results. Since the "language" of sheet-defined functions supports recursive and higher-order functions, and is dynamically typed, it is conceptually similar to a pure (side-effect free) version of Lisp [10] or Scheme, albeit with a very unusual syntax.

Some computations are difficult or impossible to express as sheet-defined functions, chiefly because we have ruled out side-effects and destructive array update. Yet we do not want to support side-effects, because that would ruin the simplicity of the model and the compiler's freedom to rearrange computations. In particular, it would complicate parallelization; see Sect. 10.

8.3   Performance

According to micro-benchmarks (not shown here) a non-trivial numerical sheet-defined function such as that in Fig. 6 can be considerably faster than a corresponding user-defined function in VBA (the macro language of MS Excel), and only 2–3 times slower than a function written in a "proper" programming language such as C, Java or C#. This is quite satisfying, given that our sheet-defined functions are dynamically typed and that the compiler is quite compact.

Moreover, benchmarking results from the case study in Sect. 7 show that financial functions built in to Excel can be implemented as sheet-defined functions without loss of efficiency. This is important because it shows that such libraries of functions need not be built-in, and hence controlled by the spreadsheet vendor, but could be developed and maintained by the relevant user communities, without resorting to external programming languages.

9   Related Work

Peyton-Jones, Blackwell and Burnett proposed [14] that user-defined functions should be definable as so-called *function sheets* using ordinary spreadsheet formulas. Similar ideas are found in Nuñez's spreadsheet system ViSSh [12, section 5.2.2]. What we have implemented is strongly inspired by Peyton-Jones et al., but extends expressiveness by permitting recursive and higher-order functions.

Cortes and Hansen in their 2006 MSc thesis [4] elaborated the concept of sheet-defined function and created an interpretive implementation. However, being based on the interpretive CoreCalc implementation [17], it did not achieve the performance goals we have set in the present work.

Resolver One [15] is a commercial Python-based spreadsheet program with a feature called RUNWORKBOOK that allows a workbook to be invoked as a function, similar to a sheet-defined function at a coarser granularity. Invocation of a workbook is implemented by loading it from file, setting the values of some cells in it, and recalculating it, which is slow. It does not appear to support recursive invocation, nor higher-order functions. Hence it does not achieve the efficiency and expressiveness goals of the present work.

We believe that the concept of evaluation condition (Sect. 5) is original with this work. The other compilation techniques presented in Sect. 4 are similar to those used by other dynamically typed languages [16].

Preliminary reports of this work includes an oral presentation [18] and a rough draft of a book-length manuscript [19]. None of these includes the case study reported in Sect. 7.

10   Perspectives and Future Work

Currently, our prototype implementation passes arguments and results of sheet-defined functions as wrapped objects. A global unboxing analysis or type-based unboxing [9] could further improve performance by avoiding such wrapping, especially for simple numerical functions.

While Peyton-Jones, Blackwell and Burnett verified that sheet-defined functions are understandable to spreadsheet users [14], our design deviates from theirs in several ways, so our design needs to be revalidated empirically.

Spreadsheets exhibit quite explicit parallelism, in contrast to Fortran, Java and C# where it is only implicit and where alias analyses are required to deal with shared data and destructive update. Chandy proposed already in 1984 to exploit spreadsheet parallelism [3], and today multicore processors and graphics processors provide the required technological platform. Sheet-defined functions may play an interesting role here: since a function may be called thousands of times in each recalculation, it is a more interesting target for optimization and parallelization than an ordinary spreadsheet formula, which is evaluated at most once in each recalculation. If parallelization is near automatic and performance is adequate, spreadsheets could become an even better framework for scientific and financial simulation [1]; a framework for "end-user high-performance computing". In fact, spreadsheets with sheet-defined functions constitute a dataflow language in the style of Sisal [11], so it may be possible to leverage the 1990es work on automatic parallelization of such languages.

Our prototype is a standalone spreadsheet implementation with a simplistic user interface. It provides very little of the ancillary functionality—graphics, formatting, auditing, pivot tables, data import—expected of a spreadsheet program, so it would be interesting to turn it into a plugin for one that does, such as Excel.

11 Conclusion

We have shown that a spreadsheet implementation can accommodate user-defined functions with sufficient convenience and performance that previously built-in functions can be user-defined instead.

By allowing more functions to be user-defined, we soften the separation between users and developers, and empower end-users. This may lead to the development of user-created function libraries and more expressive, more reliable and faster spreadsheet models.

The main *technical* innovation required to achieve this is probably the concept of evaluation conditions (Sect. 5).

Moreover, we have demonstrated that sheet-defined functions considerably increase the expressiveness of spreadsheets while preserving their dynamic interactive behavior, and with conceptual parsimony, requiring only a few new concepts and built-in functions, and no new notation.

Acknowledgments. Thanks to Bob Muller for valuable comments, and to IT University MSc students Iversen, Cortes, Hansen, Serek, Poulsen, Ha, Tran, Xu, Liton, Brønnum, Hamann, Patapavicius, Salas and Nielsen who investigated many aspects of spreadsheet technology.

References

1. Abramson, D., Roe, P., Kotler, L., Mather, D.: Activesheets: Super-computing with spreadsheets. In: 2001 High Performance Computing Symposium (HPC 2001), Seattle, USA, pp. 110–115 (2001)
2. Bolognese, L.: Excel financial functions for .NET. MSDN webpage (2009), http://archive.msdn.microsoft.com/FinancialFunctions
3. Chandy, M.: Concurrent programming for the masses (PODC 1984 invited address). In: Principles of Distributed Computing 1985, pp. 1–12. ACM (1985)
4. Cortes, D.S., Hansen, M.: User-defined functions in spreadsheets. Master's thesis, IT University of Copenhagen (September 2006)
5. Dershowitz, N., Reingold, E.M.: Calendrical calculations, 3rd edn. Cambridge University Press (2008)
6. Ecma TC39 TG3. Common Language Infrastructure (CLI). Standard ECMA-335, 6th edition. Ecma International (June 2012)
7. Hart, J., et al.: Computer Approximations. Wiley (1968)
8. IEEE. IEEE standard for floating-point arithmetics. IEEE Std 754-2008 (2008)
9. Leroy, X.: The effectiveness of type-based unboxing. In: Types in Compilation Workshop, Amsterdam (1997)
10. McCarthy, J., et al.: Lisp 1.5 Programmer's Manual. MIT Press (1962)
11. McGraw, J., et al.: Sisal. Streams and iteration in a single assignment language. Language reference manual, version 1.2. Technical report, Lawrence Livermore National Labs (March 1985)
12. Nuñez, F.: An extended spreadsheet paradigm for data visualisation systems, and its implementation. Master's thesis, University of Cape Town (November 2000)
13. Peyton Jones, S.: The Implementation of Functional Programming Languages. Prentice-Hall (1987)
14. Peyton Jones, S., Blackwell, A., Burnett, M.: A user-centred approach to functions in Excel. In: ICFP 2003: Proceedings of the Eighth ACM SIGPLAN International Conference on Functional Programming, pp. 165–176. ACM (2003)
15. Resolver Systems. Resolver one. Homepage, http://www.resolversystems.com/
16. Serpette, B., Serrano, M.: Compiling scheme to JVM bytecode: a performance study. In: International Conference on Functional Programming (ICFP 2002), pp. 259–270. ACM (2002)
17. Sestoft, P.: A Spreadsheet Core Implementation in C#. Technical Report ITU-TR-2006-91, IT University of Copenhagen, 135 pages (September 2006)
18. Sestoft, P.: Implementing function spreadsheets. Oral presentation, Fourth Workshop on End-User Software Engineering (WEUSE IV), Leipzig, Germany (May 2008), http://www.itu.dk/people/sestoft/papers/weuse-sestoft.pdf
19. Sestoft, P.: Spreadsheet Technology. Version 0.12 of 2012-01-31. Technical Report ITU-TR-2011-142, IT University of Copenhagen (January 2012)
20. Strachey, C., Wadsworth, C.: Continuations: a mathematical semantics for handling full jumps. Higher Order and Symbolic Computation 13, 135–152 (1974); Reprint of Oxford PRG-11 (January 1974)
21. Sørensen, J.Z.: An evaluation of sheet-defined financial functions in Funcalc. Master's thesis, IT University of Copenhagen (March 2012)

End-User Development
of Information Visualization

Kostas Pantazos[1], Soren Lauesen[2], and Ravi Vatrapu[1,3]

[1] Computational Social Science Laboratory (CSSL), Department of IT Management,
Copenhagen Business School, Copenhagen, Denmark
[2] Software and Systems, IT University of Copenhagen, Copenhagen, Denmark
[3] Norwegian School of Information Technology, Oslo, Norway

Abstract. This paper investigates End-User Development of Information Visualization. More specifically, we investigated how existing visualization tools allow end-user developers to construct visualizations.
End-user developers have some developing or scripting skills to perform
relatively advanced tasks such as data manipulation, but no formal training in programming. 18 visualization tools were surveyed from an end-
user developer perspective. The results of this survey study show that
end-user developers need better tools to create and modify custom visualizations. A closer collaboration between End-User Development and
Information Visualization researchers could contribute towards the development of better tools to support custom visualizations. In addition,
as empirical evaluations of these tools are lacking both research communities should focus more on this aspect. The study serves as a starting
point towards the engagement of end-user developers in visualization
development.

Keywords: End-User Development, Information Visualization, Visualization Tools.

1 Introduction

Information Visualization attempts to reduce the time and the mental effort
users need to analyze large datasets by visually presenting abstract data (e.g.
medical information such as patient name, age, treatment, dose, intake, etc) that
"has no inherent mapping to space" [1]. Unlike scientific visualization such as
radiology, in information visualization there is no spatial correspondence between
the physical information and the conceptual domain. Information Visualization
is an important topic in many domains: clinicians want a complete picture of
patient data; project managers need to obtain an overview and identify the
bottlenecks in a project; database analysts look for visualizations that can locate
trends in large datasets. Traditionally, visualization development is collaboration
between domain experts and professional programmers. Both parties spend time
and resources to design a good visualization. Usually, there are communication
problems between users and programmers [2]; users have the domain knowledge

Y. Dittrich et al. (Eds.): IS-EUD 2013, LNCS 7897, pp. 104–119, 2013.
© Springer-Verlag Berlin Heidelberg 2013

but no programming skills, while programmers do not have the domain expertise. Consequently, the process may require time and resources. From a management perspective, this collaboration can become very expensive. One solution to this problem would be to allow different domain users to construct visualizations. As a result, the cost would be significantly reduced, and better visualizations would be developed as users know their own domain-specific analytical needs and demands better.

In the last decade, a new research discipline has emerged, called End-User Development (EUD). EUD has its roots from the field of End-User Programming [3–5]. However, EUD is not limited to programming [6] and the main goal of EUD is to empower end-user developers – users who "may have little or no formal training or experience in programming" [7]– create, modify and extend *software artifacts*, and as a result gain more control over their applications by engaging them in the development process [8]. In 1995, Boehm et al. [9] estimated that by 2005, there would be 55 million end-user developers in the United States. In 2005, Scaffidi et al. [10] used and improved Boehm's method to estimate that in 2012 there will be 90 million end-user developers. They predicted that 55 million will be users of spreadsheets or databases. Some of end-user developers are: system administrators, interaction designers, teachers, accountants, health care workers, managers, etc.

This paper investigates End-User Development of Information Visualizations. More specifically, it investigates how end-user developers can create visualizations with existing visualization tools. We selected 18 Information Visualization tools form research and industry. The results of this study showed that end-user developers need more and better tools to create visualizations. Furthermore, the results of this study serve as a starting point in introducing End-User Development of Information Visualization. Also, the study aims at driving the attention of both communities towards research paths that may lead to the discovery of new development approach for end-user developers.

The remaining of this paper is structured as follows. Section 2 and 3 provide a summary of End-User Development and Information Visualization. Section 4 discusses the importance of users in visualization development. Section 5 presents a brief summary of 18 development tools from Information Visualization field focusing on how end-user developers can create visualizations. The paper concludes with a discussion of the limitations of the study and conclusions.

2   End-User Development

The End-User Development (EUD) field is a new research discipline, which has emerged from research in Human-Computer Interaction, Cognitive Science, Requirements Engineering, Software Engineering, CSCW, Artificial Intelligence, Information Systems, and the Psychology of Programming [11]. As a relatively young discipline, the field is not mature enough when it comes to definition, terminology, approaches and subject areas [11]. However, Lieberman et al. [8] defines EUD as "a set of methods, techniques, and tools that allow users of software systems, who are acting as non-professional software developers, at some point create, modify and extend a software artifact". Consequently, end-user developers are not professional programmers, but users who "may have little or no formal training or experience in programming" [7]. EUD aims at better users efficiency and effectiveness as it allows users "to develop and evolve their computer based working tools to support their specific tasks in an efficient way" [12]. Therefore, the main goal of EUD is to empower these users create, modify and extend software artifacts, and as a result gain more control over their applications by engaging them in development.

EUD takes a broader perspective than End-User Programming because it is not limited to programming when it comes to adjust application to users' needs [6]. Lieberman et al. [8] defines two types of end-user activities: *parametrization or customization* (activities that allow end-users to parametrize or customize their applications using the available presentations or interactive mechanisms) and *program creation and modification* (activities that allow end-users to create or modify software artifacts). In order to support these types of end-user activities, the system should be flexible and expressive enough to changes (e.g. set parameters, compose objects, etc.) [8]. Simple changes are not difficult, but things become more complicated as the level of complexity for a change increases. MacLean et al. [13] suggested a "gentle slope" to reduce the level of complexity and support changes on different levels. However, in cases of extensive change actions a programming language should be used [13]. EUD does not focus only on how to support end-users create an application, but also focuses on the use and adaption of the application in existing environments [14]. The second means customizing, configuring and tailoring a application, but not direct changes in the source code [15]. Customizing, configuring and tailoring are performed beyond the stage of creating a new application, and take place after the application is implemented within its organizational infrastructure. Bolmsten and Dittrich [12] presented two case-studies and discussed the challenges that infrastructure context poses to EUD. In this study, we primarily focus on program creation and modification.

As there is not an EUD taxonomy which categorizes development techniques for end-user developers, several techniques developed from the psychology of programming are inherited, and some of the main techniques useful for end-user developers are [6]: Scripting Language, Visual Programming, Spreadsheet and Programming by Example.

Rode et al. [16] investigated EUD of web application. Their study showed that web development tools focus more at supporting developers with a wide range of functionalities, and less attention is paid to ease-of-use. Further, the authors say that ideally a web development tool "would provide ease-of-use with the appropriate abstractions, absence of jargon, a library of examples and templates, wizards for complicated tasks and take a holistic approach by integrating all aspects of web development" [16]. Investigating how end-users think may help in designing better tools. Similar to this study, we investigate visualization development tools.

3   Information Visualization

Information visualization (InfoVis) enhances human cognition by visually presenting abstract data and revealing patterns, trends and outliers [1]. The InfoVis field has enabled development of visualization systems that enhance human cognitive processes by visually presenting abstract data [1]. Although, the InfoVis field emerged during the 1980's with the availability of computers, InfoVis evidence can be tracked long before. Florence Nightingale's diagram designed in 1858 shows the death rates in the hospital of Scutari, and how the rates reduce by the changes introduced by nurse Florence Nightingale [17]. Thus visualizations (when designed by a domain expert) allows viewers to get a clear picture of the situation, and derive results without any detailed explanation.

The InfoVis community has done considerable work in order to develop the field into a mature discipline. Shneiderman [18] presented a task by data type taxonomy for InfoVis. This popular taxonomy classifies visualization data types (1D Linear, 2D Map, multidimensional, temporal, tree and network) and identifies the tasks (overview, zoom, filter, details-on-demand, relate, history and extract) that have to be supported. The reference InfoVis model described by Card et al. [1] highlights end-user interactions, and it consists of three steps: (1) *Data Transformations*: convert the raw data to data tables; (2) *Visual Mappings*: convert the data tables into visual objects; (3) *View Transformations*: transform visual objects into views by means of visual objects properties. The first step is mainly related with data, while the last two have a direct impact on the visual form.

Several visualizations have been developed to present data. LifeLines [19] is an interactive visualization that presents an overview of a patient's medical record. LifeLines 2 [20] and LifeFlow [21] are two other examples of temporal data. Aigner et al. [22] provide an overview of 101 visualizations techniques for temporal data. Among them are Arc Diagrams, Circel View, Circos, Flow Map, Prespective Wall, TimeTree, etc. Many of them have been developed in close collaboration with domain experts. This collaboration has contributed in producing useful visualizations.

4   Users in Visualization Development

Considering the variety of data and user tasks, it is obvious that new visualizations are needed. However, developing new visualizations is not an easy task. Several InfoVis toolkits and tools [23–30] have been developed to improve visualization development and provide better presentation of data. Providing good data visualization is challenging as visualization creators should have a good understanding of the data, and then properly design representations that allow users to accomplish tasks effectively and efficiently. This is usually a problem according to Thomas and Cook [31], who say that: "Most visualization software is developed with incomplete information about the data and tasks. New methods are needed for constructing visually based systems that simplify the development process and result in better targeted applications."

To facilitate the visualization development process and ensure that visualizations provide complete information about the data and tasks, several InfoVis applications (e.g. [19, 32–34]) have been developed applying the user-centered method, where users participated during the entire development process. Norman[35] and Nielsen[36] describe user-centered design as the early and continuous involvement of end-users in the design and development process. Considerable work has been conducted by Slocum et al. [32], Robinson et al. [33], Roth et al. [34], and Koh et al. [2] to define the activities applied in the user-centered model for the design and implementation of InfoVis tools. For example, Robinson et al. [33] describe a six-stage user-center design process (work domain analysis, conceptual development, prototyping, interaction and usability studies, implementation, and debugging) where users are involved and provide input in each stage. Using this model [33], Roth et al. [34] present a modified user-centered design approach, which starts with prototyping, followed by interaction and usability studies, work domain analysis, conceptual development, implementation and ends with debugging. Although, the user-centered model helps producing better visualizations, still it is challenging to bridge the gap of knowledge between end-users and programmers. This gap can influence communication and create challenges such as: programmers should understand end-user needs, end-users should gain some knowledge regarding InfoVis, end-users should be devoted and actively participate in the process, etc. In their study Koh et al. [2] experienced similar challenges where simple users where more interested in the tool than on questions about their tasks and data. Also, when they tried the tool they found it limited compared to the prototypes defined during the process. The authors [2] suggested that an iterative approach may address these issues.

Although a user-centered method is a successful approach, researchers envisage approaches to facilitate visualization development and assure that visualizations provide complete information about the data and tasks. Aigner et al. [37] discuss how to support user-centered visual analysis that consists of three factors: the visualization, the analysis, and the user. They suggest that future research should focus on these three factors and lead to the convergence of user-centered visual analysis. Their vision matches the universal usability challenge defined by Plaisant [38]. According to Plaisant [38] visualization tools should be accessible to diverse users that do not have the same background, technical knowledge, or personal abilities. Other InfoVis researchers seek ways of introducing new audiences in InfoVis. Heer et al. [39] say that designing visualizations is not an easy task for users, but "we have to provide them tools that make it easy to create and deploy visualizations of their datasets" [39].

5   InfoVis Development Tools - A Survey

The purpose of this survey is to investigate how end-user developers are supported by InfoVis tools in visualization development. To the best of our knowledge, no prior study has looked at EUD of InfoVis. The results of this survey may serve as a starting point towards the engagement of end-user developers in visualization development. Before we present the tools, we describe the tool selection process and how the tools were assessed. The purpose of this study is not to analyze and compare implementation details, but to investigate the way end-user developers construct visualizations. For a deeper understanding of implementation details we encourage readers to refer to the references.

5.1 Analysis Approach

We used two professional and popular sources to find InfoVis tools and toolkits: the ACM Portal and the IEEE website. We searched for related work by combining these keywords: "information visualization", "tool", "toolkits", "graphical user interface". Initially, we ranked the results based on the total number of citations, and then we selected only the most relevant ones by reading the abstracts. Next, we read all the papers and selected the most appropriate tools and toolkits. They are: APT [40], SAGE & SageBrush [41–43], DEVise [44, 45], The InfoVis Toolkit [23], GeoVISTA Studio [46], Piccolo [47], Improvise [48], Prefuse [24], Protovis and ProtoViewer [49, 50], and Data-Driven Documents (D3) [25]. During the process of reviewing the existing literature, we identified two more tools from research that were relevant to the investigation and decided to include them in the analysis, because of their popularity and approach. They are: Processing [51] and Flare [29]. In total, we selected 12 tools from the research area. As we were reviewing the existing literature, we also found several industry tools that we decided to use. At the end we selected six popular tools: Spotfire [26], Tableau [27], Omniscope [28], MS Excel [30], Google Chart Tools [52] and Many Eyes [53]. In total, we chose only 18 tools and toolkits and we believe that the selected ones are a good sample that represents the wide-range of InfoVis tools from research and industry.

In this study, we investigated how end-user developers can construct visualizations with existing development tools. We conducted our tool analysis focusing on three main questions:

1. Can end-user developers create and modify a visualization?
2. How do end-user developers create and modify visualizations with a tool; Do they specify language specifications (e.g. Java, JavaScript, etc.), use wizards or drag-and-drop actions?
3. Can tools support development of predefined and custom (not-predefined) visualizations? A predefined visualization, for instance a bar chart in MS Excel, uses a chart where only a few visual attributes can be assigned to data. While LifeLines [19], a custom visualization, combines bars, triangles, labels, etc., into a complex visualization.

Investigating these questions will provide an overview of the current status of InfoVis development tools and reveal their accessibility to end-user developers. The assessment of the tools from academia is based on the published papers. The commercial tools were assessed using the trial or the full versions, and information from their websites. A full-fledged usability study is currently scheduled for Fall 2013 and will be reported in subsequent publications.

5.2   Tools and Toolkits

In this section, we briefly describe the selected tools. First, we present InfoVis tools and toolkits from research, and then the ones from industry.

APT (A Presentation Tool) [40] is one of the earliest tools that automatically creates effective graphical presentation of relational data. Presentations are generated in a linear model where data are extracted, synthesized and then the tool handles the rendering process to create the final output. Users of APT use predefined visual objects (e.g. bar charts, scatter plots or connected graphs) and write their graphical specifications (sentences of a graphical language that has exact syntax and semantics), and the tool creates the graphical presentation. The visual mapping is defined through APT specifications and automatically handled by the tool. Probably, end-user developers, would be able to specify graphical designs, but still they cannot create visualizations other than the supported ones.

SAGE & SageBrush: Early 1990's, Roth and Mattis [41] presented SAGE, "an intelligent system which assumes presentation responsibilities for other systems by automatically creating graphical displays which presents the results they generate" [41]. This tool uses graphical techniques to express the application data characteristics and fulfill the presentation needs. Users of SAGE query the database, and the result is used by SAGE. Based on the data, SAGE automatically defines the visual mappings and generates the visualization. After a presentation is generated, users can adjust the visual mappings of the auto-generated visualization by setting layout constraints for the data. SAGE can probably be used by end-user developers.

SAGE was extended with an interactive design tool called SageBrush [42, 43]. SageBrush aims at removing the complexity introduced by SAGE representations and operations [43]. It allows users to sketch by dragging and dropping primitives or partial controls from a palette. The sketches are used by SAGE to create a visualization. SageBrush facilitates visualization development and can be used by end-user developers. They can create predefined and custom visualizations with drag-and-drop actions.

DEVise [44, 45] allows users to create visualizations by creating, modifying or connecting visual objects. DEVise maps the data to visual objects and displays them in a view. At the end, the view uses the data and visual filters to draw the result in a window. DEVise users use a step-by-step approach to create visualizations: select an input, choose a file type for the input file, select an existing mapping or define a new mapping using *tcl* language expressions [54], select a view to display the data, select initial values for the visual filter, and finally select a window to display the view. In DEVise, end-user developers can create custom visualizations by combining and linking visual objects using the predefined visual mappings. In order to create new visual mappings, they have to use the *tlc* language. The authors says that DEVise is a powerful exploration framework, "but to appreciate this power fully, one must work with the system or at least look at several applications in some details" [45].

Processing was developed initially "to teach fundamentals of computer programming within a visual context" to newcomers, but it has grown into a more complete tool for constructing images, animations and interactions [51]. Processing has a development environment similar to a regular one. Programmers specify visual mappings by writing code in the code editor. They view the visualization in a new window after having executed the code. To create predefined and custom visualization, users have to know a programming language called Processing. This tool cannot be used by end-user developers via direct manipulation in the WYSIWYG (What You See Is What You Get) paradigm.

GeoVISTA Studio is a development environment designed to support geoscientific data analysis and visualizations [46]. It is built in Java and uses JavaBeans technology. A visualization in GeoVISTA Studio is composed by connecting visual objects (implemented as Java beans components). GeoVISTA Studio consists of three windows: the *Main* window shows the menus and JavaBeans visual object palette; the *Design* window where visual objects are placed and connected; the *Graphical User Interface (GUI)* window shows "live" the output of the used beans. Programmers can use the *Property Editor* to customize the appearance and behavior of a visual object. The application programmers (probably end-user developers) are the main users of the Studio, and they follow the following steps to construct an application: list the requirements, select the appropriate visual objects from the palette menu (new visual objects can be developed outside of the Studio and imported), place visual objects in the *Design*, link the visual objects to meet the requirements, customize a visual object using the *Property Editor*, and test the design in the *GUI*.

The InfoVis Toolkit [23] is a Java based visualization toolkit that uses several interactive controls to construct visualizations. This toolkit allows programmers to program visualizations. It allows programmers to extend the toolkit with new controls and to integrate visualization techniques into interactive applications. However, creating visualizations requires experienced programmers. Consequently, this toolkit is not appropriate for end-user developers.

Piccolo [47] is mainly used for developing graphical applications with rich user interfaces. It is developed in Java and C# and supports the development of visualizations indirectly, as it does not support visualization techniques [24]. Nevertheless, novel visualizations are based on this toolkit. Programmers can create visualizations in Java or C# and use visualization functionality and controls, such as zooming, animation and range slider. This toolkit can be used only by programmers, and the fact that it does not support visualization techniques directly, makes it challenging even for them. End-user developers cannot use this tool.

Improvise [48] is a visualization toolkit for creating multi-view coordination visualizations for relational data. It is written in Java. Visualizations are created by specifying expressions for simple shared-object coordination mechanism. Shared-objects in Improvise, which are responsible for visual mappings, are graphical attributes such as color, font, etc. Improvise has a specialized development environment where users apply a step-by-step approach interacting with four editors and creating views by adding frames, controls, defining variables and attaching data using the lexicon work area (a central repository where information related to the data and database are saved). Users of Improvise can construct visualizations based on the predefined controls. Programmers create visualizations by specifying expressions for simple shared-object coordination mechanism. Although we believe that Improvise can be used by end-user developers, this has not been empirically evaluated.

Prefuse [24] is another toolkit developed in Java. Visualizations in Prefuse are programmed in Java. Programmers construct them using a set of fine-grained building blocks and specifying operators that define the layout and behavior of these blocks. The purpose of this tool is to facilitate programmers' work, but end-user developers cannot use this toolkit.

Flare [29] is a successor of Prefuse [24], but is written in ActionScript. Flare supports programmers develop visualizations. To construct visualizations, programmers specify in ActionScript the properties of the visual objects and sequential commands. Programmers can also define new operators and visual objects, but advanced programming knowledge is required. Flare cannot be used by end-user developers.

Protovis & ProtoViewer: Protovis [49] is implemented in JavaScript and helps programmers construct visualizations using a domain specific language. They can combine primitive visual objects, called marks, bind them to data, and specify visual properties. Programmers can create visualizations by specifying Protovis specifications. The authors of Protovis have compared the specifications for a simple pie chart in Protovis, Processing and Flare, showing that the visualization in Protovis is specified in fewer lines of code [49]. This shows the simplicity of Protovis language, which has a high potential of engaging end-user developers in visualization development. Although we believe that Protovis can be used by end-user developers, there is no empirical evidence that proves it.

ProtoViewer [50] extends Protovis with a development environment. The screen is divided in three parts: *Data*, *Design* and *Code*. Programmers choose a dataset, select a visualization template and automatically the code is shown in the *Code* editor. They execute the code to view the results in the *Design*. Programmers can either use predefined visualization templates, and the code is automatically shown in the *Code* editor, or start from scratch and write Protovis specifications to specify controls. Constructing custom visualizations by end-user developers in Protovis becomes even more realistic by means of its

development environment – ProtoViewer. However, neither Protovis nor ProtoViewer has been evaluated with end-user developers.

Data-Driven Documents (D3) [25] is a successor of Protovis [49]. Visualizations are constructed using SVG, HTML 5 and CSS. In D3 the data transformation, the immediate evaluation and the browser's native representation are
handled in more effective and transparent way than Protovis, which uses more
succinct specification for static presentations [25]. However, these improvements
introduce an overhead for users: the knowledge of SVG, HTML 5 and CSS. This
toolkit is not suitable for end-user developers as it requires advanced programming skills.

MS Excel [30] is a spreadsheet program that allows end-user developers to
analyze and visualize data. With simple steps, end-user developers can construct
visualizations based on predefined visualization templates (e.g. bar chart, pie
chart, etc.) They select a visualization template (e.g. bar-chart) and specify
spreadsheet formulas or use standard wizards to map the data to the visual
object in the worksheet area. In MS Excel, visual mappings are limited and
end-user developers can set only predefined visual properties.

Tableau [27] is a commercial visualization tool, a successor of Polaris [55] developed at Stanford University. Tableau allows end-user developers to construct
visualizations by dragging and dropping fields onto axis shelves (vertical and
horizontal areas) and using visual specifications. This tool provides drag-and-
drop features and several wizards to facilitate development. Further, it has a
powerful interactive development environment where end-user developers can
interact, filter, sort data and create interactive dashboards. Tableau is a "black
box" system and constructing visualizations other than the predefined ones is
not possible.

Spotfire [26] is another commercial tool for data visualizations. It supports end-
user developers with a number of visualization techniques. End-user developers
interact with the development environment and construct visualizations based on
predefined ones. Once they select the data and choose a visualization template,
the tool automatically generates the visualization. Users can sort, filter and rearrange data by simply dragging and dropping fields in the design area. Users
can also create dashboards, by combining different predefined visualizations (e.g.
bar chart, scatter plot, etc.) in a single screen. As in Tableau, end-user developers
can only create predefined visualizations.

Omniscope [28] is in the same category as Tableau and Spotfire, and shares
similar features such as interactive dashboard, drag and drop features, etc. It
supports end-user developers in constructing predefined visualizations, as Spotfire and Tableau do. Custom visualizations cannot be constructed with this tool.

Google Chart Tools [52] is a library written in JavaScript that provides several predefined simple (line chart, scatter chart, etc.) and advanced chart types (Image multi-color bar chart, Motion Chart Time Formats, etc.) Visualizations can be constructed by end-user developers in the web-based development environment named Code Playground. In addition, Google Chart Tools has another environment named Live Chart Playground, to test charts already created in the Code Playground. In Live Chart Playground, end-user developers can change some parameters and see how the visualization changes. End-user developers are limited to predefined visualizations.

Many Eyes [53], developed at IBM Research Center, is a web-based visualization platform that can be used by end-user developers. In Many Eyes, visualizations are implemented in Java Applets. End-user developers construct visualizations in three steps: upload a dataset; choose a visualization template; customize and publish the visualization. Many Eyes automatically generates and shows the visualization on the screen. Custom visualizations are not supported.

Results

In this study, we surveyed 18 visualization tools from an end-user developer perspective. Based on published papers and subjective evaluation of the selected the tools, we found 12 InfoVis tools that have the potential to be used by end-user developers. 11 tools allow end-user developers to construct visualizations with a programming language (e.g. Java, ActionScript, JavaScript, etc.), and six with a wizard or drag-and-drop actions. Furthermore, 11 tools support development of predefined and custom (not predefined) visualizations, but only five of them can be used by end-user developers. Figure 1 provides an overview of the results.

There is a tendency that researchers mainly focus on developing visualization tools that allows users to construct predefined and custom visualizations, but users need advanced programming skills. End-user developers would not be able to benefit from these tools. Some examples are: Prefuse, Flare, D3, etc. On the other hand, industry produce visualization tools for large audiences without advanced programming skills, but at the same time limit them with predefined visualization templates. Although both communities can benefit from the engagement of end-user developers in constructing custom visualizations, they are overlooked. Only five visualization tools (SAGE/SageBrush, DEVise, GeoVISTA Studio, Improvise and Protovis/ Protoviewer) may support them in constructing visualizations other than predefined. To the best of our knowledge, none of the selected tools were empirically evaluated with potential users. As a result, it remains debatable if the five tools can support end-user developers in visualization development. This indicates that InfoVis community has to focus more on evaluation of development tools with users. In addition, a future collaboration between EUD and InfoVis researcher may address this issue and lead to better tools for the advancement of both communities.

The results also show that commercial tool provide interactive development environments where users can use wizard and/or drag-and-drop actions. These

Tools	End-User Developer	Visualization Development	Predefined Visualizations	Custom Visualizations
Processing		Programming Language	x	x
InfoVis Toolkit		Programming Language	x	x
Piccolo		Programming Language	x	x
Improvise	x	Programming Language	x	x
Prefuse		Programming Language	x	x
Flare		Programming Language	x	x
D3		Programming Language	x	x
SAGE / SageBrush	x	Programming Language & Drag-and-Drop Approach	x	x
Protovis / Protoviewer	x	Programming Language & Wizard Approach	x	x
GeoVISTA Studio	x	Wizard & Drag-and-Drop Approach	x	x
DEVise	x	Wizard Approach	x	x
ATP	x	Programming Language	x	
Google Chart Tools	x	Programming Language	x	
Tableau	x	Wizard & Drag-and-Drop Approach	x	
Spotfire	x	Wizard & Drag-and-Drop Approach	x	
Omniscope	x	Wizard & Drag-and-Drop Approach	x	
MS Excel	x	Wizard Approach	x	
Many Eyes	x	Wizard Approach	x	

a. | End-user developers: 12 | Programmers: 6 |
b. | Predefined Visualizations: 18 | Custom Visualizations: 11 |
c. | Programming Language: 9 | Drag-and-Drop Approach: 5 | Wizard Approach: 4 |

Fig. 1. 18 InfoVis surveyed from an end-user developer perspective. Classification by: a. end-user developer and programmers, b. predefined and custom visualizations, and c. visualization development approach.

environments aim at handling the gulf of execution (*How do I do something?*) and evaluation (*What happened?*) identified by Norman [35] by allowing users to easily map data to visual objects and obtain immediate feedback.

Custom visualizations in Prefuse, InfoVis Toolkit, D3, Flare, Processing and Picolo are created and modified through code. This makes them less accessible to end-user developers. Improvise and DEVise use a step-by-step approach to lower the barriers to development introduced by code and become accessible by end-user developers. While, SageBrush and GeoVISTA Studio take a different approach. Similar to commercial tools, in these two tools, end-user developers interact with visual components using drag-and-drop actions.

6   Limitations

This study investigates 18 visualization development tools. Instead of all existing InfoVis tools, we decided to include only 18 tools as that are representative of the InfoVis field and that have contributed significantly to it.

To identify InfoVis tools we searched two popular and comprehensive professional sources IEEE and ACM. InfoVis tools published in other sources such as Springer, Elsevier, Sage, etc., were not included. As a result, the findings of this study may be debatable as there might be other tools published in these sources for end-user developers. Another limitation of the selection is that we investigated tools published before 2012.

Our investigation was based on the published papers and subjective evaluation of the selected the tools. However, we do not have the knowledge that authors of these tools have. This should have facilitated the analysis process. Furthermore, a task-based evaluation with end-user developers would have enriched the results of this study, which, however, provides a first orientation towards what tools might be suitable for visualization development. Also, this study does not investigate visualization and interaction techniques a tool may support.

7   Conclusion

This paper presents a study that investigates EUD of InfoVis. We investigated how existing InfoVis tools can support end-user developers create and modify visualizations. The results of this study indicate that EUD and InfoVis community has to focus more on developing new approaches and tools to allow end-user developers create visualizations other than the predefined ones. Supporting them with more tools that provide direct manipulation, immediate feedback may be a potential research path. Furthermore, the study provides a high-level overview of the available visualization tools, which may facilitate the tool selection process for new audiences.

To the best of our knowledge, no tool has been empirically evaluated with users. Therefore, both research communities should collaborate more on this aspect in order to better address the ease-of-use and understand what makes visualization tool popular for end-user developers. In this respect, we are planning to conduct task-based usability studies and evaluate InfoVis tools with end-user developers.

References

1. Card, S.K., Mackinlay, J.D., Shneiderman, B. (eds.): Readings in information visualization: using vision to think. Morgan Kaufmann Publishers Inc., San Francisco (1999)
2. Koh, L.C., Slingsby, A., Dykes, J., Kam, T.S.: Developing and applying a user-centered model for the design and implementation of information visualization tools. In: 2011 15th International Conference on Information Visualisation, pp. 90–95 (2011)
3. Nardi, B.A.: A small matter of programming: perspectives on end user computing. MIT Press, Cambridge (1993)
4. Cypher, A., Halbert, D.C., Kurlander, D., Lieberman, H., Maulsby, D., Myers, B.A., Turransky, A. (eds.): Watch what I do: programming by demonstration. MIT Press, Cambridge (1993)
5. Lieberman, H.: Your wish is my command: programming by example. Morgan Kaufmann Publishers Inc., San Francisco (2001)

6. Lieberman, H., Paternò, F., Wulf, V.: End User Development (Human-Computer Interaction Series). Springer-Verlag New York, Inc., Secaucus (2006)
7. Pane, J., Myers, B.: More natural programming languages and environments. In: Lieberman, H., Paternò, F., Wulf, V. (eds.) End User Development. Human-Computer Interaction Series, vol. 9, pp. 31–50. Springer, Netherlands (2006)
8. Lieberman, H., Paternò, F., Klann, M., Wulf, V.: End-user development: An emerging paradigm. In: Lieberman, H., Paternò, F., Wulf, V. (eds.) End User Development. Human-Computer Interaction Series, vol. 9, pp. 1–8. Springer, Netherlands (2006)
9. Boehm, B., Clark, B., Horowitz, E., Westland, C., Madachy, R., Selby, R.: Cost models for future software life cycle processes: Cocomo 2.0. Annals of Software Engineering, 57–94 (1995)
10. Scaffidi, C., Shaw, M., Myers, B.: Estimating the numbers of end users and end user programmers. In: Proceedings of the 2005 IEEE Symposium on Visual Languages and Human-Centric Computing, VLHCC 2005, pp. 207–214. IEEE Computer Society, Washington, DC (2005)
11. Klann, M., Paternò, F., Wulf, V.: Future perspectives in end-user development. In: Lieberman, H., Paternò, F., Wulf, V. (eds.) End User Development. Human-Computer Interaction Series, vol. 9, pp. 475–486. Springer, Netherlands (2006)
12. Bolmsten, J., Dittrich, Y.: Infrastructuring when you don't – end-user development and organizational infrastructure. In: Costabile, M.F., Dittrich, Y., Fischer, G., Piccinno, A. (eds.) IS-EUD 2011. LNCS, vol. 6654, pp. 139–154. Springer, Heidelberg (2011)
13. MacLean, A., Carter, K., Lövstrand, L., Moran, T.: User-tailorable systems: pressing the issues with buttons. In: Proceedings of the SIGCHI Conference on Human Factors in Computing Systems, CHI 1990, pp. 175–182. ACM, New York (1990)
14. Dittrich, Y., Lindeberg, O., Lundberg, L.: End-user development as adaptive maintenance. In: Lieberman, H., Paternò, F., Wulf, V. (eds.) End User Development. Human-Computer Interaction Series, vol. 9, pp. 295–313. Springer, Netherlands (2006)
15. Ko, A.J., Abraham, R., Beckwith, L., Blackwell, A., Burnett, M., Erwig, M., Scaffidi, C., Lawrance, J., Lieberman, H., Myers, B., Rosson, M.B., Rothermel, G., Shaw, M., Wiedenbeck, S.: The state of the art in end-user software engineering. ACM Comput. Surv. 43(3), 21:1–21:44 (2011)
16. Rode, J., Rosson, M.B., Quinones, M.A.P.: End user development of web applications. In: Lieberman, H., Paternò, F., Wulf, V. (eds.) End User Development. Human-Computer Interaction Series, vol. 9. Springer, Netherlands (2006)
17. Spence, R.: Information Visualization: Design for Interaction, 2nd edn. Prentice-Hall, Inc., Upper Saddle River (2007)
18. Shneiderman, B.: The eyes have it: A task by data type taxonomy for information visualizations. In: Proceedings of the 1996 IEEE Symposium on Visual Languages, VL 1996, pp. 336–343. IEEE Computer Society, Washington, DC (1996)
19. Plaisant, C., Mushlin, R., Snyder, A., Li, J., Heller, D., Shneiderman, B., Colorado, K.P.: Lifelines: Using visualization to enhance navigation and analysis of patient records. In: Proceedings of the 1998 American Medical Informatic Association Annual Fall Symposium, pp. 76–80 (1998)
20. Wang, T.D., Plaisant, C., Quinn, A.J., Stanchak, R., Murphy, S., Shneiderman, B.: Aligning temporal data by sentinel events: discovering patterns in electronic health records. In: Proceedings of the Twenty-Sixth Annual SIGCHI Conference on Human Factors in Computing Systems, CHI 2008, pp. 457–466. ACM (2008)

21. Wongsuphasawat, K., Guerra Gómez, J.A., Plaisant, C., Wang, T.D., Taieb-Maimon, M., Shneiderman, B.: Lifeflow: visualizing an overview of event sequences. In: Proceedings of the 2011 Annual Conference on Human Factors in Computing Systems, CHI 2011, pp. 1747–1756. ACM (2011)

22. Aigner, W., Miksch, S., Schumann, H., Tominski, C.: Visualization of Time-Oriented Data, 1st edn. Springer Publishing Company, Incorporated (2011)

23. Fekete, J.D.: The infovis toolkit. In: Proceedings of the IEEE Symposium on Information Vizualization 2004, pp. 167–174 (2004)

24. Heer, J., Card, S.K., Landay, J.A.: prefuse: a toolkit for interactive information visualization. In: Proceedings of the SIGCHI Conference on Human Factors in Computing Systems, CHI 2005, pp. 421–430. ACM (2005)

25. Bostock, M., Ogievetsky, V., Heer, J.: D3 data-driven documents. IEEE Transactions on Visualization and Computer Graphics 17(12), 2301–2309 (2011)

26. Spotfire, http://spotfire.tibco.com/ (accessed August 2011)

27. Tableau, http://www.tableausoftware.com/ (accessed August 2011)

28. Omniscope, http://www.visokio.com/ (accessed August 2011)

29. Flare, http://flare.prefuse.org/ (accessed August 2011)

30. Microsoft Excel, http://office.microsoft.com/en-us/excel/ (accessed August 2011)

31. Thomas, J.J., Cook, K.A.: A visual analytics agenda. IEEE Comput. Graph. Appl. 26(1), 10–13 (2006)

32. Slocum, T.A., Cliburn, D.C., Feddema, J.J., Miller, J.R.: Evaluating the Usability of a Tool for Visualizing the Uncertainty of the Future Global Water Balance. Cartography and Geographic Information Science, 299–317 (October 2003)

33. Robinson, A.C., Chen, J., Lengerich, E.J., Meyer, H.G., MacEachren, A.M.: Combining usability techniques to design geovisualization tools for epidemiology. Cartography and Geographic Information Science 32(4), 243–255 (2005)

34. Roth, R., Ross, K., Finch, B., Luo, W., MacEachren, A.: A user-centered approach for designing and developing spatiotemporal crime analysis tools. In: GIScience 2010 (2010)

35. Norman, D.A.: The Design of Everyday Things. Doubleday Business (1990)

36. Nielsen, J.: Usability Engineering. Morgan Kaufmann Publishers Inc., San Francisco (1993)

37. Aigner, W., Miksch, S., Müller, W., Schumann, H., Tominski, C.: Visual methods for analyzing time-oriented data (January 2008)

38. Plaisant, C.: The challenge of information visualization evaluation. In: Proceedings of the Working Conference on Advanced Visual Interfaces, AVI 2004, pp. 109–116. ACM (2004)

39. Heer, J., van Ham, F., Carpendale, S., Weaver, C., Isenberg, P.: Creation and collaboration: Engaging new audiences for information visualization. In: Kerren, A., Stasko, J.T., Fekete, J.-D., North, C. (eds.) Information Visualization. LNCS, vol. 4950, pp. 92–133. Springer, Heidelberg (2008)

40. Mackinlay, J.: Automating the design of graphical presentations of relational information. ACM Trans. Graph. 5(2), 110–141 (1986)

41. Roth, S.F., Mattis, J.: Automating the presentation of information (1991)

42. Roth, S.F., Kolojejchick, J., Mattis, J., Chuah, M.C.: Sagetools: an intelligent environment for sketching, browsing, and customizing data-graphics. In: Conference Companion on Human Factors in Computing Systems, CHI 1995, pp. 409–410. ACM (1995)

43. Chuah, M.C., Roth, S.F., Kerpedjiev, S.: Intelligent multimedia information retrieval, pp. 83–111. MIT Press (1997)

44. Cheng, M., Livny, M., Ramakrishnan, R.: Visual analysis of stream data. In: Proceedings of SPIE/The International Society for Optical Engineering, vol. 2410, pp. 108–119 (1995)
45. Livny, M., Ramakrishnan, R., Beyer, K., Chen, G., Donjerkovic, D., Lawande, S., Myllymaki, J., Wenger, K.: Devise: integrated querying and visual exploration of large datasets. In: Proceedings of the 1997 ACM SIGMOD International Conference on Management of Data, SIGMOD 1997, pp. 301–312. ACM (1997)
46. Takatsuka, M., Gahegan, M.: Geovista studio: a codeless visual programming environment for geoscientific data analysis and visualization. Comput. Geosci. 28(10), 1131–1144 (2002)
47. Bederson, B.B., Grosjean, J., Meyer, J.: Toolkit design for interactive structured graphics. IEEE Trans. Softw. Eng. 30, 535–546 (2004)
48. Weaver, C.: Building highly-coordinated visualizations in improvise. In: Proceedings of the IEEE Symposium on Information Visualization, pp. 159–166. IEEE Computer Society (2004)
49. Bostock, M., Heer, J.: Protovis: A graphical toolkit for visualization. IEEE Transactions on Visualization and Computer Graphics 15(6), 1121–1128 (2009)
50. Akasaka, R.: Protoviewer: a web-based visual design environment for protovis. In: ACM SIGGRAPH 2011 Posters, SIGGRAPH 2011, p. 85:1. ACM (2011)
51. Processing, http://www.processing.com/ (accessed August 2011)
52. GOOGLE CHART TOOLS, http://code.google.com/apis/chart/ (accessed October 2011)
53. Viegas, F.B., Wattenberg, M., van Ham, F., Kriss, J., McKeon, M.: Manyeyes: a site for visualization at internet scale. IEEE Transactions on Visualization and Computer Graphics 13, 1121–1128 (2007)
54. Welch, B.B.: Practical programming in Tcl and Tk, 2nd edn. Prentice-Hall, Inc., Upper Saddle River (1997)
55. Stolte, C., Hanrahan, P.: Polaris: a system for query, analysis and visualization of multi-dimensional relational databases. In: IEEE Symposium on Information Visualization, InfoVis 2000, pp. 5–14 (2000)

Resolving Data Mismatches in End-User Compositions

Perla Velasco-Elizondo[1], Vishal Dwivedi[2], David Garlan[2], Bradley Schmerl[2],
and José Maria Fernandes[3]

[1] Autonomous University of Zacatecas, Zacatecas, ZAC, 98000, Mexico
pvelasco@uaz.edu.mx
[2] School of Computer Science, Carnegie Mellon University, Pittsburgh, PA, 15213, USA
{vdwivedi,garlan,schmerl}@cs.cmu.edu
[3] IEETA/DETI, University of Aveiro, 3810-193 Aveiro, Portugal
jfernan@ua.pt

Abstract. Many domains such as scientific computing and neuroscience require end users to compose heterogeneous computational entities to automate their professional tasks. However, an issue that frequently hampers such composition is data-mismatches between computational entities. Although, many composition frameworks today provide support for data mismatch resolution through special-purpose data converters, end users still have to put significant effort in dealing with data mismatches, e.g., identifying the available converters and determining which of them meet their QoS expectations. In this paper we present an approach that eliminates this effort by automating the detection and resolution of data mismatches. Specifically, it uses architectural abstractions to automatically detect different types of data mismatches, model-generation techniques to fix those mismatches, and utility theory to decide the best fix based on QoS constraints. We illustrate our approach in the neuroscience domain where data-mismatches can be fixed in an efficient manner on the order of few seconds.

1 Introduction

Computations are pervasive across many domains today, where end users have to compose heterogeneous computational entities to perform and automate their professional tasks. Unlike professional programmers, these end users have to write compositions to support the goals of their domains, where programming is a means to an end, but not their primary expertise [10]. Such end users, often form large communities that are spread across various domains, e.g., Bioinformatics [23], Intelligence Analysis [26] or Neurosciences.[1] End users in these communities often compose computational entities to automate their tasks and *in silico*[2] experiments. This requires them to work within their domain-specific styles of construction, following the constraints of their domain [8]. They often treat their computations and tools as black boxes, that can be reused across various tasks. Developers in these domains have been using approaches based on Service-Oriented Architecture (SOA) [9] to enable rapid composition of computations from third-party tools, APIs and services. There exist large repositories of

---

[1] http://neugrid4you.eu
[2] Tasks performed on computer or via computer simulation.

Y. Dittrich et al. (Eds.): IS-EUD 2013, LNCS 7897, pp. 120–136, 2013.

Table 1. Common types of data mismatches

Type	Description
DataType	Results from conflicting assumptions on the signature of the data and the components that consume it, e.g., a computation requires different data type.
Format	Results from conflicting assumptions on the format of the data being interchanged among the composed parts, e.g., xml *vs.* csv (comma separated values).
Content	Results from conflicting assumptions on the data scope of the data being interchanged among components, e.g., the format of the output carries less data content than is required by the format of the subsequent input.
Structural	Results from conflicting assumptions on the internal organization of the data being interchanged among the composed parts, e.g., different coordinates system such as Polar *vs.* Cartesian data or different dimensions such as 3D *vs.* 4D.
Conceptual	Results from conflicting assumptions on the semantics of the data being interchanged among the composed parts, e.g., brain structure *vs.* brain activity or distance *vs.* temperature.

reusable services such as BioCatalogue, BIRN and INCF,[3] and supporting domain-specific environments to compose them, e.g., Taverna [11] and LONI Pipeline.[4]

However, despite the popularity of such composition environments and repositories, the growing number of heterogeneous services makes composition hard for end users across these domains. Often end users have to compose computational entities that have conflicting assumptions about the data interchanged among them (as shown in Table 1).[5] That is, it is common for their inputs and outputs to be incompatible with those of the other computational entities with which they must be composed. This claim is supported by recent studies that have shown that about 30% of the services in scientific workflows are data conversion services [28]. Some composition frameworks today provide data mismatch detection facilities and special-purpose data converters that can be inserted at the point of the mismatch. In spite of this, data mismatch detection and resolution continues to be time-consuming and error-prone for the following reasons: (*a*) most current composition environments detect only type mismatches, while other mismatches are often undetected (e.g., format, content, structural, and conceptual), (*b*) due to the prevalence of converters in repositories such as BioCatalogue or BIRN, end users frequently have several converters to select from, often manually, (*c*) instead of a single converter, a solution might involve a combination of converters. This results in a combinatorial explosion of possibilities, and (*c*) among several repair alternatives, end users need to choose the best one with respect to multiple QoS concerns, e.g., accuracy, data loss, distortion. Today, this assessment is done by "trial and error," a time-consuming process often leading to non-optimal solutions.

The key contribution of this work is an approach that automates the detection and resolution of data mismatches, thus reducing the burden to end users. Specifically, our

---

[3] www.biocatalogue.org, www.birncommunity.org and www.incf.org

[4] pipeline.loni.ucla.edu

[5] We studied the literature in data mismatches and organized them in common types. However, this should not be considered as a complete list.

approach uses: (i) *architectural abstractions* to automatically detect different types of data mismatches, (ii) *model-generation* techniques to support the automatic generation of repair alternatives, and (iii) *utility theory* to automatically check for satisfaction of multiple QoS constraints in repair alternatives. We demonstrate the efficiency and cost-effectiveness of the approach for workflow composition in the neuroscience domain. The remainder of this paper is organized as follows. In Section 2 we introduce the background and related work. In Section 3 we describe the proposed approach and in Section 4 we demonstrate it in practice via an example. In Section 5 we present a discussion and evaluation of the approach. Finally, in Section 6, we discuss the conclusions and future work.

2   Background and Related Work

Garlan et al. [14] introduced the term *architectural mismatch* to refer to conflicting assumptions made by an architectural element about different aspects of the system it is to be a part of, including those about data. Regarding data-related aspects, there is work focused on: (a) *categorizing and detecting (architectural) data mismatches* and (b) *automatically resolving them*. In this section, we relate our work to other literature in these two categories.

Categorizing and Detecting Data Mismatches. There have been numerous efforts in the categorization and formal definition of data mismatches. Cámara et al. [5] defined the term "data mismatch" while in [3] Bhuta and Boehm defined "signature mismatch"; both mismatches highlight the differences that occur among two service components' interfaces with respect to the type and format of their input and output parameters. Similarly, Grenchanik et al. [19] defined "message data model mismatch" to describe differences in the format of the messages to be interchanged among components. Mismatch 42 in [13] refers to "sharing or transferring data with differing underlying representations." Previously, Belhajjame et. al. [2], Bhuta and Boehm [3] and Li et. al. [24] described mismatches for service compositions. Our data-mismatch resolution approach extends these previous efforts on categorizing data mismatches and formalizes them as rules to detect them amongst architectural components. In particular, we: (*i*) identify a set of relevant classes of data mismatches as constraint failures, (*ii*) use this error information to characterize the mismatches in an architectural style, (*iii*) build specific analyses to support the detection of the identified mismatches, and (*iv*) have constructed a prototype tool to detect them during system composition. In contrast to these works, we can detect more specialized data mismatches such as the ones shown in Table 1 using an architectural approach that is more suitable for automated formal analysis.

Resolving Data Mismatches. There exists some literature that addresses data-mismatch through automatic resolution approaches. The common approach across this work has been to use adapters, which are components that can be plugged between the mismatched components to convert the data inputs and outputs as necessary. Kongdenfha et al. [22] and Bowers and Ludascher [4] used adapters to convert among formats and internal structures of services' data. Several end-user composition environments today also use adapters for data mismatch resolution. For example, Taverna introduces *shims* that could implement data conversion services[6]. Similarly, LONI Pipeline provides the notion of *smartlines* [25] that encapsulate data conversion tools that resolve data format compatibility issues during workflow composition. However, unlike our approach, these works primarily focus on the automatic generation of adapters rather than on the selection and composition of existing ones. Besides that, these approaches work only for specific data types and formats (e.g., XML) and do not provide support for handling QoS concerns of end users to drive the selection of converters. Even when some environments provide selection support, they do not consider the scenario of having multiple adapters to choose from to solve the same data mismatch.

In the following sections, we describe how our approach addresses the shortcomings in the above discussed works.

3 Approach

As depicted in Figure 1, the approach presented in this paper is comprised of three main phases: (Data) Mismatch Detection, (Data) Mismatch Repair Finding and (Data) Mismatch Repair Evaluation. These three phases use (i) *architectural descriptions* for components and compositions to automatically detect different types of data mismatches, (ii) *model-generation* techniques to support the automatic generation of repair alternatives, and (iii) *utility theory* to automatically check for satisfaction of multiple QoS constraints in repair alternatives.

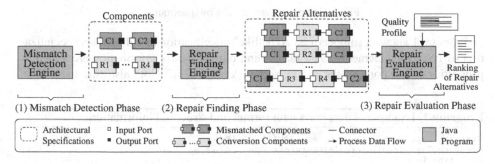

Fig. 1. The three main phases of the approach to data mismatch detection and resolution

Note that it is not the end users who create such architectural descriptions; such descriptions already exist and are created by component developers and domain experts through means like SCORE [8] and SCUFL (from Taverna) [11]. We build on our previous work on the SCORE architectural style, which provides a *generic modeling vocabulary* for the specification of data-flow oriented workflows that comprises the following elements: *component types* –which represent the primary computational elements, *connector types* –which represent interactions among components, *properties* –which represent semantic information about the components and connectors, and *constraints* –which represent restrictions on the definition and usage of components or connectors, e.g., allowable values of properties and topological restrictions.

---

[6] www.taverna.org.uk/introduction/services-in-taverna/

SCORE can be specialized to various domains through *refinement* and *inheritance*. This requires style designers and domain experts to construct substyles that extend the SCORE style and add properties and domain-specific constraints that allow end users to correctly construct workflows within that domain. In the example presented in this paper we use the FSL (Sub)Style, which includes components, properties, and constraints specific to neuroscience compositions. Figure 2 illustrates the specialization of some of SCORE's components types (i.e., Data Store, Service and User Interface) for the neuroscience domain via inheritance. The FSL (Sub)Style, shown on the left-hand side of the figure, includes specializations of service components that provide the functionality of some of the tools offered by the FSL neuroscience suite.[7] In previous work we have also demonstrated the refinement of SCORE for the dynamic network analysis domain [8]. Figure 2 shows some of the components in the resulting substyles, i.e., Dynamic Network Analysis and SORASCS.

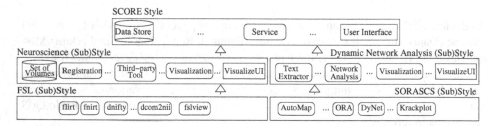

Fig. 2. Component refinement by inheritance

Program 1 shows a snippet of an ADL-like[8] specification that illustrates specialization of FSL Style elements. Data *format* and data *structure* information are added as properties of the ports of the `flirt` service component.[9] Note also that the `flirt`

Program 1. Example of data ports with format and structural information

```
Property Type legalFormats = Enum {NIfTI, DICOM};
Property Type legalInternalStructure = Enum {Aligned, NotAligned};
Port Type In = {
    Property format: set of legalFormats;
    Property structure: legalInternalStructure;
}
Port Type Out = {
    Property format: set of legalFormats;
    Property structure: legalInternalStructure;
}
Component Type flirt extends Registration = {
    Port In: in;
    Port Out: out;
}
```

---

[7] http://www.fmrib.ox.ac.uk/fsl/

[8] We assume familiarity with Architectural Description Languages (ADL) syntax.

[9] In various architectural styles data ports are used to denote data elements produced (output) and consumed (input) by components.

service component inherits from the `Registration` service component in the Neuro-science (Sub)Style, which in turn inherits from the `Service` component in the SCORE Style as shown in Figure 2. The specialization of the SCORE style can be as detailed as needed in a particular domain. The resulting architectural specifications can be used to automatically check constraints to detect various types of violations in compositions. As we will show later, in this work we take advantage of all these aspects to detect data mismatches and construct legal repair alternatives.

3.1 Mismatch Detection Phase

End users are often constrained by their domain-specific styles of construction while composing computations. By enforcing constraints that restrict the values of the properties of a composition, end-user compositions can be analyzed for data mismatches. Architectural specifications are particularly useful for such a verification, as they embed constraints that are evaluated at design time. In our approach, the *Mismatch Detection Engine* analyzes compositions with respect to the mismatches described in Table 1 by using the properties and constraints defined by SCORE (and the additional substyles). For example, this predicate can be used to define an analysis to detect a data mismatch involving both format and structural aspects:

```
for all c1, c2 : Service | connected (c1, c2) ->
   size(intersection(c1.out.format, c2.in.format)) > 0
   AND (c1.out.structure == c2.in.structure)
```

The predicate states that it is not enough for a pair of connected Services $c1$ and $c2$ to deal with data of the same format (e.g., DICOM or NIfTI[10]), but the data must also have the same structural properties (e.g., Aligned or NotAligned). Predicates are implemented as type checkers that take end-user specifications and detect data mismatches. Once a mismatch is detected via the defined analyses, the Mismatch Detection Engine retrieves the architectural specifications of the pair of mismatched components and outputs this to the repair finding phase.

3.2 Repair Finding Phase

Selecting correct composition elements with appropriate properties, with right connections, has always been a tricky process, as people often make mistakes. In this phase, our approach attempts to solve this problem by taking declarative specifications of the pair of mismatched composition elements, along with the constraints in which they could be combined, and use a model generator to find a configuration that satisfies them.

Fig. 3 outlines how our approach uses the Alloy Analyzer [18] (as a model generator) to generate valid compositions that satisfy the domain-specific constraints. These form the repair alternatives for the compositions. The *Repair Finding Engine* takes architectural specifications of both the (pair of) *mismatched components* and a set of *conversion components* as input and translates them into Alloy specifications. For an accurate model-generation, our approach also requires an Alloy model of the *architectural style of the target system* to which the mismatched components belong, that includes the constraints in which the components can be used (as denoted in Fig. 3).

---

[10] DICOM and NIfTI are data formats used to store volumetric brain-imaging data.

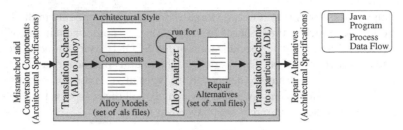

Fig. 3. The Repair Finding Engine

In recent years, various approaches to model architectural constructs in Alloy have been developed, e.g., [20,17]. In our work, we have adopted the approach in [20] where architectural types are specified as signatures (`sig`) and architectural constraints are specified as facts (`fact`) or predicates (`pred`). To provide a general idea of this translation method, consider the following ADL-like specification of the `dinifti` service component shown in the FSL (Sub)Style in Figure 2:

```
Component Type dinifti extends ThirdPartyTool = {
    in.format = DICOM;
    ...
}
```

The component extends the generic component type `ThirdPartyTool` and defines one port of the type `In` with a `DICOM` format value. Using the adopted translation method, results in the Alloy specification shown in Program 2. In this specification the `extends` keyword specifies style-specific types extending the signatures of generic ones, while the `format` and `in` relations model containment relations among types.

Program 2. A component specification in Alloy

```
sig legalFormats {}
sig NIfTI, DICOM extends legalFormats{}
sig In {format: legalFormats}
sig ThirdPartyTool extends Service { in: In, ... }
sig dinifti extends ThirdPartyTool {}

fact {  dinifti.in.format = {DICOM}  ...  }
```

While generating the legal repair, we use the *constructibility of specific architectural configuration analysis* described in [20]. A simple version of this analysis can be performed by instructing the Alloy Analyzer to search for a model instance that violates no assertions and constraints within the specified scope number (using the `run for 1` command). The Repair Finding Engine thus finds all the valid instances of a repair alternative by having multiple runs of this command. As depicted in Fig. 3, the Alloy Analyzer stores these instances as XML files. These files are then automatically transformed to architectural specifications to be processed in the next phase of the approach.

3.3   Repair Evaluation Phase

Service repositories often have a large number of converters available that could lead to multiple repair choices for a data mismatch. In this phase, our approach automates a solution for such scenarios through a utility based strategy. We assume that most composition scenarios have some quality of service criteria such as speed, number of computation steps, quality of output etc., which can enable the selection of an appropriate repair strategy that maximizes the utility value of the resulting composition. Therefore, *architectural specifications of the set of repair alternatives* and a *QoS Profile* are inputs to the *Repair Evaluation Engine* (see Figure 4). This information is used to calculate an overall QoS value for each repair alternative by using *utility theory* [12].

We implemented a simple repair evaluation strategy using QoS profiles for compositions. A QoS Profile is a XML-based template that is meant to be filled in by the end user with two main types of QoS information: (i) *QoS expectations* for a repair alternative and (ii) *importance of each QoS concern* in the profile compared to other concerns. QoS concerns are defined as quality attributes and expectations on them are characterized as *utilities*. Here, *utility* is a measure of relative satisfaction –received by the consumer of a service that explains some phenomenon in terms of increasing or decreasing such satisfaction. For instance, let x_1, x_2, x_3 be in a set of alternative choices. If the decision-maker prefers x_1 to x_2 and x_2 to x_3, then the utility values u_{xi} assigned to the choices must be such that $u_{x1} \leq u_{x2} \leq u_{x3}$. In utility theory, a utility function of the form: $u : X \rightarrow R$ can be used to specify the utility u of a set of alternatives, where X denotes the set of alternative choices and R denotes the set of utility values. For example, the "accuracy" quality attribute could have a utility function defined by the points $\langle$(Opt, 1.0), (Ave, 0.5), (Low, 0.0)$\rangle$ to represent that an optimal accuracy (Opt) gives an utility of 1.0, an average accuracy (Ave) gives the utility of 0.5, and a low accuracy (Low) gives no utility. An end user might need to specify preferences over multiple quality attributes to denote their relative importance. For example, in some situations the designer may require the urgent execution of the workflow. Thus, a repair alternative should run as quickly as possible, perhaps at the expense of fidelity of the result. Conversely, when converting among data formats, minimizing distortion can also be an important concern. In the QoS Profile this information is specified as weights.

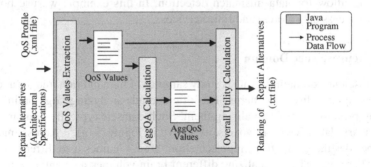

Fig. 4. The Repair Evaluation Engine

To calculate the utility of a repair alternative, it is necessary to first calculate a set of aggregated quality attribute values ($aggQA$) for a repair alternative. These values, computed via a set of built-in domain-specific functions, are analogous to the quality attributes values exposed by each converter but they apply to a whole repair alternative.

For example, suppose that a repair alternative comprises a sequence of three converters C exposing the following values for the distortion quality attribute: *Average* (e.g., 0.5), *Average* (e.g., 0.5) and *Optimal* (e.g., 1.0). A distortion aggregated value for the whole repair alternative in this case could be *Average* (i.e., 0.5) when using the following domain-specific function:[11] $aggQA_{Dist} : 1/m \sum_{i=1}^{k} = Dist(C_k)$, with $m = n + 1$.

There is one function for each quality attribute in the QoS Profile. In this approach, converters must define values for the quality attributes to be considered in the QoS Profile in order to apply these functions.

Using the above information, and based on the ideas presented in [6], we have defined a straightforward way to compute the overall utility of a repair alternative. Given a set of repair alternatives, each defining a set of q quality attributes, a set of aggregated quality attributes values $aggQA$, a utility function u that assigns an utility value to each $aggQA$ and an importance value w for each one of these q quality attributes; a utility function U of the form: $U : \sum_{i=1}^{q} = w_i * u(aggQA_i)$, with $\sum_{i=1}^{q} w_i = 1$, can be used to calculate the overall utility for each repair alternative. The utilities for the alternatives are used to provide a ranking that the end-user can use to select the best repair alternative to the detected mismatch.

4   Example

In this section we illustrate our approach with an example of workflow construction in the neuroscience domain via a prototype tool called SWiFT [8], which provides a graphical workflow construction environment. The tool uses a simplified version of the SCORE architectural style to drive workflow construction and incorporates some analyses to verify their validity at design time. We have extended it, as described in Section 3, to allow for data mismatch detection. In this example we use both Data Services (to access data stores) and FSL Services.

4.1   The Neuroscience Domain

In the neuroscience domain, scientists study samples of human brain images and neural activity to diagnose disease patterns. This often entails analyzing large brain-imaging datasets by processing and visualizing them. Such datasets typically contain 3D volumes of binary data divided to voxels, as shown in Figure 5 (a).[12] Across many such datasets, besides the geometrical representation, brain volumes also differ in their orientation. Therefore, when visualizing different brain volumes a scientist must "align" them by performing registration. When two brain volumes A and B are *registered*, the same anatomical features have the same position in a common brain reference system, i.e., the nose position in A is in the same position in B, see Figure 5 (b). Thus, registration of brain volumes allows integrated brain-imaging views.

---

[11] *Dist* stands for distortion.

[12] A voxel is a unit volume of specific dimensions, e.g. width, length and height.

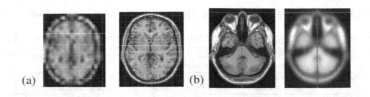

(a)   (b)

Fig. 5. (a) Volumes in voxels and (b) registered volumes with same brain reference

Processing and visualizing data sets require scientists in this domain to compose a number brain-imaging tools and services provided by different vendors. The selection of tools and services is carried out manually and often driven by analysis-dependent values of domain-specific QoS constraints, e.g., accuracy, data loss, distortion. In this context, the heterogeneous nature of services and tools often leads to data mismatches; thus, scientists also need to select conversion tools and services to resolve them.

4.2 Workflow Composition Scenario

Consider that during workflow composition a scientist needs to visualize a set of brain-image volumes. These volumes store brain images of the same person as 3D DICOM volumes. The volumes are not registered, i.e., they are not aligned to the same brain reference system. To visualize this data, the scientist tries to compose the Set of Volumes data service – which can read the actual store where the volumes are, and the Visualize Volumes service – which enables their visualization. Table 2 shows an excerpt of the specifications of the operations' parameters of these two services. As can be seen, the Visualize Volumes service requires data that is already registered and in 'NIfTI' format (see its registered='Yes' and format='NIfTI' input parameters). Thus, these two services cannot be composed as they have both a *format* and a *structural mismatch*, i.e., the interchanged data has both a different format and internal organization.

Table 2. An excerpt of the parameter specifications of the services in the example

Service	Operation	Input parameters	Output parameters
Set of Volumes	read Volumes		name='out' type='files' format='DICOM' registered='No' sameSubject='Yes'
Visualize Volumes	view	name='in' type='files' format='NIfTI' registered='Yes' sameSubject='Yes|No'	
dinifti	DICOM toNIfTI	name='in' type='files' format='DICOM' registered='No|Yes'	name='out' type='files' format='NIfTI' registered='Yes|No'
dcm2nii	dc2nii	name='in' type='files' format='DICOM' registered='No|Yes' sameSubject='Yes|No'	name='out' type='files' format='NIfTI' sameSubject='Yes|No' registered='Yes|No'
flirt	register	name='in' type='files' format='NIfTI' registered='No' sameSubject='Yes|No'	name='out' type='files' format='NIfTI' registered='Yes' sameSubject='Yes|No'
fnirt	register	name='in' type='files' format='NIfTI' registered='No' sameSubject='Yes|No'	name='out' type='files' format='NIfTI' registered='Yes' sameSubject='Yes|No'

Table 3. Some brain-imaging tools to perform registration and format conversion

Operation	Description	Name
LINEAR REGISTRATION	Align one brain volume to another using linear transformations opera- tions, e.g., rotation, translations.	*flirt*
NON-LINEAR REGISTRATION	Extends linear registration allowing local deformations using non-linear methods to achieve a better alignment, e.g., warping, local distortions.	*fnirt*
FORMAT CONVERSION	Converts images from the DICOM format to the NIfTI format used by FSL, SPM5, MRIcron and many other brain imaging tools.	*dinifti, dcm2nii*

4.3 Data Mismatch Detection and Resolution

Figure 6 (a) shows how the data mismatch is presented to the scientist in our tool once it is detected by an analysis based on the predicate presented in Section 3.1. In order to compose these two services, the scientist should invoke the Repair Finding Engine by clicking on the "Resolve Data Mismatch" button in the tool interface (shown on the left hand side of Figure 6 (a)). We illustrate the case of a repair involving a combination of converters, see Table 3. Format conversion can be performed by using either the *dinifti* or the *dcm2nii* service converters. Registration can be performed by using the either the *flirt* or the *fnirt* FSL services. Part of the operations' parameter specifications of such services is also shown in Table 2. Based on these specifications and the corresponding Alloy Models, the Repair Finding Engine finds the following repair alternatives (RA):

RA_1: Set of Volumes - dinifti - flirt - Visualize Volumes
RA_2: Set of Volumes - dinifti - fnirt - Visualize Volumes
RA_3: Set of Volumes - dcm2nii - flirt - Visualize Volumes
RA_4: Set of Volumes - dcm2nii - fnirt - Visualize Volumes

All of these alternates are legal, as they obey the architectural style's constraints that restrict their structure and properties. However, because the constituent conversion services have different quality attribute values –see Program 3, the overall QoS of each repair alternative is different. Let's assume that the scientist has specific QoS requirements for a repair. He would like to have no distortion in the brain-image; he would like to have an optimal speed and accuracy, but would be OK with their average values. However, low value of speed or accuracy, or distortion is not acceptable for this composition. This information, specified in the QoS Profile, can be summarized as follows: *Accuracy*: ⟨(Optimal, 1.0), (Average, 0.5), (Low, 0.0)⟩, *Speed*: ⟨(Optimal, 1.0), (Average, 0.5), (Low, 0.0)⟩ and *Distortion*: ⟨(Y, 0.0), (N, 1.0)⟩, with the 0.5, 0.1 and 0.4 weight values respectively.

Based on the QoS information, and using a set of built-in domain-specific functions, the Repair Evaluation Engine calculates the following aggregated quality attribute values:[13]

RA_1: $aggQA_{Dist}$ = N, $aggQA_{Sp}$ = Ave, $aggQA_{Acc}$ = Opt.
RA_2: $aggQA_{Dist}$ = Y, $aggQA_{Sp}$ = Ave, $aggQA_{Acc}$ = Opt.
RA_3: $aggQA_{Dist}$ = N, $aggQA_{Sp}$ = Opt, $aggQA_{Acc}$ = Opt.
RA_4: $aggQA_{Dist}$ = Y, $aggQA_{Sp}$ = Ave, $aggQA_{Acc}$ = Opt.

---

[13] Dist = Distortion, Sp = Speed, Acc = Accuracy, Opt=Optimal, Ave=Average.

Program 3. QoS specifications of the FSL services

```
<QoSSpecification> <!-- dinifti -->
 <att><name>Distortion</name><val>N</val></att>
 <att><name>Speed</name><val>Average</val></att>
 <att><name>Accuracy</name><val>Optimal</val></att>
</QoSSpecification>
<QoSSpecification> <!-- dcm2nii -->
 <att><name>Distortion</name><val>N</val></att>
 <att><name>Speed</name><val>Optimal</val></att>
 <att><name>Accuracy</name><val>Optimal</val></att>
</QoSSpecification>
<QoSSpecification> <!-- flirt -->
 <att><name>Distortion</name><val>N</val></att>
 <att><name>Speed</name><val>Optimal</val></att>
 <att><name>Accuracy</name><val>Optimal</val></att>
</QoSSpecification>
<QoSSpecification> <!-- fnirt -->
 <att><name>Distortion</name><val>Y</val></att>
 <att><name>Speed</name><val>Average</val></att>
 <att><name>Accuracy</name><val>Optimal</val></att>
</QoSSpecification>
```

With all this available information, the Repair Evaluation Engine can compute the overall utility of each repair alternative via the utility function U described in Section 3.3.

$$U_{RA_1} = w_{Dist} * u(aggQA_{Dist}) + w_{Sp} * u(aggQA_{Sp}) + w_{Acc} * u(aggQA_{Acc})$$
$$= 0.5 * 1.0 + 0.1 * 0.5 + 0.4 * 1.0 = 0.95$$
$$U_{RA_2} = w_{Dist} * u(aggQA_{Dist}) + w_{Sp} * u(aggQA_{Sp}) + w_{Acc} * u(aggQA_{Acc})$$
$$= 0.50 * 0.00 + 0.10 * 0.50 + 0.40 * 1.0 = 0.25$$
$$U_{RA_3} = w_{Dist} * u(aggQA_{Dist}) + w_{Sp} * u(aggQA_{Sp}) + w_{Acc} * u(aggQA_{Acc})$$
$$= 0.5 * 1.0 + 0.1 * 1.0 + 0.4 * 1.0 = 1.0$$
$$U_{RA_4} = w_{Dist} * u(aggQA_{Dist}) + w_{Sp} * u(aggQA_{Sp}) + w_{Acc} * u(aggQA_{Acc})$$
$$= 0.5 * 0.0 + 0.1 * 0.50 + 0.4 * 1.00 = 0.45$$

Fig. 6. (a) Data mismatch detection in our tool, (b) Workflow after mismatch resolution

The obtained results are ranked and alternative 3, which has the highest utility, allows automatic generation of the workflow shown in Figure 6 (b). This mismatch resolution strategy not only generates a correct workflow, but it also alleviates the otherwise painful task of manual search and error resolution by the end users.

5   Discussion and Evaluation

In this section we discuss and evaluate our approach with respect to (a) its usefulness for the targeted end users, (b) its implementation cost and flexibility, and (c) the efficiency and scalability of the used techniques.

Usefulness for the Targeted End Users. Traditional composition requires low-level technical expertise, which is not the case for many end users in some domains. For software systems, architectural abstractions for components and composition help to bridge the gap between non-technical and technical aspects of the software. We exploit this to address the problems in end-user composition. Our approach is aided by architectural abstractions, which allow a generic system modeling vocabulary that does not deal with low-level technical aspects, and therefore can be more easily understood and used by non-technical users. Such abstractions are designed once (by experts and component developers) and can be reused multiple times by the end users.

Another aspect of our approach is the need for end users to specify multiple QoS values. Although end users do not think explicitly about QoS attributes, they certainly think implicitly about them. Informal discussions with end users highlights that they are concerned about how long an analysis will take (i.e. performance), whether information will leak (i.e. privacy), whether resulting images are suitable for a particular diagnostic goal (i.e. precision, data loss) and the like. Our approach asks them to think about and quantify these explicitly to help them identify better compositions for their requirements.

Implementation Cost and Flexibility. Because of the nature of our approach, its implementation cost can be significantly minimized by reusing or refining several artifacts such as the architectural styles, the analyses, the translation rules to Alloy, the domain-specific aggregation functions and the overall QoS utility function. Although some effort is needed for creating these artifacts, this effort is required *only once* by a style designer and a domain expert and the resulting artifacts can be *reused later many times* by end-users during workflow construction. Moreover, as discussed before, many of these artifacts can be reused through refinement. Note that the modeling constructs of languages such as BPEL or the domain-specific ones used by composition environments such Taverna and LONI Pipeline can be reused many times, but cannot be refined to specific domains, like ours. Moreover, our approach is flexible enough to be integrated in composition tools; for example the SWiFT tool, used in the examples described in Section 4.

Efficiency and Scalability. A large number of languages today support the composition of computational elements. Examples include, BPEL, code scripts, and domain-specific composition languages (DSCLs) used by Taverna and LONI Pipeline. However, most of these provide very low-level and/or generic modeling constructs, and hence are not very efficient for end-user tasks [8]. Architectural specifications, in contrast, provide high-level constructs that can be reused and refined to address composition in specific application domains. The formal nature of architectural specifications enables various analyses to be performed *automatically*. We illustrated this by reusing and refining some architectural definitions in SCORE; specifically by adding properties to data ports and constraints on them, we were able to handle a bigger scope and tackle data mismatch detection in the neuroscience domain. Thus, as shown in Table 4, we claim that architectural specifications are more efficient and scalable than BPEL, code scripts or the mentioned domain-specific languages.

Table 4. Efficiency and scalability aspects for some composition specification languages

	Architectural Specifications	BPEL, Scripts, DSCLs
Efficiency (in terms of): Automated Analysis	Robust	Limited
Scalability (in terms of): Refinement of abstractions	Robust	No support

In comparison, several formal methods have been used to support the automated composition of architectural elements at design time. A majority of existing work in web-service automation focuses on using Artificial Intelligence (AI) planning techniques [1].[14] Although, many such AI planning techniques guarantee correctness of the generated compositions based on logic, a correct composition *might not be the optimal composition*, as it is recognized that planners tend to generate unnecessarily long plans [21] and little consideration is given to QoS aspects while selecting the services in a plan [1]. Additionally, AI planning based service composition tools such as SHOP2 [27] do not consider the scenario of having more than one service for a plan's action. Therefore, multiple composition plans cannot be generated. Another interesting line of work has been towards assisted mash-up composition using pattern-based approaches, e.g. [7] –despite the fact that not all the evaluation aspects presented in Table 5 apply for them. A mashup consists of several components, namely mashlets, implementing specific functionalities. Thus, pattern-based approaches to mashup composition aim at suggesting pre-existing "glue patterns", made of mashlets, in order to autocomplete a mashup. Most of this work relies on an autocompletion mechanism based on syntactic aspects of the signatures of the mashlets and the "collective wisdom" of previous users that have successfully use the glue patterns. Thus, optimal composition generation is limited. Moreover, the number of composition alternatives depends on the number of existing patterns rather than the number of individual mashlets. Finally, approaches using ontologies based on description logic are also used to assist users in selecting and composing workflow components, e.g. [16]. However, most of these approaches offer limited support for resolving mismatches that require a collection of converters.

We address the limitations of existing work in automated composition through model checking and model generation using Alloy. Two important aspects motivated its use in our work. First, by using the model finder capabilities of Alloy Analyzer it is easy

---

[14] Service composition based on AI planning considers services as atomic actions that have effects on the state. Given a list of actions that have to be achieved and a set of services that accomplish them, a plan is an ordered sequence of the services that need to be executed.

Table 5. Efficiency and scalability aspects of some approaches to automated composition, i.e. Model Checking with Alloy (MC), Artificial Intelligence Planning (AIP) and Pattern-based (PB)

	MC	AIP	PB
Efficiency (in terms of):			
- *Automated composition*	Robust	Robust	Robust
- *Composition correctness*	Robust	Robust	Robust
- *Optimal composition generation*	Limited	Limited	Limited
- *Multiple composition alternatives*	Robust	Limited	Limited
- *Translation to architectural constructs*	Robust	No Support	Not Apply
Scalability (in terms of):			
- *Processing large models*	Limited	Limited	Not Apply

Table 6. Results of the scalability experiment. All times are measured in milliseconds.

No. of Converters	No. of Signatures	Translation Time (TT)	Solving Time (ST)	TT + ST
4	13	256	47	303
10	21	827	141	968
15	26	1,077	234	1,311
25	36	1,575	453	2,028
50	61	9,376	2,215	11,591

to generate *multiple alternative compositions*. Secondly, Alloy provides a simple modeling language, based on first-order and relational calculus, that is well-suited for representing abstract end-user compositions. Additionally, we used several *ADL to Alloy automated translation* methods developed in recent years, e.g. [20,17,29].

One of the widely known problems of using model checking is the combinatorial explosion of the state-space that limit their scalability when working with large models. We believe that it is not a major concern in our case. To support this claim, we performed an experiment in which we increased the number of converters from 4 to 50 to work with bigger models.[15] Table 6 summarizes the results obtained, including those for the example presented in this paper with 4 converters. TT is the translation time, ST is the solving time, and the summation of TT+ST is the total time to generate the first possible solution –following solutions take negligible time.[16] Note that the time to generate a repair alternative in a scenario with 50 converters is about 11 secs. This time is a drastic improvement over the complexity of resolving such mismatches manually.

6   Conclusions and Future Work

Many composition frameworks today provide support for data mismatch resolution through special purpose data converters. However, as end users often have several converters to select from, they still have to put significant effort in identifying them and

---

[15] The experiment was performed on a 2.67 GHz Intel(R) Core i7 with 8 GB RAM.

[16] TT is the time that the analyzer takes to generate the Boolean clauses; ST is the time it takes to find a solution with these clauses.

determining which meet their QoS expectations. In this paper we presented an approach that automates these tasks by combining architectural modeling, model-generation and utility analysis. We demonstrated our approach with SWiFT –a web-based tool for workflow composition, using a simple data-flow composition scenario in the brain imaging domain. However, we have been working with other domains with different computation models [15].

Our future work includes exploring the integration of our approach with popular composition environments and performing usability studies on these environments. We also plan to study means to make QoS specification more approachable to end users by considering more real-life situations in specific domains, e.g. in the neuroscience domain, distortion could refer to a situation in which a converter obscures tumours of certain diameter. Similarly, as new converters and quality attributes may appear over time, we plan to define means to evolve the domain specific-functions and QoS profiles. We are also considering to explore applying the techniques used in this work to other forms of repairs. e.g. service substitution in workflows with obsolete services.

Acknowledgments. This material is based upon work funded by the Department of Defense under Contract No. FA8721-05-C-0003 with Carnegie Mellon University for the operation of the Software Engineering Institute, a federally funded research and development center. Further support for this work came from Office of Naval Research grant ONR-N000140811223, the Center for Computational Analysis of Social and Organizational Systems (CASOS) and the FCT Portuguese Science and Technology Agency under the CMU-Portugal faculty exchange program. The authors would like to thank to Aparup Banerjee, Laura Gledenning, Mai Nakayama, Nina Patel, and Hector Rosas –MSE students at CMU, and Diego Estrada Jimenez –MSE student at the CIMAT for their contributions in development of the SWiFT tool and the integration of the engines into it respectively.

References

1. Baryannis, G., Plexousakis, D.: Automated Web Service Composition: State of the Art and Research Challenges. Technical Report ICS-FORTH/TR-409, ICS-FORTH (2010)
2. Belhajjame, K., Embury, S.M., Paton, N.W.: On characterising and identifying mismatches in scientific workflows. In: Leser, U., Naumann, F., Eckman, B. (eds.) DILS 2006. LNCS (LNBI), vol. 4075, pp. 240–247. Springer, Heidelberg (2006)
3. Bhuta, J., Boehm, B.: A framework for identification and resolution of interoperability mismatches in COTS-based systems. In: Proc. of the Int. Workshop on Incorporating COTS Soft. into Soft. Syst.: Tools and Techniques. IEEE Comp. Soc. (2007)
4. Bowers, S., Ludäscher, B.: An ontology-driven framework for data transformation in scientific workflows. In: Rahm, E. (ed.) DILS 2004. LNCS (LNBI), vol. 2994, pp. 1–16. Springer, Heidelberg (2004)
5. Cámara, J., Martín, J.A., Salaün, G., Canal, C., Pimentel, E.: Semi-automatic specification of behavioural service adaptation contracts. ENTCS 264(1), 19–34 (2010)
6. Cheng, S.W., Garlan, D., Schmerl, B.: Architecture-based self-adaptation in the presence of multiple objectives. In: Proc. of the Int. Workshop on Self-adaptation and Self-managing Systems, pp. 2–8. ACM (2006)
7. Chowdhury, S.R.: Assisting end-user development in browser-based mashup tools. In: Proc. of the Int. Conf. on Software Engineering, pp. 1625–1627. IEEE Press (2012)

8. Dwivedi, V., Velasco-Elizondo, P., Fernandes, J.M., Garlan, D., Schmerl, B.: An architectural approach to end user orchestrations. In: Crnkovic, I., Gruhn, V., Book, M. (eds.) ECSA 2011. LNCS, vol. 6903, pp. 370–378. Springer, Heidelberg (2011)
9. Erl, T.: Service-Oriented Architecture: Concepts, Technology, and Design. Prentice Hall PTR, Upper Saddle River (2005)
10. Ko, A.J., et al.: The state of the art in end-user software engineering. ACM Comput. Surv. 43(3), 21 (2011)
11. Hull, D., et al.: Taverna: A tool for building and running workflows of services. Nucleic Acids Research 34(Web Server Issue), W729–W732 (2006)
12. Fishburn, P.C.: Utility theory for decision making. Pub. in operations research. Wiley (1970)
13. Gacek, C.: Detecting architectural mismatches during systems composition. PhD thesis, University of Southern California, Los Angeles, CA, USA (1998)
14. Garlan, D., Allen, R., Ockerbloom, J.: Architectural mismatch: Why reuse is so hard. IEEE Software 12, 17–26 (1995)
15. Garlan, D., Dwivedi, V., Ruchkin, I., Schmerl, B.: Foundations and tools for end-user architecting. In: Calinescu, R., Garlan, D. (eds.) Monterey Workshop 2012. LNCS, vol. 7539, pp. 157–182. Springer, Heidelberg (2012)
16. Gil, Y., Ratnakar, V., Deelman, E., Spraragen, M., Kim, J.: Wings for Pegasus: A semantic approach to creating very large scientific workflows. In: Proc. of the Int. Conf. on Innovative Applications of Artificial Intelligence, pp. 1767–1774. AAAI Press (2007)
17. Hansen, K., Ingstrup, M.: Modeling and analyzing architectural change with Alloy. In: Proc. of the ACM Symposium on Applied Computing, pp. 2257–2264. ACM (2010)
18. Jackson, D.: Software Abstractions - Logic, Language, and Analysis. MIT Press (2006)
19. Grechanik, M., Bierhoff, K., Liongosari, E.S.: Architectural mismatch in service-oriented architectures. In: Proc. of the Int. Workshop on Systems Development in SOA Environments. IEEE Comp. Soc. (2007)
20. Kim, J.S., Garlan, D.: Analyzing architectural styles. Journal of Systems and Software 83, 1216–1235 (2010)
21. Klusch, M., Gerber, A.: Evaluation of service composition planning with OWLS-XPlan. In: Proc. of the Int. Conf. on Web Intelligence and Intelligent Agent Technology, pp. 117–120. IEEE Comp. Soc. (2006)
22. Kongdenfha, W., Motahari-Nezhad, H.R., Benatallah, B., Casati, F., Saint-Paul, R.: Mismatch patterns and adaptation aspects: A foundation for rapid development of web service adapters. IEEE Transactions on Services Computing 2, 94–107 (2009)
23. Letondal, C.: Participatory programming: Developing programmable bioinformatics tools for end-users. In: End User Development. Human-Computer Interaction Series, vol. 9, pp. 207–242. Springer, Netherlands (2006)
24. Li, X., Fan, Y., Jiang, F.: A classification of service composition mismatches to support service mediation. In: Proc. of the Sixth Int. Conf. on Grid and Cooperative Computing, pp. 315–321. IEEE Comp. Soc. (2007)
25. Neu, S.C., Valentino, D.J., Toga, A.W.: The LONI debabeler: a mediator for neuroimaging software. Neuroimage 24, 1170–1179 (2005)
26. Schmerl, B., Garlan, D., Dwivedi, V., Bigrigg, M.W., Carley, K.M.: SORASCS: a case study in SOA-based platform design for socio-cultural analysis. In: Proceedings of the Int. Conf. on Software Engineering, pp. 643–652. ACM (2011)
27. Sirin, E., Parsia, B., Wu, D., Hendler, J., Nau, D.: HTN planning for web service composition using SHOP2. Web Semant. 1(4), 377–396 (2004)
28. Wassink, I., van der Vet, P.E., Wolstencroft, K., Neerincx, P.B., Roos, M., Rauwerda, H., Breit, T.M.: Analysing Scientific Workflows: Why Workflows Not Only Connect Web Services. In: Proc. of the Congress on Services, pp. 314–321. IEEE Comp. Soc. (2009)
29. Wong, S., Sun, J., Warren, I., Sun, J.: A scalable approach to multi-style architectural modeling and verification (2008)

Co-production Scenarios for Mobile Time Banking

John M. Carroll

Center for Human-Computer Interaction/College of Information Sciences and Technology
The Pennsylvania State University
University Park, Pennsylvania 16803 USA
jmcarroll@psu.edu

Abstract. *Time banking* facilitates generalized reciprocity among neighbors by rewarding contributions in proportion to the time entailed in contributing. Contributions can be person-to-person services, such as driving another person to an appointment. They can also be *co-productions*, in which the provider and recipient jointly enact a service, such as giving/receiving a guitar lesson. Co-production is an important category of time banking interaction; it has been identified as a key to strengthening the core economy of home, family, neighborhood and community, and is becoming integrated into government social service schemes. As part of a requirements analysis for mobile timing banking infrastructures, we identified and analyzed co-production scenarios. Our objective is to contribute to the social movements of co-production of social services and of time banking through designing and developing a socio-technical infrastructure that mutually leverages both to build up the core economy and to enable societal-scale time banking.

Keywords: time banks, co-production (social services), scenario based design, community informatics, ubiquitous computing, socio-technical infrastructures.

1   Introduction

In this paper, we consider *co-production* of social services as a *time banking* interaction, drawing upon our on-going work developing new models for mobile time banking, and new software infrastructures and tools for time banks. Time banking is valuing contributions by the time it takes to produce them, and mediating exchanges of effort and other contribution among community members by adjusting time credit balances (Cahn, 2000; Cahn & Rowe, 1992; Seyfang, 2004a,b; Seyfang & Smith, 2002). For example, one person might have a car, and can drive neighbors to appointments and grocery shopping, while another knows how to garden. Each can contribute their effort to the time bank, and also draw against their time balances to make requests, for example, having someone mow their lawn. Time banking is an alternative economic paradigm to exchanges of money. Because it emphasizes person-to-person interactions, and because everyone's contributions are valued on the same scale (time), time banking strengthens local social ties and social capital, enhances personal dignity in ways that the money-based economy does not (Coleman, 1988; Collom, 2005, 2008b; Putnam, 2000; Ozanne, 2010; Molnar, 2011; Seyfang, 2002, 2003, 2009).

Y. Dittrich et al. (Eds.): IS-EUD 2013, LNCS 7897, pp. 137–152, 2013.

In the context of modern market economies and government bureaucracies, time banking is radical. It is a generalized exchange economy not based on money, and values everyone's contribution on the same scale (time expended). Although accounts, debits and credits are explicitly managed in time banks, there is a high level of consensual self-management on the part of time bank members, based on moral obligation. Thus, although time credits can be used to obtain goods and services, they also serve to recognize engagement in and contribution to the community (Glynos & Speed, 2013). Time banking has spread rapidly in recent years; for example, the non-profit organization, TimeBanks USA facilitates 276 time banks in North America through 27,000 members, as well as in other countries, including Australia, Canada, Costa Rica, Italy, the Netherlands, New Zealand, Portugal, Russia, Saint Martin, Ukraine, the United Arab Emirates, Uruguay, and Vietnam (TimeBanks USA, 2013). The number of time banks in Spain has doubled during the past three years, to about 300 (Moffett & Brat, 2012); the number of time banks in the United Kingdom is also about 300 (TimeBanking UK, 2013).

Co-production of social services is producing social service outcomes through collaborations of recipients, social service professionals, and other stakeholders, in which all the stakeholders have power and responsibility to identify and achieve successful outcomes, and in which recipients or clients of services work directly with service providers to produce services. The concept of co-production originated in the observation that effective delivery of social services sometimes depends upon the active involvement of the service recipients. The signature example is Ostrom's (1993, 1996) analysis of the increase in Chicago street crime that coincided with police switching from walking a neighborhood beat to patrolling in cars. Ostrom argued that patrolling in cars reduced contact with residents, and thereby diminished the extent to which neighborhood safety could be effectively pursued as a joint project of police (service providers) and residents (service recipients/clients). The police officer in the street is in a better position to co-produce public safety with active involvement of the public: Police and residents can get to know one another better, trust one another more, share and display awareness of events, and directly and indirectly collaborate to provide neighborhood safety.

Co-production is not passive cooperation, such as a patient answering a doctor's diagnostic questions in a medical interview. And it is more than participation in planning what will be done. It is direct sharing in the work itself; it makes a service provision into reciprocal support in which the client works with the service provider to achieve an outcome better for both. An institutional example is Habitat for Humanity, an international non-governmental organization that builds low-income housing with volunteer labor, including the labor of the people who will later live in the house being built and of people who previously received housing assistance from group.

Edgar Cahn (2010) extended the concept of co-production arguing that effective co-production involves partnerships among communities and agencies, as well as among individual community members and service professionals. In this view, co-production relies on individual initiatives and relationships but in the context of a broader transformation of roles and responsibilities, including roles and responsibilities of municipal and other government entities. In Cahn's notion, social service professionals are facilitators more than providers, and services themselves are nego-tiated and produced by all stakeholders working toward collective goals. Time bank credit and peer recognition is a key social regulatory mechanism in this conception (Glynos & Speed, 2013).

In fall of 2011, we proposed to TimeBanks USA the project of creating smart phone software to support mobile time banking. TimeBanks USA agreed to work with us; they were in the midst of defining and developing a new version of the web-based Community Weaver platform, used by hundreds of time banks throughout the world (Community Weaver, 2013). Initially, our effort was focused on designing and developing a mobile client or clients that could access the database server of the Community Weaver platform. We began to envision and analyze mobile time banking scenarios. Design scenarios are intended to represent and to problematize designs, that is, to both initially codify and also raises issues about design approaches. As part of a requirements analysis for mobile timing banking infrastructures, we identified and analyzed co-production scenarios (Carroll, 2000).

In this paper, we describe scenario development for mobile time banking. We be-gan inspired by the idea that community members could leverage one another to carry out small tasks, reducing the overall busyness of the ensemble of people throughout the community. In the course of developing and analyzing this idea and our initial scenarios for envisioning it, we discovered time banking as a pre-existing concept for what we had in mind, and reconceived our idea as mobile time banking. Coming at mobile time banking from the angle of reducing busyness probably biased us toward a somewhat task oriented notion of the services that community members might exchange in a time bank.

Our partners in TimeBanks USA were pleased with our initial prototyping work, and indeed asked us to consider that the mobile platform might be the new default platform for time banking. But they also urged us to emphasize co-production scena-rios, scenarios in which time banking services and social effects are more collective. Initially it seemed to us that co-production scenarios were just a broadening of para-meters for community-based exchanges. However, the logic and the motivational dynamics underlying co-production are entirely different. We operationalized this transition as one from scenarios that emphasize "doing for" to scenarios that also emphasize "doing with". We present our experience both as a concrete instance of shifting from an individual to a collective perspective in service design, and as a general reflection on the potentially cascading effects of what at first seem small refinements in a design concept.

2   Scenarios for Mobile Time Banking

Our initial scenarios for mobile time banking sought to identify ways people can do things for other people (1) with relatively minimal effort, (2) leveraging the affordances of mobile devices, such as GPS (Global Positioning System) information and being pre-situated in a flow of embodied activity. We saw this as a source of new value for time banking, which we understood to be highly transactional and managed through a web-based content management system, Community Weaver (2013). Our reasoning was that small favors at just the right time and place might generate outsized benefit for the recipient to the actual time and trouble they cost the producer. We saw this as a novel and opportune approach to generating and strengthening social ties and social capital in a local community (Carroll, Bellotti & Han, 2013).

Our initial touchstone scenario for mobile time banking is the Get Aspirin scenario in Table 1.

Table 1. Get Aspirin scenario (from Carroll et al. 2013)

> Mary was in the market to buy some groceries. While she was shopping, she quickly checked Mobile Time Bank (MTB) requests. One of her neighbors, John, had posted a request for a bottle of aspirin an hour ago. John was at home with his daughter, who had a cold. Mary would be driving right past his home anyway. Since she already knew John, she called him up and told him the aspirin was on the way. She also accepted the request in her MTB app. She had a brief chat with John while dropping off the aspirin. As she left, she felt good about helping someone, but also was struck by how easy it was to do, earning time bank credit as well.

This scenario was effective in evoking ubiquitous interaction possibilities, but also in raising requirements issues. On the upside, it conveys a new possibility for John to both get his aspirin quickly, and without having to drag his daughter to the store, and also to experience social support from his neighbor, Mary. On the downside, the scenario emphasizes how stringent the timing relationships are: If Mary has more shopping to do, and arrives three hours later, John may be frustrated. He may have made other arrangements for the aspirin and no longer need it. It also emphasizes the social risks implicit in such interactions. Perhaps John will be anxious about posting such a request to a community time bank, depending on a stranger for something vital like aspirin, and inviting a stranger to his home. On Mary's side, she may be reluctant to accept John's request, if she does not already know him.

We generated and analyzed a set of scenarios that emphasize needs and opportunities that involve relatively small efforts whose value is magnified by being timely and co-located. For example, someone's car breaks down on a highway as they are driving across town, or they miss the last bus, and they post a time bank request to get picked up.

We identified a type of scenario that involves transactions in which one person's efforts can be almost entirely leveraged by another person. For example, one person might want to get tickets to a Bruce Springsteen concert, or purchase a textbook for the Psychology 101 course. She/he could post a request to the time bank asking for someone else, who is already planning to carry out that transaction, to do it for both of them, that is, to get an extra ticket or textbook. In this type of scenario, the extra work is only the work required to manage the time banking transaction itself (e.g., exchange money for ticket or book), the person was going to wait on line and go through the purchase protocol anyway. We imagined real time versions of these scenarios that could depend more critically on mobile interactions, such as arranging for someone to buy your ticket while you are in the queue, and so that you can leave the queue and still get the ticket. These scenarios have downsides in that money is involved: Someone buys something for someone else and either must front them the money, or must collect it advance, and then be trusted to deliver the purchase.

These first scenarios for mobile time banking, modeled on time banking scenarios but emphasizing finer grained coupling of participants with respect to time and place, all involve voluntary service provision, in which a doer provides a service to a recipient). We communicated regularly with our partners in TimeBanks USA as we developed our first set of scenarios, and implemented an Android prototype for a user study. Our prototype closely models the dialogs of Community Weaver (2013): Members can post requests and offers for other time bank members to accept. Accepting a request/offer initializes a handshake in which the original requestor/offeror confirms the arrangement. The confirmation step could include message exchanges, setting times and places, and checking one another's profile information (profiles include a summary of previous requests, offers, and accepts, though with names of other members involved). After the service exchange, the recipient notifies the time bank to award time credit to the service provider's account, and to debit the recipient's account (see Bellotti, Carroll & Han, 2013; Carroll et al., 2013, for details).

3   Co-production Scenarios

Our partners were pleased with our initial work, but also suggested that we consider including co-production scenarios. In fact, we had included co-production scenarios, but not emphasized co-production. Indeed, any interaction that involves tutoring or coaching is ipso facto a co-production scenario. This is because in any kind of teaching, the learner is an agent and collaborator in the activity. Once co-production had been specifically called out to us, we noticed that most time banks included these interactions in their basic descriptions of how time banking works. For example, in its overview description on the Web, Community Exchange (a large time bank located in Allentown, Pennsylvania, USA) describes several "typical" time banking interactions, as quoted in Table 2 (next page). Tony installs an air conditioner for Carol and drives Ellen to the doctor; these are both service contributions that are good examples of concrete helping, but are not co-productions. However, Tony helps Linda move furniture; this is a co-production, because Linda is involved too. Tony uses his time dollars to have Frank help him install tile; this is also co-production. Carol teaches drawing, though her students are not named in the scenario sketch, those students are co-producers of the drawing lessons. Linda assists time bank members with word processing; again, this is co-production.

Once we "got" the general co-production schema, it was, of course, everywhere. It suggested variations on the person-to-person mobile time banking interactions we had already identified. For example, in the Get Aspirin scenario, if Mary is a neighbor who is going shopping anyway, and takes John along so that he can get aspirin, that is co-production in that the two actors jointly achieve the outcome. Similarly, if someone's car has broken down and they request help to get it started (e.g., to borrow jumper cables for a battery charge up), that could be co-production. And for the scenario of waiting online for tickets and books, if instead of asking someone to wait *for* you, you ask someone to wait *with* you, that is co-production. We summarized the general distinction to ourselves as "doing for" (service provision) versus "doing with" (co-production).

Table 2. Co-production scenarios illustrating the lessons pattern and the helping pattern (from the overview of Community Exchange, 2013)

"Tony needed help tiling his bathroom before his new baby arrived. He earned "time dollars" by installing an air conditioner for Carol, driving Ellen to the doctor and helping Linda move furniture. He earned enough "time dollars" to have Frank help him with the tiling.

In exchange for Tony's help, Carol teaches drawing and transports Community Exchange members to the grocery store. Linda uses her computer skills to assist members with word processing, and Ellen serves on Community Exchange's advisory board and offers telephone assistance and companionship.

Over and over and over, members exchange their time and skills, building healthy community connections, while learning that receiving is as valuable as giving."

Co-production initially appeared to us as an elaboration of the service contribution scenarios we had been developing. The examples we found on websites of TimeBanks USA members overwhelmingly were instances of what we might call the "lessons" pattern (using the term *pattern*, loosely, in the sense of a schematic design solution; Alexander et al., 1977), as in Table 2 where Carol and Linda actually provide instruction to time bank members, and the "helping" pattern, where Tony helps Linda move furniture, and Frank helps Tony install tile: In both patterns, the doer provides a service to the recipient, but the service entails close collaboration, and thus the recipient also must be a doer. The lessons and helping patterns illustrate "doing with" in contrast to "doing for".

We found examples in which helping co-productions were integrated into government social service provision (Ryan-Collins, Stephens & Coote, 2008). For example, in the Rushley Green time bank in London, members receive credit for accompanying elderly members who are shopping, visiting elderly people in their homes, etc. to enable the elderly to live on their own. In this case, local doctors, working for the British National Health Service, refer their patients to the time bank for co-produced social support, in effect, having their patients do their own social services with the help of fellow citizens. Current policy debate in the United Kingdom is considering broader incorporation of co-production into social service programs (Glynos & Speed, 2013; Seyfang, 2006).

Table 3. Pay-forward co-production pattern (from Stephens, Ryan-Collins & Boyle, 2008)

If you are discharged from the Lehigh hospital outside Philadelphia, you will be told that someone will visit you at home, make sure you're OK, if you have heating and food in the house. You are also told that the person who will visit you is a former patient, not a professional, and that – when you are well – you will be asked if you could do the same for someone else.

As we focused on co-production, we were able to identify further patterns. For example, we call the time banking interaction described in Table 3, the *pay-forward pattern*: A doer renders a service contribution to a recipient (while mobile), but subsequently that recipient becomes a doer with respect to an analogous service provided to another recipient. In this example the service co-production is mediated by a community institution, the hospital; it is not an interaction between two community members, as in the helping and lessons examples of Table 2.

Also, the service that is produced and exchanged is quite specific, not generalized; the recipient is expected to do something more specific than just contribute the same amount of time to the time bank, though it is important to emphasize that in this interaction, as in all time banking interactions, the reciprocity is based only on moral obligation. Habitat for Humanity is another example of the pay-forward pattern; the organization helps you build your home with the expectation that in the future you will help others to build their homes. As is also the case with participation in Habitat for Humanity, recipients in this pay-forward service exchange often become longer-term doers, providing visits not just for *one* other patient, but adopting the role of patient visitor and visiting many other patients (Stephens, Ryan-Collins & Boyle, 2008). Note also that the lessons pattern and the helper pattern become versions of the pay-forward pattern if the recipient goes on to share what they learned through the lessons or helping interactions (e.g., Frank helps Tony with tiling, then Tony helps someone else; Carol teaches someone drawing, and then that person teaches someone else).

Another interesting fact about this example is that it was based upon practices in the Community Exchange time bank, from whose website Table 2 was excerpted. Thus, the more radical form of co-production that is very much a part of the time bank's practice (Table 3) is nevertheless invisible in the short examples they present on the overview page (Table 2). Community Exchange is affiliated with TimeBanks USA and this type of mobile time banking scenario was one of their specific motivations for establishing the partnership with our group.

We identified another example of co-production in which members initiate a service for other members, in this case sharing telephone conversations with housebound people who may be lonely (Ryan-Collins, Stephens & Coote, 2008). As described in Table 4, the service is intended to be reciprocated (and thereby is a co-production), but we might go further and consider that the interaction could be a social model for the housebound members to reach out to community members beyond the specific people who initiated the contact. Because many people have mobile telephone service, these interactions can be mobile time banking scenarios; indeed, this is the type

Table 4. Cascading communication co-production pattern (from Ryan-Collins, Stephens & Coote, 2008)

Volunteers telephone an older person regularly for a chat. Many of the volunteers receive as well as make phone calls providing opportunities for reciprocity and enabling house bound people to make a contribution.

of telephone interaction many people now carry out in interstitial time (Dimmick, Feaster & Hoplamazian, 2011). We call this the *cascading communication pattern.*

This pattern is like the pay-forward pattern in that the service exchange is specific to telephone chats. Indeed, to the extent that the recipients (the housebound people) return calls only to those who first called them, it is entirely dyadic, generalized neither with respect to what service is rendered nor to whom it is rendered. However, we suggest that housebound people might come to see that telephone chatting is a role they can play, and a general way they can contribute. In that case, seeding the initiation of the calls could create a cascade of (co-produced) support network activity throughout the community.

Another category of co-production scenarios involves *community programs* that aggregate and focus collective effort on various community interests and concerns. Timebanking Wales created the "Time for Young People" program through which young people helped to run a summer festival, participated in environmental projects, and produced concerts for the community, earning time credits, and contributing directly to the community (Ryan-Collins, Stephens & Coote, 2008). As in the Rushley Green and Community Exchange examples above, this is an example where time banks are becoming integrated with public services. The young people in Wales are in effect co-producing their own social service program, which in turn is producing services to the broader (festivals, concerts, environmental projects). This is a good example of Cahn's (2010) elaborated view that effective co-production involves partnerships between communities and agencies, as well as between particularly community members and service professionals, co-production can also be taken as a policy and design principle, urging that recipients, providers and society all benefit more when recipients play an active role in the services they receive.

The community program pattern does not require direct involvement of government. In our Nostalgia project (Carroll et al., 1999), we helped a group of community elders carry out a community program in which they posted stories about community life when they were young adults, and other community members commented on these posts, creating an online discussion about community history by the community itself, and enhancing awareness, knowledge and engagement in community history. The elders co-produced this service with all those who posted comments, or even read posts and comments. The community program pattern has a mobile time banking variant through services like Lost State College (Carroll & Ganoe, 2008), which allows participants to tour community heritage sites, to access site-specific heritage information via GPS coordinates, and to participate in social media interactions referring to the heritage sites.

We also reconsidered two examples of co-production that are widely cited as touchstone examples: Ostrom's example of the help residents provide to police when the police walk a beat (cited above), and Jacobs' (1961) example of the contribution longtime residents make in awareness of street activity for ensuring neighborhood safety. In Ostrom's example, policemen and community members casually interacted, neither classified most of that interaction as instrumental, but it nonetheless has the consequence of building trust between the police and the community and of keeping police apprised of what was going on. This is an example of community work, of community members playing an active role in maintaining their own safety, but in the example no one is really being called upon to do anything beyond being sociable. In Jacobs' (1961) example older residents in a neighborhood keep an eye on what is going on more so than residents who have recently arrived. The older neighbors would be able to do this because they know more about what is normal for a given day of week or time of day (Table 5). This is not the same as a neighborhood watch, where a community member is designated and actually patrols; it is more a matter of vigilance or active awareness.

Table 5. Street life vigilance (based on Jacobs, 1961)

> Harry and Maude are a retired couple who have lived in neighborhood for many years. They walk their dog several times a day, and like to sit on their porch in good weather. They recognize many of their neighbors, and like to say Hello. They have a sense of what is normal and keep an eye on things.

These examples seem to be instances of a *community awareness pattern:* Community members, especially long-term residents, have rich local knowledge; they recognize neighbors, and they know what is normal activity. These resources allow them to co-produce safety and security with service professionals, like the police, and collectively with their fellow community members. In Ostrom's example, the residents are human sensors to inform the police, but the interaction works best when the police walk a beat, and regularly chat with the residents, in effect pulling information. In Jacobs' example, the long-time residents are acting as push sensors; they incidentally see and hear what is going on in the street in front of their homes, and in the community around them. If something is amiss, they can detect it early and report it.

Mobile time banking variants of the community awareness pattern are easy to identify. Community members who are out and about in the community space and carrying mobile devices are all potentially human sensors. They can report suspicious activity to police or other authorities, and they can in principle be directly queried. As in Jacobs' example (Table 5), more established and connected neighbors would be expected to make especially good mobile human sensors.

4   Institutionalizing Co-production

Our analysis of co-production scenarios for time banking raises questions about valuing contributions in time banking. The principle that contributions are valued by the time required to perform the contribution makes clear sense for lessons and helping: Recipients are collaborating to produce the services but it is also clear that they are receiving services and from whom they are receiving services. Time-based valuing seems somewhat less relevant to pay-forward and cascading communication cases since these are specifically targeted, and also include a sort of "chain letter" logic to achieve a fan out of reciprocated service contributions. Looking specifically at the economic exchange, pay forward and cascading communication are really barters of specific acts of social support. Thus, the issue of time credits, of generalized exchange, seems secondary. The time bank in such cases seems to be functioning more as an instrument of recognition than of value exchange.

In the community program pattern it seems like all the active participants – teenagers, counselors/advisors, people who participate in or attend program, elder storytellers, younger story commenters, story and comment readers – are providing services for one another. Indeed, although these seem to be good examples of co-produced community services, it is difficult to pin down all the recipients of the service in these cases, raising the question of who or what would be debited for time credits for the service exchange. This problem of identifying the service recipient also seems critical for Ostrom's and Jacobs' community awareness co-productions; these are co-productions because the human sensors are both recipients and providers of the service. However, many other residents are also recipients of enhanced neighborhood safety, but would never even realize that they had received this benefit. Indeed, many of the co-producers of the services – people who chat with police on the beat, neighbors who keep an eye on cars pulling into driveways – might not even realize that they are in fact participating in producing a community service.

One way to think about this is that the exact magnitude of the valuation of a time bank contribution matters less than *the fact that it is valued at all*. Thus, in many of the more difficult examples, those beyond the lessons and helping patterns, people generally receive nothing at all for doing this, and yet they do it. The key to Ostrom's example was not that the police paid for this service, but merely that they made themselves available to it by being in the streets walking a neighborhood beat, instead of insulated from residents by riding in a patrol car. In this analysis, time credit for co-production is an issue of community visibility and validation, that is, of making community contributions more visible to the community, including those that participate in producing the contributions, and conveying to community members that such active participation is indeed valued by the community.

This reconception, however, has design implications for time banking infrastructures. The logic of recognition is different than the logic of generalized exchange. The latter emphasizes that the time required to make a contribution is a general way of valuing contributions, and regulating exchanges of contributions through the time bank. The former emphasizes making contributions visible and legitimate to the community. One way to achieve recognition is to award significant time credit, though as discussed above, complications arise in co-production scenarios as to who was a recipient of the contribution. But achieving recognition goals through award of time credits also undermines the generalized exchange of time credits. Thus, if Harry and Maude (Table 5) get 6 time credits for merely being home and occasionally looking out their front window, will it seem equitable to you to wash my car for one time credit? Conflicts between the logic of recognition, which seems critical to implement co-production scenarios for time banking, and the logic of generalized exchange, which is the basis for person-to-person scenarios like Get Aspirin (Table 1).

We have confronted the tension around recognition and exchange with respect to co-production scenarios both by trying to envision designs that could mitigate the tension, and by investigating how this issue manifests and is managed in current time banking practices. One approach to this challenge is to award *nominal time credit* for relatively continuous co-production for which it is difficult to identify a specific recipient. Thus, Harry and Maude might receive just one time credit. In many cases, indeed in Ostom's and Jacobs' original observations, community members are already making these contributions with neither recognition nor reward; a nominal reward publicly and tangibly acknowledges the contribution, makes what might have been invisible more visible, and does not disturb the overall economy of generalized exchange "too much".

Another design approach would be a separate mechanism for time banks to manage recognition. In this approach, Harry and Maude would not get time credits for co-producing neighborhood safety through their street life vigilance. They would instead receive recognition for contributing to community awareness. This might be implemented as a notification subsystem in the time bank to apprise members of recognitions. This approach has the advantage of avoiding the "deficit spending" of awarding time credits when there is recipient account to debit, but it has the great downside of disaggregating contributions into categories, which is economically chaotic and socially fragmenting.

In addition to envisioning design interventions, we consulted research literature and best practices in time banking. There is a well-documented tendency for time bank members to provide more services than they request (Ozonne, 2010; Seyfang, 2006). In some respects, this is a flaw with respect to the logic of exchange, and signals some sort of problem with respect to reciprocity. However, just with respect to tallying time credits, it suggests that time banks may often run a surfeit, and therefore could fund the "deficit spending" approach of awarding nominal, or perhaps more than nominal credit for co-production interactions in which the recipients were difficult to enumerate. This is complicated by observation of the opposite pattern among minority users of one time bank; namely, receiving more services than they provided (Collom, 2008).

Cahn (personal communication) added to this his observation that members often do not bother to account for services they render to or participate in producing with other members who they regard as personal friends. He also mentioned that time bank members may donate time credits that they have eared back to the time bank, and that this is a standard practice in time banks. Both of these points also identify sources of unused time credit that could be invested in generalized co-productions. Finally, Cahn mentioned that the pay-forward pattern (Table 3) technically requires deficit spending in that people are provided services first, and then subsequently are given an opportunity to co-produce and earn time credits.

Our analysis of co-production scenarios for time banking indicated that co-production is already pervasive in time banking, that it is not a single pattern or interaction, and that it can be problematic. Time banking is not just the substitution of hours for dollars; it is intended to signal an alternative foundation for exchange and for services. We all already have time; we can invest it, exchange it, share it, and donate it. Doing with is more inclusive, participatory, and empowering. It affirms skills and knowledge, efficacy and control. Nevertheless, in a global context in which governments are reducing resources for social services there is an inherently coercive edge to co-production if one must cooperate with the development regime to get services; there is the risk that "empowering" recipients to co-produce their own social services will encourage government bureaucrats not to encourage and support co-production, but to use it as justification for further resource reductions. These downsides must be monitored by socio-technical designers.

Our scenario analysis of requirements for mobile time banking initially focused on individual value exchanges, person-to-person interactions. Identifying the importance of co-production specifically strengthens and simplifies some of our problematic initial ideas. For example, we had identified having someone else wait in line to purchase tickets as a plausible mobile time banking interaction, but also identified as one downside the fact that a significant amount of money might be involved. An interesting co-production variant of the purchase ticket scenario is finding someone to wait *with you* in the queue: Viewed as a service, the doing with alternative is more modest, but it is also more social, and does not put anyone's money at risk.

The other co-production patterns we identified provide specific ideas to explore in design. One implication of co-production is that the time bank itself should hold time credits that it can invest on behalf of the community to provide recognition for generalized co-production contributions, to support pay-forward interactions, etc. The exact way this should be implemented is not clear at all, but it is an important direction for us to investigate through prototyping.

5   Discussion and Implications

Contemporary life can be busy and alienating. Putnam (2000) detailed the decline of civic and political participation, neighborliness, sociality, and volunteerism, as well as citizen perceptions of trust, honesty, interdependence, and social and moral values in contemporary American society. Putnam analyzes these patterns as evidence of a decline in *social capital*, defined as societal norms of generalized reciprocity (Coleman, 1988; Putnam, 2000: 18-27). The famously dystopian title of his book, *Bowling Alone* (Putnam, 2000), depicts a world of solitary individuals who trust, care about, depend upon, and interact with one another less than their parents did. Time banking is a remarkable counter-current to this dismal social trajectory.

Co-production and time banking are key elements of an alternative social/economic paradigm for social service provision, community service exchange, and personal/community health and well being in which community members collaborate with one another and with service professionals and institutions to produce and exchange services and other contributions throughout the community. Our objective is to contribute to these social movements through designing and developing a socio-technical infrastructure that mutually leverages both to build up the *core economy* (Cahn, 2010) of family and local community, and to enable societal-scale time banking.

In this paper, we described the scenario analysis front-end of a project to develop mobile time banking infrastructures, focusing on the distinction between service exchange scenarios and co-production scenarios. As we began this work, we focused on service exchange scenarios, and from that perspective, broadening consideration to co-production scenarios seemed at first a modest elaboration. However, through the scenario work and our prototyping (still underway) we have come to regard this distinction as more fundamental. Service provision scenarios can surely strengthen an alternate economy of people helping people in a value framework of unusual equity that gauges contributions to the collective good purely with respect to the time required to make the contribution. Strengthening networks of such person to person helping generates social capital and enhances communities. Better software infrastructures to support such service exchanges can contribute to this social innovation.

However, co-production scenarios of mobile time banking are more than a modest elaboration of this paradigm. Co-production seems to be governed by a logic of recognition not contribution: Members who contribute to a collective good are recognized, but not necessarily compensated hour-for-hour. Thus, the elderly neighbors who keep an eye on street activity and enhance neighborhood safety are not actively producing a service for someone in particular; rather, through their awareness and local knowledge, they are co-producing a generalized public good. Publicly recognizing such co-production is itself a generalized public good – a validation and encouragement for civic responsibility.

Our analysis of co-production scenarios for mobile time banking has specific design implications for our prototype. Our current approach, as described earlier, was based directly on Community Weaver (2013). It involves a closed exchange loop initialized by posting of service requests and offers for time bank members to accept, followed by a confirmation handshake (optionally including dyadic message exchanges, setting times and places, and checking one another's profile information), the service exchange itself, and then closed with the service recipient notifying the time bank to award time credit to the service provider's account, and to debit the recipient's own account (Bellotti et al., 2013; Carroll et al. 2013).

Based on the foregoing analysis of co-production scenarios we suggest that all stakeholders in a service be enabled to allocate credit – for co-production. Thus, as in Table 2, after Frank helps Tony with the tiling, Tony would notify the time bank to award credit to Frank, and to debit Tony's own account; this is standard time bank protocol. In our design proposal, Frank would be also be able to notify the time bank to credit Tony's account for his co-production of the tiling. Similarly, as in Table 4, the housebound member would award time credit to the person who called him/her for a chat, but that person, the caller, could also award credit to the housebound person who reciprocates and calls back.

Interestingly, and more challengingly, the notion of "stakeholders" in the service appears to be broader than that of stakeholders in the exchange itself, as in the original co-production scenarios from Ostrom and Jacobs. The retired couple in Table 5 are co-producing safety for their neighborhood but, in our example, have neither accepted an explicit request or made an explicit offer. They have not initiated or responded to a time bank interaction. Similarly, as in our mobile extension of community awareness scenarios, members who are out and about throughout the community, whose presence is continually co-producing community safety, are not doing so because of an explicit time bank interaction. In our design proposal, any member can assign nominal time bank credit for this sort of generalized co-production. For example, any of the neighbors up and down the street can assign Harry and Maude credit for their street life vigilance. As in a standard time bank interaction, the service that was co-produced (e.g. street life vigilance) would be entered into the system, and the co-producer(s) would be notified of the time credit.

Time credits earned through co-production interactions would appear, categorized as such, in a member's profile. Thus, when any member was checking another member's profile in the course of confirming a service arrangement (or in the course awarding co-production credit), he/she would see prior time bank activity, including prior co-production contributions. This elaboration of the basic time bank interaction is our initial design proposal for responding to the challenge of co-production. Although it seems odd at first to contemplate the approach of having exchanges of time credits beyond the basic recipient-to-provider exchange, broadening the concept of legitimate credit is, we believe, what the logic of recognition is telling us. Perhaps it is just odd in the context of a lifetime of socialization into a hard currency world of zero-sum economic games.

Community informatics is action research; it does not merely seek to understand community and technology, it seeks to transform and enhance community through new information infrastructures (Gurstein, 2007). Time banking and co-production are social concepts and mechanisms, but also social movements; they are alternative paradigms for economic exchange and social service provision, respectively, and they both entail and require new information infrastructures. By pushing beyond the basic "doing for" mobile time banking scenarios, as in Table 1, and extending our tools and infrastructure to address co-production scenarios, Tables 2-5, we are moving, in the terms of Glynos and Speed (2013), from *additive* to *transformative* conceptions of time banking. That is, we are investigating not just how voluntary time banking exchanges can exist within the broader context of a bureaucratic and market-based framework for social services and exchange, but how time banking and co-production could change our sense of value and valuation, and the ways we exchange services, appreciate one another, and develop as human beings.

Acknowledgements. We thank Edgar Cahn for generously answering the same questions several times. This research was supported by the US National Science Foundation (IIS 1218544) and by the Edward M. Frymoyer Chair Endowment.

References

1. Alexander, C., Ishikawa, S., Silverstein, M., Jacobson, M., Fiksdahl-King, I., Angel, S.: A pattern language. Oxford Univ. Press (1977)
2. Bellotti, V., Carroll, J.M., Han, K.: Random acts of kindness: The intelligent and context-aware future of reciprocal altruism and community collaboration. In: Proceedings of IEEE CTS 2013: International Conference on Collaboration Technologies and Systems, San Diego, CA, May 20-24, pp. 1–12. IEEE (2013)
3. Burrows, K.: Signs of health & emerging culture: Stories of hope and creative change from 2010 and 2011. In: Censored 2012. Seven Stories Press, New York (2012)
4. Cahn, E.S.: No more throw-away people: The co-production imperative. Essential Books, Washington, D.C. (2000)
5. Cahn, E.S.: Co-production 2.0: Retrofitting human service programs to tap renewable energy of community. Community Currency Magazine, 36–39 (March-April 2010)
6. Cahn, E.S., Rowe, J.: Time dollars: The new currency that enables Americans to turn their hidden resource-time-into personal security and community renewal. Rodale Press, Emmaus (1992)
7. Carroll, J.M.: Making Use: Scenario-Based Design of Human-Computer Interactions. MIT Press, Cambridge (2000)
8. Carroll, J.M.: The neighborhood in the Internet: Design research projects in community informatics. Routledge, New York (2012)
9. Carroll, J.M., Bellotti, V., Han, K.: Mobile time banking: Building social capital through ubiquitous interactions (submitted, 2013)
10. Carroll, J.M., Ganoe, C.H.: Supporting Community With Location-Sensitive Mobile Applications. In: Foth, M. (ed.) Handbook of Research on Urban Informatics: The Practice and Promise of the Real-Time City, pp. 339–352. Information Science Reference, IGI Global, Hershey, PA (2008)
11. Carroll, J.M., Rosson, M.B., VanMetre, C.A., Kengeri, R., Kelso, J., Darshani, M.: Blacksburg Nostalgia: A Community History Archive. In: Sasse, M.A., Johnson, C. (eds.) Proceedings of Seventh IFIP Conference on Human-Computer Interaction, INTERACT 1999, Edinburgh, August 30-September 3, pp. 637–647. IOS Press/IFIP, Amsterdam (1999)
12. Collom, E.: The motivations, engagement, satisfaction, outcomes, and demographics of time bank participants: survey findings from a U.S. system. International Journal of Community Currency Research 11, 36–83 (2007)
13. Collom, E.: Engagement of the elderly in time banking: The potential for social capital generation in an aging society. Journal of Aging & Social Policy 20(4), 414–436 (2008)
14. Coleman, J.S.: Social capital in the creation of human capital. American Journal of Sociology 94, S95–S120 (1988) (Supplement: Organizations and institutions: Sociological and economic approaches to the analysis of social structure)
15. Community Exchange, Overview page, http://www.lvhn.org/wellness_resources/classes_support_groups_and_events/community_programs/community_exchange (accessed January 4, 2013)
16. Community Weaver, http://groups.drupal.org/node/180979 (accessed January 8, 2013)
17. Dimmick, J., Feaster, J.C., Hoplamazian, G.J.: News in the interstices: The niches of mobile media in space and time. New Media & Society 13(1), 23–39 (2011)
18. Garfinkel, H.: Studies in ethnomethodology. John Wiley & Sons (1987, 1991) (Original work published 1967)

19. Gasser, L.: The integration of computing and routine work. ACM Transactions on Office Information Systems 4, 257–270 (1986)
20. Glynos, J., Speed, E.: Varieties of co-production in public services: Time banks in a UK health policy context. Critical Policy Studies 6(4), 402–433 (2013)
21. Gregory, L.: Spending time locally: The benefit of time banks for local economies. Local Economy 24(4), 323–333 (2009)
22. Gurstein, M.: What is community informatics (and why does it matter)? Polimetrica, Milano (2007)
23. Jacobs, J.: The death and life and great American cities. Random House, New York (1961)
24. Lasker, J., Collom, E., Bealer, T., Niclaus, E., Keefe, J.Y., et al.: Time banking and health: The role of a community currency organization in enhancing well-being. Health Promotion Practice 12(1), 102–115 (2011)
25. Moffett, M., Brat, I.: For Spain's jobless, time equals money. The Wall Street Journal, A1 (August 27, 2012)
26. Ostrom, E.: A communitarian approach to local governance. National Civic Review, 226–233 (Summer 1993)
27. Ostrom, E.: Crossing the great divide: Co-production, synergy, and development. World Development 24(6), 1073–1087 (1996)
28. Ozanne, L.K.: Learning to exchange time: benefits and obstacles to time banking. International Journal of Community Currency Research 14, 1–16 (2010)
29. Putnam, R.: Bowling Alone: The Collapse and Revival of American Community. Simon & Schuster, New York (2000)
30. Ryan-Collins, J., Stephens, L., Coote, A.: The new wealth of time: How time banking helps people build better public services. New Economics Foundation, London (2008), http://www.neweconomics.org (accessed January 4, 2013)
31. Seyfang, G.: Tackling social exclusion with community currencies: learning from LETS to Time Banks. International Journal of Community Currency Research 6(3), 1–11 (2002)
32. Seyfang, G., Smith, K.: The time of our lives: Using time banking for neighbourhood renewal and community capacity-building. New Economics Foundation, London (2002)
33. Seyfang, G.: "With a little help from my friends." Evaluating time banks as a tool for community self-help. Local Economy 18(3), 257–264 (2003)
34. Seyfang, G.: Time banks: rewarding community self-help in the inner city? Community Development Journal 39(1), 62–71 (2004a)
35. Seyfang, G.: Working outside the box: community currencies, time banks, and social inclusion. International Journal of Social Policy 33(1), 49–71 (2004b)
36. Seyfang, G.: Harnessing the potential of the social economy? Time banks and UK public policy. International Journal of Sociology and Social Policy 26(9-10), 430–443 (2006)
37. Seyfang, G.: The New economics of sustainable consumption: Seeds of change. Palgrave Macmillan, New York (2009)
38. Stephens, L., Ryan-Collins, J., Boyle, D.: Co-production: A new manifesto for growing the core economy. New Economics Foundation, London (2008), http://www.neweconomics.org (accessed January 4, 2013)
39. Timebanking UK, http://www.timebanking.org (accessed January 1, 2013)
40. TimeBanks USA, http://timebanks.org/ (accessed January 8, 2013)

Co-evolution of End-User Developers and Systems in Multi-tiered Proxy Design Problems

Daniela Fogli[1] and Antonio Piccinno[2]

[1] Dipartimento di Ingegneria dell'Informazione, Università degli Studi di Brescia, Brescia, Italy
fogli@ing.unibs.it
[2] Dipartimento di Informatica, Università degli Studi di Bari, Bari, Italy
antonio.piccinno@uniba.it

Abstract. This paper aims at analyzing the category of multi-tiered proxy design problems, where end-user developers do not necessarily coincide with the actual end users of the system, but can be considered as end users' proxies. This situation can be found in a variety of application domains, from home automation, where electricians defining home automation systems for energy saving are different from house occupants, to e-government, where administrative employees creating e-government services are different from citizens using those services. The analysis leads to the definition of a new interaction and co-evolution model, called ICE², which, on the basis of the model discussed in a previous work, considers not only the case of end users that directly make their system evolve by means of end-user development activities, but also the case where a proxy figure is present, namely an expert in the application domain that creates and modifies software artifacts for others (the actual end users). Finally, a design approach is proposed, which aims at generalizing the solutions suggested in different application domains, and at sustaining the interaction and co-evolution processes that involve end users, end-user developers, and systems.

Keywords: interaction model, co-evolution, end-user developer, meta-design, meta-model, multi-tiered proxy design problem.

1   Introduction

The communication gap often existing between users and developers usually leads to developing interactive systems that are difficult to use and to learn. To cope with this problem, since the eighties, the human-computer interaction (HCI) community is promoting design approaches that give users a voice, such as user-centered design [1] and participatory design [2], just to mention the most widespread approaches.

Another phenomenon has however been observed around HCI: users evolve by using software systems, and, to satisfy new users' needs, designers must make systems evolve. Carroll and Rosson describe this phenomenon as the *task-artifact cycle* [3]; while, subsequently, others (see [4], [5]) characterize this phenomenon as the *co-evolution of users, systems, and organization*, highlighting that also a technology-organization cycle occurs, beyond the task-artifact one.

Y. Dittrich et al. (Eds.): IS-EUD 2013, LNCS 7897, pp. 153–168, 2013.

To synthesize the communication gap and co-evolution phenomena, the Interaction and Co-Evolution (ICE) model has been defined in [6]; then, on the basis of this model, End-User Development (EUD) has been suggested as the most suitable solution to cope with co-evolution [5]. Actually, EUD encompasses techniques and applications that empower end users to develop and adapt systems themselves, by carrying out activities that are traditionally performed by software developers [7]. Moreover, according to [8], enabling end users to act as designers and contribute to the evolution of their systems requires to conceive design as a *meta-design* activity. Indeed, "meta-design extends existing design methodologies focused on the development of a system at design time by allowing users to become co-designers at use time" [9].

This view on EUD and meta-design is usually focused on those situations where end users create or adapt software artifacts for personal rather than public use, thus distinguishing it from professional programming, which has the goal of developing code for others to use [10]. For instance, in [11], the situation of a geoscientist is described: he decided to spend three months in acquiring programming knowledge, in order to be able to develop software for himself to analyze the data he collected; even though the geoscientist declares that software development is now an essential task for his research, he is aware that he is not a software developer, but just an end-user developer. As in many other application domains (e.g., medical diagnosis [12], mechanical engineering [5], business intelligence [13], CAD [14]), the end-user developer is a domain expert that, to cope with her/his specific problems, needs to adapt or create software artifacts. With reference to workgroups, Gantt and Nardi call this domain expert a *local developer* or *gardener* [14], namely a person who customizes a software environment and creates programmatic extensions of applications for her/his purpose that, possibly, will be made available to other users working in the same group with a shared objective.

However, there are also several situations, in different application domains, where the communities of end users and end-user developers remain separated: on the one hand, there are the actual end users that cannot be required to carry out EUD activities because of their specific goals, interests, and abilities; on the other hand, there are domain experts, not knowledgeable in information technology, who are called to play the role of end-user developers and create and/or adapt programs for end users by means of EUD environments and tools. A typical example is the case of e-government (discussed in detail in Section 3.4), where citizens using e-government services constitute the community of end users, whilst administrative employees developing services for citizens belong to the community of experts in government issues. Obviously, an administrative employee is a citizen as well, and it may happen that s/he will use at some point an e-government service s/he has created (for instance, to enroll her/his children at the municipality school through a proper online service); in this case s/he is changing role from end-user developer to end user.

This paper analyzes a variety of such cases by framing them in the category of *multi-tiered proxy design problems* [15]. We argue that this kind of problems deserves additional reflection in the EUD field, in order to:

1. characterize the role, competencies, and objectives of end-user developers, with respect to software developers and actual end users;
2. generalize EUD techniques and meta-design activities to face multi-tiered proxy design problems.

As to point (1), we propose ICE^2 (ICE square) model, an extension of the ICE model; as to point (2), we provide a design approach that aims at generalizing the different experiences discussed as case studies.

Furthermore, we would like to provide a reflection on the role played by meta-designers in multi-tiered design problems with respect to the role they play in 'standard' EUD situations, also with reference to the co-evolution cycles.

The paper is organized as follows. Section 2 analyses existing work and presents the starting point of the research; Section 3 describes different multi-tiered proxy design cases; Section 4 presents the model of co-evolution of end users, end-user developers and system (ICE^2); Section 5 discusses the design approach proposed for multi-tiered proxy design problems; Section 6 provides an additional discussion on the themes presented in the paper; Section 7 concludes the paper.

2   Background and Related Work

The Interaction and Co-Evolution (ICE) model discussed in [6] is at the basis of a model-based approach to the design of usable and easy-to-tailor interactive systems. This model provides a synthesis of the interaction and co-evolution models proposed in HCI literature.

Interaction models aim to identify the causes of interaction difficulties affecting software systems, namely usability issues. For example, the seminal model proposed by Hutchins, Hollan and Norman focuses on the human side of the interaction process and identifies the existence of evaluation and execution gulfs as the primary sources of usability difficulties [16]. The model proposed by Abowd and Beale highlights, on the other hand, the problems arising on the computer side, i.e. capturing and interpreting the events generated by the user [17]. Finally, the model proposed in [18] aims at balancing the roles that both human and system play in the interaction. Here, HCI is described as a cyclic process, in which the user and the system communicate by materializing and interpreting a sequence of messages (e.g., the images on the screen in visual interaction) at successive points in time. Materialization and interpretation are performed by the user, depending on her/his role in the task, as well as on her/his culture, experience, and cognitive and physical skills; whilst, on the other side, interpretation occur internally to the system, which associates the message with a computational meaning, as determined by the programs implemented in the system, and reacts to user events accordingly by materializing a new message.

This last model gives emphasis to the two different interpretation processes occurring inside the human and the machine. These interpretation processes are considered as the main source of usability problems and are related to the *communication gap* existing between users and designers [5]. Indeed, users need to perform their tasks by reasoning in accordance to their mental models, and to express this reasoning in notations familiar to them; whilst, designers usually develop the systems by focusing primarily on the computational and management aspects; therefore, the message interpretation performed by the system reflects the designers' understanding of the task at hand, rather than the users' point of view. User-centered and participatory design approaches are being promoted by the HCI community for more than twenty-five years [1], [2], with the purpose to cope with the communication gap phenomenon and favor the development of systems that end users find easy to use and to learn.

A further important phenomenon observed in HCI is the *co-evolution of users and systems,* namely the possibility that the users evolve by using the systems and that the systems evolve - through designers' work - to satisfy the new users' needs. Specifically, Carroll and Rosson describe this phenomenon as the task-artifact cycle [3], which highlights how the software artifacts created to support some user's tasks usually suggest new possible tasks; to support these new tasks, new artifacts must be created. Other HCI scholars provide a wider view of the co-evolution phenomenon: since technology advances give computer scientists new possibilities of improving interactive systems once they are already in use, new interaction possibilities occur that might change users' working habits, thus making their social and work organization evolve itself with technology [4], [5].

The three cycles – interaction cycle, task-artifact co-evolution cycle and organization-technology co-evolution cycle – are illustrated in Figure 1 (adapted from [6]).

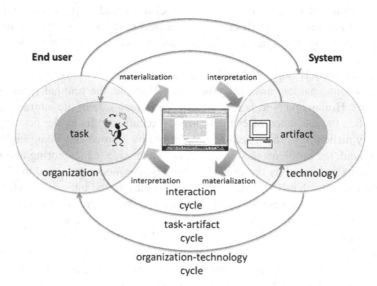

Fig. 1. Interaction and Co-evolution cycles (adapted from [6])

Both co-evolution cycles can be sustained and favored by EUD techniques, which empower end users to develop and adapt systems themselves [7]. In this way, whenever end users would like to carry out new or different tasks, they can directly modify the artifact by means of EUD activities, ranging from simple selection among alternative behaviors already available in the artifact (customization), to actual program creation carried out through programming-by-example, incremental programming, model-based development, and extended annotation. Due to the task-artifact co-evolution cycle, end users also improve their knowledge, update their procedures in the real world, and modify their working organization, possibly requiring the adoption of more advanced technologies. The organization-technology co-evolution is thus itself a long-term side effect of end-user development.

The ICE model is able to describe the several proposals that can be found in EUD and End-User Software Engineering (EUSE) [10] literature. For example, *component-based* techniques allow end users tailoring their own systems, thus making them evolve [19]. More recently, scholars studying tools for mash-up creation adopt component-based approaches as well [13], [20]. Another technique widely used in EUD is *extended annotation* [12]: a number of EUD tools based on this technique have been recently proposed (e.g., [21], [22]).

As far as EUSE is concerned, a methodology is presented for instance in [23], which supports end-user programmers to carry out testing and debugging in spreadsheet environments. Many other proposals in this field are discussed in [10].

In all these works, emphasis is given to end users developing software per se and not for third or public use; indeed, EUD activities are usually distinguished from professional programming, which has the goal of developing code for others to use. In this paper we would like to analyze case studies that can be framed in the category of multi-tiered proxy design problems [15], where end users and end-user developers may form different communities, with different goals, skills, and competences. As we will discuss in Section 6, considering this kind of problems pushes further in the direction of adopting a meta-design approach: indeed, meta-design aims at creating the socio-technical conditions that empowers end users to behave as end-user developers [8]; in multi-tiered proxy design problems, meta-design should have a wider perspective by providing all stakeholders (including domain experts) with suitable languages and tools to foster their personal and common reasoning about the development of software systems that support end users [5].

The following section discusses multi-tiered proxy design problems and some literature case studies.

3   Multi-tiered Proxy Design Problems

The main purpose of EUD is to support new needs at use time, by taking into account changing tasks. In many application domains, however, end users cannot act as developers, but a third figure must accept this role. This is the case of the so-called multi-tiered proxy design problems [15]. They can be characterized by the identification of the following figures:

- *end users*, who are usually not able to completely describe their needs and design requirements;
- *end-user developers*, who are able to articulate what should be developed, even if they have no software programming competencies;

- *software developers,* who know how to develop the required system, but are unable to completely satisfy end users' needs without the help of end-user developers, since they are not expert in the domain as end-user developers are.

In the following, several case studies in very different domains, which can be framed in this problem category, are presented.

3.1   Cognitive Disability Support

Memory Aiding Prompting System (MAPS) [15], [24] aims at supporting the independence and safety of people with cognitive disabilities in their daily activities, such as going to the grocery or taking a bus. MAPS is a platform that provides a simple, wireless prompting system for individuals with cognitive disabilities (end users), along with an editing tool that allows caregivers to customize the prompting system for the end users. This is a typical case in which the adoption of a multi-tiered proxy design approach has to be adopted, since the end users cannot act as end-user developers and caregivers are called to play this role.

More precisely, the system comprises the following components:

- *MAPS-Design-Environment (MAPS-DE)*: a PC-based interface that enables the caregiver (usually a family member) to edit, store, and reuse multimedia scripts that prompt instructions for task support (i.e., sequences of video and verbal instructions); this environment is designed according to the needs and capabilities of caregivers;
- *MAPS-Database*: an information storage space that is accessible both at the level of the local PC where the MAPS-DE is installed and via the Internet. It stores script images and sounds, user and task modeling metadata, and a repository of tested scripts to be used as templates by caregivers using their MAPS-DE;
- *MAPS-Prompter*: a PDA-based device that prompts instructions supporting the person with cognitive disabilities in the accomplishment of her/his daily tasks.

Software developers have created the infrastructure to make these three components work together and to allow end-user developers, i.e., caregivers, to create instances of the PDA-based application for specific end users.

3.2   Cultural Heritage

In [25], the authors present an approach to the design of interactive art guides, where cultural domain experts are provided with a proper design environment to organize and tailor multimedia content of heterogeneous nature by instantiating a set of predefined templates on actual visit paths for a wide range of end users. The role of visitors of interactive exhibitions (end users) is obviously distinguished from that of cultural domain experts (end-user developers), since the latter are the persons in charge of developing guides for the former people.

In this approach, the development of the structure for multimedia art guides is based on an abstract model, represented by a directed graph specification, which exploits the notions of "topic" and "visit". Each topic is in turn specified as a finite state automaton, whilst the visit is the sequence of automaton states experienced by the visitor. Each art guide page will thus correspond to a node of the graph: the cultural domain expert can act on node data and external multimedia files to create content that will be applied to the pre-existing templates, in order to generate new node instances. S/he can also compose data files to insert new nodes and, by defining relationships between them, create new thematic, spatial, or logical organizations of artworks in the guide. Cultural domain experts work with interface designers and programmers to design the guide conceptual structure; instead, they are more independent in the organization of the multimedia material, by using a customized Content Management System (CMS).

In the traditional development of interactive guides, knowledge about art exhibitions possessed by cultural domain experts is usually transferred, with many ambiguities and misunderstandings, to software programmers; the adoption of a multi-tiered proxy design approach allows overcoming this problem, by transforming cultural domain experts into end-user developers.

3.3   Home Automation

The paper [26] presents an approach and a tool (Pantagruel), which supports the development of home automation environments dedicated to helping house occupants (end users) in their everyday life, e.g. for home security, energy consumption, or assisted living. A domain expert, for example a caregiver expert in assisted living or an electrician expert in energy consumption, who knows end users' needs, plays the role of end-user developer: s/he provides an environment description, which consists of a declaration of entity classes along with their attributes and methods; this description is then used to define a concrete environment by instantiating entity classes.

A visual language is provided in the Pantagruel tool to create orchestration rules, which are based on the environment description and foster environment composition. More precisely, the development process starts when the end user expresses her/his requirements to the domain expert. On the basis of requirements analysis, the domain expert defines the application goals and entities. The latter are then further specified into a Pantagruel taxonomy by the entity expert, based on the needs expressed by the domain expert. Once specified, the entities are used as the building blocks to be orchestrated by Pantagruel. The domain expert, using the Pantagruel visual development editor, ensures application development.

3.4   E-Government

A novel approach to the development of e-government services has been presented in [27]. In this approach, administrative employees (end-user developers) first collaborated with software engineers and HCI specialists to define the characteristics of online services to be made available to citizens (end users). In particular, the design team examined the class of services for reserving appointments at the different counters of a government agency, in order to speed up identity card release, deal with foreign people permits, and so on. Such services have been characterized by a form-based, step-by-step interaction style, thus recalling the traditional way of communication between citizens and government agencies. The design activity led to define a meta-model representing the considered class of services, which was then represented by software engineers through an XML schema [28]. In addition, the team designed an EUD environment able to support administrative employees in creating instances of the XML schema, namely XML documents describing the steps of specific appointment reservation services. The EUD environment does not require end-user developers to write any XML code, neither to know the underlying meta-model: they only have to fill in some forms that define the requests for citizens in each step of the service. A form generator exploits XML documents created through the EUD environment to generate the actual service pages for citizens.

Also in this case, the need for a multi-tiered proxy design approach emerged from existing work practice: the idea of transferring to administrative employees the responsibility of developing e-government services allows avoiding misunderstandings with software engineers and better satisfying citizens' needs [27].

3.5   Electronic Patient Record

The case study discussed in [29] about the development of the Electronic Patient Record (EPR) can be regarded as a multi-tiered proxy design problem as well. Patient records are official artifacts that practitioners write to preserve the memory or knowledge of facts and events that occurred in the hospital ward [30]. The patient record is a many-sided document: it is read by very different people, not only physicians and nurses, but also the patients themselves, their relatives, etc., thus it must have the ability to speak different "voices" to convey different meanings according to people using it [31]. The patient records are actually composed of modules, each one containing specific fields for collecting patient data. Various hospital employees are only interested in a subset of such modules, and use them to accomplish different tasks, i.e. the nurse records the patient's measurements, the reception staff records the patient's personal data, the physician examines the record to formulate a diagnosis, and so on. The following main stakeholders who are involved in the EPR management were identified: (1) practice manager; (2) head physicians; (3) physicians; (4) nurses; and (5) administrative staff. In particular, the head physician has the right and the responsibility of the EPR to be adopted by physicians and nurses of her/his ward.

EPR project has been managed by applying the software shaping workshop methodology [5], [32]. A team composed of software engineers, HCI experts and physicians designed the software environments (software shaping workshops) for the different stakeholders, as well as the data modules, which are the basic component of the EPR, and the application template to allow each head physician to design the EPR for her/his ward by directly manipulating data modules in her/his software environment. In this case study, end users are physicians and nurses of a specific ward, while the head physician is the end-user developer in charge of creating the EPR for them. The adoption of a multi-tiered proxy design approach is here required because the head physician is the only stakeholder responsible for the EPR adopted in the ward.

4   The ICE² Model

As already mentioned in Section 2, EUSE and EUD are usually intended as design techniques that aim to support the development of systems enabling people to create, modify and adapt software artifacts per se. However, as observed in multi-tiered design problems, end-user developers are often called to develop for others; therefore, since they are not professional developers, they should be able to interact easily with a software environment to create, modify or adapt software systems devoted to end users.

The ICE² model presented in Fig. 2 encompasses this second type of end user. As in the ICE model, the three cycles model the mutual influence that systems and technology have with end users, end-user developers, and respective organizations.

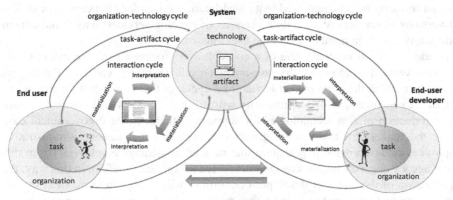

Fig. 2. The ICE² model

The co-evolution process involving end users (left-hand side of the figure) is the same as in the ICE model; this process is *sustained* by the other co-evolution process, described by the right-hand side of the figure and involving end-user developers. The artifact is the boundary object [33] between the two co-evolution processes, which can be regarded as composed of two parts: 1) the software system devoted to the end user, and 2) the EUD tools (including the EUD environment and/or software components as building blocks of the software system being developed) that are used by the end-user developer to generate and/or adapt the software system for end users.

Interesting interactions between the two co-evolution processes occur at use time; they are discussed in the following with reference to the case studies illustrated in sections 3.4 and 3.5, where authors of this paper have been personally involved.

Requests for system evolution coming from end users reach end-user developers, who may directly operate on the system through EUD tools or, if necessary, may in turn ask software developers for the evolution of their own tools. In this way, the left task-artifact cycle of Fig. 2 (involving end users) affects the right task-artifact cycle of end-user developers. For example, when citizens ask for an additional e-government service, administrative employees may create it, if their EUD environment already includes that type of service (e.g., appointment reservation); otherwise, administrative employees will ask software developers to extend the EUD environment to include the new type of service (for example, paying local taxes). In the EPR case, ward physicians can get aware that new data are needed (for example, in case of specific pathologies), but they cannot find the related module in the EPR. Thus, they have to ask for a new specific module to the head physician, who, using EUD tools, will evolve the current EPR accordingly or make a request to software developers for creating the new type of module.

The external cycle in the right-hand side of Fig. 2 may influence the organization-technology cycle that involves the end-user community. Indeed, technology advances give new possibilities for improving systems during their use, bringing to new interaction possibilities that might change working habits and organization of end users, and possibly lead to include new end users in the end-user community. For example, in the e-government case, new online services may be devoted to further categories of citizens formerly not encompassed (e.g., healthcare services for old people), or different versions of services (e.g., mobile versions of existing services) may make citizen community evolve in number and in the user classes.

In addition, each internal cycle of a co-evolution process affects the external one and vice versa. For example, the task-artifact cycle involving end-user developers may in turn affect the organization-technology cycle, in that it may call for the extension of the end-user developer community with further members, and possibly require the introduction of new technologies for supporting them. In the e-government case study, the request for additional e-government services that current administrative employees cannot provide may require that new administrative employees (from different agency departments) be engaged in service design and creation; in this way, the organization of the end-user developer community will change in terms of composition, power, and relationships; the artifact may change in turn, as a consequence of a possible extension of the EUD environment to cope with the new end-user developers' needs. The task-artifact cycle also means the end-user developers may evolve during their interaction with the EUD environment, since they may acquire new skills related to software technology and discover new possibilities for enhancing end users' tasks. For example, in the EPR case, it has been observed that the head physician involved in the project has been strongly affected by the technology advances: whilst in the beginning he was almost scared by the EPR system, he is now using regularly advanced mobile devices and asks to adapt EPR tools to be used in mobility.

Finally, the organization-technology co-evolution cycle can have an impact on the task-artifact one, since rules and guidelines may change over time, especially as a consequence of a consolidation or other types of re-organization. For example, in the EPR case, rules about data visualization in the EPR changed after the recent consolidation of "Giovanni XXIII" Children Hospital of Bari with the Polyclinic of Bari.

Beside the communication, mediated by the system, between end users and end-user developers, a further communication channel always exists (see arrows at the bottom of Fig. 2) that is outside the system. In fact, end users and end-user developers usually exchange information also through traditional means, e.g., face-to-face, phone, email, etc.

5   Addressing Multi-tiered Proxy Design Problems

In [9], the authors discuss an approach to the meta-design of socio-technical systems. In particular, the conceptual framework for meta-design is described through a three-level model including: 1) a meta-level, which contains the beliefs and concepts of meta-design; 2) an intermediate level, which refers to a framework to be meta-designed in accordance with the higher level and that serves as an environment within which socio-technical systems are developed; 3) a basic level, including socio-technical systems developed within the framework in the intermediate level.

In order to cope with the co-evolution processes represented in the ICE^2 model, we deepen the three-level model in the case of multi-tiered proxy design problems, by generalizing the solutions encountered in the case studies described in section 3 (and in many others) and making the above three levels more concrete in terms of design activities.

The resulting design approach here proposed develops along three main phases:

1. the *meta-design phase*: in this phase, a multidisciplinary team carry out meta-design activities to create an environment for end-user development able to generate software systems for end users;
2. the *design phase*: in this phase, end-user developers carry out design activities in a creative but guided way, by using the EUD environment;
3. the *use phase*: in this phase, the system generated through EUD is used by end users, who possibly personalize it by setting some parameters, in order to choose among alternative behaviors (or presentations or interaction mechanisms) already available in the system [12].

At a beginning, these phases are carried out sequentially; whilst, along the system lifecycle, they are more entwined: for example, new needs emerging at the use phase may ask for new design activities, which in turn, in some cases, may require further meta-design activities. In order words, the three phases influence each other and allow responding to co-evolution requests. These phases are illustrated in the following.

5.1   The Meta-design Phase

In the meta-design phase, a multidisciplinary team, including at least software engineers, HCI specialists and domain experts, defines at first the conceptual model of the software systems devoted to end users. This activity could be carried out through participatory design techniques, for example by means of scenario-based analysis or mock-up development. The metaphor and interaction style of the systems for end users are thus defined; they will strongly depend on domain characteristics and users' habits. For example, different conceptual models have been defined in the case studies discussed in Section 3: video help in MAPS, guide tour in cultural heritage, composition of virtual sensors and actuators in home automation, form-based interaction in e-government and EPR systems.

After the conceptual model definition, the design team defines a meta-model that describes and generalizes the structure and properties of the software systems for end users. This meta-model can be formally represented as a UML class diagram, an ontology, an XML schema, a finite state automaton, etc., or informally, as a natural language description of the application domain. For example, in MAPS, script templates and script rules constitutes the meta-model; in the cultural heritage case study, the meta-model is composed of the graph and the finite state automaton; class diagrams are used in Pantagruel (home automation); an XML schema is adopted in the e-government case; the conceptual schema of the underlying database is the meta-model in the EPR case.

Then, members of the design team will collaborate to the development of the EUD environment that supports the creation of instances of the meta-model, namely of models that will play the role of specification for the software systems devoted to end users. For example, in the e-government case study, the EUD environment created for administrative employees allows them to generate instances of the meta-model, namely XML documents, which specify form-based web applications for citizens; whilst in the culture heritage case, cultural domain experts collaborate to design the guide conceptual structure, which will be then instantiated with multimedia material; in the MAPS project, MAPS-DE supports caregivers in creating multimedia scripts through the instantiation and composition of available templates.

Finally, software engineers must create an interpreter of the meta-model instances, capable of generating the actual software systems described by such instances. This interpreter must generate systems that satisfy the conceptual model previously defined by the design team.

5.2   The Design Phase

In the second phase of the approach, end-user developers use the EUD environment developed during the meta-design phase to create the software systems for end users. As end-user developers, they should be able to easily interact with the EUD environment, possibly by following their traditional way of reasoning and operating when a similar service was supplied to end users without the help of information technology (e.g. paper-based forms in e-government, human tourist guide in art exhibitions, paper-based patient record in an hospital). For example, MAPS-DE allows caregivers to easily generate scripts that are instances of the meta-model, from which videos for disabled persons are automatically generated. In a similar way, in the cultural heritage domain, end-user developers may use the CMS to create a guide for visitors, which is actually an instance of the graph, namely the meta-model previously defined. In the home automation case, the visual development editor allows domain experts to create a taxonomy that models a specific domain and is used to generate the application for end users. In the EPR case, the software shaping workshop devoted to the head physician of a specific ward allows her/him to create EPRs customized to the different stakeholders of the ward.

5.3   The Use Phase

Finally, in the third phase, end users use the software systems designed for them by end-user developers. Thanks to meta-design and meta-modeling, such systems may have some flexibility degrees, and thus be personalized by end users. For example, in the e-government case, citizens can change service forms on the basis of their input; in the cultural heritage case, visitors can provide their profile, and the tourist guide adapts itself accordingly; in the EPR case, ward nurses, who primarily input data about patients, can modify the layout of the EPR modules by moving, for example, the parts they are interested in to the top, in order to find them quickly.

Mechanisms for providing feedback to end-user developers at use time should be integrated in the systems for end users, in order to foster more rapidly the co-evolution processes modeled by the ICE^2 model. These mechanisms could be based for example on annotation tools, as reported in [6].

6   Discussion

End-User Software Engineering proposes a variety of methods to adequately manage the code quality of software artifacts created by end-user developers [10]. However, usability of such software artifacts is usually considered an immaterial issue, since the underlying assumption is that end users carry out development activities to adapt or develop software artifacts for their personal use. In few words, end users who develop per se *may create unusable systems*. However, in multi-tiered proxy design problems this is not true anymore: end-user developers who develop software artifacts for others *must develop usable systems* [34].

These different needs lead to a reflection on the meta-design activity and the role of meta-designers. In the former case, meta-designers work for end users and must sustain the interaction and co-evolution cycles encompassed by the ICE model (Figure 1). To this aim, many meta-design guidelines have been proposed [9], [11]; among them, it is interesting to remember that meta-designers must i) provide end users with building blocks to be composed freely and in unexpected manners, ii) underdesign for emergent behavior during use, ii) establish cultures of participation, so that end users should be encouraged to make their contributions, and iv) reward and recognize contributions, in order to motivate end users to participate in system evolution.

In multi-tiered proxy design problems, meta-designers work for people having different characteristics, needs and objectives with respect to the actual end users. Indeed, meta-designers are called to provide end-user developers with domain-oriented design tools that allow them, not only to co-evolve with such tools, but also to support the co-evolution cycles involving end users (Figure 2).

In the design approach proposed in this paper the meta-design phase plays a crucial role to guarantee the usability and modifiability of the software artifacts to be created by end-user developers. Here, the meta-design team has the responsibility to define the conceptual model and the meta-model of a class of systems for end users. The team is then called to develop an EUD environment suitable to the knowledge and capabilities of end-user developers, as well as a generator of software systems for end users that reflect the defined conceptual model. In this way, EUD is not conceived as a mere code creation or adaptation, but as the "instantiation of a meta-model", carried out by end-user developers through an easy and natural interaction with the EUD environment.

We argue that the multi-tiered structure of the described problems, due to the diversity of the involved communities and the specific nature of EUD activities proposed in the design approach, should lead to additional reflections on the meta-design guidelines.

7　Conclusion

The contribution of this paper is three-fold. First, we have analyzed a set of case studies in different application domains that can be classified as multi-tiered proxy design problems, which, in our opinion, deserve a special attention within the EUD community. Second, we have proposed a novel interaction and co-evolution model for this kind of problems. Beyond the interaction and co-evolution cycles referred to the end-user community, the ICE^2 model also encompasses the co-evolution cycles that explicitly involve end-user developers. Indeed, in multi-tiered proxy design problems, end-user developers form a separated community, whose activity supports the co-evolution of end users and systems, and who may in turn co-evolve with EUD tools and the technology used to develop them. Third, we have presented a design approach, structured in three phases, to address multi-tiered proxy design problems.

The design approach is based on a deep understanding of the domain of end users and end-user developers, which can be accomplished by adopting traditional user-centered and participatory design during the meta-design phase. However, suitable software tools to support meta-designers in carrying out their activities are still lacking. We are planning to study and develop in the near future a proper meta-design environment that supports the definition of the conceptual model of artifacts to be created, the specification of meta-models, and the development of domain-dependent EUD environments.

Acknowledgments. The authors wish to thank Maria Francesca Costabile and Gerhard Fischer for their insightful comments and suggestions to an earlier version of this paper.

References

1. Norman, D.A., Draper, S.W.: User Centered System Design; New Perspectives on Human-Computer Interaction. L. Erlbaum Associates Inc., Hillsdale (1986)
2. Schuler, D., Namioka, A.: Participatory Design: Principles and Practices. Lawrence Erlbaum Associates, Inc. (1993)
3. Carroll, J.M., Rosson, M.B.: Getting around the Task-Artifact Cycle: How to Make Claims and Design by Scenario. ACM Trans. Inf. Syst. 10(2), 181–212 (1992)

4. Bourguin, G., Derycke, A., Tarby, J.C.: Beyond the Interface: Co-Evolution inside Interactive Systems - a Proposal Founded on Activity Theory. In: IHM-HCI, pp. 297–310. Springer (2001)
5. Costabile, M.F., Fogli, D., Mussio, P., Piccinno, A.: Visual Interactive Systems for End-User Development: A Model-Based Design Methodology. IEEE T. Syst. Man Cy. A 37(6), 1029–1046 (2007)
6. Costabile, M.F., Fogli, D., Marcante, A., Piccinno, A.: Supporting Interaction and Co-Evolution of Users and Systems. In: International Conference on Advanced Visual Interface, pp. 143–150. ACM Press (2006)
7. Lieberman, H., Paternò, F., Wulf, V. (eds.): End User Development. Springer, Dordrecht (2006)
8. Fischer, G., Giaccardi, E.: Meta-Design: A Framework for the Future of End User Development. In: Lieberman, H., Paternò, F., Wulf, V. (eds.) End User Development, pp. 427–457. Springer, Dordrecht (2006)
9. Fischer, G., Herrmann, T.: Socio-Technical Systems: A Meta-Design Perspective, pp. 1–33. IGI Global (2011)
10. Ko, A.J., Abraham, R., Beckwith, L., Blackwell, A., Burnett, M., Erwig, M., Scaffidi, C., Lawrance, J., Lieberman, H., Myers, B., Rosson, M.B., Rothermel, G., Shaw, M., Wiedenbeck, S.: The State of the Art in End-User Software Engineering. ACM Comput. Surv. 43(3), 1–44 (2011)
11. Fischer, G., Nakakoji, K., Ye, Y.: Metadesign: Guidelines for Supporting Domain Experts in Software Development. IEEE Software 26(5), 37–44 (2009)
12. Costabile, M.F., Fogli, D., Mussio, P., Piccinno, A.: End-User Development: The Software Shaping Workshop Approach. In: Lieberman, H., Paternò, F., Wulf, V. (eds.) End User Development, pp. 183–205. Springer, Dordrecht (2006)
13. Cappiello, C., Matera, M., Picozzi, M., Sprega, G., Barbagallo, D., Francalanci, C.: Dashmash: A Mashup Environment for End User Development. In: Auer, S., Díaz, O., Papadopoulos, G.A. (eds.) ICWE 2011. LNCS, vol. 6757, pp. 152–166. Springer, Heidelberg (2011)
14. Gantt, M., Nardi, B.A.: Gardeners and Gurus: Patterns of Cooperation among Cad Users. In: CHI 1992, pp. 107–117. ACM, New York (1992)
15. Carmien, S., Dawe, M., Fischer, G., Gorman, A., Kintsch, A., Sullivan Jr., J.F.: Socio-Technical Environments Supporting People with Cognitive Disabilities Using Public Transportation. ACM T. Comput.-Hum. Int. 12(2), 233–262 (2005)
16. Hutchins, E.L., Hollan, J.D., Norman, D.A.: Direct Manipulation Interfaces. In: Norman, D.A., Draper, S.W. (eds.) User Centered System Design: New Perspectives on Human-Computer Interaction, pp. 87–124. Lawrence Erlbaum, Hillsdale (1986)
17. Abowd, G., Beale, R.: Users, Systems and Interfaces: A Unifying Framework for Interaction. In: VI Conference of the British Computer Society Human Computer Interaction Specialist Group - People and Computers (HCI 1991), pp. 73–87. Cambridge University Press, Cambridge (1991)
18. Bottoni, P., Costabile, M.F., Mussio, P.: Specification and Dialogue Control of Visual Interaction through Visual Rewriting Systems. ACM T. Progr. Lang. Sys. 21(6), 1077–1136 (1999)
19. Mørch, A.I., Stevens, G., Won, M., Klann, M., Dittrich, Y., Wulf, V.: Component-Based Technologies for End-User Development. Commun. ACM 47(9), 59–62 (2004)
20. Ghiani, G., Paternò, F., Spano, L.D.: Creating Mashups by Direct Manipulation of Existing Web Applications. In: Costabile, M.F., Dittrich, Y., Fischer, G., Piccinno, A. (eds.) IS-EUD 2011. LNCS, vol. 6654, pp. 42–52. Springer, Heidelberg (2011)

21. Avola, D., Bottoni, P., Genzone, R.: Light-Weight Composition of Personal Documents from Distributed Information. In: Costabile, M.F., Dittrich, Y., Fischer, G., Piccinno, A. (eds.) IS-EUD 2011. LNCS, vol. 6654, pp. 221–226. Springer, Heidelberg (2011)
22. Dittrich, Y., Madsen, P., Rasmussen, R.: Really Simple Mash-Ups. In: Costabile, M.F., Dittrich, Y., Fischer, G., Piccinno, A. (eds.) IS-EUD 2011. LNCS, vol. 6654, pp. 227–232. Springer, Heidelberg (2011)
23. Burnett, M., Rothermel, G., Cook, C.: An Integrated Software Engineering Approach for End-User Programmers. In: Lieberman, H., Paternò, F., Wulf, V. (eds.) End User Development, pp. 87–113. Springer, Netherlands (2006)
24. Carmien, S.P., Fischer, G.: Design, Adoption, and Assessment of a Socio-Technical Environment Supporting Independence for Persons with Cognitive Disabilities. In: CHI 2008, pp. 597–607. ACM (2008)
25. Celentano, A., Maurizio, M.: An End-User Oriented Building Pattern for Interactive Art Guides. In: Costabile, M.F., Dittrich, Y., Fischer, G., Piccinno, A. (eds.) IS-EUD 2011. LNCS, vol. 6654, pp. 187–202. Springer, Heidelberg (2011)
26. Drey, Z., Consel, C.: Taxonomy-Driven Prototyping of Home Automation Applications: A Novice-Programmer Visual Language and Its Evaluation. J. Vis. Lang. Comput. 23(6), 311–326 (2012)
27. Fogli, D., Parasiliti Provenza, L.: A Meta-Design Approach to the Development of E-Government Services. J. Vis. Lang. Comput. 23(2), 47–62 (2012)
28. Fogli, D., Parasiliti Provenza, L.: End-User Development of E-Government Services through Meta-Modeling. In: Costabile, M.F., Dittrich, Y., Fischer, G., Piccinno, A. (eds.) IS-EUD 2011. LNCS, vol. 6654, pp. 107–122. Springer, Heidelberg (2011)
29. Ardito, C., Buono, P., Costabile, M.F., Lanzilotti, R., Piccinno, A.: End Users as Co-Designers of Their Own Tools and Products. J. Vis. Lang. Comput. 23(2), 78–90 (2012)
30. Berg, M.: Accumulating and Coordinating: Occasions for Information Technologies in Medical Work. Comp. Support. Coop. W. 8(4), 373–401 (1999)
31. Cabitza, F., Simone, C.: LWOAD: A Specification Language to Enable the End-User Develoment of Coordinative Functionalities. In: Pipek, V., Rosson, M.B., de Ruyter, B., Wulf, V. (eds.) IS-EUD 2009. LNCS, vol. 5435, pp. 146–165. Springer, Heidelberg (2009)
32. Costabile, M.F., Fogli, D., Marcante, A., Mussio, P., Parasiliti Provenza, L., Piccinno, A.: Designing Customized and Tailorable Visual Interactive Systems. Int. J. Softw. Eng. Know. 18(3), 305–325 (2008)
33. Star, S.L.: The Structure of Ill-Structured Solutions: Boundary Objects and Heterogeneous Distributed Problem Solving. In: Gasser, L., Huhns, M.N. (eds.) Distributed Artificial Intelligence, vol. II, pp. 37–54. Morgan Kaufmann Publishers Inc., San Mateo (1989)
34. Fogli, D., Piccinno, A.: Enabling Domain Experts to Develop Usable Software Artifacts. In: Organization Change and Information Systems. Springer, Heidelberg (2013)

Meta-design in Co-located Meetings

Li Zhu[1] and Thomas Herrmann[2]

[1] Dipartimento di Informatica, Università degli Studi di Milano
Via Comelico 39/41 20139 Milano, Italy
zhu@dico.unimi.it
[2] Information and Technology Management, Ruhr-University of Bochum,
Universitaetsstr. 150, 44780 Bochum, Germany
thomas.herrmann@rub.de

Abstract. In this paper we present a web-based design-environment – MikiWiki – which demonstrates how the concept of meta-design can be practically supported. It enables and fosters collaboration between meta-designers, designers and end-users. By running a case study to evaluate the appropriateness of MikiWiki in a co-located setting, the effects on interaction between these roles and the support of creativity were observed to derive socio-technical options for improvement. Conducting such an evaluation requires clarifying the basic properties of meta-design in a way that makes its effects observable.

Keywords: Meta-design, creativity, Creativity Barometer, MikiWiki, Hive-Mind Space Model, co-located collaborative design.

1 Introduction

Meta-design is a powerful concept that helps designers and end-users to elaborate needs and requirements, but also to iteratively specify what a software solution should look like. We characterize meta-design by referring to the following principles (Fischer and Herrmann 2011):

- Support of a fluid transition between design for use and design in use.
- Underdesign: representations of solutions (e.g. models or prototypes) do not only include determined specifications but also preliminary, incomplete or imprecise specifications so that designers and end-users are inspired to think about variations or to add further ideas.
- Cultures of participation where several roles and stakeholders can contribute with respect to their interests and find a space of communication and collaboration to exchange their perspectives.
- Empowerment of adaptation by helping end-users or their supporters (software-developers, administrators, power-users, facilitators etc.) to modify a software design with respect to their needs.

By complying with these principles we expect that meta-design provides a framework within which end-user and designer closely interact to conduct the development of a system. The advantage of meta-design can become evident with respect to:

Y. Dittrich et al. (Eds.): IS-EUD 2013, LNCS 7897, pp. 169–184, 2013.

- Creativity support covering divergence (the generation of multiple ideas) as well as convergence (Guilford 1950) (building synergy and merging a variety of ideas) which leads to a concrete design.
- Integration of the knowledge and experience of meta-designers, designers and end users.

The role of the meta-designers is *to provide an environment,* which is used by designers *to draft or develop a solution and to demonstrate it* as immediately as possible so that end users can *directly influence the design of the solution by communicating with the designer or by interacting with electronic media.*

The research challenge is to give examples for concrete meta-design environments to demonstrate how it can be brought to reality, and how its features and benefits can be specified in a way that helps to make them observable within an empirical evaluation. This is necessary to understand the extra effort, which is caused by offering flexibility and multiple solutions with the meta-design approach, and whether the resulting benefits justify an additional workload.

In this paper a concrete web-based meta-design environment – MikiWiki (Zhu 2011) is introduced and evaluated within a co-located meeting support setting (Herrmann 2010). The leading question is how far small groups of people with various roles (such as meta-designer, designer or end user) can use MikiWiki as a collaboration space, how far they are supported to express and to creatively elaborate their needs and ideas, and what hints can be derived for improving socio-technical meta-design environments. Focusing on co-located design is guided by the intention to understand how situated creativity in action (comparable with reflection in action (Schön 1983)) can become possible when people can easily describe their ideas to others by using various tools and material.

The next section will introduce the Hive Mind Space model, a meta-design conceptual model focused on supporting collaborative design. It serves as a framework to summarize related work in the context of meta-design. Subsequently, this model will be illustrated by a concrete environment – MikiWiki. On this basis, the following sections will describe the methodology of a case study being based on five co-located meeting sessions using MikiWiki, our findings and the conclusion.

2   Mikiwiki

In order to evaluate a meta-design model and provide some concrete guidelines for implementing a meta-design model, we implemented MikiWiki (Zhu 2011) as an Hive-Mind Space model (HMS) model prototype.

2.1   The Hive-Mind Space Model

The HMS-model is grounded on several paradigms and frameworks. It aims to bring collaborative design and social creativity together to achieve better collaboration.

The Hive-Mind Space model is a meta-design framework derived from the Software Shaping Workshop methodology (SSW) (Costabile et al. 2007) that integrates the "seeding, evolutionary growth, reseeding" model (Fischer et al. 2001). The bottom-up approach inherent in this framework breaks down static social structures so as to support richer ecologies of participation. It provides the means for structuring communication and appropriation. The model's open mediation mechanism tackles unanticipated communication gaps among different design communities (Zhu 2012).

2.2   Deriving Features of the MikiWiki from the HMS-Model

MikiWiki is a structured programmable wiki, with a hierarchical page organization made of "pages" and "folder pages".

Table 1. Feature of MikiWiki derived from HMS model

HMS conceptual model (Model)	MikiWiki (System features)
Habitable environments	Folders, Environment Page, Lookup mechanism
HMS – boundary objects (Star and Griesemer 1989)	Nuggets (Social application units)
Communication channel (Konkola 2001)	Accessible pages, open environments (folders accessible by design communities)
Mediation mechanism (Ardito et al. 2011)	Format page, environments and Lookup mechanism
Different levels of participation (Costabile et al. 2007) Different levels of tailoring (Mørch 1997)	Meta-design level: design environments, creating format page with JavaScript editor Design level: use design environment, browsing, editing visualization pages, data pages and format pages with JavaScript editor or rich-text editor Use level: browse visualization pages, creating visualization pages with rich-text editor
Open infrastructure (Fischer and Giaccardi 2006)	End-user development approach to allow client-side programming and programming by examples Enabling flexible switching between different design levels Extensibility to the existing Web ecosystem
SER model (Fischer et al. 2001)	Providing just enough features to be useful, and at the same time leaving code short and simple to be quickly understood and modifiable so that the set of features can be easily extended.

Table 1 depicts how each feature of the HMS model maps to MikiWiki. A habitable environment can be seen as a folder containing an environment page. In the environment page, users can specify certain behaviors and attributes that apply to all pages in the environment. Within MikiWiki, nuggets are drafted in analogy to boundary objects. Open environments accessible to all groups or communities can be seen as the boundary zone. The mediation mechanism and support for the different levels of participation and tailoring are also reflected in MikiWiki. This might not be precisely a one-to-one mapping, as many theoretical concepts, such as boundary objects, cannot be reduced to simple software system components.

Collaborative and communication features in MikiWiki are not in-built in the system, but they are made available as underdesigned "nuggets" on top of the system. Hence, they are also seeds (Fischer et al. 1994) for encouraging appropriation and modification.

2.3   Nuggets

In MikiWiki, nuggets are explicitly designed to support the instantiation of the HMS model's boundary objects. A nugget is a page, which can be used as an embeddedable component within another page, in order to create sharable remixable components.

Fig. 1. Using the note nugget for brainstorming

Nuggets are MikiWiki pages, written in HTML, CSS and JavaScript. Non-programmers can easily start using and remixing existing nuggets, while advanced users can clone and modify these nuggets and consequently introduce new behaviors. To support collaborative design, we categorize nuggets in order to address collaborative design from different perspectives - for instance, *chat, comment* and *wall* nuggets support communication; *notify* and *activeuser* nuggets can be used to enhance awareness among design communities; and *todo* and *list* nuggets can be used to coordinate co-located and distributed activities (Hutchins 1995). Figure 1 gives an example of a nugget which supports participants creating PostIt notes, writing down their ideas and clustering them in different colors, while Figure 2 demonstrates participants designing a mobile interface with various nuggets, e.g. different *toolbox, canvas* and *trash* nuggets, etc. A decisive characteristic of nuggets is that the representation of ideas, which can be created with different nuggets, can be interrelated to each other. Therefore nuggets can intertwine the

Fig. 2. Designing a mobile interface with various nuggets

various perspectives of different participants and they can bridge various phases of the design (see also Table 3).

3 A Case Study

The design study was done in collaboration with the Information and Technology Management Group at the Ruhr-University of Bochum, Germany. Meta-designers, designers and users were tasked to collaboratively design an Android phone version of a micro-survey tool, the creativity barometer (Herrmann et al. 2011) which is currently under development. The purpose of the creativity barometer is to conduct surveys to continuously understand and assess the climate of employee creativity.

Increasing economic pressure, competition and emergent project problems require employees to come up with creative campaigns, services or strategies in a very short time and cope with high workload under high pressure. However, these very high workloads and employee uncertainty about continued employment are major obstacles to creativity (Amabile 1999).

The creativity barometer allows companies to periodically repeat surveys and get immediate feedback. It can also provide a good opportunity for employees to reflect on the development of their own attitude and comprehend how their colleagues perceive the creativity climate. After a pre-specified time period (e.g. eight months), the company can summarize the feedback and plan interventions to improve the creativity climate. Since continuous surveying can disturb the employees, the idea is to support them to post their answers as "en passant" as possible, e.g. with smart phones. To draft the design of an appropriate smart phone solution seemed to be a reasonable task to test the meta-design concept by employing MikiWiki.

The case study was intended to evaluate:

1) Whether MikiWiki supports a fluid transition between design for use and design in use, as well as the interplay between meta-designers, designers and users.

2) Whether MikiWiki supports cultures of participation by providing lightweight means to allow participants with different background and different roles to articulate and share their ideas, which in turn enhance social creativity.

A decisive criterion with respect to these questions is creativity is   supported or employed:

- Do design environments support the creativity of designers and users, in that participants continuously adapt nuggets to form a design space in order to perform their design tasks at that moment and use the design space to externalize their thoughts immediately?
- Does it allow designing the design environment as an activity at the meta-design level, in that the meta-designer sets up the initial design environment for the design session and constantly evolves it opportunistically to cope with emergent socio-technical issues without needing to change server-side code?

3.1   Environment Setting: Features of the Modlab

The design study was conducted in the modlab of the Information and Technology Management Group. It was established to develop and evaluate computer support for facilitated, co-located meetings. The following characteristics provided an appropriate setting for five collaborative design sessions supported with MikiWiki:

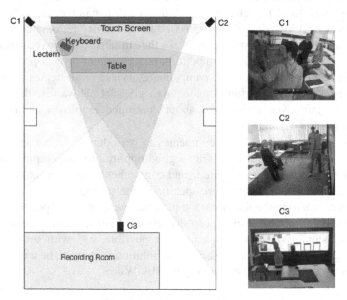

Fig. 3. Environment setting

- A large, high-resolution interactive wall (4,80m x 1,20m; 4320x1050 pixels) which seamlessly integrates three rear projection boards (see Figure 3). The touch screen displayed the MikiWiki mockup environment. Touch is recognized via six cameras which view the reflection of infrared light caused by fingers (Herrmann 2010). The view cones of the cameras are overlapping to support uninterrupted dragging actions over the entire wall.
- A table for users to sit down and get an overview of the design stage;
- A lectern where designers could use a keyboard to input text and interact with the screen;
- iPads as additional input devices which are connected via WLAN, since the interactive wall does not support multi-user interaction. This allows participants to input text and operate actions directly on the screen or via iPads.
- Three cameras recording the sessions from different angles to support observational analysis.

The screen-capture software records all the interactions on the interactive wall and outputs video clips, which can be used to further reflect on the design process, and on how users create new artifacts, interact, reuse, arrange and extend them.

While MikiWiki works for synchronous as well as asynchronous and distributed design collaboration, the modlab is focused on synchronous, co-located meetings. This focus has the advantage that the interaction between the participants and the possibilities of observing them are very direct. Furthermore, less coordination is needed and more attention is available for the actual design task. The disadvantage of co-located meetings is that people cannot freely switch between working in solitude, communication or incubation phases. However, the focus on co-location is a reasonable start for gathering immediate feedback on the strengths of MikiWiki and the underlying meta-design concept or on needs for improvement,

3.2   Methodology

The evaluation approach is an empirical and explorative observation-based field method. A design session follows these steps:

- Meta-designers (in this case the authors) prepare an environment for gathering ideas and sketching mockups in MikiWiki, with which designers drafted the Creativity Barometer user-interface for Android phones.
- Designers and users employ the environment to design the interface. Designers are participants who have designed applications, while users are participants who do not have design experiences, but have used the desktop version of the Creativity Barometer.
- Afterwards, meta-designers observe and interview designers and users to collect feedback on how to improve the design environment. Furthermore, the interviews trigger the reflection among the participants and help the meta-designer to understand how the participants have perceived the design process.
- Based on the empirical data, meta-designers refine the design environment for improving the next design cycle.

Semi-structured Interviews: After each design session, the meta-designer conducts follow-up semi structured interviews, for a total of 13 interviews. Open-ended questions are used in qualitative research rather than to quantify the answers. We aim to find out what participants think about MikiWiki, their design experiences and the rationale behind their opinions (Dawson 2002).

These are the guiding questions for the interviews:

• How does MikiWiki support participants in generating, expressing, structuring and connecting their ideas with respect to different design phases?

• What is the level of the satisfaction with their design results? How does MikiWiki support participants' creativity on an individual level and on a collaborative level?

• Do participants have any difficulties in using MikiWiki, how do they cope with them and what can be improved for the next design sessions?

• How do participants reach final agreement on design decisions?

• What are the important differences between MikiWiki and other groupware and what are the best parts of using MikiWiki?

[In01] to [In13] are used in the text to identify the 13 interviews.

Observation: Furthermore, we focus on observing and reflecting upon situations related to meta-design principles. Therefore the meta-designer took notes during the sessions with respect to the following questions.

1) How do participants and the meta-designers cope with the transition between meta-design, design and use?

2) Do nuggets encourage participants' appropriation with respect to underdesign?

3) How do participants with different perspectives exchange their ideas and find a balance between individual preferences and collective decisions?

4) How do participants shape their design space?

5) How do participants brainstorm, articulate and finalize their creative ideas via different nuggets at different design phases with respect to divergence and convergence of ideas?

It was possible to refine these notes by employing the video recordings afterwards.

3.3   Participants

The design sessions involved 11 participants (P), all with the following characteristics (Table 2):

Table 2. Participants Profile Information

Education and Expertise (Age)
Master in Sociology and Historical Science; Organizational and Migration Research, Urban Planning, Qualitative Research Methods (26-30)
Master in Political Science & Oriental Science; German Policy Development; Cooperation Development in the Middle East/ North Africa (26-30)
Master in Computer Science (CS); Privacy, CSCW, CSCL (26-30)
Master in CS; Creativity, User-Experience Design, Ubiquitous Computing (26-30)
Bachelor in CS; Video Analysis, Interaction and Experimental Design with Groups (26-30)
Master in CS; CSCW, Collaborative modeling, End-user Participation (31-35)
Master in CS; CSCW, Creativity, Collaborative Modeling (31-35)
Master in Social Science; Storytelling; Ambient Assisted Living (36-40)
Master in Engineering; Communication Technologies, Computer Sciences and Business Administration, CSCL, New Media (41-45)
Master in Computer Science; Interfaces, Interaction, Usability, Cognition, CSCW (41-45)
PhD in Engineering; Applied Work Science, Innovation and Process Modeling (50-)

1) Researchers who are involved in innovation, creativity, CSCW and CSCL related research and are willing to try out new technology

2) All participants have some experience with interdisciplinary creative collaborations, and are used to use different groupware systems

3) Some participants are directly involved in creativity related research.

4) Every participant has interdisciplinary focus, ranging from computer science,. usability engineering to social, history and political science.

Design sessions were organized to involve different types of participants. Group 1 and 2 consisted of designers; group 3 consisted of users and designers from the previous design session; group 4 was made purely of users; group 5 consists of one designer and two users.

The meta-designer introduced participants the use of MikiWiki to participants and answered any usage question during the design process. Between design sessions, the meta-designer improved the design environment according to feedback given by the latest group.

Two participants from group 1 also attended the third design session in order to validate the previous experience and evaluate improvements of the mockup design environment.

Table 3 lists the main initial nuggets used to create the design environment for design session 1 (DS1).

Table 3. Initial nuggets

Design phases	Nuggets	Usage
Collaborative Writing	note	Creates PostIt notes
	sync-imagenote	Translate text into images
Collaborative Sketching	doodle	A sketch canvas for users to sketch
Collaborative Design	toolbox	Contain Android design elements
	canvas	Android phone canvas
	trash	Deletes design elements
	iconsearch	Searches for icons from the web

3.4   Design Phases

Each design session lasted approximately 60 minutes and it was divided into three phases.

Phase 1: Brainstorming and Collaborative Writing (15 minutes)

1) Define the design needs and goals of the design of Creativity Barometer for mobiles

2) Agree on suitable categories to describe design elements, structure, requirements, and pages

3) Create a mood-board and agree on the proposed "look and feel"

Phase 2: Sketching Ideas and Collaborative Drawing (15 minutes)
1) Basic illustrations of the structure and components of web pages
2) Focus on the interaction and navigation structure

Phase 3: Designing with the Mockup Environment and Collaborative Design (30 minutes)
1) Use the mockup environment to design the creativity barometer interfaces
2) Final wrap up: suggest possible elements for improving the design process

4   Selected Findings: Creative Interaction

This section describes some of our findings with respect to participants' creative interaction with MikiWiki.

Interplay between Artifacts and Communication: We observed that using MikiWiki leaves continuous traces of the participants' interaction to support their knowledge sharing. The nuggets offered various modes of externalizing and documenting their ideas. Referring to these externalizations on the large screen allowed them to explain their design rationale and to intertwine their perspectives and foster synergy building. Furthermore, the documented ideas were a continuous basis for refining and extending them.

However, starting to work with the interactive wall and the MikiWiki-environment presented some barriers: at the beginning, designers were mostly talking rather than interacting with the wall, not leaving a trace of their thoughts and discussion on the system. After a while they forgot what they had said or had in mind previously. Others (e.g. designer 2) were goal oriented and questioned the benefits of creating something such as a moodboard for their mobile application design. In these situations, it became obvious that the meta-designer has an influential role as a facilitator since her interventions helped the participants starting to use the environment. After this initial phase, no further intervention was necessary – the participants continued to use the wall.

The sharing of perspectives led to negotiations and to creative proposals. For example, the participants had different opinions about the "look and feel" of the barometer interface. Eventually they designed two different mockup styles: a *robotic* style

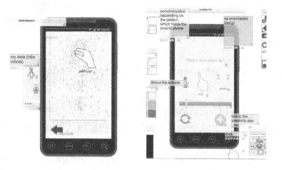

Fig. 4. Two different perspectives

Fig. 5. Repurposing color icons

and a *hello kitty* pink style (Figure 4). The difference between these two styles also demonstrates that the participants were encouraged to transfer their moods, and their emotional attitudes towards the interface, as well as their feelings about the expected context of use to the design.

Another example demonstrates the wide range of possibilities for externalizing ideas: In DS2, designers wanted to use a vertical slider to symbolize the barometer. However, the existing toolbox only provided a horizontal slider. P3 proposed that *"maybe it would be easier to just try to draw something like a box, just tell that it's a vertical slider..."* He then used colored box icons (Figure 5) to create a vertical graduated slider.

This case demonstrates the advantage of meta-design. On the one hand a wide range of features and materials is offered to inspire the participants and to promote the expressing of ideas. For example, the meta-designer intended the color toolbox to provide simple and more generalized design elements. On the other hand she meta-designed them to be easily appropriated and to be used in many different situations, so that the initial set of design elements could be spontaneously extended.

Meta-design before and in between: The interplay between meta-designers, designers and users also which benefitted from the MikiWiki approach: after each design cycle, in accordance with the participants' feedback and the meta-designer's observations, nuggets were modified and evolved for the next cycle to better support the collaborative design process. As such the nuggets were constantly evolving and improving, which also demonstrates how the meta-designer coped with the emerging socio-technical issues via bricolage (Lévi-Strauss 1968) and opportunistic programming (Brandt et al. 2008).

As an example Figure 6 illustrates from the meta-design level how a doodle nugget was evolved in-between each design session based on the meta-designer's observations as well as the feedback given by participants, e.g. adding the auto-saving function in DS2, combining the *page* nugget and the *doodle* nugget to provide better dragging, and hiding and expanding interaction in DS3. Figure 6 also presents the progression of design sessions and the co-evolution that took place between users, designers and meta-designers.

The evolution of the meta-design environment took place iteratively, and was also re-enforced and perpetuated by designers' and users' creative contributions. For the meta-designer, MikiWiki strongly supported a design-in-use option making it both possible and easy to adapt the design space from session to session. It is through this cyclical process that meta-designers, designers and users enhanced their mutual understanding by interacting with the concretely available tools and materials.

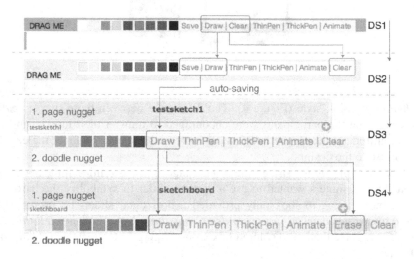

Fig. 6. Evolving the doodle nugget in between sessions

Tools for Creativity Support: An essential aspect of meta-design is to continuously support creativity throughout the whole span between design-for-use and design-in-use to fill the gaps being left by underdesign. During the sessions, it became apparent that MikiWiki provided various features, which supported creativity in design. The combination of MikiWiki with an interactive large wall meets several published creativity criteria (Herrmann 2010; Hailpern et al. 2007; Resnick et al. 2005). The interactive screen is especially useful to provide an overall picture of what has been proposed so that nothing is lost and the various ideas can be flexibly grabbed to generate variations, played around with or become the basis for following ideas. The following features were identified as creativity support:

Simple Tools: a whole palette of tools is offered [In02, In07, In13]; they are small enough to foster appropriation (Pipek 2005) and adaptation; and different tools can be used together to achieve new behaviors [In04, In11].

Ease of use: low threshold of use, simple interactions, system trust (e.g. given by the auto-saving feature meta-designed in DS3) [In05] and perceived feasibility breed satisfaction [In01, In07, In13]. The appropriate tools can also greatly reduce the risk of misunderstanding, and unproductive discussions (Mamykina et al. 2002) as well as provide each individual with suitable means to be creative [In01, In07, In08, In09].

Reconfigurable spaces: restructuring personal workflow [In04], coping with and exploiting the initial lack of structure. As nuggets are independent and loosely coupled, participants can recombine them to create either a structured design space [In01] or a more chaotic space on the canvas [In03].

Adding structure: users can structure and transform ideas by connecting them and indicating their relationships (Figure 1)[In10]. This process also supports reflection and the articulation of previous creative ideas towards a convergent design result [In04].

Perceptibility: providing an overview of all ideas and the big picture they compose [In01, In06, In11]; inspection of details is possible and process history can be reconstructed from the traces left in the design environment [In04].

Quick experimentation: it is possible to explore what-if scenarios with easy drag-and-drop actions (Figure 2)[In01, In11]. As undo is also available, both creating and erasing content could be safely conducted [In09, In12].

One shortcoming of the environment that emerged from the interviews is that there was no private space where participants could draft ideas in isolation, without being observed by others – as required by Lu and Mantei (Lu and Mantei 1991). Currently MikiWiki does not support the differentiation between various layers which can be assigned to certain participants of design aspects and can be easily hidden or shown, although it could be extended on the client side to do so.

A Sandbox for Tinkering: One shared reason for appreciation was that MikiWiki acted as a sandbox that the users could play with, tinker and try things out. It is important to support participants to explore solutions and "what-if" scenarios (Shneiderman 2000; Mamykina et al. 2002) scenarios, trying out assumptions to assess design proposals. One participant [In02] stated: "*It was quite nice that we didn't jump from tool to tool to do different things. Brainstorming feels more like a different tool, starting from simple GUI. We just tried what we had there to achieve what we want. It really felt like a little playground, when you had quite many possibilities. [...]*" Therefore, using MikiWiki with an interactive large screen can be characterized as a 'sandbox for tinkering' which allows the participants to collaboratively prototype design proposals, try out, evaluate, and eventually discard or use them as a basis for ongoing work. We believe that the perception of the sandbox is supported by the easy reach and availability of a range of small tools and the easiness of designing by selecting, dragging and dropping ready-made design elements.

From Reciprocal Inspiration to Convergence: When participants were seeing the wealth of icons made available by the meta-designer, they were inspired even if the icons were not related to their actual ideas. Those items that were not in the initial center of the participants' interest yet acted as a stimulus for creative thought and enriched participants' design ideas. For instance, in DS3 they noticed the audio icon, and subsequently had the idea to use audio input. The possibility to visualize abstract concepts helped them to detect similarities between their design approaches and to refine them thus supporting a process of convergence. It could be observed that MikiWiki promoted the building of relations between design ideas and the merging of individual approaches. Therefore, in MikiWiki it is not only feasible to support divergent phases of brainstorming but also building synergy in a later phase by using the initial results from the brainstorming process.

Appropriation Kits: Not only were designers and end-users inspired but also the creativity of meta-designers was stimulated. By observing how nuggets were appropriated by participants, what they tried to do with them and which expectations came up, the meta-designer developed new ideas on how to enhance or modify the nuggets. Nugget pages act as a mechanism and interface for supporting the creation and evolution of software artifacts and are themselves subject to creative redesign. Moreover, nuggets capture and embody knowledge via their continuous adaptation process. In a reflexive process, this knowledge affects the medium itself by triggering its adaptation. Participants can incrementally construct knowledge via nuggets during collaboration and communication between themselves and with the meta-designer.

5   Summary and Implications for Design

The empirical evaluation of co-located MikiWiki sessions and of the underlying HMS reveals that meta-design is not only an abstract concept but can be instantiated in real settings. The instantiation is not only a technically issue (MikiWiki, large screen etc.) but also relies on the whole socio-technical context - e.g.: the influence of a facilitator, who has to encourage the participants to sketch their ideas, and to get them initially used to employing the variety of the meta-design features available. Further influential factors are the duration of sessions, their cyclical repetition, the appropriate mixture of the participants with respect to their abilities and experiences, and the characteristics of the design task. The facilitator must be able to act as a meta-designer who can instantaneously add new features to the design-environment or modify its features. If the meta-designer's activities do not only include bug fixes or simple adaptations but are the result of a more substantial reflection, they can be considered as re-seeding in terms of the SER-model. The adaptability of the design-environment is the most central characteristic of meta-design and can be achieved by flexibly combining small components. This is exemplarily demonstrated with the MikiWiki nuggets. Each of them represents an independent aspect of the design process and they can be closely related to each other and easily connected to a network.

The way MikiWiki instantiates meta-design does not only support rational problem solving, but also takes emotions and moods into account. It offers participants an asset to transfer their mood and emotional approach to the product being under design – and therefore supports a design outcome that is highly compliant with cultural issues or aspects of experience. This is a relevant aspect for further research.

MikiWiki provides a collaborative design environment for a broad spectrum of application areas, for instance iteratively prototyping interactive system design with a focus on evolutionary participatory design. MikiWiki could be used to rapidly prototype new UI designs and bring different design teams together. It is a web-based platform, allowing design results to be easily stored and shared by communities. The wide design corridor, which is opened by MikiWiki, became obvious by the way participants used it and how their design focus was broadened and enriched.

The validity of the empirical findings is limited since meta-design usually covers a much longer period than was observable within the case study. Ongoing empirical investigation and clarification of the meta-design concept should take a whole series of design cycles into account, and also include phases of asynchronous and dislocated collaboration. Furthermore, a longer time period can be taken into account where design outcomes are used and adapted during use. However, it appeared reasonable to start with short cycle experiments to get an immediate feedback on:

- The needs for adapting the MikiWiki environment or increasing its adaptability.
- The characteristics of the socio-technical context into which MikiWiki has to be embedded.
- The kinds of explanations and interventions that have to be provided by the meta-designer.
- The characteristics of the design task and of the involved participants.

The chosen setting is a reasonable basis to proceed with the empirical investigation of meta-design. Further design studies can help in concretizing and exploring meta-design principles and their interplay with collaborative creativity in participatory design processes.

References

Amabile, T.M., Conti, R.: Changes in the work environment for creativity during downsizing. Academy of Management Journal, 630–640 (1999)

Ardito, C., Barricelli, B.R., Buono, P., Costabile, M.F., Piccinno, A., Valtolina, S., Zhu, L.: Visual mediation mechanisms for collaborative design and development. In: Stephanidis, C. (ed.) Universal Access in HCI, Part I, HCII 2011. LNCS, vol. 6765, pp. 3–11. Springer, Heidelberg (2011)

Brandt, J., Guo, P.J., Lewenstein, J., Klemmer, S.R.: Opportunistic programming: how rapid ideation and prototyping occur in practice. Paper Presented at the Proceedings of the 4th International Workshop on End-User Software Engineering, Leipzig, Germany (2008)

Costabile, M.F., Fogli, D., Mussio, P., Piccinno, A.: Visual Interactive Systems for End-User Development: A Model-Based Design Methodology. IEEE Transactions on Systems, Man and Cybernetics, Part A: Systems and Humans 37, 1029–1046 (2007), doi:10.1109/TSMCA.2007.904776

Dawson, C.: Practical Research Methods: A User-Friendly Guide to Mastering Research Techniques and Projects. How to Books Ltd. (2002)

Fischer, G., Giaccardi, E.: Meta-Design: A Framework for the Future of End User Development. In: Lieberman, H., Paternò, F., Wulf, V. (eds.) End User Development, pp. 427–457. Kluwer Academic Publishers, Dordrecht (2006)

Fischer, G., Herrmann, T.: Socio-Technical Systems: A Meta-Design Pers-pective. International Journal of Sociotechnology and Knowledge Development (IJSKD) 3(1), 1–33 (2011)

Fischer, G., McCall, R., Ostwald, J., Reeves, B., Shipman, F.: Seeding, Evolutionary Growth and Reseeding: Supporting Incremental Development of Design Environments. In: Adelson, B., Dumais, S., Olson, J. (eds.) Proceedings of ACM Conference on Human Factors in Computing Systems (CHI 1994), vol. 1, pp. 292–298. ACM, New York (1994)

Guilford, J.P.: Creativity. American Psychologist 5, 444–454 (1950)

Hailpern, J., Hinterbichler, E., Leppert, C., Cook, D., Bailey, B.P.: TEAM STORM: demonstrating an interaction model for working with multiple ideas during creative group work. Paper Presented at the Proceedings of the 6th ACM SIGCHI Conference on Creativity & Cognition, Washington, DC, USA (2007)

Herrmann, T.: Support of Collaborative Creativity for co-located Meetings. In: Randall, D.S., Pascal (eds.) From CSCW to Web 2.0: European Developments in Collaborative Design. Computer Supported Cooperative Work, pp. 65–95. Springer, London (2010), doi:10.1007/978-1-84882-965-7_4

Herrmann, T., Carell, A., Nierhoff, J.: Creativity barometer: an approach for continuing micro surveys to explore the dynamics of organization's creativity climates. Paper Presented at the Proceedings of the 8th ACM Conference on Creativity and Cognition, Atlanta, Georgia, USA (2011)

Hutchins, E.: Cognition in the Wild. The MIT Press, Cambridge (1995)

Konkola, R.: Harjoittelun kehittämisprosessi ammattikorkeakoulussa ja rajavyöhyketoiminta uudenlaisena toimintamallina. In: Tuomi-Gröhn, T., Engeström, Y., Young, M. (eds.) Koulun ja Työn Rajavyöhykkeellä. Uusia Työssäoppimisen Mahdollisuuksia, pp. 148–186. University Press, Helsiniki (2001)

Lévi-Strauss, C.: The Savage Mind. University of Chicago Press (1968)

Lu, I.M., Mantei, M.M.: Idea management in a shared drawing tool. Paper Presented at the Proceedings of the Second Conference on European Conference on Computer-Supported Cooperative Work, Amsterdam, The Netherlands (1991)

Mamykina, L., Candy, L., Edmonds, E.: Collaborative creativity. Commun. ACM 45(10), 96–99 (2002)

Mørch, A.: Three Levels of End-User Tailoring: Customization, Integration, and Extension. In: Kyng, M., Mathiassen, L. (eds.) Computers and Design in Context, pp. 51–76. MIT Press, Cambridge (1997)

Pipek, V.: From tailoring to appropriation support: Negotiating groupware usage. University of Oulu, Oulu (2005)

Resnick, M., Myers, B., Nakakoji, K., Shneiderman, B., Pausch, R., Selker, T., Eisenberg, M.: Design Principles for Tools to Support Creative Thinking. In: IJHCI, 36th edn.

Schön, D.A.: The Reflective Practitioner: How Professionals Think in Action. Basic Books, New York (1983)

Shneiderman, B.: Creating creativity: user interfaces for supporting innovation. ACM Transactions on Computer Human interaction 7(1), 114–138 (2000)

Star, S.L., Griesemer, J.R.: Institutional Ecology, 'Translations' and Boundary Objects: Amateurs and Professionals in Berkeley's Museum of Vertebrate Zoology, 1907-1939. Social Studies of Science 19(3), 387–420 (1989)

Zhu, L.: Cultivating collaborative design: design for evolution. Paper Presented at the Proceedings of the Second Conference on Creativity and Innovation in Design, Eindhoven, Netherlands (2011)

Zhu, L.: Hive-Mind Space: A Meta-Design Approach for Cultivating and Supporting Collaborative Design. Università degli Studi di Milano, Milano (2012)

Designed by End Users: Meanings of Technology in the Case of Everyday Life with Diabetes

Anne Marie Kanstrup

Aalborg University, Department of Communication, Nyhavnsgade 14, 9000 Aalborg, Denmark
kanstrup@hum.aau.dk

Abstract. This paper presents end users' ability to work across boundaries in design. The point of departure is a research project in which 60 end users participated as co-designers of ICT to support their everyday lives with the chronic illness diabetes. In additional to a series of digital co-designs, 22 mock-ups designed by the end users emerged from the project. These mock-ups/end-user designs are analyzed, with a focus on boundaries. This design case presents end users' ability to create continuities across boundaries through their willingness to step into the unknown territory of ICT design and through their fusion of meanings of technology, diabetes, and everyday life experience in their designs. The paper concludes with reflections on engagement in boundary relations and call for embracing end users' contributions to design by focusing on horizontal and hybrid cooperations.

Keywords: End-user design, diabetes, eHealth, boundaries, dichotomies.

1 Introduction

We have taken three pictures: where and when we want to learn. The first one is in relation to relaxing and reading. That one gets the data directly into the brain. Like with the Internet...

The quote above and the related photo (Fig. 1) are from Marie Glasemann's work with the design of mobile technology support for children living with the chronic illness diabetes. Glasemann participated in two diabetes youth camps in Germany – 14-day camps where children with type 1 diabetes (T1D) stayed over the summer holiday to learn about their illness, have a good time, and meet new friends. Glasemann explored designs to support the youngsters' learning and cooperated with the children via participant observation, interviews and questionnaires, design workshops, and prototyping [16-18].

The photo in Fig. 1 presents three boys' design of a mobile diabetes supporter. It was designed at a design workshop at the camp. The theme of the workshop was learning. The children were aided by materials like Polaroid cameras, paper, pens, stickers, cardboard boxes, Plasticine, and toys, to create mock-ups of designs for mobile devises to support their learning about diabetes [15]. The three photos in Fig. 1 are visualisations of where and when the boys would like to learn – they prefer areas

Y. Dittrich et al. (Eds.): IS-EUD 2013, LNCS 7897, pp. 185–200, 2013.

for "relaxing and reading" (cf. quote). The green mobile devise created in Plasticine is the boys' design of a mobile supporter for learning about diabetes: "That one gets the data directly into the brain", they explain (cf. quote). You put the headphones in your ears, and then whatever you need to know about diabetes goes into your brain.

Fig. 1. Photo taken by Marie Glasemann at a design workshop at a diabetes youth camp. Three boys' design of a mobile diabetes supporter.

Marie Glasemann's work with the design of mobile technology support for children living with diabetes is a wonderful example of how end users of all ages can contribute to the design of technology for their everyday practices if this is facilitated in an appropriate language. However, it is also an example of how difficult it can be to understand end users' designs and cooperate with them. This is especially true if we, as professional designers, think and work in terms of traditional production, thus trying to understand designs like those above as merely technological products.

In this paper, I will elaborate on this challenge. Along with Glasemann and colleagues at Aalborg University, I have supervised the creation of a series of mock-ups designed by end users at design workshops. In this paper, I reflect on the quality of these designs. First, I present perspectives on design as working across boundaries (section 2). Second, I offer the example of end-user designs, which are characterised by their ability to work across boundaries, here in the case of design of Information and Communication Technology (ICT) for everyday living with diabetes (section 3). Third, I discuss and offer some conclusions on challenges of engaging in boundary relations (section 4).

2   Design as Working across Boundaries

In 1964 Alexander [1] presented a view of end users as "unselfconscious" designers whose designs were characterised by "a dynamic process in which both form and context change continuously, and yet stay mutually well adjusted all the time" [1: 37]. Alexander presented examples of designs made in "unselfconscious cultures", for example, buildings and clothing, and called attention to the puzzling fact that these designs were characterised by a "good fit" between "form" and "context", in contrast to most designs made by professionals. Work by "selfconscious" designers, taught academically, was often characterised by a mismatch between form and context. Alexander argued that the difference in quality between these two types of design cultures could not be explained by the increased complexity in professional "selfconscious" design alone [1: 32]. Nor can the nature of "unselfconscious" design be boiled down to a story of "adaptation" [1: 37]. Instead, we need to understand the "self-organizing" process, which supports "dual coherence" – processes in which, e.g., operations, maintenance, constraints, surroundings, and daily life are "fused in the form" [1: 31]. Alexander argued that the common problems of misfit in designs made by "selfconscious" designers were caused by design processes, which are often "broken down", thereby cutting the production of the form off from its context [1: 38].

Alexander's "notes" from 1964 still contribute to the research on how to bridge established boundaries between form and context, technology and use, and professional designers and end users. The field of End User Development (EUD) is occupied by bridging the dichotomies of "design time" and "use time" [13], and designers and users [31], and in general working "across boundaries" [35]. As presented by Suchmann, the reconstruction of the relationship between technology production and use is an enormously difficult task, since boundaries defining professional practices of technology production are institutionalised arrangements. Boundary crossing involves "encountering difference; entering into territory with which one is unfamiliar and, to some significant extent therefore, unqualified to act" [35: 93]. EUD research presents rich examples of end users' steps into unknown terrain through engaging in software design despite a lack of formal education. With this research, EUD also presents the need for professional software designers to be able to understand end users' designs in order to participate in and facilitate the bridging of boundaries in design. This might sound simple, but even in recent literature we find examples of how difficult it is to break free from the traditional perception of users as receivers of technology who need help from professional designers. One honest example is Buxton's own admission of the assumption that end users exposed to multiple designs would be the most creative and constructive, i.e., the assumption that end users come to the design process "empty" and therefore need to be given ideas by professional designers from which to choose or upon which to elaborate. Buxton carried out a systematic analysis of 48 sketches made by end users [6: 396-399]. Some of these designs were made by end users who had been exposed to multiple designs, while other users had not. Buxton concluded that his hypothesis had been wrong. He wrote: "What is clear in these sketches, even to a lay-person, is that the users did have original ideas about alternative designs. What we had not done in the first study, however, was let them communicate them to us in an appropriate language" [6: 394]. Buxton's honesty is venerable and important to share. It reminds us to keep a perspective of users as competent designers (in contrast to testers or elaborators of ideas presented by professional designers, cf. [20]). Moreover, it reminds professional designers of our responsibility to communicate in an appropriate manner with end users – to make a true effort to work across boundaries and to understand the meanings of technology for end users (in contrast to anticipating use without local grounding [35]). Despite more than 40 years of work with engaging end users in the design of ICT, we still fall short in understanding end-user design and, consequently, in knowing how to facilitate cross-boundary work on design and use. The constant technological development of platforms supporting end-user design is, on the one hand, a contribution and, on the other hand, a critical challenge to software designers' goal of re-conceptualising design towards "dual coherence", as called for by Alexander [1: 31]. Returning to Suchmann, we need to move "beyond simple dichotomies in our understanding of who and where we are within the divided terrain of technology production and use, we need to begin by problematizing the terms 'designer' and 'user' and reconstructing relevant social relations that cross the boundaries between them" [35: 94].

My interest in conceptual understandings of end-user designs comes from concerns found in the literature and from my experiences in research projects. In both cases, I am concerned about understandings of end-user designs as merely products. Literature in business studies on how to "open innovation" and work across borders in companies [7] and on how to "democratize innovation" by offering lead users information and tool-kits to innovate has drawn important attention to end(/lead) users' value in design [36], though this is from a market-oriented perspective. The focus is on how to support end users in their construction of forms that hit the market in form of increased sales [37]. As argued by Björgvinsson, Ehn, and Hillgren, attention to how end users' designs contribute to "open[ing] up [...] possibilities and questions" is missing [5: 42]. In practice, I have seen software developers and even researchers become frustrated if it was difficult to see the line connecting the end-user design to the final product. In these frustrations lies a desire for a 1:1 correspondence between end-user designs and a final product. This technical-functional rationality assumes that if we provide end users with tool kits to innovate, then products that will hit the market will emerge. Of course, there are best practice examples of lead users designing such products [37]. However, these processes do not tend to follow causal lines of activity. In most cases, design, including when it involves and/or is carried out by end users, is far more complex. This is because most people, and also most projects [14], are not based on rationality alone.

During a series of research projects on how to support end users in design [23], it was clear that the end-user designs – the forms that surfaced in these projects from the hands of end users – were not just products (cf. Fig. 1). In practice, in many cases it was impossible to implement them in formal language, which especially frustrated the software engineers. Because of this clash of understandings and expectations about end-user design, it has become important to find conceptual understandings that can support professional design teams in their cooperative work with end users as co-designers. In this conceptual and analytical work, the end users' designs came to be understood not as products, but rather as some type of artefacts of meanings. As such, the end-user designs from such research projects are wonderful examples of how unsound (and frustrating) it is to insist on a division between the objective and the subjective.

Because the end-user designs from the research projects expressed meanings (rather than functionality), they recall Krippendorf's definition of design as "making sense (of things)", emphasising the *sense*-making role of products, in contrast to a focus on *making* objectively existing products [27: 9]. Thus, I suggest understanding these end-user designs as "expressions", and, therefore, working with end-user designs as communicative artefacts, as suggested several years ago by, e.g., Ehn and Kyng [11]. Additionally, I have suggested to understand the end-user designs as "partly unconscious communications" [22]. This suggestion is made in reference to Bateson's definition of messages communicated in art as falling in between the self-conscious and unself-conscious, a kind of expression that Bateson termed "partly unconscious communication" [4]. Such "partly unconscious" messages would be "falsified" if made fully conscious. Instead, to understand them, we must engage in a particular sort of "partly unconscious communication" [4: 138]. Returning to Such-mann [35], this is a call for professional designers to step into unknown territory, and to leave the comfort zone of "making" and step into the zone of "sense", as suggested by Krippendorf [27: 9]. This means leaving behind the frustrated attempts to translate end-user designs like those in Fig. 1 as conscious specifications. On the contrary, professional designers must engage in partly unconscious communication and, as emphasised by Buxton in his reflections, work on how to facilitate communication "in an appropriate language" [6: 394].

In the following section, I will present how we worked through these challenges of bridging boundaries in design in a case of ICT for everyday living with diabetes.

3   ICT for Living with Diabetes – Boundary Challenges

The data presented in this paper are from the maXi project, an acronym for "master-ing chronic illness with information technology". Since 2007, the maXi project (www.maxi-projektet.dk) has worked on the design of interactive systems to support everyday living with the chronic illness diabetes. During the course of the project, this came to include explorations of prototypes for grocery shopping, restaurant visits, glucose simulation, and training tools [24]. 17 Danish families (60 family members in total) participated in the project. Glasemann's work with learning technology at a diabetes youth camp was part of the maXi-project. The research focused on re-thinking health, and user-driven innovation was explored as a method to bring end users, normally excluded from the design of technology for their everyday lives with chronic illness, to the forefront of the design process. The ambition was to bring new perspectives to technology production in eHealth, which is traditionally driven by healthcare professionals and engineers [26]. EUD perspectives on end users as com-petent designers – the genuine belief in end users' contribution to design and an insis-tence in opening up the world of technology production to end users [31] – has formed the basis for the empirical research in the maXi project. The design process was organised according to three themes [23]:

- Cooperation: focused on finding end users for participation, establishing cooperation, and planning the process.
- Context: focused on insights on current practice and visions for future practices.
- Concept: focused on materialising concepts as sketches and presentations.

Two iterations were carried out. Eight families participated in the first iteration in year 2008. Nine families participated in the second iteration, in year 2009. All families participated in: 1) two-hour home interviews; 2) a three-hour workshop at the University; and 3) one weekend of exploring prototypes for digital health services in a living laboratory. The participants were selected to represent a broad variety of the target group. Diabetics were between 4 and 68 years old. Approximately 50% had T1D and 50% had T2D. Some were newly diagnosed diabetics, while others had more than 20 years of experience with diabetes. Additionally, 9 service providers (restaurants, bakeries, supermarket, tourist office, and butcher shops) from the city of Skagen in North Denmark participated in establishing a living laboratory for digital health services [25].

A series of co-designed digital prototypes were designed and explored [24]. Additionally, the users designed a series of low-fi prototypes on their own at the concluding design workshops. It is this activity – the end users' design of low-fi prototypes at design workshops – that is presented here. These design workshops concluded the design iteration (both in 2008 and in 2009). At the workshops, the users formed groups of 5-8 people. All groups worked to design one or more IT-service to support everyday living with diabetes. To express their ideas, all users had access to several objects, including paper, pencils, Plasticine, post-its, cardboard imitations of computers and mobile phones, stickers, and Polaroid cameras.

The design workshop took place over 60 minutes followed by 30 minutes of joint sharing and reflection on the designs. The design workshop concluded the end users' participation in the maXi project. It was organised and presented as the end of the design inquiry, with the goal of summing up the needs and ideas that emerged through the design activities in the project. All groups presented their designs to each other and participated in a concluding qualitative interview on their experiences as designers in the project.

The data that form the basis of the analysis of the end-user designs are photos and recordings of end users' presentations of designs. This was further supported by tape recording of end users' conversations during the 60-minute design activity and of their reflections in follow-up interviews. The 22 end-user designs are numbered below. I will refer to these numbers in my discussion of how the end-user designs work across boundaries.

1. A PC solution that supports daily use for monitoring
2. A mobile application for grocery shopping combined with personal glucose management and social community
3. A necklace and earrings to monitor and measure glucose level

4. A watch to monitor and measure glucose level
5. A monster that helps to remember medicine
6. A variety (14 designs) of mobile applications that support communication between family members on glucose levels and everyday activities like sports, groceries, friends, whereabouts, etc.
7. An information infrastructure that supports data catch-up and use from supermarket systems (via bar-codes) to mobile phones, refrigerators, interactive cookbooks, and personal glucose management systems
8. Two beepers that monitor and send an alarm to family members if glucose levels get too low.

Fig. 2. At a design workshop, end users design mock-ups of ICT to support their everyday lives with diabetes

The maXi project faced a series of boundary challenges in the design of ICT for everyday living with diabetes. The following section will summarise the core boundary challenges and illustrate how end-user designs from the design workshops worked across boundaries.

3.1   Boundaries of Individual and Cooperative Practice

A core challenge faced in the maXi project was how to bridge the boundary between the medical practice of self-management, on the one hand, and the cooperation practised in families and communities, on the other. Diabetes is a serious illness for which, at present, there is no cure. From a medical perspective, a diabetic, especially with T1D, needs strict control of blood glucose levels, obtained by balancing the trio of food, exercise, and insulin. This includes measuring blood glucose levels several times a day, calculating carbohydrate, insulin doses, and physical activity. These activities are termed "self-management". In Denmark, those diagnosed with diabetes consult a physician only twice a year unless complications occur.

Between these consultancies (i.e., over six months), the diabetic manages her own illness, typically with help from blood glucose meters, applications on mobile phones or personal computers, cookbooks with information on carbohydrates, and simple tools to support ongoing monitoring and calculation, like watches with alarms and mobile calculators. The growth in social media over recent years has supported user contributions to everyday life services. There is an endless array of networking possibilities for diabetics (e.g., forums, chats, weblogs, and video or picture-sharing sites). In these network facilities, information is primarily user-generated. Through such networks, people strengthen and encourage each other by articulating thoughts, problems, and fears, but also by sharing their experiences and offering advice for a better life. The term "health 2.0" has emerged [21]. What had emerged through 2.0 technologies shows that diabetes is not simply an individual activity focused on the illness from a purely medical or rational perspective. In practice, diabetes is a cooperative activity that takes place in groups, like among families, friends, trusted people at institutions like school and work, and even through "reaching out across the web" in "emphatic communities" [33].

Figure 3 presents a design of a beeper that monitors the glucose level and sends an alarm to family members if it gets too low (left) and a design of a mobile application to support communication between family members regarding glucose levels and everyday activities like sports, groceries, friends, and whereabouts (right).

Fig. 3. Left: end-user design 8: a design of a beeper that monitors glucose level and sends an alarm to family members if it gets too low. Photo right: end-user design 6: a design of a mobile application to support communication between family members regarding glucose levels and everyday activities like sports, groceries, friends, and whereabouts.

End-user designs 8 and 6 are examples of how *mock-ups designed by end users work across boundaries of individual self-management and co-operative communities of practice.* These designs represent the primary types of end-user designs (with 14 examples of end-user design 6 and two examples of end-user design 8), and they were characterised by a focus on creating and supporting relations across communities of practice, such as healthcare professionals, family members, friends from the diabetes community, friends from school, colleagues at work, associations, and service providers of interests. The designs all touched upon the diabetics' need to feel safe and connected to trusted people in relation to their illness. A child explains design 6 to his mother as follows:

Child: "It is a mobile beeper where you can see how I am"
Mother: "so I can see if you are ok or not?"
Child: "Yes"

At the same time, the designs emphasise the need for privacy and to break free from interactions related solely to diabetes – to step across communities and integrate interactions involving fun, friendship, and work. One child emphasises the need for privacy: "I don't want the school to see my data". An adult points out the need for integration with non-diabetic activities: "It has to support me at work. Not make it more complicated". The end-user designs focus on relationships at the community level, with an emphasis on membership in multiple communities of practice, i.e., connection to a wide range of relations without requiring a specific shared practice. The end-user designs are types of boundary objects [34], calling for a nexus of interpretations, objectives, structures, and scales. These end-user designs call attention to the importance of designing for participation across boundaries, rather than just use. As Wenger noted, on boundary objects, such perspectives are important:

The crucial issue is the relationship between the practices of design and the practices of use. Connecting the communities involved, understanding practices, and managing boundaries become fundamental design tasks. It is then imperative to consider a broader range of connections beyond the artifact itself, both to reconcile various perspectives in the nexus and to take advantage of their diversity. [38: 108]

3.2   Boundaries of Clinical and Everyday Life Settings

Another core challenge in the maXi project was to work across the boundaries between clinical settings and the settings of everyday life. In general, and not only in relation to diabetes, there has been growing interest in how to decrease hospitalisation time and treatment costs by supporting patients with ICT in their homes and everyday life environments. New technologies and practices of telemedicine [32] and self-management tools are expanding, and the private sphere has become a design setting for eHealth. Rules and practices in what here I broadly term "everyday life", such as private households and service settings like restaurants and supermarkets, are different from clinical settings like hospitals. Following Barker's studies of "Ecological Psychology" [3], "the environment is seen to consist of highly structured, improbable arrangement of objects and events which coerce behavior in accordance with their own dynamic patterning" [3: 4]. The clinical setting and the private setting have different styles, agendas, and, in general, different "patterns" [3: 4].

Fig. 4 illustrates the differences in structure, arrangements, objects, and patterns between a clinical setting and everyday life settings. The first photo (left) shows a clinical setting, while the middle and right photos are two examples of everyday life settings in the maXi project: the city of Skagen and a bakery. Even a layperson can see that these settings call for different designs and can foresee the danger of "misfit" [1] if we attempt merely to fuse clinical settings onto the settings of everyday life.

Fig. 4. Left: a clinical setting – a Danish hospital ward. Middle: a maXi setting, end users on a city tour in Skagen. Right: a maXi setting, end users at a bakery.

Fig. 5 presents examples of end-user designs in which the home setting is addressed, with emphasis on the designs' ability to support a home-like atmosphere. End-user design 5 (left photo), which is a monster to help remember treatment, was designed by a child who envisioned this design as a decoration in her room. End-user design 2 is a kind of collage of functionality, combining a mobile application for grocery shopping with personal glucose management and social community.

Fig. 5. Left: end-user design 5: a monster helping to remember medicine. Right: end-user design 2: a mobile application for grocery shopping combined with personal glucose management and social community.

When designing mock-up 2, the end users (women aged 40 to 65) placed candles in the middle of the design and had the following conversation:

End user 1: let's put these candles in the middle 'cause we want it to be cosy
End user 2: candles, yes, we need candles
End user 1: ok, so we want candles, let's place them in the centre like this. Cosy we write like that. It must not be too technical. Cosy.

Aarhus and Ballegaard's studies of professionally designed technology to assist with self-care at home showed how end users engage in boundary work "to maintain the order of the home when managing disease and adopting new healthcare technology" [2]. End-user designs 2 and 5 are examples of how *mock-ups designed by end users work across boundaries of clinical settings and everyday life settings*, such as home.

3.3   Boundaries of Illness and Identity

Fig. 6 presents examples of end-user designs in which lived life and identity are put at the forefront, and diabetes is integrated into this life and identity. The photo on the left shows one of the project participants' technologies for diabetes management: a professionally designed insulin pen with a self-administering clinical focus: it can inject the suggested dosage of insulin and display insulin dosages. In contrast with this are two end-user designs, shown in the middle and right photos. The former shows jewellery and the latter a watch; both were designed to wear for fashion and to monitor blood glucose levels. The end users who designed these were teenagers who emphasised the need for technology that is not just designed for illness or medical activities. One of these end user designers stated: "I say, 'I am Anna'. I don't say 'I am diabetic'" (teen diabetic). Emphasis in these designs was on how to blend into everyday life with friends at school, in the city, at sport activities, cafés, etc. Anna explains: "I would prefer not to say that I am diabetic" (teen diabetic). The end user who designed the watch explained: "It has to be fashionable" (teen diabetic). Similar examples are found in Glasemann's end-user designs, e.g., covers for diabetes technology inscribed with "love", unlike to existing professional designs, which are typically black or blue with medical business logos [19].

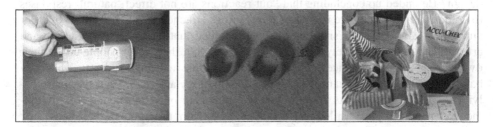

Fig. 6. Left: a professionally designed insulin pen. Middle: end-user design 3: jewellery to monitor and adjust glucose levels. Right: end-user design 4: a watch to monitor blood glucose levels.

Studies of how people experience living with a chronic condition have shown that they feel predominantly healthy [28]. When expressing how it feels to be healthy, they report central themes like honouring the self, being connected with others, creating opportunities, and celebrating life. Studies like these support an understanding of health and illness as coexistent. A predominant focus on illness will mean that "a large part of a person's whole is missing and therefore denied" [28: 466]. End-user designs 3 and 4 are examples of how *mock-ups designed by end users work across boundaries of illness and identity*.

3.4   Coherent Connections between Objects and Context

It is important to remember that the motivations and values of diabetics and health-care professionals differ. Generally speaking, there is a boundary between medical ideals and everyday life practices. Healthcare is evidence–based, with clinical proce-dures as the fundamental rationale for decisions and actions. In contrast, research in ICT support for diabetes shows that it is naïve to assume that such health rationales are a fundamental part of people's everyday lives [9, 29].

Krippendorf has shown evidence of how people's sense-making is primarily re-lated to non-causal relationships, like family belonging, associations, and harmony. Simply put, "The perception of how something fits into a cognitively constructed context has no causal base" [27: 13]. Krippendorf was referring here to Csikszentmi-halyi, who carried out a study with nice examples of such a lack of causal base. Csik-szentmihalyi was interested in the psychological effects of art. However, in his study of 82 homes, he found that these homes contained "a symbolic ecology, a network of objects that referred to meanings that gave sense to the lives of those who dwelt there" [8: 119]. Even when art and design objects were clearly visible in the house-hold, they played an insignificant role. In contrast, respondents showed strong at-tachments to several other artefacts, such as a cheap plastic statuette appreciated for its memory of success, an old bible, which symbolised family continuity, a stereo that was helpful when the person felt depressed, and a trombone used when responsibili-ties felt overwhelming [8: 119]. From this observation, Csikszentmihalyi asked if it actually mattered how objects looked – if people were attached to experiences related to objects, rather than to the colour or form, then what was the importance of art and design? He ended up concluding that "our reactions are not direct 'natural' responses to color and form. They are responses to meanings attached to configurations of color and form" [8: 124-125]. Csikszentmihalyi concluded that there was good design and art with an impact on society and on people's lives, but that "most people create their own private set of references singling out objects that will give order to what they have experienced". The nuances of layers of technology are visible in Csikszentmiha-lyi's studies, where objects that are merely objects are only the ground (or environ-ment) of people's lives, while objects with meaning form the figure of their lives.

During home visits in the maXi project, we asked the 17 participating families to show us what they used as support in their everyday life with diabetes. They all found cookbooks from the diabetes association, glucose meters, and insulin pens; most also showed their mobile phones, and some a personal computer. In addition, they showed artefacts with indirect functions in the task of monitoring and regulating glucose lev-els. One such example is seen in Fig. 7, where the family has added a photo of their dog because "I love the dog. He makes me so happy". The red watch at the table was presented as the diabetic's favourite technology. It was a private item (not a medical devise), and its best feature was its look, which made it "cool", and its alarm, which was invisible to others but was set to remind the diabetic to measure glucose levels.

It is clear which objects make meaning for this family (the dog and the watch) and which objects are "merely objects" (presented to us and used every day in the ongoing tasks of monitoring and regulating glucose levels). As elaborated by Krippendorf

[27], meaning is a cognitively constructed relationship. It selectively connects features of an object and features of its (real environment or imagined) context into a coherent unit. The end-user designs from the maXi project, and the end users' sharing of objects and meanings of technology provide insight into already existing and potential *coherent connections between objects and context*.

Fig. 7. At this home visit, the family has displayed technology they use in their everyday living with diabetes. They insist on showing a photo of the dog and presenting a personal watch as their favourite technology.

4   Engagement in Boundary Relations – Concluding Remarks

The aim of this paper has been to present:

- design as working across boundaries. The case is a glimpse into how engagement in boundary relations can be fruitful in terms of ideals of dual coherence.
- end users' ability and contributions in working across boundaries in design, here specifically in relation to the design of ICT support for everyday life with diabetes.
- the variety of meanings found in end-user designs and, consequently, the need for professional designers to go beyond offering end users tools and platforms for design and step into unknown terrains of meanings of technology.
- the notion that communication in and about design is not purely conscious and causal, i.e., directed towards product development. Instead, it is flexible when it comes to interpretation across boundaries and dual when it comes to the meanings of technology.

Design is occupied with creating qualitative transformations of form and context, aimed at transcending existing practices by fomenting new and better ones.

Engeström et al. [12] and Wenger [38], among others, have shown how boundary crossing is a crucial theoretical concept in the processes of innovation and learning. These authors emphasised the horizontal, hybrid character of boundary crossing: "Boundary crossing entails stepping into unfamiliar domains. It is essentially a creative endeavour which requires new conceptual resources. In this sense, boundary crossing involves collective concept formation" [12: 333].

Working across boundaries in design – to bridge and blur dichotomies of design and introduce horizontal and hybrid cooperations – calls for new ways of thinking. Ehn [10] has suggested that we work with design as "staging", in contrast to envisioning a project as including the phases of analysis, design, construction, and implementation. Ehn explained: we could then ask: How *to construct the initial object of design* for the project? That is, how to align the participants around a shared, though problematic, object of concern? [10: 93].

In this paper, I have presented examples of end users' engagement in boundary work. My encounters with professional designers' frustrations with translating end-user designs directly into product chains, along with the business literature's presentation of traditional production-oriented end-user design, are my primary concerns as I call attention to boundaries and boundary concepts in design. I argue that such re-conceptualisation will support the fluency, flexibility, heterogeneity, and dynamic organisation of ICT design, meaning, and use.

References

1. Alexander, C.: Notes on the synthesis of form. Harvard University Press (1964)
2. Aarhus, R., Ballegaard, S.A.: Negotiating Boundaries: Managing Disease at Home. In: Proceedings of the SIGCHI Conference on Human Factors in Computing Systems, CHI 2010, Atlanta, Georgia, USA, April 10-15, pp. 1223–1232 (2010)
3. Barker, R.G.: Ecological Psychology: Concepts and methods for studying the environment of human behavior. Stanford University Press (1968)
4. Bateson, G.: Steps to an ecology of mind. University of Chicago Press, Chicago (2000)
5. Björgvinsson, E., Ehn, P., Hillgren, P.A.: Participatory design and "democratizing innovation". In: PDC 2010, Sydney, Australia, pp. 41–50 (2010)
6. Buxton, B.: Sketching User Experiences – getting the design right and the right design. Morgan Kaufmann (2007)
7. Chesbrough, H.W.: Open Innovation – The new imperative for creating and profiting from technology. Harvard Business Press (2003)
8. Csikszentmihalyi, M.: Design and Order in Everyday Life. In: Margolin, V., Buchanan, R. (eds.) The Idea of Design – A design Issues Reader, pp. 118–126. The MIT Press (1995)
9. Danholt, P.: Interacting Bodies: Posthuman Enactments of the Problem of Diabetes – Relating Science, Technology and Society-studies, User-Centered Design and Diabetes Practice. PhD thesis. Computer Science, Department of Communication, Business and Information Technology, Roskilde University, Denmark (2008)
10. Ehn, P.: Participation in Design Things. In: PDC 2008 Proceedings of the Tenth Anniversary Conference on Participatory Design 2008, pp. 92–101. Indiana University (2008)

11. Ehn, P., Kyng, M.: Cardboard Computers: Mocking-it-up or Hands-on the Future. In: Greenbaum, J., Kyng, M. (eds.) Design at Work: Cooperative Design of Computer Systems. Lawrence Erlbaum Associates, New Jersey (1991)

12. Engeström, Y., Engeström, R., Kärkkäinen, M.: Polycontextuality and boundary crossing in expert cognition: Learning and problemsolving in complex work activities. Learning and Instructions 5, 319–336 (1995)

13. Fischer, G., et al.: Meta-design: a manifesto for end-user development. Communications of the ACM 47(9), 33–37 (2004)

14. Flyvbjerg, B.: Rationality & Power: Democracy in Practice. The University of Chicago Press (1998)

15. Glasemann, M., Kanstrup, A.M.: Evoking Creativity: Young Diabetics Design Their Own Mobile Diabetes Supporter. In: Proceedings of the Eighth Danish Human-Computer Interaction Research Symposium, Aalborg University, November 20, pp. 37–41 (2008)

16. Glasemann, M., Kanstrup, A.M., Ryberg, T.: Design and Exploration of a Mobile Game Scenario in a Diabetic Youth Camp. In: Proceedings of the IADIS International Conference Mobile Learning 2010, Porto, Portugal, pp. 132–140 (2010)

17. Glasemann, M., Kanstrup, A.M., Ryberg, T.: Making Chocolate-covered Broccoli: Designing a Mobile Learning Game about Food for Young People with Diabetes. In: Halskov, K., Petersen, M.G. (eds.) Proceedings of the 8th ACM Conference on Designing Interactive Systems, pp. 262–271. Association for Computing Machinery (2010)

18. Glasemann, M., Kanstrup, A.M.: IT for Learning Diabetes. Studies in Health Technology and Informatics 157, 154–159 (2010)

19. Glasemann, M., Kanstrup, A.M.: Emotions on diabetes: a design case of user mock-ups by young living with diabetes. CoDesign 7(2), 123–130 (2011)

20. Greenbaum, J., Kyng, M. (eds.): Design at Work: Cooperative Design of Computer Systems. Lawrence Erlbaum Associates, New Jersey (1991)

21. Hughes, B., Joshi, I., Wareham, J.: Health 2.0 and Medicine 2.0: Tensions and Controversies in the field. Journal of Medical Internet Research 10(3), e23 (2008)

22. Kanstrup, A.M.: A small matter of design: an analysis of end users as designers. In: PDC 2012: Proceedings of the 12th Participatory Design Conference: Research Papers, vol. 1, pp. 109–118. ACM, New York (2012)

23. Kanstrup, A.M., Bertelsen, P.: User Innovation Management – a handbook. Aalborg University Press (2011)

24. Kanstrup, A.M., Glasemann, M., Nielsby, O.: IT-services for everyday life with diabetes: learning design, community design, inclusive design. In: Proceedings of the 8th ACM Conference on Designing Interactive Systems, DIS 2010. ACM Press (2010)

25. Kanstrup, A.M., Bjerge, K., Kristensen, J.: A Living Laboratory Exploring Mobile Support for Everyday Life with Diabetes. Wireless Personal Communications 53(3), 395–408 (2010)

26. Kanstrup, A.M., Bertelsen, P., Glasemann, M., Boye, N.: Design for more – an ambient perspective to diabetes. In: Proceedings of the Tenth Anniversary Conference on Participatory Design, PDC 2008. Indiana University, Indianapolis (2008)

27. Krippendorf, K.: On the Essnetial Contexts of Artifacts or on the Proposition that "Design Is Making Sens (of Things)". In: Margolin, V., Buchanan, R. (eds.) The Idea of Design – A design Issues Reader, pp. 156–184. The MIT Press (1995)

28. Lindsey, E.: Health within illness: experiences of chronically ill/disabled people. Journal of Advancd Nursing 24, 465–472 (1996)

29. Mamykina, L., Mynatt, E., Kaufman, D.: Investigating Health Management Practices of Individuals with Diabetes. In: CHI 2006, Montéal, Québec, Canada, April 22-27 (2006)

30. Muller, M.: Participatory Design: The Third Space in HCI. In: Jacko, J., Sears, A. (eds.) Handbook of HCI, 2nd edn. Erlbaum (2007)
31. Nardi, B.: A small Matter of Programming – Perspectives on end user computing. MIT Press (1993)
32. Norris, A.C.: Essentials of Telemedicine and Telecare. Wiley (2001)
33. Preece, J.: Empathic Communities: Reaching Out Across the Web. Interactions, 32–43 (March + April 1998)
34. Star, S.L.: This is Not a Boundary Object: Reflections on the Origin of a Concept. Science, Technology, & Human Values 35(5), 601–617 (2010)
35. Suchman, L.: Located accountabilities in technology production. Scandinavian Journal of Information Systems 14(2), 91–105 (2002)
36. Von Hippel, E.: Democratizing Innovation. MIT Press (2005)
37. Von Hippel, E.: The Sources of Innovation. Oxford University Press (1988)
38. Wenger, E.: Communities of Practice: Learning, Mearning, and Identity. Cambridge University Press (1998)

Cultures of Participation in Community Informatics: A Case Study

Daniela Fogli

Dipartimento di Ingegneria dell'Informazione
Università degli Studi di Brescia
Via Branze 38, 25123 Brescia, Italy
fogli@ing.unibs.it

Abstract. This paper describes a participatory design project aimed at developing FirstAidMap, a collaborative web mapping application to be used by an Italian non-profit association for public assistance and first aid. Volunteers of this association, and specifically ambulance drivers, need to know the characteristics of the territory where the association ensures its assistance, in order to reach a given place quickly and in a safe manner. Despite the new opportunities offered by Web 2.0 technologies, paper-based maps are the only means used by volunteers to spread and share knowledge within the association, while training sessions through Powerpoint™ presentations are regularly held to train novice drivers about the dangers existing in the territory and possible changes to traffic and road signals. The two design cycles carried out to develop FirstAidMap, which are described in this paper, gave the chance to observe how a culture of participation may progressively emerge in a community informatics domain and how the related issues may be addressed.

Keywords: collaborative web mapping, meta-design, cultures of participation, community informatics.

1 Introduction

In many application domains, managing and sharing knowledge is a fundamental activity that needs to be sustained by favoring a culture of participation [3-4], namely by providing all actors in the application environment with the proper means to participate in activities of their interest. Creating and exchanging up-to-date knowledge about the territory is a crucial need at COSP (Centro Operativo Soccorso Pubblico), a non-profit association that provides first aid and public assistance in a wide area near Brescia, in Italy, to a population of more than 20000 inhabitants. The association has grown over the years from 10 to 220 volunteers, providing today about 5000 first aid interventions a year. At COSP, volunteers play different roles, from driving ambulances to acting as rescuers, to coordinating the activities of other volunteers at the switchboard. COSP volunteers actually constitute a 'community of practice' [27], and share a high motivation and a strong desire to participate in the achievement of an important goal, namely saving human lives.

Y. Dittrich et al. (Eds.): IS-EUD 2013, LNCS 7897, pp. 201–216, 2013.

The activities at the non-profit association could be naturally sustained by Web 2.0 technologies, and especially by collaborative web mapping systems, which may help COSP volunteers obtain detailed and up-to-date information about the territory. Nevertheless, members of COSP still prefer keeping on using traditional paper-based maps to plan their interventions, as well as going on taking training sessions through PowerPoint^{TM} presentations to transfer knowledge about the territory from senior to novice drivers. The reasons underlying this situation are manifold. First of all, most volunteers come from different professional fields, have different cultural background, and are generally not so confident in computer-based systems. Lack of trust in new technologies is often the main problem for this type of user communities. As reported in [22], with reference to the fire response domain, firefighters still keep on using printed A5 cards representing parts of the city map, instead of using GPS navigators. Similarly, COSP volunteers do not rely on navigator satellite systems the ambulances are equipped with, because they do not generally suggest optimum routes for emergency vehicles. Some COSP volunteers currently use Google Maps, but they would not use it for COSP activities since it is considered too general and not well-suited to their domain and needs: they would fear making mistakes while using it or loosing precious time while preparing an intervention, if they do not find quickly the necessary indications to reach the target place.

Consolidated paper-based practices, lack of trust in information technologies, inexperienced and heterogeneous users, need for self-sufficiency, and limited budget are some of the typical problems that one usually finds in 'community informatics', intended as the design and management of computer-based systems for non-profit communities, non-governmental social service providers and local government agencies [1].

A first goal of our design project was thus to develop, with the collaboration of COSP volunteers, a web mapping application, which, on one hand could exploit existing web mapping services (including Google Maps), but, on the other, encapsulate relevant knowledge of COSP domain, being customized to the first aid domain and the skills of COSP volunteers. During the design of the first version of the application, volunteers' expectations on the system under design increase. In particular, a more collaborative application was required: volunteers asked for a virtual space they could directly shape and enrich to actively build their knowledge about the territory and share it within the COSP community. In other terms, volunteers felt the natural need of transforming themselves from mere consumers to producers of knowledge useful to their domain, namely, with Fisher's words, they required "a shift from consumer cultures to cultures of participation" [4, p. 42]. A second design cycle was thus carried out to obtain a collaborative web mapping system satisfying these new demands.

The paper presents the experience concerning the design and development of this system, called FirstAidMap. It illustrates how the components of the culture-of-participation framework discussed in [4] – meta-design, social creativity, and richer ecologies of participation – progressively emerged in the project. The considered case study shows that, in community informatics more than in other domains, users must be directly involved in system design, and called to be active participants at use time.

The paper is organized as follows: Section 2 discusses related work. Section 3 presents the first design cycle of the application. Section 4 illustrates the second design cycle, carried out to integrate functionality for knowledge creation and system adaptation in FirstAidMap. Section 5 aims to draw the main lessons learnt from this experience and delineate future research directions.

2   Related Work

Geographic maps are one of the most ancient and useful tools for displaying and creating knowledge about the places where we live [17]. This characteristic is emphasized in the digital era, where maps become dynamic and interactive. They are dynamic since they usually display data from a database and, if these data change, map visualization changes accordingly. Maps are also interactive in that different users working on the displayed map can add, reorganize or change the information to be displayed, thus creating new knowledge about a territory.

Geographic information systems (GIS) are the early software systems introducing digital maps as displays for information located in databases. They allow one to perform sophisticated operations on geographic information organized in map layers. However, GISs are usually designed for communities of geographers or expert in geographic information generally, whilst inexperienced users are often unable to use them [26], [12]. Even though GIS usability has been considered in some studies (e.g., [20]) and methods have been proposed for user-centered design of GISs [14], [24], the research in this area is mainly focused on effective knowledge visualization and retrieval, also called 'geovisualization' [18], rather than on the design of easy-to-use GISs. Particularly, geovisualization is playing an important role in the emergency domain (see for example: [18], [25], [2], [11]). In this context, geovisualization tools are aimed at representing cartographic content about the occurrence of certain events (e.g. a fire, a chemical disaster, a flu epidemic) and their evolution. Less emphasis is given to the representation of territory knowledge necessary to reach a given place with an emergency vehicle, with the exception of the study presented by Nadal-Serrano [22] for the design of web cards that resemble the printed cards used by firefighters for incident response preplanning.

As an alternative to GISs and geovisualization systems, collaborative web mapping systems can be used for free by a vast population of users, because they do not require particular competencies and they are generally usable. Collaborative web mapping systems allow users to visually define spaces by enabling them to choose what to map according to their own goals, knowledge and practices [10]. Furthermore, web maps can be regarded as virtual spaces created by end users and totally evolved at their hands and thus become social media [19]: while accessing and managing the information associated with the map, users interact directly or indirectly with other people, by sharing and exchanging knowledge related to the territory.

Among collaborative web mapping systems, Google Maps is certainly the most famous and used worldwide. It enables users to create personalized maps and share them with relatives and friends. Particularly, users can create their own maps by using place markers, shapes, and lines to define a location, an entire area, or a path. However, the interaction with tools for map personalization is still too much programmer-oriented, with terminology and interaction style that often intimidate some users. Furthermore, working on a shared map, possibly with different roles, is not supported adequately. Last but not least, Google Maps is not domain-oriented, being general enough to address the needs of different user communities, and enabling a wide range of activities and different kinds of knowledge to be represented on the map.

Other systems, like WikiMapia (www.wikimapia.org), allow map sharing, even though their main goal seems the creation of social networks rather than virtual places where to accumulate and share knowledge for specific and common purposes. User-generated street maps are supported in OpenStreetMap as well, an extensive and effective project involving a user community that is increasing exponentially [13]. Anyway, in these applications, users constitute informal groups, characterized by common interests in a same place. In other terms, they are aimed at supporting communities of interest; whilst, according to the characterization presented in [15], in our case, there is a need for a system to be used by a community of practice that has to share knowledge about territory for faster first aid [9]. Furthermore, it must be regarded as a system that belongs to the community informatics tradition.

Community informatics is characterized by an increasing need of participation on behalf of community members, due both to the continuing growth in the request for services by the community and to limited budget flexibility reserved in such organizations to information technology. Therefore, in a community informatics domain, an interactive system must be inexpensive, easy to use, and customizable by the community members; moreover, its configuration, management and enhancement must be carried out within the community, by limiting as much as possible the intervention of software professionals. However, as observed in several projects [1], [7-8], community members do not usually have high competencies and expertise in information technologies; in addition, their motivation to learn a new work practice or technical skills strongly depends on the goal value with respect to the individual effort.

To cope with these problems, a culture of participation [3-4] should be adopted, in order to provide users "with the means to participate and to contribute actively in personally meaningful problems" [4, p. 42]. Particularly, three major components constitute the theoretical framework for cultures of participation [4]: 1) *meta-design*, that is the creation of a socio-technical infrastructure in which new forms of collaboration can come alive by allowing systems to be modified at use time [5]; 2) *social creativity*, which allows all voices being heard to frame and solve a complex problem and to support people interacting each other and through shared artefacts; 3) *richer ecologies of participation*, which foresee the creation of different levels of participation on the basis of the different roles that community members can play or would like to play.

In the following, we illustrate how these three components progressively emerged in the FirstAidMap project as a consequence of an iterative design work carried out with representative end users.

3   Supporting Driver Training: First Design Cycle

In the FirstAidMap project, two participatory design cycles have been carried out: the former to build a first version of the application to support ambulance drivers and driver instructors in training activities; the latter to cope with the new emerged requirements and collaboration needs. In both design cycles, three volunteers of the COSP association participated in the design process. They have a deep knowledge of the non-profit association and its needs. Two out of them are experienced ambulance drivers, also playing the role of instructors of new drivers. The last volunteer is an ambulance driver who has been collaborating with the association for more than 5 years. In this section we present the main results of the first design cycle.

3.1   User Profile and Task Analysis

Interviews and brainstorming sessions with the three COSP volunteers allowed exploring the characteristics of the COSP association, identify the profiles of the intended users, analyze their tasks, and define the requirements for the new system.

At the beginning of the project, FirstAidMap was intended for ambulance driver instructors who possess deep knowledge of the territory and have a long experience in driving ambulances as volunteers. It was also intended for all ambulance drivers and driver assistants interested in keeping themselves up-to-date. These volunteers share a common motivation in helping others, offering their time to COSP activities, but their primary job ranges among a variety of possibilities. Most of them are not young people and have no specific competence in information technology. Usually, they are able to browse the web and use web mapping applications, such as Google Maps. Furthermore, driver instructors are able to use office applications as novice users, especially PowerPoint[TM].

As emerged from the interviews, navigator satellite systems are not considered sufficient and satisfactory to carefully assist ambulance drivers and the whole emergency crews in bringing medical care to serious patients timely. Navigator systems, indeed, do not take into account critical issues when suggesting quickest paths to a place, such as roads with humps or uneven road surfaces (really dangerous in case of patients on board), road yards in progress or weekly open-air markets causing detours that can irreparably delay the provision of first aid. Due to these limitations, COSP volunteers do not rely on navigator systems, but they rather prefer trusting in their knowledge and expertise of the territory to decide how to reach a given place quickly and in a safe manner. For this reason, driver instructors regularly carry out training sessions for the other volunteers. During a training session, instructors describe the most important characteristics of the territory where COSP operates (including about fifteen different villages), and show possible changes occurred since the last training session. Driver instructors carry out training sessions by preparing PowerPoint[TM] slides with annotated maps of the different villages that they comment and illustrate in detail.

3.2   Data and Functional Analysis

Representative volunteers participating in the domain and task analysis revealed soon their interest in a system for map navigation similar to Google Maps, but customized to the specific needs and characteristics of their community.

Therefore, the first requirement was to develop a web application based on existing mapping services, which could be specifically suited to the training of new ambulance drivers.

The digital map should have been the main component of the application; its interactive nature obviously should have increased the ability of instructors to explore the map with respect to the static versions.

Furthermore, the map should have been easy to explore by users with limited experience and competencies in information technology. Particularly, map zooming and panning activities should have been facilitated. In this respect, a 'direct zoom' function to a selected set of villages was explicitly required, because instructors, during training sessions, are used to present and describe all the characteristics of a single village simultaneously.

Finally, the map should have contained all the information the specific community requires about the territory. Three types of information were recognized as crucial for COSP work: *zones*, *points of interests* and *notifications*. Such information are all necessary to guide ambulance drivers to the place where a medical assistance is needed. A *zone* is an area on the map with common characteristics; it groups together several points of the map satisfying some condition, namely a set of roads or neighborhoods reachable through a same ambulance route from the COSP offices. A *point of interest*, or briefly POI, is a place on the map, more precisely a fixed and stable element on the territory that acts as a reference point for ambulance drivers and can help drivers to find their way to a place. As in navigator satellite systems, a POI can be a church, a sports ground, a square and so forth. However, it can also be a more specific reference point for an ambulance driver such as a bridge, a dangerous road or a traffic light. Finally, a *notification* provides alert information about a critical situation that can interfere with first aid interventions. It describes a critical condition occurring in a given place and for a period of time that may hamper the attainment of a certain place, e.g. the work in progress in a specific area of interest or the temporary modification of the road network of a neighborhood due to a demonstration. Differently from zones and POIs, notifications:

1. Often convey critical information about the territory;
2. May have a limited validity, e.g. the closing of a motorway tollbooth due to work in progress that may last one week;
3. May refer to events occurring with a certain frequency, e.g. the open-air market that takes place in a square each Wednesday morning.

All these types of information should enrich the map with semantics relevant for the COSP domain. However, they can constitute a lot of information, which altogether may confuse the map user. Therefore, to avoid information overload, such information should have been organized in different levels to be enabled/disabled, according to users' needs and preferences.

3.3   Design

After the requirements analysis, a set of static mock-ups have been prepared and used during the meetings with representative COSP volunteers to discuss whether the needs they had previously expressed have been satisfied, to obtain their suggestions for improving the system look-and-feel and possibly to collect new requirements.

An interactive prototype was then designed and developed. Figure 1 shows a screenshot of this first version of FirstAidMap.

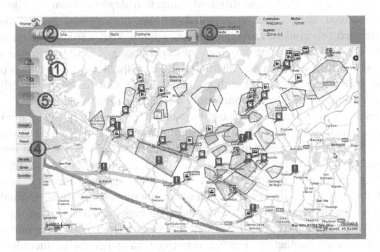

Fig. 1. The first version of FirstAidMap

As the reader can notice, the screen space is almost totally filled with the map. Different types of map (road, satellite, or hybrid) can be selected and retrieved on the fly through different web mapping services (Google Maps, Yahoo! or Visual Maps). The information relevant for the COSP domain is included within proper information levels: zones are represented as interactive semi-transparent orange polygons; POIs are represented through icons that resemble POI meaning (a church, a soccer balloon to indicate a soccer field, a train to indicate the railway, etc.); notifications are represented by square red icons with an exclamation mark inside.

The map is surrounded by a variety of widgets to carry out the following activities:

- Navigate the map through the common tools for panning and zooming in/out (widget no. 1 in Figure 1), or by using the mouse left button and wheel;
- Search for a place, by inserting an address in the search bar (widgets no. 2) or selecting a village from the combo box through the 'direct zoom' component (widget no. 3);
- Personalize the visualization (through the selector widgets no. 4) to choose the type of map to be displayed or the web mapping service;

- Enable/disable the information levels for zones, POIs and notifications (selector widgets no. 5);
- Select an element (zone, POI, or notification) by a mouse click on the element itself, in order to access a pop-up presenting some detailed information about the selected element.

3.4   Evaluation

To gather preliminary user feedback and assess to which extent this first prototype satisfied COSP needs and expectations, an experiment has been conducted with a group of seven COSP volunteers (five males and two females). Their ages ranged from 24 to 49 years. They held different education degrees, from middle to high school, till laurea degree, and represented various professional backgrounds: the sample included two civil servants, an artisan, a housewife, a student and a software developer. They all had at least two years of experience at COSP by playing the role of ambulance driver and/or driver instructor. Five of them were using the computer daily and had already accessed online maps, using Google Maps mainly. Two volunteers declared to use the computer only a few times in a week.

Participants were asked to carry out two tasks for evaluating the searching and exploration functionality offered by the system. The test was performed at the COSP office at the end of participant shifts. An introduction session was carried out before the experiment to show test participants the main functionality of the application. During task execution, qualitative data about FirstAidMap usability have been collected through direct observation. Then, an anonymous post-questionnaire was submitted to participants to investigate their opinions about the easiness of the interaction with the application, the effectiveness and efficiency of its components, and the application aesthetics. Further questions have been also included in the questionnaire to gather additional user comments and ideas for improving the application.

In the experiment, all participants were able to interact soon with the map and the tools offered by the system. They successfully completed both the assigned tasks. The most significant problems experienced by test participants were related to the identification of a target point within the map (its marker was hardly distinguishable from POIs), and the map dragging when information levels were active.

User opinions gathered through the post-questionnaire provided the design team with important feedback. Participants expressed their desire to contribute to content insertions, with the aim of sharing their knowledge of the territory with other volunteers and thus contributing to improve the COSP service. They also recognized, in some cases, the need of defining new types of POIs and notifications.

4   Fostering Cultures of Participation: Second Design Cycle

After the evaluation of the first prototype, the design team, including the three representative volunteers, met again to discuss the results of the test with users. In that meeting, the design team reflected on the emerging motivation of users to participate in content creation and system evolution.

As a consequence, representative volunteers realized that a system where users could apply their knowledge of the territory in a more extensive and collaborative way would have better supported their daily practice. They realized that what they need was not simply a training system through which they could learn and teach the characteristics and the dangers of the territory, but also an interactive space that all volunteers could shape to build and share their knowledge on the territory, and thus collaborating to bring first aid to patients timely.

The emerging idea, which subsequently permeated the second phase of the project, was therefore considering all COSP volunteers as a fundamental source of knowledge related to the management and provision of first aid in a given territory.

This opened up a different perspective on system design where the components of the framework for cultures of participation described in [4] naturally emerged.

4.1   Meta-design

Sustaining and encouraging COSP volunteers to participate in shaping the map according to their needs and preferences became the new goal to be pursued, and thus led to the adoption of a meta-design approach.

Indeed, it was necessary to provide users with proper tools for enriching the map with significant and up-to-date information, along with functionality for customizing map visualization and monitoring users' activities. Moreover, this should have been achieved without forcing COSP volunteers to become expert neither in information technology nor in cartography, as many commercial geographic information systems require [26], [12]. The aim was to create a community able to manage and evolve the system without the intervention of software professionals.

A new usage scenario has been identified, beyond driver training: using FirstAidMap as a support tool while preparing an emergency intervention, in order to identify the characteristics of the area around the ambulance destination place. Indeed, to carry out this task, ambulance drivers still use traditional paper-based maps available at COSP offices and annotated with their comments and notes.

Thus, the design team started to study how 'to transform' COSP volunteers from passive users into co-designers of map content. The aim was to design and develop a new version of FirstAidMap enriched with end-user development (EUD) [16] features that, not only could support users in creating and sharing knowledge on the territory in an easy and natural way [9], but also that could encourage and motivate them to participate. To this end, the level of complexity of activities should have been appropriate to the COSP volunteers' individual skills and situations, and possibly allow them to easily move up from less complex to more complex activities. In this way, advanced functionalities should have been made available to users progressively, without forcing them to learn such functionalities soon. Advanced functionalities should not have been intrusive and distract users from their primary task; at the same time, they should have encouraged users in experimenting system adaptation and modification. Moreover, some form of acknowledgement should have been foreseen, such as a clear association between contents and their creators.

4.2   Towards a Rich Ecology of Participation

For the new version of FirstAidMap different user roles have been identified, which correspond to the different roles that volunteers may play in contributing content.

All COSP volunteers should be able to access the system easily, without any authentication mechanism[1], as *visitor* users, just to explore the map-based content, visualize the map based on their needs and interests, and eventually point out a danger or a real-time update (e.g. a detour, an hazard), which can interfere with first aid interventions, by adding a new notification.

Like visitor users, ambulance *drivers* can access the map and the associated information, visualize active notifications, and possibly insert new ones. However, they are required to log in FirstAidMap and consult the map before each emergency intervention, in order to check possible alert situations in the route to the emergency site. This organization rule suggested by volunteers that participated in design was a consequence of the new usage scenario of FirstAidMap.

A volunteer logged in the system as *contributor* user is provided with advanced tools and functionality to create and modify zones, POIs and notifications in addition to access and explore the knowledge base as visitors or drivers.

Finally, more active and experienced COSP volunteers should be able to perform activities to let both the content and the whole system evolve according to the COSP community's needs, thus acting as *administrator* users. An administrator is a power user who manages user profiles, system accesses and all the information associated with the map (POIs, zones and notifications). Furthermore s/he is responsible for configuring the system according to the COSP volunteers' needs.

This classification of end-user roles (see Figure 2) is characterized by a gradual increase in the complexity of the activities assigned to them, according to the principle of "gentle slope of complexity" [21]. The usage of the application should motivate and encourage COSP volunteers to become more active in their collaboration to map enrichment. It is worth noticing that a migration path of users [3] is foreseen in this classification: after a first period of basic interaction with the system as visitor or driver users, COSP volunteers may wish to become contributors to add and manage zones and POIs, beyond inserting notifications only. In a similar way, a contributor could wish to become an administrator, possibly collaborating with other administrators in the definition of new kinds of POIs and notifications.

The different participation mechanisms may foster a mutual support for knowledge accumulation and sharing. Volunteers that are more knowledgeable of some particular area, or that occasionally discover some new information, may make their knowledge available to the community as soon as possible, even accessing the system just as visitors to add notifications. Each volunteer's contribution may stimulate reciprocity, especially when information is regarded as crucial to find the best path for an intervention. The idea of associating zones and POIs with the authors' name allows recognizing not only each volunteer's contribution, but also the relationships that the different volunteers have with specific places. In this way, knowledge on the map may stimulate interactions among volunteers, beyond the use of the system for first aid interventions, and re-enforce the sense of belonging to the community.

---

[1] The underlying assumption is that the system is accessible only on the COSP intranet.

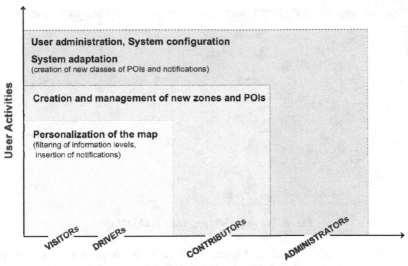

COSP volunteers participating in map shaping

Fig. 2. The rich ecology of participation of FirstAidMap

4.3   Encouraging Social Creativity

To include functions concerned with insertion of new content and system administration, it was necessary redesigning the layout of FirstAidMap and enriching its interaction experience. The three representative COSP volunteers have been involved again in the participatory design of the new version of FirstAidMap. In this way, system appropriation by volunteers further increased, while considering their perspective helped designing the EUD mechanisms to be made available to the different user roles.

In this second version of the application, after selecting the map consultation button in the home page, a visitor or a driver user accesses the map view page shown in Figure 3[2]. Here, the user can interact with the map by clicking on the zoom in/out and pan widgets or using the mouse wheel and left button. S/he can also select an icon on the map, so as a pop-up window appears to display its textual details (in the example, it is a notification informing about traffic deviation due to the construction of a new roundabout). On the right of the map there is a navigation panel where the user can: i) customize the map visualization by selecting its type (road, hybrid or satellite map) and the web mapping service (Google, Yahoo!, Visual Maps); ii) filter the map-related information to be displayed (zones, POIs, notifications); iii) search a specific place by specifying its address or selecting a village from a list.

---

[2] The figure refers to a driver user authenticated in the system. A driver is allowed to perform the same activities of visitor users, but FirstAidMap logs his/her activities. This feature allows checking a posteriori if drivers consulted the map before starting their interventions.

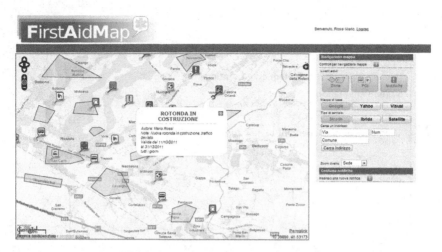

Fig. 3. The map view page of FirstAidMap

Under the navigation panel in Figure 3, there is a notification manager panel allowing the user to insert notifications by characterizing them with a name, a description, a validity period, a frequency and a severity degree. This feature is a result of the social creativity in design: indeed, it was an explicit request of representative end users, because every COSP volunteer should have the possibility to notify to the community new dangerous situations. This also allows volunteers to become confident with content creation, according to the idea that providing everyone with (few) tools for participating encourages changes in human behavior and social organization, and thus social creativity at use time.

Obviously, social creativity increases if a consistent number of volunteers log in the system as contributor users. To this end, these users find in the interface three more panels to manage zones, POIs and notifications respectively (Figure 4). Each item in these panels can be selected by the user to perform a specific action, namely *insertion, modification* or *deletion* of zones, POIs and notifications respectively; the corresponding sub-panel is thus expanded to show all the information necessary to carry out the selected action. Only a sub-panel, and thus only one functionality, can be active at any time. This allows reducing errors and increasing user performance while updating content. For example, to insert a new zone (Figure 4), the user should select the 'manage zones' panel, and within this panel, open a sub-panel for zone insertion. In this state of the application, the interaction with the map allows drawing a new zone, and a simple form allows completing the data about the zone being drawn.

Finally, most experienced and skilled COSP volunteers can log in the system as administrator users. As a member of the COSP staff, an administrator user will not necessarily be an expert in system administration, but just a power user, with some deeper knowledge in information technology with respect to the other volunteers. Therefore, s/he must be supported by easy-to-use tools and user-oriented terminology. To this end, a separate section of the application has been created to carry out monitoring activities, manage user profiles, configure and adapt the application.

Figure 5 shows the page devoted to system adaptation. At the top, the user can select the base map to be loaded when the application starts. Then, s/he can manage the types of POIs and notifications by changing the existing ones or defining new types. In this way, the visual aspect of POIs and notifications can change at use time. The administrator can define a new type of POI or notification by inserting a name and selecting an icon from those available in a group of radio buttons. If the user does not find a suitable icon, s/he can load a new image on the system (Figure 5).

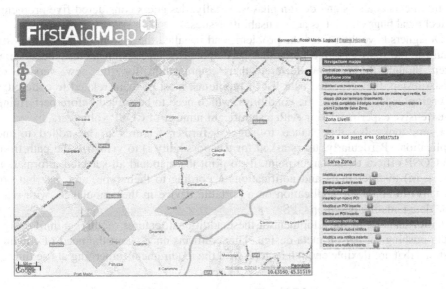

Fig. 4. Adding a zone to FirstAidMap

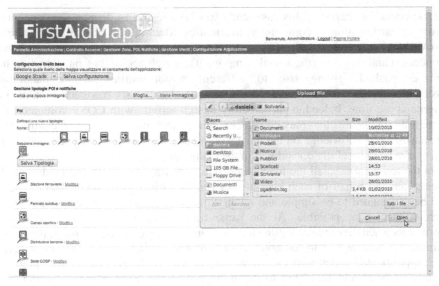

Fig. 5. The page for managing POI and notification types

4.4   Evaluation

Two outside evaluators have carried out a heuristic evaluation [23] of the second version of FirstAidMap. They identified 60 usability problems, which were then discussed with the design team, in order to identify possible solutions and their priorities. During this meeting, four usability problems were judged false positives. More precisely, evaluators classified as usability problems the appearance and behavior of some widgets that were explicitly discussed and decided during the requirements analysis and design phases. Finally, designers considered five problems as technical bugs and not as actual usability issues.

Designers have then fixed the problems and installed the system at COSP, in order to allow the representative users that participated in the design to test the system. Even though these users declared their appreciation for the new version of FirstAidMap, they reported us a list of problems, most of them related to code bugs emerging under some specific conditions, which need to be solved before performing an extensive experimentation with a significant number of COSP volunteers.

Users took also the chance to suggest further features to be added to the application. Particularly, users asked for the possibility i) to visualize the path from the COSP offices to the target point, ii) to print the map and all selected information levels, iii) to filter POIs and notifications according to their type, and, last but not least, iv) to enjoy the application on a portable device in the ambulance, with real-time data updating based on GPS.

Unfortunately, the development of these additional features requires a third design cycle pushing further on meta-design. This confirms once again the need of creating systems that are flexible enough to cope with the requirements emerging at use time.

5   Discussion and Conclusion

The experience gathered in this case study has been useful to deepen the concept of culture of participation in community informatics. Meta-design contributed to create FirstAidMap as a living entity [6], composed by a software system (the technical component) and its users (the social component). A rich ecology of participation has been established, giving rise to different responsibilities and collaboration possibilities for COSP volunteers. Moreover, social creativity has been sustained at design and use time. Indeed, a participatory design activity with COSP volunteers led to create EUD features that may engage, encourage and motivate users in contributing and sharing their knowledge on the territory. In particular, usability aspects and social issues have been carefully considered in the design of such features.

On the technical side, all the functionalities for inserting new data and modifying the existing ones on behalf of each kind of user (visitor, driver, contributor, administrator) have been designed to be simple and intuitive, in order to foster the participation of as much volunteers as possible. At the same time, users are not forced to become contributors when they are not willing to: for example, they can first approach the system as simple visitors, then try to add notifications and finally ask for the possibility to access more sophisticated functionalities. Moreover, in FirstAidMap, objects and tools are properly grouped and presented to the users only when needed, thus limiting error possibilities and supporting a more efficient interaction.

On the social side, it is crucial to let each user contribute her/his knowledge as in the traditional paper-based practice. The main motivation for this activity - underlying also the traditional practice - is that it is carried out for an important cause, namely saving lives. However, FirstAidMap creates further opportunities for social rewards: for example, the contributor's name is associated with zones, points of interests and notifications, and this can be recognized by all volunteers using that information. Participation may yield personal, social and professional benefits: personal benefit is achieved when "I feel better" by realizing the importance of my participation; social benefit can emerge from the fact that "colleagues may use and appreciate my contribution" or, more importantly, that "lives are saved also thanks to myself"; professional benefit could be a consequence of approaching a software system as a non-expert in information technology, who progressively migrates from the role of visitor to that of administrator ("I can learn some more IT").

For the future, we plan to integrate the system with further mechanisms for the evolution of its technical and social components. Thus, on the one hand, EUD tools must be implemented to extend the system with advanced functionalities, such as the possibility for users to create new information levels or develop content filters; on the other hand, different forms of rewarding must be studied to encourage user migration path towards co-developing roles. Personal, social and professional benefits must be understood better and sustained by studying further EUD mechanisms, by going beyond the mere technological aspects. Finally, we would like to test the system in other application domains where knowledge about territory is a fundamental source for problem solving, e.g. logistics, transport by courier, and so on.

Acknowledgments. The author wishes to thank Loredana Parasiliti Provenza for her support in carrying out the FirstAidMap project. The volunteers of COSP Mazzano are also acknowledged. I am then grateful to Francesca Facchetti, Paolo Melchiori, Maddalena Germinario and Annamaria Percivalli for their contribution to the design, implementation, and evaluation of the prototypes.

References

1. Carroll, J.M., Rosson, M.B.: Participatory design in community informatics. Design Studies 28(3), 243–261 (2007)
2. De Groeve, T., Riva, P.: Early flood detection and mapping for humanitarian response. In: Proc. of the 6th Int. ISCRAM Conference, Gothenburg, Sweden (2009)
3. Fischer, G.: End-User Development and Meta-Design: Foundations for Cultures of Participation. J. of Organizational and End User Computing 22(1), 52–82 (2010)
4. Fischer, G.: Understanding, Fostering, and Supporting Cultures of Participation. Interactions XVIII(3), 42–53 (2011)
5. Fischer, G., Giaccardi, E.: Meta-Design: A Framework for the Future of End User Development. In: Lieberman, H., Paternò, F., Wulf, V. (eds.) End-User Development, pp. 427–457. Kluwer Academic Publisher, Dordrecht (2006)
6. Fischer, G., Grudin, J., McCall, R., Ostwald, J., Redmiles, D., Reeves, B., Shipman, F.: Seeding, Evolutionary Growth and Reseeding: The Incremental Development of Collaborative Design Environments. In: Coordination Theory and Collaboration Technology, pp. 447–472. Lawrence Erlbaum Associates, Mahwah (2001)

7. Fogli, D., Colosio, S., Sacco, M.: Managing Accessibility in Local E-government Websites through End-User Development: A Case Study. Int. J. Universal Access in the Information Society 9(1), 35–50 (2010)
8. Fogli, D., Parasiliti Provenza, L.: A Meta-Design Approach to the Development of E-Government Services. J. of Visual Languages and Computing 23(2), 47–62 (2012)
9. Fogli, D., Parasiliti Provenza, L.: Knowledge Sharing in the First Aid Domain through End-User Development. In: Fred, A., Dietz, J.L.G., Liu, K., Filipe, J. (eds.) IC3K 2010. CCIS, vol. 272, pp. 307–321. Springer, Heidelberg (2013)
10. Giaccardi, E., Fogli, D.: Affective Geographies: Towards Richer Cartographic Semantics for the Geospatial Web. In: Proc. AVI 2008, Naples, Italy, pp. 173–180 (2008)
11. Gupta, S., Knoblock, C.A.: Building Geospatial Mashups to Visualize Information for Crisis Management. In: Proc. of the 7th Int. ISCRAM Conference, Seattle, USA (2010)
12. Haklay, M., Jones, C.: Usability and GIS – why your boss should buy you a larger monitor. In: AGI GeoCommunity 2008, Stratford-upon-Avon, UK (2008), http://discovery.ucl.ac.uk/13850/1/13850.pdf
13. Haklay, M., Weber, P.: OpenStreetMap: User-Generated Street Maps. Pervasive Computing, 12–18 (October-December 2008)
14. Haklay, M., Zafiri, A.: Usability Engineering for GIS: Learning from a Screenshot. The Cartographic Journal 45(2), 87–97 (2008)
15. Herranz, S., Diez, D., Diaz, P., Hilz, S.R.: Classifying Communities for Design – A review of the Continuum from CoIs to CoPs. In: Proc. COOP 2012, Marseille, France (2012)
16. Lieberman, H., Paternò, F., Wulf, V. (eds.): End-User Development. Kluwer Academic Publishers, Dordrecht (2006)
17. MacEachren, A.M.: How Maps Work. The Guilford Press, New York (1995)
18. MacEachren, A.M.: Geovisualization for knowledge construction and decision support. IEEE Computer Graphics and Application 24(1), 13–17 (2004)
19. Marcante, A., Parasiliti Provenza, L.: Social Interaction through Map-based Wikis. PsychNology Journal 6(3), 247–267 (2008)
20. Masud, M., Hossain, D.: Usability Analysis of Geographic Information System Software: A Case Study. Int. J. of Software Engineering 2(2), 1–22 (2009)
21. Myers, B.A., Smith, D.C., Horn, B.: Report of the End-User Programming Working Group. In: Languages for Developing User Interfaces, pp. 343–366. Jones and Bartlett, Boston (1992)
22. Nadal-Serrano, J.M.: Towards very simple, yet effective on-the-go incident response preplanning: using publicly-available GIS to improve firefighters' traditional approach. In: Proc. of the 7th Int. ISCRAM Conference, Seattle, USA (2010)
23. Nielsen, J.: Heuristic evaluation. In: Nielsen, J., Mack, R.L. (eds.) Usability Inspection Methods. Wiley. New York (1994)
24. Sebillo, M., Tortora, G., Vitiello, G.: Special Issue on Visual Languages and Techniques for Human-GIS Interaction. J. of Visual Languages and Computing 18, 227–229 (2007)
25. Schafer, W.A., Ganoe, C.H., Carroll, J.M.: Supporting Community Emergency Management Planning through a Geocollaboration Software Architecture. Computer Supported Cooperative Work 16, 501–537 (2007)
26. Traynor, C., Williams, M.G.: Why are Geographic Information Systems Hard to Use. In: Proc. CHI 1995 Mosaic of Creativity, Denver, CO, pp. 288–289. ACM Press (1995)
27. Wenger, E., McDermott, R., Snyder, W.: Cultivating communities of practice: a guide to managing knowledge. Harvard Business School Press, Boston (2002)

End-User Development: From Creating Technologies to Transforming Cultures

Gerhard Fischer

Center for LifeLong Learning & Design (L3D)
Department of Computer Science and Institute of Cognitive Science
University of Colorado, Boulder USA
gerhard@colorado.edu

Abstract. In a world that is not predictable, improvisation, evolution, and innovation are more than luxuries: they are necessities. The challenge of design is
not a matter of getting rid of the emergent, but rather of including it and making
it an opportunity for more creative and more adequate solutions to problems.
End-User Development (EUD) provides the enabling conditions for putting
owners of problems in charge by defining the technical and social conditions
for broad participation in design activities. It addresses the challenges of fostering new mindsets, new sources of creativity, and cultural changes to create
foundations for innovative societies.

Grounded in the analysis of previous research activities this paper explores
(1) *conceptual frameworks* for EUD (including: socio-technical environments;
meta-design; and cultures of participation), (2) *models* guiding and supporting
EUD (including: the seeding, evolutionary growth, reseeding process model;
and richer ecologies of participation). These frameworks and models are briefly
illustrated in one specific application domain.

The paper concludes by articulating new discourse concepts and design-
tradeoffs to shape the future of EUD being understood as a *cultural transformation*
rather than only as a technology in creating software artifacts.

Keywords: socio-technical environments, meta-design, cultures of participation,
personally meaningful problems, control, participation overload, future research
agenda for EUD.

1 Introduction

In a world where change is the norm, EUD is a necessity rather than a luxury because
it is impossible to design artifacts (including software systems, socio-technical environments, and learning environments) at design time for all the problems that occur at
use time. The co-evolution of systems and users' practices requires socio-technical
environments that can evolve and be tailored continuously. An important objective for
the EUD perspective articulated in this article is that design as a process is tightly
coupled to use and it continues during the use of the system [1]. It sees the "unfinished" as an opportunity (by extending design time indefinitely) rather than as an

Y. Dittrich et al. (Eds.): IS-EUD 2013, LNCS 7897, pp. 217–222, 2013.

obstacle or as something to be avoided. Figure 1 provides an overview and illustrates the structure of this paper that tries to articulate a theoretically-guided and empirically-supported vision for the future of EUD as a cultural transformation rather than only as a technology to create software artifacts.

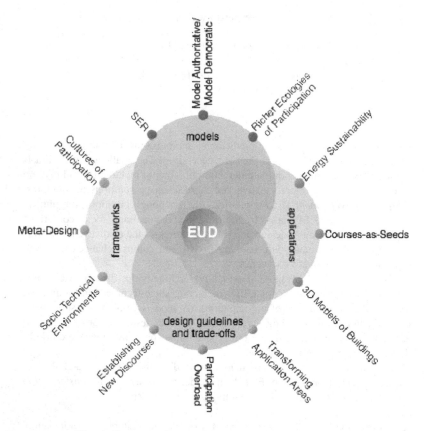

Fig. 1. Conceptualizing EUD as Cultural Transformation

2   EUD: From Creating Technologies to Transforming Cultures

EUD is instrumental for the ability to create, reformulate, externalize and share new knowledge rather than simply to comprehend existing knowledge. It appeals to diverse audiences by supporting them in designing and building their own artifacts by situating computation in new contexts, by generating content, and by developing tools that democratize design, innovation, and knowledge creation [2]. This broad vision of EUD complements and transcends a technological perspective of EUD [3] derived from *End-User Programming (EUP) and End-User Software Engineering (EUSE).*

Addressing Important Problems. A cultural transformation perspective of EUD includes technological developments as essential components but transcends them with additional objectives addressing requirements derived from the following fundamental problems [4]: (1) problems of a *magnitude* which individuals and even large teams cannot solve thus requiring the contribution of all interested citizens; (2) problems of a *systemic nature* requiring the collaboration of many different minds from a variety of backgrounds; and (3) problems modeling *changing and unique worlds* supported by open and evolvable systems based on fluctuating and conflicting requirements.

Inspirations, Perspectives and Influences for Conceptualizing EUD as a Transformational Culture. An early inspiration for conceptualizing EUD as a transformational culture was articulated by Ivan Illich with *convivial systems* envisioned to *"give each person who uses them the greatest opportunity to enrich the environment with the fruits of his or her vision"* [5]. To cope with the unattainable challenge of fully anticipating or envisioning use before actual use takes place, *participatory design* *("design for use before use")* needs to be complemented with *meta-design ("design for design after design")* [6].

Related Research Efforts. The conceptualization of EUD as a transformational culture has been explored by a number of research activities including: (1) the *Software Shaping Workshops* environment [7]; (2) the *hive-mind space (HMS) model* [8]; (3) the exploration of meta-design in *virtual worlds* [9]; and (4) the impact of *different relationship between design and use* [10].

3   Frameworks and Models for EUD as a Transformational Culture

Our research over the last decade has articulated and assessed different conceptual frameworks and models providing foundations to explore, to foster, and to support EUD as a transformational culture, including:

- *Socio-technical environments* [11] are focused on the systematic integration of two sets of design requirements: (1) *technical* components (computers, networks, building materials, and software substrates) and (2) *social* components (people, procedures, laws, collaboration, and communication policies).
- *Meta-design* is "design for designers" [12]: (1) allowing systems to be flexible and to evolve because they cannot be completely designed prior to use and (2) empowering end-users to drive the evolution.
- *Cultures of participation* providing all people with the means to participate and to contribute actively in personally meaningful problems [4].
- the *Seeding, Evolutionary Growth, Reseeding (SER) Process Model* is a descriptive and prescriptive model for creating the social and technical infrastructures in which new forms of collaborative design (designing seeds that can grow rather than complete systems) can take place that best fit an emerging and evolving context.
- *Rich Ecologies of Participation* break down the strict designer-user distinction. For cultures of participation to become viable and be successful, it is critical that a

sufficient number of participants take on the more active and more demanding roles. EUD research needs to analyze the necessary requirements associated with the more active roles, and develop social and technical interventions to support participants in their *migration paths* towards more demanding roles.

These developments support moving away from a world in which a small number of people define rules, create artifacts, make decisions for many consumers towards a world in which everyone has possibilities to actively participate by creating widely accessible artifacts.

4   Application: "Courses-as-Seeds"

The conceptual frameworks and models articulated in the previous sections have been explored (1) in a large number of major applications (including: open source software, Wikipedia, YouTube, Instructables, etc.), (2) by other members of the EUD research community (see section "Related Research Efforts" above), and (3) in our own work [4, 12]. One specific application illustrating the cultural transformation perspective of EUD is teaching courses at a university. Providing learners of all ages with the means to become co-creators of new ideas, knowledge, and products in personally meaningful activities presents one of the most exciting innovations and transformations in education with profound implications in the years to come.

Courses-as-seeds [13] is an educational approach that explores EUD in the context of fundamentally changing the nature of courses taught in universities (a large number of them being available at: http://l3d.cs.colorado.edu/~gerhard/courses/). It complements the currently increasingly popular approach of Massive Open Online Courses (MOOCs) with their promise and hype that online learning will give millions of students access to the world's best teachers. The goals of courses-as-seeds are (1) to overcome the impoverished conception that a course provides a learning experience in which an all-knowing teacher tells or shows unknowing learners something they presumably know nothing about; and (2) to foster *cultures of participation* [4] by providing all students with the opportunity to contribute.

5   New Discourses and Design Trade-Offs

EUD: Establishing New Discourses. EUD can and should establish new discourses, including an exploration of the following concepts:

- *Motivation:* Human beings are diversely motivated beings acting not only for material gain, but for psychological well-being, social integration, connectedness, social capital, recognition, and for improving their standing in a reputation economy. The motivation for going the extra step to engage in cultures of participation is based on the overwhelming evidence that people are more likely to like a solution if they have been involved in its generation; even though it might not make sense otherwise. Creating something personal (such as hand-knitted sweaters, home-cooked meals, etc.) even of moderate quality, has for many people a different kind of appeal than consuming something of possible higher quality made by others.

- *Control:* EUD supports users as active contributors who can transcend the functionality and content of existing systems. By facilitating these possibilities, *control* is distributed among all stakeholders in the design process. EUD erodes monopoly positions held by professionals, educational institutions, experts, and high-tech scribes. Empirical evidence gathered in the context of the different design activities indicates that EUD is less successful when users are brought into the process late (thereby denying them ownership) and when they are "misused" in fixing problems and in addressing weaknesses of systems that the developers should have taken care of themselves.
- *Changing Human Behavior:* Technology alone does not determine social structure nor does it change human behavior, but it can create feasibility spaces for new social practices [14] and can persuade and motivate changes at the individual, group, and community level.

Design Trade-Offs. There are numerous trade-offs to consider in establishing a EUD culture. Two important ones are:

- *Division of Labor versus Empowerment of Individuals:* Democratizing design by putting owners of problems in charge does not mean that there is no place for professionals in the future. By arguing for the independence of owners of problems from high-tech scribes, a legitimate question to ask is whether this will reverse the division of labor that has been a major driving force in advancing our societies. Professional designers play an important role in our society: most people are not able to and nor want to build their own houses, design their own cars, or write their own software systems or sorting routines. People do not have the time to participate equally in all aspects of human life in order to become fully engaged and informed, and therefore they rely on intermediaries to act in their interests.
- *Participation Overload and Personally Meaningful Problems.* Information overload has been discussed as a fundamental problem for the information society. Participation overload will be one of the most serious problems for EUD societies. Two pitfalls should be avoided: individuals (1) should not be forced to act as active contributors in situations where they want to be consumers (this is mostly the case in the context of problems and activities which are irrelevant to people); and (2) should not be restricted to consumers when they want to be active contributors and decision makers (this is mostly the case in personally meaningful situations).

6   Conclusions

EUD has moved from nonexistent to center stage. EUD perceived as a cultural transformation will create new social realities: public and private media will co-exist and blend together and professional and amateur contributions will complement each other. Providing all citizens with the means to become co-creators of new ideas, knowledge, and products in personally meaningful activities presents one of the most exciting innovations and transformations with profound implications in the years to come. This objective characterizes the vision behind EUD as a cultural transformation.

Acknowledgements. The author thanks (1) the members of the Center for LifeLong Learning & Design who have made major contributions to the frameworks, models, and systems described in this paper, and (2) Daniela Fogli, Monica Maceli, Julie Zhu, David Diez, Ben Koehne, Stefano Valtolina, and Tony Piccino who provided insightful comments and suggestions to an earlier version of this paper. The research was supported in part by several grants from the National Science Foundation. The writing of this article was facilitated by the support of a "Chair of Excellence" fellowship granted to the author by the University Carlos III of Madrid.

References

1. Henderson, A., Kyng, M.: There's No Place Like Home: Continuing Design in Use. In: Greenbaum, J., Kyng, M. (eds.) Design at Work: Cooperative Design of Computer Systems, pp. 219–240. Lawrence Erlbaum Associates, Inc., Hillsdale (1991)
2. von Hippel, E.: Democratizing Innovation. MIT Press, Cambridge (2005)
3. Burnett, M.M., Scaffidi, C.: End-User Development. In: Soegaard, M., Dam, R.F. (eds.) The Encyclopedia of Human-Computer Interaction, 2nd edn. The Interaction Design Foundation, Aarhus (2013)
4. Fischer, G.: Understanding, Fostering, and Supporting Cultures of Participation. ACM Interactions XVIII(3), 42–53 (2011)
5. Illich, I.: Tools for Conviviality. Harper and Row, New York (1973)
6. Binder, T., et al.: Design Things. MIT Press, Cambridge (2011)
7. Costabile, M.F., et al.: End User Development: The Software Shaping Workshop Approach. In: Lieberman, H., et al. (eds.) End User Development, pp. 183–205. Springer, Dordrecht (2006)
8. Zhu, L.: Hive-Mind Space: A Meta-design Approach for Cultivating and Supporting Collaborative Design, PhD, Dipartimento di Informatica e Comunicazione, Università degli Studi di Milano, Milano (2012)
9. Koehne, B., Redmiles, D., Fischer, G.: Extending the Meta-design Theory: Engaging Participants as Active Contributors in Virtual Worlds. In: Costabile, M.F., Dittrich, Y., Fischer, G., Piccinno, A. (eds.) IS-EUD 2011. LNCS, vol. 6654, pp. 264–269. Springer, Heidelberg (2011)
10. Maceli, M.G.: From Human Factors to Human Actors to Human Crafters: A Meta-Design Inspired Participatory Framework for Designing in Use, Ph.D. Dissertation, Drexel University (2012)
11. Fischer, G., Herrmann, T.: Socio-Technical Systems: A Meta-Design Perspective. International Journal of Sociotechnology and Knowledge Development 3, 1–33 (2011)
12. Fischer, G.: End-User Development and Meta-Design: Foundations for Cultures of Participation. Journal of Organizational and End User Computing 22, 52–82 (2010)
13. dePaula, R., et al.: Courses as Seeds: Expectations and Realities. In: Dillenbourg, P., et al. (eds.) Proceedings of the European Conference on Computer-Supported Collaborative Learning, Maastricht, Netherlands, pp. 494–501 (2001)
14. Benkler, Y.: The Wealth of Networks: How Social Production Transforms Markets and Freedom. Yale University Press, New Haven (2006)

Objects-to-think-with-together

Rethinking Papert's Ideas of Construction Kits for Kids in the Age of Online Sociability

Gunnar Stevens, Alexander Boden, and Thomas von Rekowski

University of Siegen, Human Computer Interaction, Siegen, Germany
{gunnar.stevens,alexander.boden,
thomas.vonrekowski}@uni-siegen.de

Abstract. The spread of the Internet has led to a change from a TV-childhood to a computer-childhood. We investigate how this shift towards networked forms of communication is reflected in constructionist learning environments and elaborate the concept of objects-to-think-with-together in the context of using computers as tool and social medium at the same time. In doing so, we propose four design aspects that should be considered in the context of socially-oriented constructionist learning environments: providing an integrated platform for construction and socializing, supporting re-mixing and re-using as well as self-expression and appreciation, allowing collaborative projects of non-collocated learners, and supporting enculturation and team-building.

Keywords: End User Development, Constructionism, Social learning, Social Media, Scratch, Logo, Constructionist Learning Environments.

1 Introduction

Several representative empirical studies have shown that children's media use has been changing over the last years. For example, in Germany a majority of children's households provide Internet access and 50% of children state that they are using the Internet on a regular basis; furthermore, 31% of the children state to (rather) conduct this activity on their own. This trend has been described by Hammer and Schmitt (2002) as a change from a TV-childhood to a computer-childhood, indicating the replacement of television as the lead medium in favor of computers and the Internet. At the same time, there has been a significant increase of social networks usage in the last years. One out of three children regularly use communication services such as online communities, chats and instant messengers and assert those as their online favorites.

These empirical findings demonstrate that online sociability has become a common part of children's everyday life worlds. Based on this situation, it is important to investigate how this shift towards networked forms of communication and creating/sharing could be integrated into collaborative learning environments for children, especially with regard to artifact-centered approaches of supporting learning such as constructionism.

Y. Dittrich et al. (Eds.): IS-EUD 2013, LNCS 7897, pp. 223–228, 2013.
© Springer-Verlag Berlin Heidelberg 2013

2   The Social Turn in Constructionist Learning

Constructionism as a learning approach has been developed by Seymour Papert in the 1970ies, adopting ideas from Piaget's constructivism as well as from Activity Theory (Papert 1980). His key thought is that knowledge cannot be exchanged in abstract forms. Instead, knowledge exchange is considered to be dependent on practical and cognitive re-construction on behalf of the learner. Hence, the construction of tangible and personally meaningful artifacts plays a seminal role for the learning process. Against this backdrop, a number of computer based environments for supporting constructionist learning have been developed, called constructionist learning environments (CLE, see for example Figure 1b, left).

The initial focus of Papert's work lay on the domain of technical sciences and individual learning approaches, where the computer serves as an "object-to-think-with" (Papert 1980) that allows learners to realize their personal objectives. At that time, it was a common necessity to edit the source code in one tool, then use another tool for compiling the code, and afterwards execute it manually. This cycle created a "gulf" between code and behavior analog to the gulf of evaluation and execution as outlined by Norman (1986). The seminal innovation of Papert's Logo environment was to bridge that gulf, by making the effects of coding directly visible for the learner.

Beyond the individual focus, recent research has a stronger focus on communities and social aspects of constructionist learning (Bruckman 1997; Chapman 2004; Shaw 1995). One example of this second generation approaches the concept of distributed constructionism elaborated by Resnick (1996) as a socially oriented enhancement of Papert's work. Intellectually, this second generation of constructionism is shaped by learning theories that emphasize the social and distributed nature of learning in practice (Wenger 1998; Salomon 1997). They are typically focused on collaborative learning efforts in communities, where the constructionist learning activities include several participants. In such settings, learning becomes richer and more effective, as

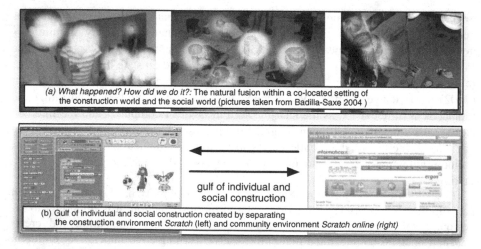

(a) *What happened? How did we do it?:* The natural fusion within a co-located setting of the construction world and the social world (pictures taken from Badilla-Saxe 2004)

gulf of individual and social construction

(b) Gulf of individual and social construction created by separating the construction environment *Scratch* (left) and community environment *Scratch online (right)*

Fig. 1. Social learning in (a) co-located learning environments and (b) computer mediated environments

affective, social and cognitive development is fostered reciprocally through the interaction with one's social environment (see Badilla-Saxe 2004 and Figure 1a).

Within settings such as schools, a shared social context is naturally given. The question of how to establish and support constructionist learning environments beyond this context, for instance on a local community level, has been a recent topic in research. Institutions like the Intel Computer Clubhouses (Resnick and Rusk 1996) or the Come_IN Computer Clubs (Stevens et al. 2005) in Germany demonstrate that by providing local, publicly accessible places to use computers, the participation of educationally deprived groups of society can be improved. In addition, several constructionist learning systems (e.g. Barricelli et al. 2011; Bruckman 1997; Shaw 1995) have been designed following the concept of distributed constructionism (Resnick 1996). The aim of these systems is to enhance computer based learning environments by incorporating social and cultural aspects (see also Figure 1b, right).

2.1   Providing Objects-to-think-with-together

So far we have outlined two topics that are mainly studied independently: the increased online sociability of children and the new insights about the social contexts of constructive learning. Bringing these topics together, we believe that it is time to reconsider Papert's influential idea in the light of the mentioned developments.

Given the potentials of the collaborative web, we think that it is time to extend this principle with regard to the mentioned social turn of education science represented e.g. by Wenger (1988). According to this view, social constructionism should be fostered by making the social relations that are conciliated by the artifacts visible in the learner's use context, embedding the children's online sociability into the context of the construction activities (much similar to the upheaval of initial constructionist approaches resolving the detachment between the design and use of learning artifacts). The integration of the social context is meant to transform the objects-to-think-with of individual community members to objects-to-think-with-together for the whole community, addressing both individual and community-contexts of learning in a unified approach where the computer serves as a medium and tool at the same time.

This thought is also related to recent threads in Activity Theory (Engeström 2005) which consider artifacts as boundary objects which have to be sufficiently tangible in order to be adoptable by users of various backgrounds, and at the same time robust enough to establish a common identity among social worlds. In this regard, digital construction kits as computational boundary objects can serve two major purposes, as noted by Fischer (2001): "(1) they can serve as objects to support the interaction and collaboration between different communities of practice, and (2) they can support the interaction between users and (computational) environments".

2.2   Bridging the Gulf between the Individual and the Social Construction

In the following, we want to elaborate the concept of "objects-to-think-with-together" in terms of design by using the concept as an analytic lens to study existing approaches discussed in the literature. Based on our considerations outlined above, we propose four design aspects that illustrate how the social dimension of artifacts could be supported.

Integrated Platform for Construction and Socializing

At a basic level, there is a need for an integrated platform that supports socializing between different learners and fosters the sharing of ideas and artifacts in a project based learning environment. In this platform, the construction editor and social tools should be tightly integrated with each other to avoid a gap between the social activities and the construction activities (see also the gap mentioned in Fig 1b). In the literature, we find game-oriented approaches that extend multi-player games by integrating collaborative game construction kits like MOOSE Crossing (Bruckman 1997) or that discuss multi-player construction games like Minecraft (Zuzanna 2011) as collaborative learning environments. Such approaches illustrate how construction and social interaction can be integrated with each other. However, existing work in this area is usually limited to games and does only support highly specific kinds of design projects.

Concerning this topic, the evolution of Scratch and Scratch online (Resnick et al. 2009) to Scratch 2.0 (see http://beta.scratch.mit.edu/) is highly interesting. Like Scratch, the new approaches rest on traditional programming ways of sharing projects that group code blocks and additional resources. However, Scratch 2.0 aims at developing this idea further by integrating Web 2.0 features, most notably by integrating an online code editor into their social platform. Other notable examples from outside the domain of CLE are Mash-up platforms such as Yahoo Pipes that combines mash-up editors with community services, thus minimizing the divide between editing and sharing of mash-ups (Grammel und Storey 2010).

Re-mixing, Re-using, Self-expression and Appreciation

Kids learn from observing and mimicking actions of others. In this context, artifacts of others typically serve as inspiration and blueprints for one's own project. This "monkey see-monkey do" style of construction (Gamma and Beck 2004) implies a need for supporting re-using and re-mixing of digital artifacts as well as a need for supporting their appropriation. In addition, the created artifacts also have an emotional side as these artifacts serve kids as a way for self-expression. Hence, in becoming an object of discourse, artifacts are used to share common interests, perspectives and ideas. In particular, they allow appreciating each other by appreciating each other's work. With regard to design, this implies a need for reusing artifacts made by others as well as commenting and rating them.

The first solutions that explicitly support the "monkey see monkey do" were the mentioned mash-up platforms, which allow users to re-use and -assemble existing web services to create their own solutions. In addition, users can tag and receive recommendations during construction activities based on the tagging information (Grammel und Storey 2010). With regard to CLE, Scratch online (Resnick et al. 2009) was maybe the first to provide tagging as well as re-mixing support. In addition, the system allows kids to comment and rate projects as well as inspect which project was re-mixed by whom in order to support the promote mutual appreciation among the community.

However, in a further step to realize the vision of objects-to-think-with-together, these features should also be embedded into the context of the construction activities (in order to provide for instance awareness about expertise and artifacts that fit the situated context). Regarding this aspect, CLE design might learn from newer Software

Engineering approaches. For instance, the tool STeP_IN (Nishinaka et al. 2007) uses existing recommendation algorithms to make software developers aware about local experts and documentation to Java components that are used in the actual context.

Collaborative Projects

Creating artifacts is a common goal and motivation for joint projects, in which the artifact will be constructed in a collaborative manner. This implies a need for synchronous and/or asynchronous environments for collaborative construction. There is a long vast body of work on supporting collaboration in synchronous and asynchronous contexts (for example in environments such as Wikipedia or Google Docs). Because of this, we were quite surprised that most of the existing project-oriented solutions like Scratch 2.0 or Mash-up editors do not support this social dimension of artifacts. Instead, projects are still owned by one person and collaboration can only be organized by sharing copies which each other.

However, quite interestingly, the situation is totally different in the case of game oriented CLE like MOOSE Crossing or construction-oriented games such as Minecraft. In these environments, kids can create virtual objects, spaces, and characters while interacting with one another e.g. through chats. Therefore, ethnographical studies would be highly interesting, how kids appropriate these systems and use them to work together.

Enculturation and Team Building

Last but not least, CLE 2.0 platforms should support enculturation and team building, as well as further aspects of social learning in the sense of Communities of Practice (Wenger 1998). For example, CLE should allow legitimate peripheral participation, enable gentle transitions from being a lurker to becoming a core team member, and allow scaffolding as well as seeking and offering help within the community. This topic is sporadically discussed in the literature, for example by Bruckman (1997) who notes that such ideas inspired her. In addition, Korn and Veith (2009) outline how Scratch could be extended through scaffolding mechanisms into that direction. Yet, what is missing is a systematic investigation of the design patterns that support enculturation and team building in online communities for kids as well as empirical studies about how such features are used in practice.

3   Discussion and Conclusion

In this paper, we have outlined that computational constructions are social artifacts that can serve as boundary objects between the self and the computational environment and the social world. Yet, this quality is hardly covered by the current CLE designs. In order to bridge the gulf between individual and social constructionist learning in communities, we have outlined the concept of objects-to-think-with-together that rethinks Papert's original idea in the age of online sociability and brings together the different facets of computational boundary objects by means of an integrated collaboration infrastructure within the application (Stevens 2009). We further identified a number of interesting examples that show steps towards how the concept could be realized. In our future work, we have to study how the different design concepts could be integrated in a coherent framework to improve the boundary object quality of artifacts mediating social relations. In particular, we plan on conducting ethnographical studies on how these features are being appropriated to understand the concept from within the construction and learning practices of the children.

References

Barricelli, B.R., von Rekowski, T., Sprenger, M.A., Weibert, A.: Supporting Collaborative Project Work in Intercultural Computer Clubs (2011)

Badilla-Saxe, E.: Constructionism, Complex Thinking and Emergent Learning. Constructionism 2010, Paris (2004)

Bruckman, A.S.: MOOSE Crossing. PhD Thesis, MIT, USA (1997)

Chapman, R.: Pearls of wisdom. In: Social Capital and Information Technology, pp. 301–331 (2004)

Engeström, Y.: Developmental work research. Bd. 12. Lehmanns Media (2005)

Fischer, G.: External and shareable artifacts as opportunities for social creativity in communities of interest. In: Computational and Cognitive Models of Creative Design (2001)

Gamma, E., Beck, K.: Contributing to Eclipse. Add.-Wesley (2004)

Grammel, L., Storey, M.-A.: A survey of mashup development environments. In: Chignell, M., Cordy, J., Ng, J., Yesha, Y. (eds.) The Smart Internet. LNCS, vol. 6400, pp. 137–151. Springer, Heidelberg (2010)

Korn, M., Veith, M.: Learning support through scaffolding collaborative project work. In: Proc. of CSCL 2009 (2009)

Hammer, V., Schmitt, C.: Computer in der Familie. Staatsinst. für Familienforschung an der Univ., Bamberg (2002)

Nishinaka, Y., Asada, M., Yamamoto, Y., Ye, Y.: Please STeP_IN: A Socio-Technical Platform for in situ Networking. In: Proc. of APSEC 2005 (2005)

Norman, D.A.: Cognitive engineering. In: User Centered System Design, pp. 31–61 (1986)

Papert, S.: Mindstorms: Children, computers, and powerful ideas. Basic Books (1980)

Resnick, M.: Distributed constructionism. In: Proc. of the 1996 International Conference on Learning Sciences, pp. 280–284 (1996)

Resnick, M., et al.: Scratch: programming for all. CACM 52(11), 60–67 (2009)

Resnick, M., Rusk, N.: The Computer Clubhouse: Preparing for life in a digital world. IBM Systems Journal 35(3.4), 431–439 (1996)

Salomon, G.: Distributed cognitions. Cambridge Univ. Pr. (1997)

Shaw, A.: Social constructionism and the inner city. Ph.D. Thesis, MIT (1995)

Stevens, G.: Understanding and Designing Appropriation Infrastructures. PhD Thesis, Universität Siegen, Germany (2009)

Stevens, G., Veith, M., Wulf, V.: Bridging among ethnic communities by cross-cultural communities of practice. In: Proc. of C&T 2005, pp. 377–396 (2005)

Wenger, E.: Communities of practice. Cambridge Univ. Pr. (1998)

Zuzanna, M.: Constructing identity in games: a case study of Minecraft on YouTube, University of York

End-User Development
in Tourism Promotion for Small Towns*

Augusto Celentano, Marek Maurizio, Giulio Pattanaro, and Jan van der Borg

Università Ca' Foscari Venezia, Italy
{auce,marek,giulio.pattanaro,vdborg}@unive.it

Abstract. This paper discusses the design and implementation of a system for promoting small towns based on the mash-up of various data sources for personalized mobile access. The positive issues and the open problems are discussed and evaluated in the frame of an experiment made in a region in Northern Italy.

1 Introduction

The increasing popularity of the Web has considerably affected the way business and marketing are conducted in every sector. Tourism is no exception: more and more travelers use Internet services to plan, document, and share their journeys; furthermore, they are often active contributors of social networks and personal blogs. Thanks to their richness in personal experiences and trustworthiness of electronic word-of-mouth, social contents are a very influential factor in travellers decision-making [1,2]: contributions (feedbacks, videos, etc.) uploaded by other web users are increasingly accessed during the vacation planning process [3]. These direct contributions add up to already existing sources like the official websites of a local tourism board; as a consequence, it is often difficult for a tourist to analyze and compare information available in several sources.

Central for the success of online tourism promotion are two behaviors of tourism operators: they need to provide complete and up-to-date information about a destination, and encourage a constant exchange of information with tourists [4,5]. This situation is particularly relevant when the chosen destination is a small town or a village, i.e., it is not among the most famous and discussed locations in a region. Such minor locations could, however, benefit from suggestions coming from shared information on the web more profitably than well known places who are adequately "self-promoting" at one side, and often overloaded with almost useless repeating standardized comments at the other side.

Here Web 2.0 applications may be very helpful: thanks to mash-up, third-party resources can be presented in a different way or used to create new web contents. Websites can make their information accessible via Application Program Interfaces (APIs), which define the way data can be retrieved and re-used. Although being a fairly recent topic, mash-ups have gained more and more importance in both the academy and industry. They are becoming an important instrument in the field of End-User Development (EUD), where experts who are not professional developers can use tools to

* Project supported by Regione Veneto, Italy, under the FSE programme.

Y. Dittrich et al. (Eds.): IS-EUD 2013, LNCS 7897, pp. 229–234, 2013.

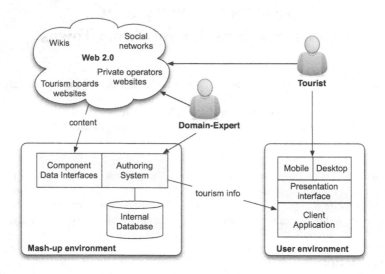

Fig. 1. The system architecture

create or modify software and organize complex data structures mixing existing information according to their needs. In tourism, mash-ups and EUD technologies are used to make the information about a destination easier to access and integrate [5]. Actually, although tourism destinations tend to be perceived and consumed by tourists as "*a brand comprising of a collection of suppliers and services*" [1], different actors are involved in the provision of tourism services. There are direct players like, e.g., hotel owners, but also community members and associations. As it has been underlined by public funding schemes as well [6], collaboration among these stakeholders is a general precondition for the successful development and promotion of a tourism destination. In such a scenario, domain experts can play a relevant role in integrating and delivering the information produced by the different actors.

This project wants to give tourism players the possibility to find, filter, aggregate, merge, and organize syndicated contents coming from different and heterogeneous sources. Three main issues are addressed: (1) the creation of an environment promoting tourism through the collaboration of different stakeholders; (2) the use of EUD techniques to implement such an environment; (3) the generation of a virtuous cycle to improve the quality of the information provided on the web. The system is expected to be cost-effective (already existing and open contents are extracted and re-used) and easy to maintain (if the integrated contents are updated in the original source, there will be an automatic update in the system as well). Since material directly generated by tourists (e.g., WikiTravel guides) is also integrated, the system is also expected to adopt a user-friendly language.

One could argue that, for small towns and villages, the information available on the Internet is not sufficient to provide a complete and up-to-date overview of these destinations. While in some cases this statement is valid, this is considered as an opportunity rather than as a definitive limit: if the required information is not present, it is easier and more effective to create it by using collaborative websites authoring tools, promoting the usage of well-know social networks from visitors, or accessing the already existing infrastructures (e.g. a regional tourism boards website content management system). In fact, the generation of open and accessible contents rather then that of closed and platform-specific ones is encouraged.

2 System Architecture

Figure 1 shows the systems architecture and actors. A domain expert accesses Web resources to be included in the guides through a set of *component data interfaces* to Internet websites and services, either by wrapping their APIs or by employing ad-hoc parsing solutions. An *authoring system* allows him/her to retrieve, organize, and classify web contents related to destinations. An *internal database* stores the parameters used to retrieve information from the web and the structure given to information, along with an updatable cache of the extracted contents. The application runs on different desktop and mobile devices, allowing the user to experience the content in a user-friendly and visually rich environment.

Data Model and Component Data Interface. The system data model is built around the concept of *tour*: each tour is an abstract subject of interest, such as "The Medieval Tour of Veneto" or "A Food & Wine Journey". Each tour is made of one or more *places* (i.e. cities or towns such as "Marostica" or "Castelfranco Veneto"); each place is associated with a set of *topics*; each topic represents a theme or object of possible interest to tourists (e.g. "Local Food", "Local Markets", or "Onara Marsh"). Topics are organized hierarchically to allow sub-specialization of broader subjects. Each tour, place, and topic has a set of *properties* — such as name, description, picture, and so on — which are stored in a local database. However, topics have also a set of attached objects, called *components*, whose content is extracted from web sources.

The component data interfaces are responsible for collecting tourism contents from heterogeneous web sources, such as destination marketing organizations' web pages, other official on-line documents, collaborative websites, personal pages, and social networks. Each interface can be based either on the source's APIs protocol or, if the source does not allow the use of APIs, on ad-hoc parsing solutions. The component data interface system is designed to be modular: each interface is an object that responds to a set of predefined methods. With this architecture new components can be added to the system without requiring remarkable efforts. The current implementation of the system features a set of component data interfaces to interact with some of the web sites and services considered as the most relevant for tourism purposes, in particular, for a visit to the locations of interest.

More specifically, a set of tourism promotion websites which are run by different levels of local authorities was looked at (the regional tourism board for Veneto, the seven provincial tourism authorities, and the different municipalities involved). Privately run websites (e.g., tour operators' websites) were analyzed as well, although priority was given to public authorities' ones.

Two component interfaces were developed to interact with such sources: *web article* and *web fragment*. A web article has a standardized format, hence it can be fully parsed to automatically extract only the relevant content; web fragments offer a more focused way to extract contents, using regular expressions written in the XPath language. At the time of writing, the component requires knowledge of XPath and must be considered a work-in-progress, not yet tailored for end users. Both component data interfaces were successfully used to extract data from institutional websites such as *Veneto Tourism* (`http://veneto.to`), *Veneto Natural Parks* (`http://www.parchiveneto.it`) as well as personal blog posts.

From a customer's point of view, the value of using personal and collaborative web sites as a source of tourism information lies in both the trustworthiness of personal experiences, and the familiarity users have with known sites. The system allows domain experts to interact with a number of collaborative web sites such as Wikipedia, Wikitravel, Flickr, YouTube and Google Maps.

Social networks have recently become an important asset in the tourism industry. When they are planning their journey, travelers trust the personal experience and opinion of relatives and friends, but also make use of social networks during and after their trip, thus generating interest in viewers that can easily become travelers themselves [7]. The system allows to leverage such potential by including contents from some of the major social networks such as Twitter and Facebook. Finally, links to other tourism mash-up applications allow domain experts to benefit from other authors' results. Although the selected sources are only a small portion of the available Internet tourism web sites and services, they appear to provide a good selection of contents for domain experts to mash-up a high quality overview of the selected destinations. To extend the system's possibilities, the object-oriented approach used to build the system enables an easy integration of new components into the system once a correct and stable interface has been defined.

The Authoring System. The authoring system allows domain experts to create, organize and manage tours. It is accessed through a web-based application, requiring neither a specific installation nor specialized plugins, with a graphical interface based on common knowledge and clear action feedback, thus allowing domain experts to easily operate it. It is worth pointing out that the authoring system's capabilities only cover the structure and classification of the model elements. The system does not work as a middleware to edit the components' data. Should, for instance, a domain expert feel the need to edit a destination's Wikipedia page, there is no reason not to use directly the website authoring tools, or any other application the domain expert is comfortable with. The system provides a direct link to such tools.

In the tourism domain, a number of different taxonomies and catalogues already exist. Each one is designed and used to manage heterogeneous tourism data. Ontologies facilitate the semantic integration of such heterogeneous data, and several publicly available formal tourism ontologies have been identified [8]. The project employs a simple, two-level, hierarchical ontology allowing domain experts to classify the contents. When an expert inserts a new topic in the system, he/she has to select one or more *themes* to describe it: each theme is a specialization of a *category*. The categories and themes taxonomy was developed by the domain experts themselves and is made specifically for the current project.

Topics are organized hierarchically: the classification of a topic is given by an algorithm that takes into consideration the themes the domain expert selects for the topic, and the classification of the topic's subtopics, recursively. Domain experts can classify directly only *topics*. Each *place* will be automatically classified by an algorithm that takes in consideration how that place's topics were classified. In the same way, *tours* are classified automatically according to their related places' classification. This mechanism ensures that, at any given moment, tours and places are classified by the actual content present in the guide.

The User Application. Tourists access the contents through a web application. Particular care is put on the mobile version of the application, since most tourists now travel with their own devices. Users can browse the available tours and select the one that best suits their needs, or just browse the different destinations individually. Tours, places, and topics are classified following the taxonomy presented above; in the user's application each category is characterized by a specific color, while each theme has its own icon to offer an immediate, clear, and visual contextualization to each of the proposed destinations and attractions.

3   Implementation

The authoring system was implemented as a web application using *Rails 3*, a framework based on the *Ruby* programming language. The administration system is accessible by multiple users with the adequate privileges. The component interface of the mash-up environment is designed according to the object-oriented paradigm, so that it is easy to develop and add new components. If domain experts need to gather data from a new service, it is sufficient to program a new component and notify the system. The component must define: a name; a method to extract data, either using the service's APIs or by ad-hoc parsing; a web form to input the data extraction parameters; a way to visualize the extracted data in HTML; a link to the original content.

Each component is allowed to save data in the main database to allow content caching, since fetching data for each request would not have been practical. For the automatic update of the information, each component instance can define how often the fetch operation must be performed by the system. While some data, like Wikipedia pages, are quite static and can be safely updated every week or month, other data, like twitter streams, need to be updated almost in real time.

The client-side application is a set of HTML pages interfacing with the server to allow tourists to browse the different tours, places, and topics. The Twitter Bootstrap 2.0 web library was used for rapid prototyping.

4   Discussion

Mash-ups allow for the combination and integration, within the same online tool, of different web sources, thus providing complete information about a specific destination. Furthermore, once original sources are modified, the periodical update of the mash-up process makes these modifications almost immediately visible in the system. Updates are visible in real time in the case of the social networks integrated into the system, thus making these sources the direct interaction channel between visitors and tourism players but also between different groups of tourists.

For the completeness of content it provides, the system here illustrated differs from already existing tourism websites and open-access information repositories. In these existing sources, one or more types of information (e.g., sport activities or cultural events) tend to predominate; users must access, compare and combine several sources with information styled in different ways. Only the information integration within the same system can provide a complete overview of what a destination can offer. Furthermore, an online system integrating social networks and wikis may also contribute to involve in local tourism development and promotion some categories of traditionally excluded stakeholders, like local associations and individual citizens.

Being these ones the main advantages of the system, some potential implementation issues need to be taken into account. For example, it may happen that an insufficient number of sources to mash up are available. It may also turn out that existing contents do not fully satisfy adequate quality standards. It is here believed that local tourism players can successfully cope with these potential issues: e.g., local players may decide to amend wiki contents by acting as individual editors.

Finally, as confirmed by some early informal talks with regional tourism stakeholders, it is important to highlight that this system can be fully successful only if the different categories of local tourism stakeholders do actually cooperate and collaborate. If no agreement is reached on the selection of the online sources to be mashed up, the system will not meet its objectives in terms of the quality of the information provided and interaction between tourists and local players.

References

1. Buhalis, D.: Marketing the competitive destination of the future. Tourism Management 21(1), 97–116 (2000)
2. Corigliano, M., Baggio, R.: On the significance of tourism website evaluations. In: Information and Communication Technologies in Tourism, pp. 320–331 (2006)
3. Kim, H., Fesenmaier, D.: Persuasive design of destination web sites: an analysis of first impression. Journal of Travel Research 47(1), 3–13 (2008)
4. Giannopoulos, A., Mavragani, E.: Traveling through the web: A first step toward a comparative analysis of European national tourism websites. Journal of Hospitality Marketing & Management 20(7), 718–739 (2011)
5. Linaza, M., Lölhöffel, F., Garcia, A., Lamsfus, C., Alzua-Sorzabal, A., Lazkano, A.: Mash-up applications for small destination management organizations websites. In: Information and Communication Technologies in Tourism 2008, pp. 130–140 (2008)
6. European Commission: Agenda for a sustainable and competitive European tourism. Technical report, Communication of the European Communities, COM (2007) 621 Final, Brussels (2007)
7. White, L.: Facebook, friends and photos: A snapshot into social networking for generating travel ideas. In: Sharda, N. (ed.) Tourism Informatics: Visual Travel Recommender Systems, Social Communities, and User Interface Design, pp. 115–129. IGI Global (2010)
8. Prantner, K., Ding, Y., Luger, M., Yan, Z., Herzog, C.: Tourism ontology and semantic management system: state-of-the-arts analysis. In: IADIS International Conference WWW/Internet, pp. 111–115 (2007)

Get Satisfaction: Customer Engagement
in Collaborative Software Development

Renate Andersen and Anders I. Mørch

Department of Educational Research and InterMedia
University of Oslo, Norway
{renate.andersen,anders.morch}@intermedia.uio.no

Abstract. This paper presents an empirical study of social media integrated in a product development process to support mutual software development. The case is Get Satisfaction, a company and crowd-sourcing community for customer engagement employed by many product development companies as an alternative to traditional customer relationship management (CRM) systems. We have studied user-developer interactions through the company's public support tools to identify how the company enhances its own productivity tools. The method we employ is interaction analysis. We focus on some productive interactions and analyze them in detail, including: "User request and developer implementation" (a long term activity, involving many users, sometimes leading to a new version of the tool). We refer to this form of user involvement in collaborative software development as "distributed EUD," and discuss the strengths and weaknesses of using social media to mediate the activities.

Keywords: Collaborative software development, distributed EUD, empirical study, interaction analysis, mediating artifacts, mutual development, social media.

1 Introduction

The object of study is an empirical analysis of collaborative software development involving user participation and social media (Get Satisfaction tools). Get Satisfaction is a customer engagement platform with tools that go beyond socializing by centering interaction around a shared artifact (a software product to be developed). The research question guiding the data collection and analysis is: How can social media be integrated in a product development process and how may it mediate the mutual software development process? The paper is organized as follows. First, we present related work, emphasizing the theoretical notion of artifact mediation. We then describe the case, explaining Get Satisfaction as an online community. Next, we explain our methods for data collection and analysis and our empirical findings. We describe in detail one excerpt, showing one distinct feature of collaborative software development (user request and developer implementation). Next, we discuss the research question. We conclude with some open issues and directions for further work.

Y. Dittrich et al. (Eds.): IS-EUD 2013, LNCS 7897, pp. 235–240, 2013.

2   Artifact Mediation

Vygotsky defined mediation as the way tools and signs provide the means for interacting with the sociocultural environment. Wertsch developed the concept further by
stating that tools or signs mediate all human activity and that cultural mediation is
central to both social interaction and mental development [8]. Mediation as an external activity refers to the relationship between humans and their objects of activity,
which is supported by tools [4]. Tools are thus the carriers of cultural knowledge and
social experience [8].

Mediation as a theoretical concept needs to be operationalized in specific application domains. Mutual development is a model of mediation for how customers and
professional developers can collaborate in order to create new functionality and improve upon existing products [1, 5]. In previous work we have investigated the characteristics of mutual development in small communities [1, 5], and in this paper we
study the same relationship in mass collaboration [7], as profiled in user-developer
collaborations and in user-user collaborations.

Furthermore, new activities such as negotiating contributions from multiple users
become important, like filtering out bad proposals and prioritizing those that can be
transformed into product features. We follow a process that starts with end users in-
itiating changes, and identify one pattern of interaction leading to a new product feature: user request and developer implementation.

3   The Case

The data we present in this paper are from an ongoing case study in a company named
Get Satisfaction. The company was founded in 2007. The main products, Get Satisfaction tools, are bundled as an online community software and customer engagement
platform. It has today more than 63,000 online communities and boasts 9.600,000+
visitors a month. The support community is structured around questions and answers,
organized in four different topic threads: 1) ask a question, 2) share an idea, 3) report
a problem, and 4) give praise. The participants (regular users, experienced users or
champions, and professional developers) contribute in the community by posting
messages (replying to questions and refining answers) and can express engagement by
giving praise, pressing "like" on postings, and giving good points to other people's
contributions. Figure 1 shows a screenshot of a part of one of the discussion threads
of Get Satisfaction.

4   Methods

We have used a combination of quantitative and qualitative methods as part of a case
study, but for space reasons we focus on the qualitative methods here, in particular
interaction analysis. Interaction analysis is an interdisciplinary method for empirical
investigation of the interactions of human beings with each other and with objects in
their environments [3]. Conversational turn taking is the unit of analysis we use in our
interaction analysis. We followed the postings on the support community from March

2012 to July 2012, as well as reading earlier postings that have been marked as "completed ideas." In addition to this, two email interviews with two of the community managers at Get Satisfaction were conducted. In the data section, we present data from one discussion thread at the Get Satisfaction support community.

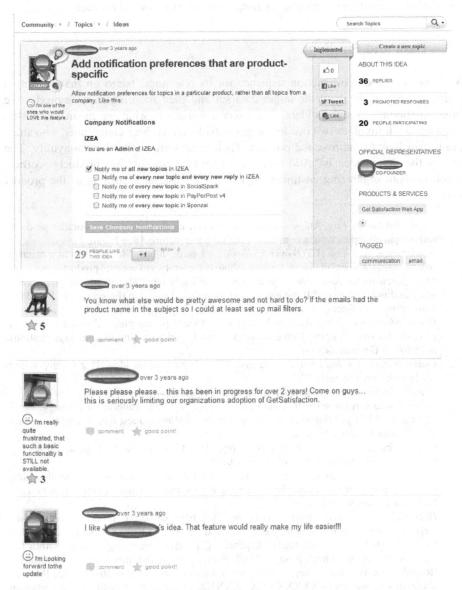

Fig. 1. Two screenshots of a discussion thread in Get Satisfaction: "Add notification preferences that are product specific." The topmost screen image shows the message that spawned the thread, and the bottom shows some replies.

The participants themselves, when updating their personal profiles, specify their role as champion, user/customer, or employee, whereas the distinction between insider and outsider are our own, between unpaid contributors (outsiders) and paid contributors (insiders). Champions take on both roles: They are outsiders who later become recruited by the company because of outstanding skills and endurance as measured by the number of highly rated postings. Champions are part-time employees.

5   Data and Findings

We have chosen one interaction sequence for its relevance, based on first running a social network analysis on the larger data set and then zooming in on a productive thread involving all stakeholders. The excerpt illustrates what we mean by "distributed EUD." It involves two insiders, eight outsiders, and three champions, who share an idea for how to improve the product. Their names are fictive for anonymity. The title of the shared idea is "Add notification preferences that are product-specific," which is about organizing customer improvement requests according to the product features.

1   *Champion Steven Fox*: Allow notification preferences for topics in a particular product, rather than all topics from a company. Like this: see picture: [See Figure 1].

2   *Insider/employee: Alan (CTO) over 3 years ago*: I agree, Jamie. We have this as a planned feature, along with email digests for both whole community and specific products.

3   *Outsider/customer Janet over 3 years ago*: You know what else would be pretty awesome and not hard to do? If the emails had the product name in the subject so I could at least set up mail filters.

4   *Outsider/customer Tony Wilkins 2 years ago*: Please please please... this has been in progress for over 3 years! Come on guys... this is seriously limiting our organizations adoption of Get Satisfaction.

5   *Outsider/customer Jon Long 2 years ago*: I like Tony Wilkins idea. That feature would really make my life easier!!!

6   *Outsider/customer Andy Barnes 2 years ago*: Yes please!

7   *Champion Lisa responds with a smiley face and states*: "I'm grateful for the suggestion! "1 year ago: I've got this idea loaded up into our feature request queue, and I'll update all y'all once I know a bit more.

8   *Outsider/customer Tony Wilkins 2 years ago*: Hey Lisa, is there any update on getting product specific notifications into the product?

9   *Champion*: Lisa 1 year ago: I'm checking in on the status of this one - I like this idea, too, but I'm not sure how complex/expensive it gets when it comes to our email system. I'll let y'all know when I know more.

10   *Outsider/customer Ted Evans 2 years ago*: We have numerous products and they all arrive as emails to "Roadrunner Records" - it'd be great if there was some differential based on what product the feedback pertained to. Even changing the line within the body of the email where it says: "Ted Evans just shared this idea in Roadrunner Records:" for instance to say "Ted Evans just shared this idea in Roadrunner Records about this product: XXXXXXXXXXXXXXXX" I could then easily set up filtering rules in Gmail (where I catch all these emails) to forward them through to other people in my organization. It's worth noting that you already do this with respect to private feedback (i.e. it states which product the feedback was in relation to) so it would seem like a super simple thing for you guys to add to the regular, non-private email alerts.

11   *Outsider/customer Tony Wilkins 2 years ago*: In our organization, different people are responsible for each product and/or service listed in our Get Satisfaction installation. As the local GS admin, I'm happy to receive all notifications but the people who look after each product have often asked me if they can limit their notifications to just the product they are responsible for. I eagerly await the development!

12   *Outsider/customer Tony Wilkins 2 years ago*: Alan, Mary, any update on the progress of this?

13   *Champion Sarah Williamson 2 years ago*: It looks like this feature is bundled into our notification improvements, but sadly I don't have an exact time frame for when this get released.

14   *Inside/Employee*: Mary (Director, Product Management) 18 months ago I'm thankful that everyone has been so patient while we worked on other stuff): Hi everyone, I'm really glad to say that we finally launched a Product follow feature. Learn more about it on our blog: url: http://product.getsatisfaction.com/2011/07/follow-products-on-get-satisfaction

The conversation in this excerpt begins with a champion sharing an idea for how to improve the product further. The suggestion is about how to organize ideas for improvements with respect to the artifacts they refer. Two outsiders support the idea in turns 3 and 4. In turn 4, the outsider Tony points out that this discussion has been ongoing for more than two years, indicating a very long-term user-development process. In response, champion Lisa answers (turn 7) by saying she is grateful for the suggestion and that "this idea is loaded up in the feature request queue." Following this, Tony asks Lisa for some feedback on the status of the idea, and champion Lisa answers (turn 9) that she does not know when it will be followed up, as it depends on "how complex/expensive it gets." In turn 10, another outsider (Ted) gives a detailed description for how to develop the feature, which is supported by outsider Tony (turn 11). When Tony in turn 12 asks for the status, the champion Sarah answers in turn 13 that she does not know, and finally in turn 14 an insider and director Mary replies that the proposal has finally been accepted and launched as a new product feature. Excerpt 1 thus illustrates end-user development as a collaborative effort between less technically skilled end users (customers) and technically skilled developers (insiders), brokered by informed end users (champions).

6   General Discussion and Directions for Further Work

The research question raised in the beginning of the paper is discussed here: How can social media be integrated in a product development process and how may it mediate mutual software development?

We have showed an example of collaborative software development initiated by users, which can be considered a type of "distributed EUD," a long-term effort of collaborative software development involving end users. The data show how a user-oriented feature request initiated by an active member of the community may be transformed from an issue within the user support community to become a feature implemented in the shared product, available to all customers of the company. The data show how different stakeholders take part in this process and how the Get Satisfaction tools (the forum, good point, mood and likes) mediate interaction [8].

Mediation is supported by both textual and emotional means. The textual means are expressed through publishing reply messages, whereas likes, good points, and mood represent the non-textual mediation. It can be seen at the top of Figure 1 that 29 people like the suggested idea in turn 1. This is likely to influence developers when they listen to, pick up, and implement the suggested idea.

However, only those who contributed with textual postings and replies are taken into consideration in our analysis. There may be "lurkers" also playing a role in the collaborative software development we have studied, who raise their voice anonymously, clicking "like" and giving out good points. Lurkers are participants that hang around, observing and reading postings posted by community members, but not explicitly raising their own voice by replying or issuing new postings [6]. Further studies (and technological features) ought to find ways to get access to lurkers.

We have scaled our previous efforts from a small group study of user-developer collaborations [1, 5] towards mass collaboration. Whether or not we see a similar phenomena occurring in large groups, as in small, depends on several conditions, some of which have been passed on lightly here, involving a new type of mediating artifact (social media rather than CRM system), and choosing new research methods (from interview to interaction analysis to social network analysis).

Open issues for further work include: how do we prevent an evolving product from being overspecialized and feature excessive, making its own use cumbersome; and will it as a result of this process also accumulate erroneous behavior and become more faulty? Can outsiders continue to request improvements of a product for the duration of its lifetime, and expect to be satisfied? What motivates the non-paid participants to contribute and spend much of their time to improve products belonging to a company that may profit from non-paid users' contributions?

References

1. Andersen, R., Mørch, A.I.: Mutual development: A case study in customer-initiated software product development. In: Pipek, V., Rosson, M.B., de Ruyter, B., Wulf, V. (eds.) IS-EUD 2009. LNCS, vol. 5435, pp. 31–49. Springer, Heidelberg (2009)
2. Fischer, G.: End-user development and meta-design: Foundations for cultures of participation. In: Pipek, V., Rosson, M.B., de Ruyter, B., Wulf, V. (eds.) IS-EUD 2009. LNCS, vol. 5435, pp. 3–14. Springer, Heidelberg (2009)
3. Jordan, B., Henderson, A.: Interaction analysis: Foundations and practice. IRL Technical Report, Palo Alto (1995)
4. Mifsud, L.: Learning with mobile technologies: Perspectives on mediated actions in the classroom. PhD thesis. University of Oslo, Norway (2012)
5. Mørch, A.I., Andersen, R.: Mutual Development: The Software Engineering Context of End-User Development. Journal of Organizational and End User Computing 22(2), 36–57 (2010)
6. Nonnecke, B., Preece, J.: Lurker demographics: Counting the silent. In: Proceedings CHI 2000, pp. 73–80. ACM, New York (2000)
7. Tapscott, D., Williams, A.D.: Wikinomics: How Mass Collaboration Changes Everything. Penguin Group, New York (2008)
8. Wertsch, J.: Voices of the mind: A sociocultural approach to mediated action. Harvard University Press, Cambridge (1991)

Lightweight End-User Software Sharing

Cristóbal Arellano and Oscar Díaz

ONEKIN Research Group, University of the Basque Country (UPV/EHU),
San Sebastián, Spain
{cristobal.arellano,oscar.diaz}@ehu.es

Abstract. This paper looks into the sharing of end-user software (referred to as "script"). Based on this study four implications are drawn: reduce the effort to make scripts shareable, minimize deployment burdens, less stringent protection mechanisms, and tap into communities of practice as for sharing. To attend these implications, we introduce a URL-based distribution schema for scripts combined with an IP-address-based authorization model. This makes scripts URL-addressable and easy to install, because choosing to install a script means that all of the necessary frameworks, plug-ins, etc. that are needed to make this script run are simultaneously installed. On the other hand, IP-based protection uses IP network prefixes as cypher keys. A script language is used as a proof of concept.

Keywords: End-User Development, Social Sharing, Domain Specific Languages, Web 2.0.

1 Introduction

Software sharing might promote three aspect of relevance in an end-user setting: (1) *participatory design* between producers and consumers; (2) *community building*; and (3), *producer engagement* as a result of the potential recognition from consumers. This begs two questions: how the sharing of end-user software differs from the sharing of commercial software, and (2), how these differences might impact the way end-user software is delivered. This work looks at these matters, and introduces a URL-based distribution schema for end-user software combined with an IP-address-based authorization model. As a proof of concept, we outline the realization of this schema for a script language.

2 End-User Software and Commercial Software: Differences on Sharing

For our purposes, sharing implies the exchange of a resource (i.e. the software) from a producer to a consumer. Two dimensions are then established: (1) the profile of the stakeholders, and (2), the characteristics of the resource (see Figure 1).

Y. Dittrich et al. (Eds.): IS-EUD 2013, LNCS 7897, pp. 241–246, 2013.

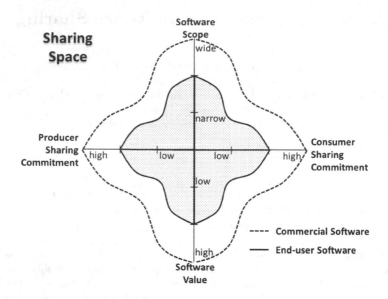

Fig. 1. Sharing: Commercial software *versus* End-user software

Stakeholder Dimension. Stakeholders differ in their commitment to share. In a commercial setting, producers make a leaving out of sharing/selling software while consumers are somehow compelled to use the company software. Their commitment is high. This is not the case for end-user software (hereafter refer to as "scripts"). First, producers are not forced to share their scripts while, on the other hand, sharing might be cumbersome (e.g. documenting, protecting, making it accessible). We should then aim at reducing the barriers for sharing scripts, ideally, making sharing "a click away". Therefore, *producers' low commitment advices scripts to be "shareable by construction"*.

Second, consumers are not forced to deploy someone-else's scripts. Rather, affiliation and membership become main inductors [4]. However, these incentives should be cautiously balanced with the availability of time and skills. In this setting, consumability turns into a main enabler. Consumable scripts are scripts that facilitate their consumption, i.e. they are easy to configure, license, share, enact, etc. When users are not obliged to consume one's software, we risk "the consumability effort" to go above the endeavour users are willing to accept to enjoy the software. Therefore, *consumers' low commitment advices to minimize the script deployment burdens*.

Resource Dimension. It includes two features: the software value and the software scope (i.e. the potential consumer base). As for the value, scripts are generally not as valuable as commercial software. Hence, there are no economic restrictions to constrain their flow. Therefore, *the lower value of scripts permits less rigorous protection mechanisms in honour of a lower footprint*.

Second, the software scope. It is commonly agreed that end-user programmers are focused on developing programs that fulfil some personal goal that exists in

Table 1. Impact of End-User Software specifics into software sharing

Script characterization	Implications for script sharing	Realization strategy
Producers' commitment: low	Minimize the effort to make a script shareable	URL-based distribution
Consumers' commitment: low	Minimize deployment burdens	Deployment-leveraged URLs
Value: low	Less stringent protection mechanisms	IP-based authorization leveraged URLs
Scope: narrow	Sharing through communities of practice	Inline social media share buttons

their domains of expertise [6]. This delimits the scope of interest to communities of practices. Script sharing is mainly bounded within the local team at the workplace or the mates at the social network [4]. In this setting, resources are traditionally shared through Web-based repositories. Example abounds: *Flickr* for pictures, *YouTube* for videos, etc. This option is certainly also possible for scripts. Indeed, *www.userscripts.org* is a repository for *JavaScript* scripts. This repository assigns a URL to each uploaded script. This URL can later be shared or bookmarked. However, software repositories impose an additional burden to end users (e.g. signing up, learning a new interface). In addition, the functionality of the script might be too focused to be of interest for a general audience while at the same time, end users might be intimidated by putting their code under public scrutiny. Indeed, studies indicate an increase in software sharing if conducted within smaller groups [1]. We can then conclude that *the limited scope of scripts favours social networks rather than repositories as sharing conduits*.

Table 1 summarizes the characterization of end-user software and the implications for software sharing. Next section looks at how these differences impact the practice of sharing, i.e. the means and ways to share scripts.

3   Implications for Software Sharing

Minimize Sharing Burdens. Our vision is for scripts to be shared as easily as other resources such as pictures (e.g. *JPG* resources) or documents (e.g. *PDF* resources). The sharing of pictures is normally achieved through the Web by turning pictures into Web resources, i.e. making pictures URL addressable. Clicking on such URLs makes the associated resources readily available. Basically, this scenario introduces two main requirements: *MIME* types and plugins. A *MIME* type is an identifier for file formats on Internet that permits user agents (e.g. browsers) understand what the associated Web resource is about. In this way, the browser is able to associate the correct behaviour to each *MIME* type. This is commonly achieved through a plugin. A plugin adds specific abilities (e.g. handling a *PDF* file) to the browser (e.g. once the *Adobe* plugin is installed, browsers know how to handle *PDF*-typed Web resources).

Likewise, turning scripts into Web resources would imply (1) making scripts URL addressable, and (2), making script file extensions become *MIME* types. The latter basically implies the existence of a plugin that takes over when a script is retrieved.

Minimize Deployment Burdens. Software deployment is all of the activities that make a software system available for use. Previous paragraph argues about the sharing benefits of making scripts URL addressable. The deployment cost of this solution would be limited to install first the *MIME* plugin and next, click on the script's URL. Despite its simplicity, this option still requires the user to locate and install the plugin before clicking on the script's URL. An even simpler approach is to code the location of the plugin as part of the URL. In this way, clicking on the script's URL not only install the script but, first, install the plugin. Consumers do no longer need to be aware of locating/installing the plugin (and checking the configuration). All is needed is the script's URL. We refer to this second kind of URLs as *"deployment URLs"*.

Less Stringent Protection Mechanisms. Unlike commercial software, scripts tend to be for self consumption or to be shared in private scopes [4]. We propose the use of IPs as a lightweight license-like approach to sharing control. IP structure tends to reflect the structure of the organization. Different studies indicate how user software tends to be distributed among co-workers within the boundaries of the organization [4]. This permits the use of IP network prefixes to denote the range of IPs within a given cluster/department/unit of the organization. User scripts can be associated with IP network prefixes and, in so doing, restricting the range of IPs which is allowed to install the script. In this way, sharing is IP scoped. The advantage is that neither the producer nor the consumer need to remember the cypher key (i.e. the IP network prefix) as it can be automatically obtained from the computer configuration.

The scenarios that can benefit from this approach should exhibit two characteristics. First, IP network prefixes are known in advance. If sharing happens within an organization, the IP structure should mimic the sharing boundaries. If sharing happens among different organizations, their respective IP network prefixes should be introduced as configuration parameters of the cryptographic algorithm. The second aspect to keep in mind is that IP network prefixes as encryption keys are weak. That is, the number of possible IP network prefixes is limited, and hence, it is possible for brute-force crackers to eventually come up with a correct IP network prefix. More to the point, this mechanism does not prevent an authorized IP subnet to download a script, and next, email it to unauthorized users on other networks. Therefore, this mechanism fits those scenarios where *sharing limitations come not so much for security reasons but the renounce from disclosing immature work to the public*. In this way, this mechanism supports more a boundary rather than a security instrument. Implementation wise, a *deployment URL* now stands for a request to install a given piece of code provided the IP of the petitioner meets a given IP network prefix that plays the role of the cypher key.

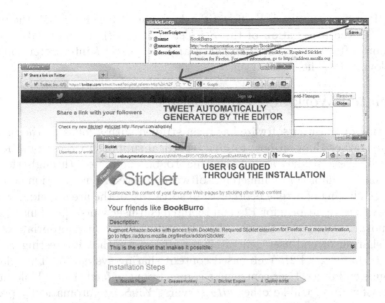

Fig. 2. Sharing in *Sticklet*: inline sharing (top) and a *deployment URL* at work (bottom). Have a go by typing: *http://tinyurl.com/a8qdl4y*.

Sharing Limited to Communities of Practice. Previous paragraphs evolved the notion of the URL. First, URLs were mere script identifiers. Next, URLs encoded the script code, and they were re-phrased as requests for the script's installation. Finally, last paragraph makes these requests IP-aware by encrypting the content of the URL with the IP network prefix of the producer. Therefore, generating a *deployment URL* requires (1) the script's code, (2) the producer's IP network prefix, and (3), the location of the plugin. Since *deployment URLs* are born to facilitate sharing, we advocate for this "url-ization" process to be provided as part of the sharing process. Since, as we believe, this sharing process will become common practice, we advocate for sharing utilities to be integrated within the *script* editors (e.g. through share buttons to social media). As a proof of concept, next section outlines how these sharing concerns were realized for the script language *Sticklet*.

4   Sharing in Sticklet

Sticklet is a *JavaScript* internal domain-specific language [3]. Broadly, a *Sticklet* expression stands for a high-level description of a *JavaScript* program. Along the aforementioned strategies, the *Sticklet* editor includes share button for *Facebook* and *Twitter* (see Figure 2). Clicking on the *Twitter* button generates a *tweet* whose content includes the *deployment URL* for the script at hand (*e.g. http://tinyurl.com/a8qdl4y*). On receiving the *tweet*, the consumer can click on this URL to readily start consuming the script. If so, the user is assisted in the installation process provided his IP network prefix matches the script's IP network prefix. For a first-time deployment (see Figure 2), the process includes (1) the installation of the *Sticklet* plugin, (2) the installation of the companion software (e.g. *Greasemonkey* and the *Sticklet* interpreter), and (3), the deployment of the script itself.

5   Related Work and Conclusions

The sharing of end-user software has been studied with a focus on the practices of sharing rather than on how to give technical support to these practices [4]. In general, these studies assume sharing to be conducted through the same mechanisms available for commercial software. Therefore, inspiration should be look at the sharing of artefacts other than software. In the area of video gaming, *12seconds.tv* is a platform for 12second-length end-user videos [2]. This platform is yet another example of the use of social networks as an appropriate conduit for the sharing of end-user generated resources. Another interesting example is that of *YouServ*, a P2P Web-based content sharing system [5]. This platform also targets end users. User centricness comes from the facilities in deploying the P2P infrastructure. Unlike other *http* servers, *YouServ* automatically provides a domain name, replicates the content in other Web servers, and automatically secure content without accounts or passwords. That is, they considerably reduce the user burden to deploy this P2P solution. The main difference with *Sticklet* rests on the communication paradigm. Our approach is push, i.e. the producer decides in a script basis when and to whom the script is to be shared without requiring the consumer to be part of the P2P network.

References

1. Bogart, C., Burnett, M.M., Cypher, A., Scaffidi, C.: End-User Programming in the Wild: A Field Study of CoScripter Scripts. In: Proceedings of the 24th IEEE Symposium on Visual Languages and Human-Centric Computing, VL/HCC 2008, pp. 39–46 (2008)
2. Bornoe, N., Barkhuus, L.: Video Microblogging: Your 12 Seconds of Fame. In: Proceedings of the 28th ACM Conference on Human Factors in Computing Systems, CHI 2010, pp. 3325–3330 (2010)
3. Díaz, O., Arellano, C., Azanza, M.: A Language for End-user Web Augmentation: Caring for Producers and Consumers Alike. Accepted for Publication at ACM Transactions on the Web (2013)
4. Huang, X., Ding, X., Lee, C.P., Lu, T., Gu, N.: Meanings and Boundaries of Scientific Software Sharing. Proceedings of the 16th Conference on Computer Supported Cooperative Work and Social Computing, CSCW 2013 (2013)
5. Bayardo Jr., R.J., Agrawal, R., Gruhl, D., Somani, A.: YouServ: A Web-Hosting and Content Sharing Tool for the Masses. In: Proceedings of the 11th International Conference on World Wide Web, WWW 2011, pp. 345–354 (2002)
6. Ko, A.J., Abraham, R., Beckwith, L., Blackwell, A., Burnett, M., Erwig, M., Scaffidi, C., Lawrance, J., Lieberman, H., Myers, B., Rosson, M.B., Rothermel, G., Shaw, M., Wiedenbeck, S.: The State of the Art in End-User Software Engineering. ACM Computing Surveys 43, 21:1–21:44 (2011)

Decision-Making Should Be More Like Programming

Christopher Fry and Henry Lieberman

MIT Media Lab
20 Ames St., Cambridge, MA 02139 USA
{cfry,lieber}@media.mit.edu

Abstract. *Justify* is an interactive "end-user development environment" for deliberation. Justify organizes discussions in a hierarchy of *points*, each expressing a single idea. Points have a rich ontology of types, such as *pro* or *con*, *mathematical*, or *aesthetic* arguments. "Programs" in this environment use inference rules to provide *assessments* that summarize groups of points. Interactive browsing modes serve as *visualizers* or *debuggers* for arguments.

1 Introduction

Online social media have given us a new opportunities to have large-scale discussions that help us understand and make decisions. But large-scale discussions can quickly get too complex. Who said what? Did anybody reply to a particularly devastating criticism? Is this redundant? Do the pros outweigh the cons?

Most people know basic concepts in decision-making, like weighing evidence, voting, or understanding dependencies. But an intuitive understanding is not enough to express ideas unambiguously, or when situations get complex.

We are proposing, essentially, an end-user development environment for online deliberation. Just like Eclipse is a development environment for Java, and Excel is a development environment for numerical constraints, we introduce the *Justify* system as an end-user development environment for rational arguments.

2 The Analogy between Deliberation and Programming

The analogy between deliberation and programming runs deep. Discussions are hierarchies of ideas. Programs are hierarchies of statements. In a discussion, people express reasons for believing or rejecting a single idea. Each of those reasons can, recursively, have reasons for accepting or rejecting it. Justify calls each idea, a *point*.

2.1 Points and Point Types

Since an argument is frequently a hierarchy, we adopt an outline view for the user interface. A point is shown as a single line in the outline, but it can be selected to see details or expanded to see subpoints.

Y. Dittrich et al. (Eds.): IS-EUD 2013, LNCS 7897, pp. 247–253, 2013.

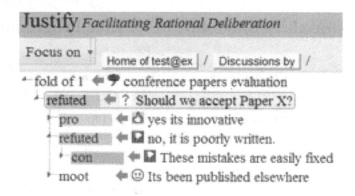

Fig. 1. An argument about whether or not to accept a conference paper

Programming has data types. Justify has *point types*. These are shown by icons that precede the one-line point description. Common point types are *question*, (question mark icon) which introduces an issue to be debated, and, for subpoints of a question, *pro* (thumbs-up icon) and *con*, (thumbs-down) for positions on the question.

Fig. 1 shows a Justify argument about the acceptance of a conference paper. The *question* is "Should we accept Paper X?". Below it are a *pro* point, "Yes, it's innovative", and a *con* point, "No, it is poorly written".

Below that appears another *con*, "The mistakes are easily fixed". Arguments are recursive. This refutes the criticism of poor writing directly above it. It is a *con* point because it is arguing against the criticism, so therefore it is an argument *in favor* of accepting the paper.

> Point type doc ▾   Help ▾
>
> **The Most Important Points**
> **question**: pro_or_con prioritize clarification
> **folder**: discussion Object
> **pro**:
> **con**:
> **math**: number add
> **meta**: use_assessment get_by_title
> **moot**: insignificant redundant
> **fix**: suggestion not_one_point

Fig. 2. Justify point types

2.2   Assessments

What does it mean to "evaluate" a discussion? An *assessment* is the result of evaluating a subtree of the discussion, and can be computed by arbitrary program code. Assessments for subpoints are like intermediate values in programming.

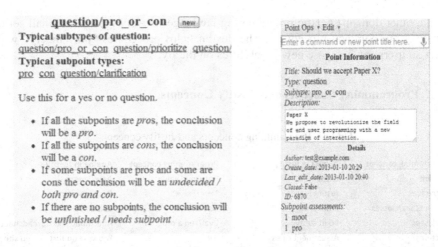

Fig. 3. Documentation on the question/pro_or_con point type, and a particular question's details

Assessments *summarize* their subtrees. A user can read an assessment and learn the result of the sub-arguments without reading through them.

Assessments appear to the left of the arrow on each line. Each point type has its own rules to compute its assessment. For example, an objection, with no subpoints, is assessed as *refuted*. So the "poorly written" criticism is refuted by the assertion that the "mistakes can be fixed".

The *moot* point type asserts that its superpoint is worthless, trumping any other assessment of that argument. Here we have a *moot* point, "It's been published elsewhere". Thus, the entire "Should we accept Paper X?" question is marked *refuted*.

2.3   Justify's Computational Model Is Like a Spreadsheet

The computational model of Justify is like a spreadsheet. Each Justify point is like a spreadsheet cell. The assessment, to the left of the arrow, is like the value of a cell. To the right of the arrow, the point type, represented by its icon, is like a spreadsheet formula that determines how the value of the cell is computed. The subpoints of a point, appearing below, are like the arguments to the computational rule that is represented by the point type. The point title is essentially a domain-specific comment.

For example, the math point type has subtypes that apply a given function to its subpoints; they can perform arithmetic makeing end-user programming in Justify like spreadsheet programming.

Like spreadsheets, Justify has a continuous computation model. When a point is changed, everything that depends on it is immediately recomputed. Assessments, which represent intermediate values, are always visible, facilitating debugging, as in the ZStep debugger [Lieberman and Fry 97].

Like other domain-specific programming languages, Justify presents a small set of primitives for common procedures. The design helps procedures "play nicely" with others so users can compose new capabilities on the fly.

2.4   Programming Concepts and Justify Concepts

Table 1. Programming concepts and Justify concepts

Programming concept	Analog in Justify	Programming concept	Analog in Justify
Program	Discussion	Returned value	Assessment
Source files	Justify shared repository	True/False	Pro/Con points
Built-in types/classes	Point types	List or array	Folder point
Subclasses	Point subtypes	Eval/run a program	Automatic (like spreadsheet)
Functions	Assessment rules	IDE	Browser on Justify web site
Object system	Prototype objects for points	Debugger	Expand/contract points
Expression in source code	Point in discussion hierarchy		View assessments

3   A More Substantial Example: A Program Committee Meeting

Let's return to the example about reviewing conference papers. Imagine that you are the Program Chair. The initial paper are completed. You would like to prepare for the Program Committee meeting.

Many conferences use prepackaged conference management software, such as EasyChair or Precision Conference. If the users follow the software's workflow, these work well.   But with Justify, conference organizers can program their own.

3.1   Papers Reviewed by External Reviewers

Reviewers can use Justify to identify pro or con points about the paper, or assert a rating (on the conventional 1-5 scale).

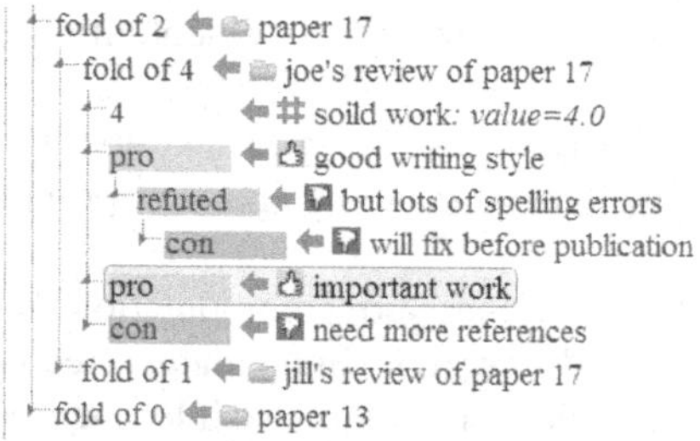

```
  ┬ fold of 2  ⟸ ▦ paper 17
  ├ fold of 4  ⟸ ▦ joe's review of paper 17
  │ ┬  4           ⟸ ♯ soild work: value=4.0
  │ ├ pro       ⟸ ♨ good writing style
  │ ├ refuted   ⟸ ▣ but lots of spelling errors
  │ │ ├ con     ⟸ ▣ will fix before publication
  │ ├ pro       ⟸ ♨ important work
  │ ├ con       ⟸ ▣ need more references
  ├ fold of 1  ⟸ ▦ jill's review of paper 17
  ┴ fold of 0  ⟸ ▦ paper 13
```

Fig. 4. Reviewers' discussion of Paper 17

3.2   Program Committee Discussion

Author rebuttal and reviewer discussion can be implemented as Justify points, as can the Program Committee discussion itself.   Justify has access control via the *discussion* point type,   allowing comments visible to the Program Committee only.

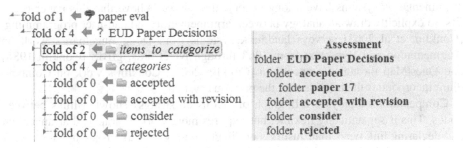

Fig. 5. Program Committee discussion. A PC member argues in favor, referencing a point made by one of the reviewers, who thought it uses "important work".

Rebuttals or PC discussions can target specific points of a review, packaging up the whole discussion for easy perusal by the Program Committee.

An author can rebut a reviewer point by creating a *use_assessment* point that references what the reviewer had to say in a different part of the hierarchy. In Fig. 5, the first *pro* point is a *use_assessment point* references the "important work" point.

3.3   Categories

Finally, the whole discussion is organized by using the *categorize* point type.

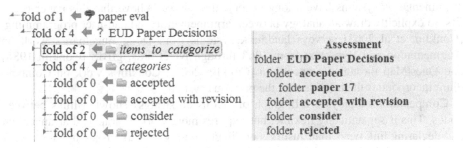

Fig. 6. Paper categories established by the Program Chair, and decisions

The Program Chair has set up four categories, accepted, accepted with revision, consider, and rejected. We might add other categories, for example, demote from long to short paper.   The result is to put each paper in one of the four categories.

4   Usability Evaluation

We conducted a small usability study to answer: Did people understand the concept of Justify? What is its intended purpose? Would they use Justify ? We were worried that the complexity of Justify's ontology of point types might limit usability. Although we only tested a few point types, results were positive. The point types, and hierarchical structure, did not prove a barrier to usability.

4.1   Experimental Method

Participants were shown a demonstration, then walked through two examples:
"Should I subscribe to a public bicycle sharing system? Should I purchase an iPad? They then used Justify on whether or not to take a vacation in Hawaii.

4.2   Experimental Results

We tested 8 college students in their 20s. 88% said they understood the purpose of Justify (agree/strongly agree), 100% were confident in the basic operations on points, while 75% felt that way about using the more advanced point types. Respondents were split halfway about whether the ease of use was appropriate to the complexity of the example discussions, perhaps not surprising considering the example discussions were simple and Justify shines mainly in more complex discussions. 63% said they would be willing to use Justify for their own (presumably more complex) discussions. The one participant who strongly disagreed later clarified that her answer was due to the simplicity of the examples. Later work will test more complex scenarios.

5   Related Work

Argumentation systems have a long history, though we believe that this paper is the first to explicitly draw an analogy between argumentation and end-user programming. [Conklin, et al 2003] surveys landmark systems from Doug Engelbart's work on Augmentation and Hypertext from 1963 through NoteCards, gIBIS [Conklin 1988] and QuestMap through Compendium [Conklin 2003]. Conklin's work on Compendium incorporates the best ideas of the previous systems.

Compendium employs a 2-D graph of "icons on strings" showing links between nodes. This is semantically flexible, but requires more work in graphical arrangement and declaring link types than Justify's outline/hierarchy. We like Buckingham's work on Cohere and the conceptual framework described in [Buckingham Shum 2010].

We also like SIBYL [Lee 91] by Jintae Lee at the Center for Coordination Science directed by Thomas Malone. Fry worked in the early 1990's there. Malone's work of planet-wide importance continues at MIT's Center for Collective Intelligence.

Iyad Rahwan [Rahwan 11] tackles representing argumentation in the Semantic Web technologies of XML, RDF and OWL. This can standardize and share an ontology across the web, but pays little attention to the accessibility of the interface.

References

1. Buckingham Shum, S., De Liddo, A.: Collective intelligence for OER sustainability. In: OpenED 2010: Seventh Annual Open Education Conference, Barcelona, Spain, November 2-4 (2010)
2. Conklin, J., Selvin, A., Buckingham Shum, S., Sierhuis, M.: Facilitated Hypertext for Collective Sensemaking: 15 Years on from gIBIS. In: Weigand, H., Goldkuhl, G., de Moor, A. (eds.) Keynote Address, Proceedings LAP 2003: 8th International Working Conference on the Language-Action Perspective on Communication Modelling, Tilburg, The Netherlands, July 1-2 (2003), http://www.uvt.nl/lap2003
3. Conklin, J., Begeman, M.L.: gIBIS: a hypertext tool for exploratory policy discussion. In: Proceedings of the 1988 ACM Conference on Computer-Supported Cooperative Work (CSCW 1988), pp. 140–152. ACM, New York (1988)
4. Lee, J.: SIBYL: A qualitative decision management system. In: Winston, P.H., Shellard, S.A. (eds.) Artificial Intelligence at MIT Expanding Frontiers, pp. 104–133. MIT Press, Cambridge (1991)
5. Lieberman, H., Fry, C.: ZStep 95: A Reversible, Animated, Source Code Stepper. In: Stasko, J., Domingue, J., Brown, M., Price, B. (eds.) Software Visualization: Programming as a Multimedia Experience. MIT Press, Cambridge (1997)
6. Malone, T.W., Lai, K.Y., Fry, C.: Experiments with Oval: A radically tailorable tool for cooperative work. ACM Transactions on Information Systems 13(2), 177–205 (1995)
7. Mason, C., Johnson, R.: DATMS: A Framework for Assumption Based Reasoning. In: Distributed Artificial Intelligence, vol. 2. Morgan Kaufmann Publishers, Inc. (1989)
8. Malone, T.W., Klein, M.: Harnessing Collective Intelligence to Address Global Climate Change. Innovations 2(3), 15–26 (2007)
9. Minsky, M.: The Society of Mind. Simon & Schuster, New York (1988)
10. Rahwan, I., Banihashemi, B., Reed, C., Walton, D., Abdallah, S.: Representing and Classifying Arguments on the Semantic Web. The Knowledge Engineering Review 26(4), 487–511 (2011)
11. Speer, R., Havasi, C., Lieberman, H.: AnalogySpace: Reducing the Dimensionality of Commonsense Knowledge. In: Conference of the Assocation for the Advancement of Artificial Intelligence (AAAI 2008), Chicago (2008)

Back to the Future of EUD: The Logic of Bricolage for the Paving of EUD Roadmaps

Federico Cabitza, Carla Simone, and Iade Gesso

Università degli Studi di Milano - Bicocca
Viale Sarca 336, 20126 Milano, Italy
{cabitza,gesso,simone}@disco.unimib.it

Abstract. Several recent approaches to EUD increasingly recognize an active role of users in the construction of the tools that support their daily practices. However, there is still a lack of a general framework that could play a role in the comparison of existing proposals and in the development of new EUD solutions. The paper proposes a conceptual framework and a related architecture, called Logic of Bricolage, that aims to be a step further in this direction. The concluding remarks point to the potential value of this conceptualization effort in the EUD field.

1 Introduction

Irrespective of the different underlying disciplinary stances and of the historical evolution of the approaches that promote an active participation of end-users in the construction of the applications supporting their work practices [16, 11, 13], we see researchers reach an increasing agreement upon a set of tenets that are common in their solutions. First, the awareness that approaches to design that are rooted in the so called "rational mould" have to be abandoned in favor of a more collaborative relationship between designers and actual end-users. Second, the awareness that there is a continuity between design and use of a technology and that times are ripe for a re-interpretation of the traditional roles of "user" and "designer", in the light of the new understanding of what can guarantee a better technological outcome. Third, the awareness that there is a need for methods and environments that coherently support the involved stakeholders in EUD activities in light of the former two principles. See for example, the notion of meta-design proposed by Fischer et al. [e.g., 10]; and the hierarchical framework described in [9], in which the concept of Software Shaping Workshops (SSW) allows for the definition of environments that are shaped according to specific user communities and where users can use or tailor the software tools that support their working practices. Besides this widespread awareness, also some terms have been (increasingly) used in the related literature and have so far become familiar to EUD researchers: terms like bricolage [12, 3], facilitator [11], appropriation, task-artifact cycle and the like (although often with slightly different interpretations by different authors).

The paper aims to contribute a step further in this direction to fill an apparent gap in current EUD debate, where a purposely general framework has

Y. Dittrich et al. (Eds.): IS-EUD 2013, LNCS 7897, pp. 254–259, 2013.

not yet submitted as a concrete reference that could help interested researchers bridge existing EUD initiatives, as well as help EUD practitioners use concepts that are unambiguous in meaning and definite in scope. We call this still intrinsically on-progress conceptual framework for the conception of EUD enabling environments "Logic of Bricolage" (LOB), after Lanzara seminal contribution to the field [12]. This short paper presents the LOB framework and the related conceptual architecture. The concluding section discusses the advantages of such a conceptual framework and the research agenda that is necessary to make it a common reference for truly EUD environments.

2   Toward a Logic of Bricolage for EUD Systems

The expression *Logic of Bricolage* was used by Lanzara [12] to point to some general features that the "environments" supporting bricolage as a collaborative practice should provide. We chose this expression to denote a framework by which to characterize EUD environments that support this collaborative practice, namely both the *editing* and *execution* environments where tools are *co-defined*, and *used*, respectively. The framework and the environments with the underlying platform constituting the LOB conceptual architecture are described in what follows (see also Figure 1).

The LOB conceptual framework: Constructs, Structures and Annotations - Unlike traditional approaches that aim to provide users with sophisticated (i.e., semantically rich) modeling tools and facilitate the top-down construction of applications, the LOB framework takes a clear bottom-up approach starting from the basic building blocks that users deem as necessary to conceive – and possibly build – their working spaces and the related behaviors. These latter are called *structures*: these are discussed in the next paragraph together with the related editing environment. The LOB framework calls end-users *bricolants* (i.e., people actively involved in bricolage activities), and *constructs* the basic building blocks used to build more complex structures in such activities.

The LOB framework further distinguishes between *Operand Constructs* and *Operator Constructs*: operands are the most atomic data structures, constants and variables that make sense in a work setting and application domain; operators are all the operations that users deem necessary to be performed over the operands in their setting; these latter can be either *functional* or *actional* to indicate something either akin to the evaluation of a function, or related to the production of some actual effect in the computational environment: for example, the evaluation of a predicate and the storing or retrieving of a piece of information, respectively. In particular, functional Operator constructs can be applied to operands to allow for the recursive construction of more complex operands from simpler ones. What the users consider as "atomic" (black box) constructs at their own level of description to use and invoke while working with their artifacts can be of increasing complexity: for this reason, the community of end-users may request the assistance of IT professionals to implement the constructs that they want to employ.

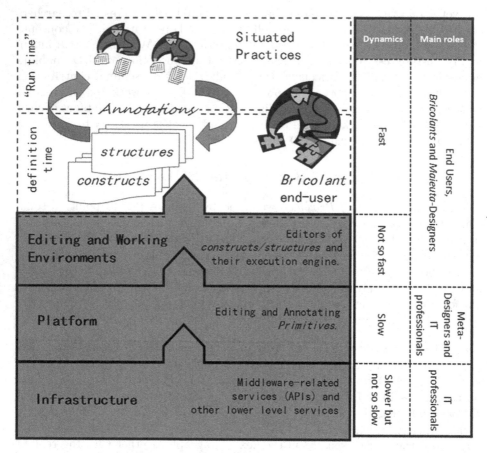

Fig. 1. A conceptual architecture for environments supporting EUD bricolage. LOB keywords are in italics.

Moreover, the LOB framework contains *annotations* as a first-class concept, as they play a central role in collaborative work articulation, knowledge sharing and mutual understanding [14, 8, 2, 9, 1, 4]. In order to play these roles *annotations* can be either stigmergic signs and marks attached to the contents of a document or any extempore comment and semantic tag chosen by users from either domain specific taxonomies or setting-specific folksonomies; notably annotations can have multiple targets and can express also various relationships among (elements of) Layout Structures. In addition, in LOB annotations can be increasingly nested, that is users should be able to annotate annotations, so as to allow for nested threads of comments and tags [7] to support informal communication.

The LOB Editing and Working Environment and the underlying Platform - Arranging constructs into suitable *structures* requires an editing environment by which to shape both the information structures and the logic that are needed for the desired application: then we distinguish between *Layout structures* and *Control structures*. The former ones are the above mentioned working spaces that a community of users recognizes as the physically inscribed and computationally augmented artifacts supporting the accomplishment of its work. For this reason, *Layout structures* result from the topological arrangement of Operand constructs. In the domain of computer-aided design and collaborative drawing/editing, a Layout Structure is the working space where users arrange the docking bars of their preferred commands, symbol stencils and predefined configurations of elements that must be set up before the actual work begins. In document-based information systems, Layout Structures are the document templates of forms and charts that are used to both accumulate content and coordinate activities.

Control structures specify the behaviors of Layout structures, i.e., how the artifacts act on the content inscribed therein, e.g., in response to events generated at interface level, and how this level interacts with users during the use of the application. Control structures can be of arbitrary complexity, ranging from simple *Rewriting Rules* (among which there are input-output transformations), to (recursively defined) set of instructions that are articulated by means of *Connectors* to express both sequential and concurrent processes.

The LOB platform underlying the editing environment offers an (extensible) set of *Primitives*, that is domain-independent functionalities that are expressed in terms of lower level Application Programming Interfaces. Examples of primitives characterizing the LOB framework are: *Read* and *Write*, that represent the conceptual operations at the basis of any computation; *Bind*, which assigns constants to variables; *Aggregate*, by which to build complex operands from simpler ones; *Compose*, to build complex operators in terms of functional composition; and *Place*, to associate an *operand construct* to a position within a *Layout structure*.

Moreover, the platform exposes *primitives* for the creation, addition, deletion, etc. of annotations; and *primitives* implementing the *Connectors* to be used in the definition of the *Control structures*.

The LOB conceptual architecture: between transiency and permanency -
The LOB conceptual architecture depicted in Figure 1 encompasses the different layers described above. In so doing it recognizes the main point made by Mansfield [15, p. 25] who submits the adoption of a layered architecture where some layers are allowed to change at different rates (see the column called dynamics in Figure 1). Going from the upmost layer where structures and constructs are defined and instantiated together with their annotations to support situated practices, down to the technological infrastructure through the editing and execution environments and their supporting platform, the change rate decreases in normal conditions: this implies that the layers have to guarantee the corresponding degree of flexibility to manage the occurring changes and their propagation, irrespective of the layer at which they occur.

At each layer, the tasks and the reaction to changes (either generated by technological evolution or users' needs) are in charge of specific roles (see the column called main roles). Beside the role of *bricolant* end-users and that of *meta*-designer (who "designs for designers" [10]) we envision also a specific role, the *maieuta*-designer (see [6] for a detailed characterization of this particular *meta*-designer), to help bricolant users "help themselves" and reach an increasing level of autonomy with respect to traditional IT professionals (i.e., designers, architects and programmers).

3   Concluding Remarks

We are convinced that in EUD "the best is yet to come". This is not to discard what has been done so far in this research field, but rather to recognize that the last ten years or so of proposals and solutions that have been brought forth to allow end-users to create and maintain their computational tools autonomously have now reached a maturity level that requires a sort of backward reflection, as well as an effort to generalize local solutions and intuitions into general insights and concepts for future reuse and discussion. To this aim, we have presented a general framework, called Logic of Bricolage. According to [11, p. 308], who provides a lens through which to consider the utility of conceptual proposals, we propose the LOB framework to: i) facilitate EUD researchers in describing their and others' solutions (descriptive power); ii) help them talk about their solutions by providing them with a common vocabulary (rhetorical power), i.e., a very concise lexicon whose available terms cover few but essential aspects that often recur in EUD models and solutions, and are defined with some degree of unambiguous formalization (see [6] for the formal grammar associated with the LOB framework). Lastly, iii) both inform and guide the design of the next EUD proposals to come in heterogeneous application domains (applicative power), or at least to foster discussion on the need of such a framework in the EUD field.

The LOB framework is intended as one step toward a shared systematization of technological approaches that could soon reach enough simplicity and generality by progressively abstracting and formalizing the lessons learned and best solutions that the field has so far proposed and discussed. This systematization would be of some value both for the designer and the informed user of new EUD solutions, as they could either conceive or address those heterogeneous solutions within a more homogeneous conceptual framework. Our current efforts are aimed toward the development of an EUD platform and related environments that are fully compliant with the LOB tenets and concepts: a preliminary version of such an effort is represented by the WOAD framework initially presented in [5].

References

[1] Ardito, C., Buono, P., Costabile, M.F., Lanzilotti, R., Piccinno, A.: End users as co-designers of their own tools and products. Journal of Visual Languages & Computing 23(2), 78–90 (2012)
[2] Bringay, S., Barry, C., Charlet, J.: Annotations: A functionality to support cooperation, coordination and awareness in the electronic medical record. In: COOP 2006: Proceedings of the 7th International Conference on the Design of Cooperative Systems, France, Provence (2006)

[3] Buescher, M., Gill, S., Mogensen, P., Shapiro, D.: Landscapes of practice: Brico-lage as a method for situated design. Computer Supported Cooperative Work (CSCW) 10(1), 1–28 (2001)

[4] Cabitza, F., Colombo, G., Simone, C.: Leveraging underspecification in knowl-edge artifacts to foster collaborative activities in professional communities. Inter-national Journal of Human - Computer Studies 71(1), 24–45 (2013)

[5] Cabitza, F., Gesso, I.: Web of active documents: An architecture for flexible elec-tronic patient records. In: Fred, A., Filipe, J., Gamboa, H. (eds.) BIOSTEC 2010. CCIS, vol. 127, pp. 44–56. Springer, Heidelberg (2011)

[6] Cabitza, F., Simone, C.: Design ltd.: Renovated myths for the development of socially embedded technologies. arXiv:1211.5577v2 [cs.HC] (2012)

[7] Cabitza, F., Simone, C., Locatelli, M.P.: Supporting artifact-mediated discourses through a recursive annotation tool. In: GROUP 2012: Proceedings of the 17th ACM International Conference on Supporting Group Work, pp. 253–262. ACM, New York (2012)

[8] Cadiz, J.J., Gupta, A., Grudin, J.: Using web annotations for asynchronous col-laboration around documents. In: CSCW 2000: Proceedings of the 2000 ACM Conference on Computer Supported Cooperative Work, pp. 309–318. ACM Press, New York (2000)

[9] Costabile, M.F., Fogli, D., Mussio, P., Piccinno, A.: Visual interactive systems for end-user development: A model-based design methodology. IEEE Transactions on Systems, Man and Cybernetics, Part A: Systems and Humans 37(6) (November 2007)

[10] Fischer, G., Scharff, E.: Meta-design: Design for designers. In: DIS 2000: Proceed-ings of the 3rd Conference on Designing Interactive Systems, pp. 396–405. ACM, New York (2000)

[11] Halverson, C., Ackerman, M., Erickson, T., Kellogg, W.A. (eds.): Resources, Co-Evolution and Artifacts: Theory in CSCW. Computer Supported Cooperative Work, 1st edn. Springer, Berlin (2008)

[12] Lanzara, G.: Between transient constructs and persistent structures: designing systems in action. Journal of Strategic Information Systems 8, 331–349 (1999)

[13] Lieberman, H., Paternò, F., Wulf, V. (eds.): End User Development. Human-Computer Interaction Series, vol. 9. Springer, Netherlands (2006)

[14] Luff, P., Heath, C., Greatbatch, D.: Tasks-in-interaction: paper and screen based documentation in collaborative activity. In: CSCW 1992: Proceedings of the 1992 ACM Conference on Computer-Supported Cooperative Work, pp. 163–170. ACM Press, New York (1992)

[15] Mansfield, J.: The nature of change or the law of unintended consequences. Impe-rial College Press, London (2010)

[16] Simonsen, J., Robertson, T.: Routledge International Handbook of Participatory Design. Routledge (2012)

Guidelines for Efficient and Effective End-User Development of Mashups

Saeed Aghaee and Cesare Pautasso

Faculty of Informatics, University of Lugano (USI), Switzerland
`first.last@usi.ch`

Abstract. End-User Development (EUD) is an emerging research area aiming at empowering non-technical users to somehow create or design software artifacts. Mashups provide a high potential for EUD activities on the Web. Users on the Web can tap into a vast resource of off-the-shelf components in order to rapidly compose new lightweight software applications called mashups. In this paper, we provide a set of guidelines to design EUD systems for mashups that are widely referred to as *mashup tools*. The guidelines are derived from our experience with the (ongoing) design and evaluation of `NaturalMash`, a novel mashup tool targeted for a wide range of users to create feature-rich mashups.

Keywords: Mashup, End-User Development, Mashup Tool.

1 Introduction

Mashups are a popular type of Web applications built out of the composition of heterogeneous components available through the Web [1]. End-User Development (EUD) [2] of mashups aims at exploiting them by a wide range of users on the Web. EUD systems for mashups are referred to as *Mashup tools*. They usually provide users with an intuitive composition language and environment for the code-free development of mashups. Despite the excessive number of mashup tools emerging form both academia and industry [3], only a few of them have been successful. Tools from academia are mostly research prototypes that rarely reach a large user community. Also, many industrial mashup tools, such as Microsoft Popfly and Google Mashup Editor have been discontinued.

The designers of mashup tools face a number of key challenges, including the need for defining high level, intuitive descriptions of computations and integration logic to be combined with suitable abstractions to represent Web widgets, Web services and Web data sources as reusable components. In this paper, based on our experience with the (ongoing) design and usability evaluation of `NaturalMash` [4], we propose a set of guidelines informing the design of next-generation mashup tools.

2 NaturalMash: A Natural Mashup Tool

`NaturalMash` (Figure 1) is a mashup tool targeted to support a wide range of users, including specially non-programmers, to build sophisticated, feature-rich

Y. Dittrich et al. (Eds.): IS-EUD 2013, LNCS 7897, pp. 260–265, 2013.

mashups. The goal behind the design of NaturalMash was to enable an optimal learning experience, where not only the challenges imposed by the activities at hand are properly balanced with the users's skills, but also the users gradually learn to master new challenges and skills [5]. Also, we intended to ensure an intuitive form of interaction that users feel comfortable and familiar with.

To these ends, we have followed a formative user-centered approach in order to have access to users' feedback at a very early stage of development and make sure users were kept central in our design so as to avoid as much as possible mismatches between users' expectations versus system behavior.

NaturalMash introduce a novel composition technique based on What You See Is What You Get (WYSIWYG), Programming by Demonstration (PbD) [6], and controlled natural language programming [7]. The WYSIWYG interfaces, augmented with PbD (visual field), enables a natural means for the design and manipulation of the presentation layer, and partially the application logic layer, of mashups. Natural language programming compensates the shortcoming of WYSIWYG and PbD to express the application logic of mashups. The choice of structured natural language also fits with the need to ease the tool's learning curve. The mashup descriptions written in natural language are readable and understandable by any English-speaking end user.

One important deficiency of programming in structured natural languages, however, is that it is cumbersome to learn the restrictions of these languages. To overcome this issue, NaturalMash introduces an autocomplete menu that provides suggestions as the users types in the text field. Autocompletion also enables incidental learning. While browsing the suggestions provided by the menu, users gradually discover what are the available components that can be mashed up.

NaturalMash incorporates a stack bar that represents the components that can be used as the "ingredients" for the mashup. The stack gives an overview of the functionalities offered by the tool, representing them with an icon and a name, thus making easy to recognize and memorize. From there, users can drag-and-drop ingredients on the visual field or text field. The list of components used by the mashup being created is shown by the component dock.

In the design of NaturalMash, we have adapted the paradigm of live programming based on WYSIWYG, in which the life-cycle of edit/compile/run is fully automated by the system. As a result, users will be able to more easily bridge the gulf of evaluation (the degree of difficulty of assessing and understanding the state of the system [8]) to incrementally validate and learn from their small steps one at a time. This in turn leads towards an optimal learning experience.

To non-professional users, data flow is a very challenging concept to grasp when learning how to develop mashups [9]. NaturalMash semi-automates the data flow design using a semantic data integration framework.

Up to now, we have successfully completed two design iterations and evaluations. The results of the two usability evaluations were promising and provided us with valuable analytical insights on the ongoing design of NaturalMash. In this paper, we used the results to develop a set of design guidelines that will be presented in the next section.

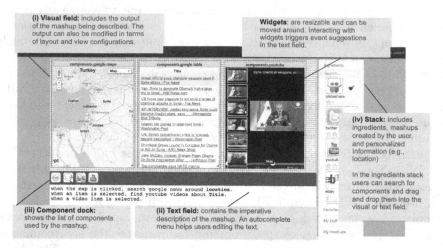

Fig. 1. `NaturalMash` environment: the ingredients stack gives an overview of the tool functionalities (available mashup components). From there, users can drag-and-drop ingredients to start building mashups. Alternatively, they can use the text field to discover desired components. With the help of the autocomplete menu, users type in the text field the imperative description of the mashup in natural language, and immediately see the result in the visual field.

3   End-User Development of Mashups: Guidelines

The design of effective and efficient mashup tools requires to trade-off abstraction against expressiveness and generality against specificity. From a technical perspective, one of the main tasks of mashup tools is to hide the heterogeneity and complexity of Web technologies behind an easy-to-understand abstraction. From a user modeling perspective, the challenge lies in the broad diversity of user skills that need to be targeted and in the large number of domains in which mashups can be applied to.

In the following we enumerate a set of guidelines resulting from our experience with the design and evaluation of `NaturalMash`. We believe these guidelines can help addressing the mentioned tradeoffs towards the design of efficient and effective mashup tools letting non-professional users create sophisticated mashups.

– **Use natural metaphors:** Bringing the user interface closer to the user's way of thinking and working can significantly increase usability. This can be achieved by, for instance, reconciling the semantics of the presentation objects with the semantics of the target application domain (domain-specific metaphors), or using metaphors that are well understood by non-professional users. For example, a recent study on the understandability of service composition languages [10] shows that the visual wiring paradigm (i.e., visual control flow and data flow diagrams) that is widely utilized by existing mashup tools, is not a familiar metaphor for non-professional users.

The `NaturalMash` interface adopts the generic metaphor of visual context and textual content, where the visual field contains the actual mashup output and the text field consists of the imperative descriptions of the output in natural language. Provided that the imperative natural language descriptions are abstract enough, this metaphor is understandable by almost everyone. This hypothesis was also supported by the results from our user studies.

– **Design at meta-level:** Mashups can be built and used in different domains of applications. These domains range from daily utilities of Web users (i.e., consumer market) to narrowly specialized domains and enterprise environments. It is important to identify the application domain in which users are willing to and have shown a clear need to develop mashups [11]. This is a well known problem in EUD, as the importance of task and domain specificity was already pointed out by Nardi [12] in the context of end-user programming. From the point of view of the tool designer, a closed approach which narrowly targets a single application domain may present some limitations. Application domains usually change over time. This may results in changes of the initial requirements and assumptions based on which the mashup tool was designed. Also, a mashup tool targeting a specific domain may not perfectly fit into, or be easily transformed into, a tool targeting another domain. Therefore we advocate a meta-design approach [13], whereby a generic mashup meta-tool is designed and from it domain-specific mashup tools can be derived by it users.

The meta-design elements in `NaturalMash` include (i) selection of the available ingredients (components), (ii) the look and naming of ingredients, and most importantly (iii) the language style used to describe them. In the latter case, the description of each ingredients used in the text field can be changed by users to tailor the "language" of the tool to their domain.

– **Support different levels of expressiveness:** Being able to only create so-called "toy" mashups is the main criticism against existing mashup tools. An effective mashup tool should provide enough expressive power to allow the creation of sophisticated mashups. On the other hand, the usability of a system may be affected by the degree of expresivenss it offers. To avoid this issue, [14] proposes three levels of user tailoring including customization, integration, and extension. In case of mashups, all these three levels are relevant and thus should be supported by a mashup tool. Customization means modifying an existing mashup through parameterization or user interface manipulation. Integration is the process of creating new mashups and should be allowed at all the levels of data, business logic, and presentation tiers. Extension allows extending the functionality of the mashup tool by developing new components.

In `NaturalMash`, customization is enabled through the visual field. Integration is mainly supported by natural language programming. The plan is to also enable extension for professional users to create and add components the tool library.

– **Avoid complex user interfaces:** Simple user interfaces can largely decrease the learning cost. We emphasis simplicity in terms of elements, content, and language used in the user interface of a mashup tool. Many existing mashup tools have a complex tab-based environment with nested user interface elements.

They also commonly use very technical terms (e.g., "regular expressions", "mashup components", etc.) in their user interface.

These are issues that we tried to avoid in the design of `NaturalMash`. We intended to keep the user interface as simple and easy-to-use as possible. As illustrated in Figure 1, the interface is composed of only four non-nested components (visual field, text field, component dock, stack). We also attempted to use non-technical and easily understandable terms in the interface (e.g., "ingredients" vs. "component library").

– **Build an online community:** Online communities are of importance in boosting the ability of users to learn how to use the tool through creating, sharing, and reusing mashups, knowledge, and experience [12]. Crowdsourcing can also be applied in an online community to persuade professional users to enrich the component library for non-professional users [15].

We plan to investigate the mentioned impacts of online communities in the context of mashup EUD. More importantly, we are interested in in-the-wild testing of our meta-design using an online community.

– **Adopt user-centered design:** We have realized that a formative user-centered design is a promising method to design "natural" mashup tools. This method ensures receiving early feedback from users and applying it on every step of the design process.

4   Related Work

Stemming from both academic and industrial research and development, a number of mashup tools have been designed. Most of existing industrial mashup tools, such as Yahoo! Pipes (`http://pipes.yahoo.com/`), IBM Mashup Center (`http://www.ibm.com/software/info/mashup-center`), and JackBe Presto (`http://www.jackbe.com/`), as well as early academic tools (e.g., Marmite [16]) are designed for expert users with advanced technical knowledge.

Recently, however, the attempt in academia has been to design mashup tools supporting non-programmer users as well. For instance, ServFace builder [17], DashMash [18], and RoofTop [19] provide a full WYSIWYG approach, which, however, does not provide as much expressive power as `NaturalMash` (thanks to natural language programming). In terms of natural language programming, IFTTT (`https://ifttt.com`) is a similar system, which, even though it is solely based on natural language, restricts the user's input using a structured visual editor. Also, IFTTT only allows to create mashups based on a single control-flow pattern (if this then that).

5   Conclusion

Mashups provide a vast potential for EUD activities on the Web. In this paper, we proposed a set of guidelines to design next-generation EUD systems for mashups (mashup tools). The guidelines were a result of our experience with the design and evaluation of `NaturalMash`. The next big step is to bring the tool to the real world and conduct in-the-wild testing.

Acknowledgments. This work has been supported by Swiss National Science Foundation with the SOSOA project (SINERGIA grant nr. CRSI22_127386).

References

1. Benslimane, D., Dustdar, S., Sheth, A.: Services mashups: The new generation of web applications. IEEE Internet Computing 12, 13–15 (2008)
2. Lieberman, H., Paternò, F., Klann, M., Wulf, V.: End-User Development: An Emerging Paradigm. In: End User Development. Springer, Netherlands (2006)
3. Aghaee, S., Nowak, M., Pautasso, C.: Reusable Decision Space for Mashup Tool Design. In: Proc. of EICS (2012)
4. Aghaee, S., Pautasso, C.: EnglishMash: Usability Design for a Natural Mashup Composition Environment. In: Grossniklaus, M., Wimmer, M. (eds.) ICWE Workshops 2012. LNCS, vol. 7703, pp. 109–120. Springer, Heidelberg (2012)
5. Repenning, A., Ioannidou, A.: What Makes End-User Development Tick? 13 Design Guidelines. Springer (2006)
6. Cypher, A., Halbert, D.C., Kurlander, D., Lieberman, H., Maulsby, D., Myers, B.A., Turransky, A. (eds.): Watch What I Do: Programming by Demonstration. MIT Press (1993)
7. Petrick, S.R.: On Natural Language based Computer Systems. IBM J. Res. Dev. 20, 314–325 (1976)
8. Norman, D.A., Draper, S.W.: User Centered System Design; New Perspectives on Human-Computer Interaction. L. Erlbaum Associates Inc. (1986)
9. Mehandjiev, N., Lecue, F., Wajid, U., Namoun, A.: Assisted Service Composition for End Users. In: Proc. of ECOWS 2010 (2010)
10. Namoun, A., Nestler, T., Angeli, A.D.: Service Composition for Non-programmers: Prospects, Problems, and Design Recommendations. In: Proc. of ECOWS (2010)
11. Casati, F., Daniel, F., Angeli, A.D., Imran, M., Soi, S., Wilkinson, C.R., Marchese, M.: Developing Mashup Tools for End-Users: On the Importance of the Application Domain. IJNGC 3 (2012)
12. Nardi, B.A.: A Small Matter of Programming: Perspectives on End User Computing. MIT Press (1993)
13. Fischer, G., Giaccardi, E., Ye, Y., Sutcliffe, A.G., Mehandjiev, N.: Meta-design: A Manifesto for End-User Development. Commun. ACM 47, 33–37 (2004)
14. Mørch, A.: Three Levels of End-user Tailoring: Customization, Integration, and Extension. In: Computers and Design in Context. MIT Press (1997)
15. Nebeling, M., Leone, S., Norrie, M.C.: Crowdsourced web engineering and design. In: Brambilla, M., Tokuda, T., Tolksdorf, R. (eds.) ICWE 2012. LNCS, vol. 7387, pp. 31–45. Springer, Heidelberg (2012)
16. Wong, J., Hong, J.I.: Making mashups with marmite: towards end-user programming for the web. In: Proc. of CHI 2007 (2007)
17. Nestler, T., Feldmann, M., Hübsch, G., Preußner, A., Jugel, U.: The ServFace Builder - A WYSIWYG Approach for Building Service-based Applications. In: Benatallah, B., Casati, F., Kappel, G., Rossi, G. (eds.) ICWE 2010. LNCS, vol. 6189, pp. 498–501. Springer, Heidelberg (2010)
18. Cappiello, C., Matera, M., Picozzi, M., Sprega, G., Barbagallo, D., Francalanci, C.: DashMash: A Mashup Environment for End User Development. In: Auer, S., Díaz, O., Papadopoulos, G.A. (eds.) ICWE 2011. LNCS, vol. 6757, pp. 152–166. Springer, Heidelberg (2011)
19. Hoyer, V., Gilles, F., Janner, T., Stanoevska-Slabeva, K.: SAP Research RoofTop Marketplace: Putting a Face on Service-Oriented Architectures. In: Proc. of SERVICES (2009)

Software Development for the Working Actuary*

David Raymond Christiansen

IT University of Copenhagen
drc@itu.dk

Abstract. We present an in-progress domain-specific language for actuaries. Due to the mathematical sophistication of actuaries and the relatively high degree of formalization of the field, we conjecture that a dependently-typed functional language with special support for actuarial models will enable actuaries to develop software that is robust and understandable.

1 Introduction

The demands on insurers and actuarial software are increasing. New rules from the European Union, called *Solvency II* [6], pose new challenges that require significant changes to pension infrastructures. The Actulus project, a collaboration between the University of Copenhagen, Edlund A/S and the IT University of Copenhagen, seeks to solve this problem through a combination of actuarial science and programming language research, taking advantage of Edlund's position as a market-leading vendor of software to the life insurance and pension industry in Denmark.

Key to our approach is empowering actuaries to develop their own analysis tools. We aim to do this by developing a domain-specific language that supports actuarial models and yet is sufficiently general to express a wide variety of programs.

Actuaries are an interesting target for end-user software development for a number of reasons:

- Actuarial science is a highly-formalized field with well-understood terms and ideas.
- Actuaries are used to formal notation and mathematical thinking.
- Many actuaries write software already in the course of their day-to-day work.

This paper describes ongoing work on a domain-specific language for actuaries that will enable them to safely develop models of life insurance and pension products that can be analyzed either with a standard set of utilities or with tools that the actuaries construct themselves. Sect. 2 presents just enough of the theory in question to explain the features of the language. Sect. 3 presents our preliminary solutions. Finally, Sect. 4 discusses our plans for further developing our language.

---

* Work supported by the Danish Advanced Technology Foundation (*Højteknologifonden*) (017-2010-3).

Y. Dittrich et al. (Eds.): IS-EUD 2013, LNCS 7897, pp. 266–271, 2013.
© Springer-Verlag Berlin Heidelberg 2013

2   Actuarial Theory

In this section, the basics of actuarial mathematics as relevant to Actulus are laid out. Note that the mathematical models influence the development of new products, as only products that can be effectively modeled are sold, while pressures from the market can lead to new models. It is far beyond the scope of this paper to provide a proper introduction to actuarial mathematics, but Promislow's textbook [5] contains a discussion of the multi-state, continuous-time models that are used.

An insurance or pension product is a collection of *states* that one or more people can inhabit, combined with repeating payments due during sojourn in these states and lump-sum payments due on transition from one state to another.

Both pricing of products and determination of solvency rely on calculating what is known as the *reserves* of a product. The reserve is the present value of the expected future payments, both benefits and premiums.

Two simple products will be used as running examples in this discussion: the *pure endowment* and the *temporary life annuity*.

Pure Endowment. If the policy holder is alive at some time t, then he or she receives a payment.

Temporary Life Annuity. The policy holder receives a continuous payment from time 0 until some time n or until his or her death, whichever occurs first.

More complicated products can depend on multiple related lives (such as those of a married couple and their children), track more events (such as disability), and have more complicated specifications of payments.

In Actulus, products are modeled within continuous-time Markov processes. Continuous-time Markov processes are similar to the perhaps more familiar discrete-time Markov processes, except instead of defining state-transition probabilities as a function of time, we define state-transition *intensities*. Integrating a transition intensity over an interval yields the probability of transition in that interval.

Sometimes, we also want to make use of semi-Markov models, in which transition intensities can depend on duration of sojourn in the present state. The optimal treatment of these models in the context of Actulus is ongoing work.

In addition to the Markov model representing the events in the life or lives of the insured, the payments mandated by the product must be specified. These are customarily specified in differential form, so that integrating them over an interval gives the payments due in that interval. Additionally, products can specify lump-sump payments due at state transitions.

Combining the Markov model with the payment streams and lump-sum payments allows us to construct *Thiele's differential equations*, a system of equations whose solution represents the *statewise reserves* for the product. The statewise reserves are the contribution of each state in the Markov model to the whole of the reserves, and the current reserve is the statewise reserve for the present state of the insured.

3   Actulus Modeling Language (AML)

According to the experience of Edlund A/S in the Danish insurance software industry, the present activities of the Danish life insurance and pension industry are largely centered around a compendium of well-understood products with standardized mathematical models, called *G82*. This rules out broad classes of interesting products and it can lead to the use of models that ignore important features of the actual products being modeled if these stray too far from *G82*.

When a fitting model has been chosen or developed, actuaries send the model to professional software developers. The professional programmers then implement the necessary calculations. Many actuaries are familiar to an extent with programming, especially using languages such as R or Matlab, but they are not typically skilled in modern programming languages and software development practices. Because of this disconnect, the correspondence between the model and the resulting code is not necessarily readily apparent.

By using a numerical differential equation solver combined with a domain-specific language for describing products and the calculations involving them, the Actulus project aims to make insurance calculation both more accurate and more understandable. Actulus consists of the following components: a high-performance numerical solver for differential equations called the *calculation kernel*, a language for declaratively defining the products described in Sect. 2 called the *product language* or AML-P, and a language for describing calculations called the *calculation language* or AML-C. While it is extremely important in practice for Actulus, the calculation kernel is not the focus of this paper. Instead, we describe AML, as it is the primary interface between the user and the system.

There have been a number of examples of DSLs for financial applications in the literature, dating at least back to Risla in 1995 [1]. One particularly interesting line of research is a number of Haskell-based combinator libraries for defining derivatives products that are based on work by Peyton Jones, Eber and Seward [4]. A paper by Mogensen that describes the use of a novel type system for a financial DSL [2] is also highly relevant.

While other pension administration and calculation systems present forms or tables to the actuary as a primary interaction model, Actulus will present the user with a programming language. While work on AML is not yet complete, the broad outlines of its structure are apparent. We believe that making it easy for actuaries to program their systems themselves will allow them to receive many of the benefits of modern programming languages, such as modular constructions, code re-use, and the safety provided by an advanced type system, when constructing their models.

AML is a dependently-typed total functional language with special support in the type system for checking specific properties of insurance products. These insurance products are defined using a special syntax that is designed to be particularly readable for domain experts.

Because the dedicated product syntax adheres closely to the actuarial theory described in Sect. 2, we expect that actuaries who are not skilled software developers will be able to read and write these descriptions with little additional training. This will be empirically evaluated when an implementation is ready. Additionally, we expect that the presence of a mathematically-inspired programming language will allow users to incrementally build on their knowledge of the modeling language. However, the product modeling notation alone is at least as expressive as existing forms-and-tables interfaces. All products from *G82* can be expressed in AML-P.

The AML product language consists of three primary constructions: state models, products, and risk models. Products represent a collection of (conditional) payments. Risk models describe the transition intensities. State models simply ensure that products and compatible risk models are used together. Both of our example products in Sect. 2 mention only two states: `alive` and `dead`. We call this state model `LifeDeath`:

```
statemodel LifeDeath where
  states = alive | dead
  transitions = alive → dead
```

When we define a product, we must specify the state model within which it is defined. Syntactically, this resembles a type ascription.

```
product PureEndowment(expiry : TimePoint) : LifeDeath where
  obligations = at t pay ¤1 when (t = expiry) provided (alive)
```

```
product TempLifeAnn(expiry : TimePoint) : LifeDeath where
  obligations = at t pay ¤1 per year provided (alive and t < expiry)
```

In the above DSL, **at** binds the variable t representing the current point in time, the operator ¤ constructs currency, **per year** constructs a constant-rate payment stream from an amount of money, **when** constructs a payment stream that delivers a lump sum at a particular point in time, and **provided** makes a payment stream conditional on a particular set of states or Boolean conditions.

The other half of our model, the transition intensities, is described by a risk model. An example risk model for `LifeDeath` follows:

```
riskmodel Mortality(p : Person) : LifeDeath where
  intensities = alive → dead by gm(p)
```

In the above, `gm` is a library function that takes a representation of a person (presumably some sort of record structure with fields for age, sex, and so forth) as its argument, returning a mortality intensity according to the industry-standard Gompertz-Makeham formula. As described in Sect. 2, a transition intensity is the continuous-time analog of a transition probability in discrete-time Markov chains.

The *statewise reserves* are the contributions that each state makes to the overall reserve. We can compute it for these two products by calling the appropriate library function:

```
statewiseReserves(PureEndowment(TimePoint(2035, 1, 1)), Mortality)
```

There are a few important details in the call to `statewiseReserves`. First, the fact that PureEndowment and Mortality are defined according to the same state model - `LifeDeath` - can be statically checked. Second, we don't need to write that the state model in question is in fact `LifeDeath`, because it can be inferred from the other two arguments.

One of the main features that distinguishes our work on AML from other domain-specific languages is that it is a *total* language with *dependent types*. A total language is one in which every function returns a result for every type-correct input. In other words, infinite loops are impossible and no pattern-match may miss a case. By construction, this prevents a number of errors, and it results in a language that more closely matches mathematical notions of functions. For example, we don't need to worry about the potential for an infinite recursion in a transition intensity.

Perhaps the most daring design choice in AML is the inclusion of full dependent types. Dependent types are types that can be abstracted over values, and not just other types as in traditional functional programming. In many ways, dependent types represent a quite radical departure from traditional functional programming, and a full introduction to them is beyond the scope of this paper. Oury and Swierstra [3] offer an accessible introduction to the expressive capabilities of dependent types.

Dependent types allow the type system to be much more precise. For example, a list type can encode the length of the list, and the `head` function can then, in its type, require that the list is non-empty.

For perhaps a more relevant example of the kinds of invariants that can be enforced through dependent types, consider discounting of money. Discounting is the process of using information about interest rates to compute the value of an amount of money at some other time. Because one euro in 2003 is worth a different amount than one euro in 2013, we can't simply add currency. Instead, we must *discount* the value, converting from one time to another.

For the sake of simplicity, assume that the interest rate is some constant r through the entire period. In that case, we discount from t_0 to t_1 by multiplying the value at t_0 by $e^{r(t_1-t_0)}$. In AML, we can force this discounting by adding a point in time to our currency type. We then require that these time points be equal in the types of arguments to our addition function.

We begin by defining a data type `Money` which is *indexed by* a point in time. Two instances of `Money` only have the same type if they are indexed by the same point in time, just as a Java `ArrayList<String>` has a different type than `ArrayList<File>`. Note that the types of `a` and `b` refer to the value of the parameter `t` – this is a feature of a dependent type system. The compiler will reject calls to `add` for which it cannot prove that `a` and `b` have the same time index.

```
type Money(time : TimePoint) : Type where
  Amount(x: Real) : Money(time)

function add(t : TimePoint, a : Money(t), b : Money(t)) : Money(t) where
  add(t, Amount(x), Amount(y)) = Amount(x + y)
```

We now have the ability to represent currency at a particular point in time. We can define a discounting function according to the above formula as follows:

```
function discount(t0 : TimePoint, t1 : TimePoint,
                  interest : Real, m0 : Money(t0)): Money(t1) where
  discount(TimePoint(t0'), TimePoint(t1'), r, Amount(x0)) =
    Amount(exp(r * (t1' - t0')) * x0)
```

By controlling the scope of the `Amount` constructor, the library author can prevent explicit pattern-matching on the value as was done in the definition of `discount`. An important potential source of errors is eliminated entirely through judicious use of dependent types in three short, readable definitions.

4   Future Work

The ongoing development of AML has two primary aspects:

- We want to ensure that AML is on a strong theoretical footing, with a sound type system. Users should not be able to circumvent the typechecker, whether through malice or by accident.
- We need to ensure that AML is actually usable by actuaries.

We plan to achieve the first goal through a combination of explaining the unique features of AML in terms of well-understood systems and through a mixture of machine-checked and manual mathematical reasoning. The second goal, however, requires empirical evaluation. Implementation work on an AML interpreter has begun. We will soon be in a position to begin testing the language and associated tools with actuaries.

References

1. Arnold, B.R.T., van Deursen, A., Res, M.: Algebraic specification of a language for describing financial products. Technical report, Eindhoven University of Technology (1995)
2. Mogensen, T.Æ.: Linear Types for Cashflow Reengineering. In: Broy, M., Zamulin, A.V. (eds.) PSI 2003. LNCS, vol. 2890, pp. 13–21. Springer, Heidelberg (2004)
3. Oury, N., Swierstra, W.: The power of pi. In: Proceedings of the 13th ACM SIGPLAN International Conference on Functional Programming, ICFP 2008, pp. 39–50. ACM, New York (2008)
4. Peyton-Jones, S., Eber, J.M., Seward, J.: Composing contracts: an adventure in financial engineering (functional pearl). SIGPLAN Not. 35(9), 280–292 (2000)
5. David Promislow, S.: Fundamentals of Actuarial Mathematics, 2nd edn. Wiley (2011)
6. Directive 2009/138/EC of the European Parliament and of the council

Automated Test Case Generation in End-User Programming

Nysret Musliu[1], Wolfgang Slany[2], and Johannes Gärtner[3]

[1] DBAI, Technische Universität Wien, Austria
musliu@dbai.tuwien.ac.at
[2] IST, Technische Universität Graz, Austria
wolfgang.slany@tugraz.at
[3] Ximes GmbH, Austria
gaertner@ximes.com

Abstract. Generation of test cases for end-user programmers is crucial to assure the correctness of their code. In this paper we investigate the automatic generation of test cases for programs that are written in Visual Basic for Applications and are used in MS Excel. We implement a metaheuristic search method to generate tests that achieve a satisfactory statement and branch coverage. Furthermore, in our methodology the code coverage is visualized. The generated test cases and the visualization enable end users to better understand the behavior of the programs and increase the probability of detecting errors when the code is changed at a later time.

1 Introduction

Nowadays the end-users who are not professional programmers write sometimes small programs to do their work more efficiently. A typical case is the writing of small programs in Microsoft Office using Visual Basic for Applications (VBA). In this paper we investigate the testing of VBA programs written in MS Excel, which is one of widely used spreadsheet applications.

Testing of spreadsheets has attracted the interest of many researchers working in area of end-user software engineering. Although spreadsheets contain many errors it has been shown that end-users are overconfident that their applications are working correctly ([7], [9]). Therefore, several methodologies have been proposed to minimize the number of errors in spreadsheets. Examples of such approaches include the What You See Is What You Test (WYSIWYT) methodology for white box testing ([8], [2]), the methodology proposed in [1] etc. We refer the reader to the recent survey [5] that describes different other existing approaches for testing spreadsheets.

In this paper we propose a methodology that enables end-user programmers that write VBA programs in Excel to test their code. To this aim, we propose a heuristic based search procedure to generate automatically test cases that achieve high coverage (statement and branch coverage). The test cases ensures that most parts of the code are executed and enables end-users to inspect whether

Y. Dittrich et al. (Eds.): IS-EUD 2013, LNCS 7897, pp. 272–277, 2013.

the code is giving the appropriate results by analyzing generated test cases. Furthermore, in the proposed methodology the code is also shown in the Excel sheet and is visualized with different colors to show the parts of code that are covered with the generated tests.

2   Methodology

In Figure 1 the main parts of the proposed methodology are presented. In the first step users can select the procedure for which test cases should be generated. Additionally, the range of input variables can be determined. In the current implementation our methodology enables the user to determine the range for integer variables. The specification of other type of data (e.g. strings) is also of importance and should be considered in the future.

In the next step the selected procedure is instrumented to store the information for the statements and branches that are reached by a particular test case when the instrumented code is executed during the search process for test cases.

2.1   Automatic Generation of Test Cases

The main component of our methodology automatically generates test cases. We propose a heuristic based procedure that starts from a random solution. The current solution is further improved until all statements/branches are covered or the maximum number of iterations is reached. Note that automatic generation of test cases with other metaheuristic techniques (e.g., genetic algorithms [4], tabu search [3], etc.) for imperative languages has been extensively investigated by researchers working in the area of search based software engineering. The algorithms based on simulated annealing framework have been also used for test case generation in different domains ([10], [11]). A recent review on search based software techniques has been given by Harman et al [4]. We implemented

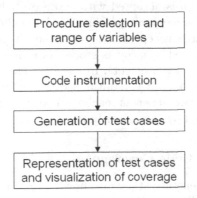

Fig. 1. Main steps in our methodology

a simple algorithm which is also based on the ideas of simulated annealing to show that even simple heuristics can be used succesfully to generate test cases in end-user programming. Our procedure is presented below:

1. Generate an initial random test case (solution) and store it.
2. Initialize the parameter called temperature (T).
3. Generate a random solution in the neighborhood and evaluate it.
4. Accept the neighborhood solution if it fulfills the acceptance criteria.
5. Store the neighborhood solution if it covers at least one uncovered statement or branch.
6. Decrease the parameter T. If the temperature reaches the value 0 assign to it the initial value.
7. Go to step 3 if the number of maximum iterations is not reached.
8. Return the generated test cases.

The algorithm first generates a solution that initializes all input variables randomly in the range given by the user. This solution is further stored as one test case and is used as current solution. The algorithm also initializes the temperature T in this phase. This parameter is used later when the decision is made whether the new test case should be accepted as the current solution. In step 3 the algorithm generates a new solution in the neighborhood of the current solution. To generate this solution one of the input variables is selected randomly. The selected variable gets another random value in its domain. The new test case is evaluated with an evaluation function that consists of two components. The first component gives the information whether the new case covers a new branch/statement or part of condition of the branch. If the test case covers at least one uncovered statement/branch, it is accepted for the next iteration. Otherwise, the second component of the fitness function is calculated from the degree of fulfillment of the conditions. This component is an aggregated sum of all distances for uncovered branches. The new generated solution is accepted if the second component is better than the component of the current solution. In other cases the solution is accepted with some probability that depends on the temperature T. In the beginning when T is large there is a higher chance that also a bad solution is accepted, whereas when T is low this probability decreases. The new accepted solution is stored as a new test case, if it covers at least one new branch (or statement). In the next step the temperature T is decreased, and if it has value 0 it is reinitialized. Steps 3 to 7 are repeated until the maximum number of iterations is reached. The stored test cases during the search are finally returned by the algorithm.

2.2 Visualization of Code Coverage

After the test cases are generated they are shown to users, and the code coverage is visualized. An example of such test cases is shown in Figure 3. These test cases are generated automatically with the described algorithm for a simple program called myGrade that is introduced in the next section. Given these test

```
Private Function myGrade(midtermEx As Integer, finalEx As Integer, assignments As Integer)

    Dim points As Single
    points = midtermEx * 0.3 + finalEx * 0.3 + assignments * 0.4

    If (points > 90) Then
        Grade = "A"
    Else
        If (points > 80) Then
            Grade = "B"
        Else
            If (points > 70) Then
                Grade = "C"
            Else
                If (points > 60) Then
                    Grade = "D"
                Else
                    Grade = "F"
                End If
            End If
        End If
    End If

End Function
```

Fig. 2. The program that determines a grade based on input points and the visualization of statement coverage (the last test case in Figure 3 is not taken into consideration). The light gray color corresponds to green, and the dark gray color corresponds to red color.

cases, end-users can check if the program is performing as expected. The selected procedure is also presented in the spreadsheet and the statement coverage is visualized. Statements with the green color are covered by the test cases whereas statements that are not covered are presented with the red color. With the generated test cases all statements of myGrade would have the green color, but if we remove the last test case the visualization would look like in Figure 2.

The visualization of code coverage is not new, and different applications that visualize the code coverage exist. The effect of code visualization on professional programmers has been investigated in [6]. In our approach the aim of visualization is limited to give more information to end-user regarding the code coverage. We believe that this information is important for the end-users, because it makes them aware regarding the parts of code that are not tested enough.

3   Preliminary Experiments

In our first experiment we wrote a program that is called myGrade. Although this is a very simple program, it is a good example to illustrate our approach. This program takes three integer variables (that can take values from 0 to 100) that represent the points students obtained in midterm exam, final exam, and assignments. The total number of points is calculated based on the weights of each variable. The function assigns a grade A, B, C, D, or F, to the global variable Grade. This function is represented in Figure 2. Our algorithm generates in less than a second the test cases presented in Figure 3.

To show the usefulness of our method for more complex functions we further experimented with an example from the literature that is used as a benchmark problem for code coverage. This program is called triangle classifier (see Figure 4) because it classifies the triangle in one of several types based on the lengths of its sides. The program has three input variables. Our current tool can deal only with integer values and in our experiment these variables can take values from 1 to 1000. Our algorithm has been able to generate test cases in less than 1 second

Midterm	Final	Assignments	Grade
31	54	58	F
31	87	71	D
57	92	84	C
93	50	93	B
98	100	85	A

Fig. 3. Test cases generated by the heuristic algorithm

```
Private Function triangleClassifierCode(A As Integer, B As Integer, C As Integer)

    If (A > 0 And B > 0 And C > 0) Then
        If (2 * A < A + B + C And 2 * B < A + B + C And 2 * C < A + B + C) Then
            If (A = B) Then
                If (B = C) Then
                    triangleClass = "Equilateral"
                Else
                    triangleClass = "Isosceles"
                End If
            Else
                If (A = C) Then
                    triangleClass = "Isosceles"
                Else
                    If (B = C) Then
                        triangleClass = "Isosceles"
                    Else
                        triangleClass = "Scalene"
                    End If
                End If
            End If
        Else
            triangleClass = "No triangle"
        End If
    Else
        triangleClass = "No triangle"
    End If

End Function
```

Fig. 4. The code for triangle classifier ([3])

that cover almost all statements and branches. We have also experimented with a more complex program (line rectangle classifier) used for example in [3] that has 8 input variables and much more branches. With our approach we could also generate test cases with satisfactory branch/statement coverage for this problem in a time that should be acceptable by end-users.

4   Conclusions

We proposed a methodology for automatic generation of test cases for VBA programs written in Excel. Our search procedure has shown good results in the preliminary experiments, and the visualization of code coverage gives users information regarding those parts of code which are (not) covered.

For the future work, it will be interesting to extend our search procedure to deal with any type of variables. Furthermore, more extensive experiments are needed, and other search techniques may also be considered. Providing users with the possibility to easily run the test cases is also an important issue.

Acknowledgments. The research herein is partially conducted within the competence network Softnet Austria II (www.soft-net.at, COMET K-Projekt) and funded by the Austrian Federal Ministry of Economy, Family and Youth (bmwfj), the province of Styria, the Steirische Wirtschaftsfrderungsgesellschaft mbH. (SFG), and the city of Vienna in terms of the center for innovation and technology (ZIT).

References

1. Abraham, R., Erwig, M.: Ucheck: A spreadsheet type checker for end users. J. Vis. Lang. Comput. 18(1), 71–95 (2007)
2. Burnett, M.M., Sheretov, A., Ren, B., Rothermel, G.: Testing homogeneous spreadsheet grids with the "what you see is what you test" methodology. IEEE Trans. Software Eng. 28(6), 576–594 (2002)
3. Díaz, E., Tuya, J., Blanco, R., Javier Dolado, J.: A tabu search algorithm for structural software testing. Computers & Operations Research 35(10), 3052–3072 (2008)
4. Harman, M., Mansouri, S.A., Zhang, Y.: Search-based software engineering: Trends, techniques and applications. ACM Comput. Surv. 45(1), 11 (2012)
5. Ko, A.J., Abraham, R., Beckwith, L., Blackwell, A.F., Burnett, M.M., Erwig, M., Scaffidi, C., Lawrance, J., Lieberman, H., Myers, B.A., Rosson, M.B., Rothermel, G., Shaw, M., Wiedenbeck, S.: The state of the art in end-user software engineering. ACM Comput. Surv. 43(3), 21 (2011)
6. Lawrance, J., Clarke, S., Burnett, M.M., Rothermel, G.: How well do professional developers test with code coverage visualizations? An empirical study. In: VL/HCC, pp. 53–60 (2005)
7. Panko, R.: Spreadsheet errors: What we know. What we think we can do. arXiv preprint arXiv:0802.3457 (2008)
8. Rothermel, G., Li, L., DuPuis, C., Burnett, M.M.: What you see is what you test: A methodology for testing form-based visual programs. In: ICSE, pp. 198–207 (1998)
9. Ruthruff, J.R., Prabhakararao, S., Reichwein, J., Cook, C.R., Creswick, E., Burnett, M.M.: Interactive, visual fault localization support for end-user programmers. J. Vis. Lang. Comput. 16(1-2), 3–40 (2005)
10. Tracey, N., Clark, J., Mander, K.: Automated program flaw finding using simulated annealing. ACM SIGSOFT Soft. Eng. Notes 23, 73–81 (1998)
11. Waeselynck, H., Thévenod-Fosse, P., Abdellatif-Kaddour, O.: Simulated annealing applied to test generation: landscape characterization and stopping criteria. Emp. Soft. Eng. 12(1), 35–63 (2007)

Component-Based Design and Software Readymades

Anders I. Mørch[1] and Li Zhu[2]

[1] Department of Educational Research and InterMedia, University of Oslo, Norway
anders.morch@intermedia.uio.no
[2] Department of Computer Science, Università degli Studi di Milano, Milan, Italy
zhu@dico.unimi.it

Abstract. End-user developers need access to tools and techniques that allow them to create, modify, and extend software artifacts without programming. Previous research has shown that visual software components can provide the right level of abstraction. However, component-based design (CBD) will succeed only if there is a good balance of standardization and flexibility (software issues) and a good balance of usefulness and usability (HCI issues). We present a vision for CBD and two approaches toward achieving it: 1) design by composition and 2) design by redesign. We claim that the latter is more user friendly but lacks the flexibility of the former. We propose the notion of "software readymade" as a theoretical concept to integrate them, inspired by the role of the "spectator" in the work of the artist Marcel Duchamp. We propose stand-alone multiperspective tailorable software components to instantiate the concept, and we give two examples (application units and nuggets).

Keywords: Application units, component-based design, nuggets, readymades, software components, tailorable components.

1 Introduction

At the 2011 EUD conference in Brindisi, Italy, Fabio Casati gave a keynote describing failed attempts of end-user application composition environments (e.g., component-based design environments, workflows, service composition, and mashup builders). A reason for the failure is that these technologies expose low-level (software program) features that are difficult for end users to make sense of. However, it is difficult for developers to anticipate end-user developers' needs because the needs are emergent and circumstantial (based on use), and arguably, more network-oriented (rooted in human relations and work organizations) than hierarchical (software organization). This discrepancy can be addressed by software engineering methods that allow applications to be modified during development in response to user requirements, but users should also be actively engaged in the process, drawing on their domain expertise and creativity. We discuss the pros and cons of component-based design (CBD) for end-user development (EUD), addressing both professional and end-user developer needs. We present a vision and two approaches to CBD toward that end: 1) design by composition and 2) design by redesign. Next, we propose a theoretical perspective to integrate the two approaches,

Y. Dittrich et al. (Eds.): IS-EUD 2013, LNCS 7897, pp. 278–283, 2013.

and we summarize our efforts at developing tools and techniques based on this perspective (multiperspective, tailorable, autonomous software components).

2 Vision of Component-Based Design

We present an illustrative example for balancing standardization and flexibility (technical issues) and for usefulness and usability (user-oriented issues). Furniture design, and chair design in particular, is a good analogy because chair designers are concerned with many of the same issues that user interface designers and software developers deal with: producing flexible variations of a generic product informed by a design concept. Figure 1 shows a picture of how we envision flexibility incorporated in CBD: enabling end-user developers to create new applications based on an application platform (generic application), without making the same application twice. In this way EUD-enabled applications will also be creativity support tools.

Fig. 1. A vision of component-based design: combining standardization and flexibility within a constrained design space of creative reconfiguration. Reprinted with permission from the artists: Martino Gamper (100 chairs in 100 days) and Angus Mill (photo) [7].

3 Component-Based Design of Software Applications

Our idea of component-based design (CBD) of software applications has been influenced by Fischer's notion of a domain-oriented design environment (DODE) [2]. He proposed that the basic building blocks are domain-oriented components that are connected by meaningful relations as defined by external criteria, ranging from design rules to user preferences. More commonly, component-based design (CBD) means to create new functionality (e.g., applications) by combining existing functionality (e.g., software components). We distinguish two approaches to CBD: 1) design by selecting from a library of basic components and a work area for composing them and 2) design by modifying a generic (tailorable) application to create new applications. We briefly review work in each of the two areas below.

3.1   Design by Composition

The FreeEvolve platform developed by Wulf, Pipek, and Won provides a palette of basic search application functionality for stitching small database applications within the domain [8]. A user study of the system revealed the strength of direct activation of tailoring functionality and the weakness of manually connecting two components. User-assistance techniques such as 3D visualization and organization (part/whole structures) were added to resolve the weaknesses.

Web services are a more recent innovation of software component integration, associated with web applications. A study conducted by Mehandjiev [3], comparing three different web service integration models, found that users preferred one with a logic that abstracted features of programming and more easily aligned with the users' mental model of the task (flowchart model) [3]. However, most application composition environments require developers to follow another logic (dataflow), exposing the various sources and sinks of data required for composition, which prevented end-user developers to participate beyond simple applications.

Mashup components are the latest trend in application composition, as they are more flexible by allowing user interfaces and data in addition to software functionality to be composed. Muhammad and colleagues [5] found evidence that domain-oriented mashup builders are more usable for end-user developers than generic builders and demonstrate this by developing a domain-oriented builder for scientific publication ratings and comparing it with Yahoo Pipes (a generic builder).

3.2   Design by Redesign

Many domain-independent application environments have turned out to be successful EUD environments. Arguably, the most famous is the spreadsheet application. With the use of a formula language (e.g., Excel macros), numerous applications of the same basic user interface have been created [6]. Several hybrid application/application builders have since been proposed (e.g., MS Office with Visual Basic for Applications), but none of them have achieved the same fame as the spreadsheet when it comes to supporting EUD. A key to success has been a combination of a generic (multipurpose) user interface and a mechanism for producing variation at a scale that is both useful and usable by application users.

Google Maps shares many of the characteristics of a spreadsheet in so far as it provides a combination of multipurpose user interface and a mechanism for generating variation without an excessive amount of programming. An early application (arguable comparable to VisiCalc in fame) is HousingMaps, a "mashup" created by Paul Rademacher in 2005. He integrated a housing-rental and for-sale listing (craigslist) with Google Maps to form a new kind of application (http://www.housingmaps.com/). Numerous Google mashups have since followed.

The variability mechanism provided by Google Maps differs from the spreadsheet formula language. Integrating the Google Map API with data sources and related components in a mashup builder is one way to create applications. Another way is to make custom maps by manually typing in addresses. The latter is more time consuming for large data sets but simpler for users without technical expertise (e.g., the My Places wizard and tutorial in Google Maps).

The tradeoff between flexibility and usability is only partially resolved by each of the two approaches. The success of "design by redesign" depends on "killer apps," and the success of the "design by composition" depends on access to a sufficient number of interesting components to choose from. We propose a framework for combining them and addressing the vision described in section 2, combining a generic application with a set of components to extend it. This framework is presented below in two parts, first as a theoretical concept (software readymade) that is later operationalized in two prototypes (application units and nuggets). This work is continually evolving and is not yet finished.

4   Software Readymade as a Theoretical Concept

The artist Marcel Duchamp coined the term *readymade* in 1913 when he started to transform everyday manufactured objects into art by a series of operations performed by the artist. He suggested how spectators should perceive, react, and make sense of the artwork. Duchamp's famous and provocative *Bicycle wheel* and *Fountain* are two examples of readymades, the latter borrowing and appropriating a porcelain urinal, the former using a bicycle wheel mounted on a kitchen stool. Despite the readymades being "locked" from conventional use, Duchamp was an advocate of active and continuous use, and he explained it by the following quote: "After all, the artist alone does not perform the creative act. The spectator brings the work in contact with the external world by deciphering and interpreting its inner qualities and thus adds his contributions to the creative act" [1].

Duchamp's concept of readymades and how they can be interacted with provides clues for how end users can be involved in composition and redesign. For example, across the two domains of art and end-user development, we find the following common themes: 1) acts of intervention in established practice (manufacturing), 2) opening-up functional objects for introspection, and 3) revealing relations and viewpoints that have previously been hidden. We have developed prototypes for exploring the second and third themes that aim to reveal hidden relations and viewpoints of functional objects (software components) in order to increase end users' awareness of modification options.

5   Tailorable Autonomous Software Components

The software components we have developed are "small applications" that can be used separately, opened up for viewing, and modified within an application framework. The first author developed "application units" [4], and the second author more recently developed "nuggets" inspired by the former [9]. We present a brief summary of our past and current work.

5.1   Application Units

Application units are components of conventional application, creating cognitive chunks that are easier to comprehend than complete applications. To support "opening up," each component is organized into views or aspects: 1) user interface, 2) design rationale, and 3) program code. Users can access each aspect by holding down a modifier key (alt, ctrl, or shift) when clicking on the application unit. Each aspect can be modified in a separate editor, and the data is then stored in an initialization file [4]. The goal of application units is to simplify access to the different parts of UI components that have to be modified during end-user tailoring.

Another goal of the application units is to support learning on demand and incremental mastery of computational complexity. We conducted a video-recorded usability test of BasicDraw with twelve users and asked them to perform end-user development modifications to the application, and we found that customization (modifying user interface) and integration (updating design rationale) could be achieved without much instruction or help. The extension (writing program code in method bodies), however, required assistance, or knowledge of programming and basic skills in object-oriented programming [4].

5.2   Nuggets

MikWiki is a user-extensible wiki [9] where the components of the system are represented by a set of web pages, referred to as *nuggets*. Nuggets are independent of each other and bundled with EUD tools. As code executes on the client side, users can change the behavior of existing nuggets or create new nuggets from and within the wiki and thus evolve the wiki at use time.

Similar to the "multiple aspects" of application units, each nugget has three perspectives: 1) visualization, 2) format, and 3) data representation. An example is the *Imagenote* nugget that allows end users to create "Post-it-like" image notes, which are synchronized between users. The data page contains the wall data in JSON format, the format page defines how to represent the JSON data in JavaScript, and the visualization page embeds the macro-like code that expands to the visible nugget on the screen.

MikiWiki provides a set of stand-alone components. These are components to support communication, coordination, and localization that track history, enhance awareness, and provide authentication and annotation services.

Empirical studies of MikiWiki extend applications units by demonstrating that EUD can be achieved in naturalistic settings (outside usability laboratory). They are uncomplicated to use once familiar with editing web pages and wiki articles [9].

One shortcoming we have found is that EUD using JavaScript still imposes a steep learning curve for many end-user developers. Additional components, user documentation, tutorials, and templates must be provided to flatten the learning curve.

6   General Discussion and Directions for Further Work

We distinguished between design by redesign and design by composition. A challenge for design by composition is specifying communication protocols between components and resolving unambiguous input-output ports. A challenge of design by redesign is to enable end-user developers to extend generic applications to create something new. We proposed a vision for CBD by the creative reconfiguration of chairs and provided a theoretical account of the vision by the notion of software readymades. Our own efforts to instantiate the concept with multiperspective, tailorable application units and nuggets revealed strengths and weaknesses. The strength is that it can give end users access to multiple aspects of a software component (e.g., user interface, code, and data) in order to simplify end-user tailoring. A weakness is that having access to code may not help, as many end-user developers find programming difficult, and scripting languages is also difficult in this regard.

Directions for further work include exploring how small applications can expose hooks, open points, and reconfiguration options, starting with what manufacturers refer to as sizes and models of standard components, and extending this to modularized generic applications that can be taken apart and recombined to make new applications. Moreover, future work should address what it means for stand-alone components to be integrated without sending or receiving data. For example, integration can be approached from a domain-oriented perspective as in the work of Fischer and colleagues (defined by design rules, perspectives, and preferences). Integration can also be achieved within a social-technical framework, being less about component interfaces and more about new tools for viewing, modifying, and sharing.

References

1. Duchamp, M.: The Creative Act. In: Lebel, R. (ed.) Marcel Duchamp, pp. 77–78. Paragraphic Books, New York (1959)
2. Fischer, G., Girgensohn, A., Nakakoji, K., Redmiles, D.: Supporting Software Designers with Integrated, Domain-Oriented Design Environments. IEEE Trans. on Soft. Eng. 18(6), 511–522 (1992)
3. Mehandjiev, N., Namoune, A., Wajid, U., Macaulay, L., Sutcliffe, A.: End User Service Composition: Perceptions and Requirements. In: Proceedings ECOWS 2010, pp. 139–146. IEEE Computer Society, Washington, DC (2010)
4. Mørch, A.I.: Aspect-Oriented Software Components. In: Patel, N. (ed.) Adaptive Evolutionary Information Systems, pp. 105–122. Idea Group, Hershey (2003)
5. Muhammad, I., Florian, D., Fabio, C., Maurizio, M.: ResEval Mash: A mashup tool that speaks the language of the user. In: Proc. CHI 2012, pp. 1949–1954. ACM, New York (2012)
6. Nardi, B.A., Miller, J.R.: The spreadsheet interface: A basis for end user programming. In: Proceedings INTERACT 1990, Amsterdam, The Netherlands, pp. 977–983 (1990)
7. Thompson, H.: Remake it Home. Thames & Hudson Ltd., London (2009)
8. Wulf, V., Pipek, V., Won, M.: Component-based tailorability: Enabling highly flexible software applications. Int. J. Hum.-Comput. Stud. 66(1), 1–22 (2008)
9. Zhu, L., Vaghi, I.R., Barricelli, B.R.: A Meta-reflective Wiki for Collaborative Design. In: Proceedings WikiSym 2011, pp. 53–62. ACM, New York (2011)

End User Architecting

Vishal Dwivedi

School of Computer Science, Carnegie Mellon University
5000 Forbes Avenue, PA, 15213, USA
vdwivedi@cs.cmu.edu

Abstract. A large number of domains today require end users to compose various heterogeneous computational entities to perform their professional activities. However, writing such end user compositions is hard and error prone. My research explores an improved approach for design, analysis and execution of such end user compositions. I propose a new technique called 'end user architecting' that associates end user specifications in a particular domain as instances of architectural styles. This allows cross-domain analyses, systematic support for reuse and adaptation, powerful auxiliary services (e.g., mismatch repair), and support for execution, testing, and debugging. To allow a wider adoption of this technique, we have designed a framework that can be instantiated across a large number of domains, with composition models varying from dataflows, pub-sub, and workflows. This approach can reduce the cost of development of end user composition platforms (compared to developing them from scratch) and improve the quality of end user compositions.

1 Research Problem

Within an increasing number of domains an important emerging need is the ability for technically naive users to compose computational elements into novel configurations. Examples include e-science (e.g., astronomers who create new analysis pipelines to process telescopic data), intelligence analysis (e.g., policy planners who process diverse sources of unstructured text to discover socio-technical trends), and medicine (e.g., researchers who process repositories of brain imaging data to discover new disease pathways). In these domains professionals typically have access to a large number of existing applications and data sets, which must be composed in novel ways to gain insight, carry out "what if" experiments, generate reports and research findings, etc.

Unfortunately, assembling such elements into coherent compositions is a non-trivial matter [1][2]. In particular, we can identify five critical barriers.

1. **Excessive technical detail:** Existing languages and tools require end users to have knowledge of a myriad of low-level technical detail such as parameters, low-level control flow decisions, exception handling, and other programming constructs.
2. **Inappropriate computational models:** The computational models provided by typical execution platforms, such as SOA, may require end users to map their tasks into a computational vocabulary that is quite different from the natural way of decomposing the task in that domain. For example, tasks that are logically represented in the end user's mind as a workflow may have to be translated into the very-different vocabulary of service orchestrations and execution scripts.

Y. Dittrich et al. (Eds.): IS-EUD 2013, LNCS 7897, pp. 284–288, 2013.

3. **Inability to analyze compositions:** There may be many restrictions on legal ways to combine elements, dictated by things like format compatibility, domain-specific processing requirements, ordering constraints, and access rights to data and applications. Today, discovering whether a composition satisfies these restrictions is largely a matter of trial and error, since there are few tools to automate such checks. Moreover, even when a composition does satisfy the composition constraints, its extra-functional properties — or quality attributes — may be uncertain. For example, determining how long a given computation will take to produce results on a given data set can often be determined only by time-consuming experimentation.

4. **Lack of support for reuse:** An important requirement in many communities is the ability for professionals to share their compositions with others in those communities. For instance, brain researchers may want to replicate the analyses of others, or adapt an existing analysis to a different setting (e.g., execute on different data sets). Packaging such compositions in a reusable and adaptable form is difficult, given the low-level nature of encodings, and the brittleness of the specifications.

5. **Impoverished support for execution.** Compared to the capabilities of modern programming environments, end users have relatively few tools for things like compilation into efficient deployments, interactive testing and debugging (e.g., setting breakpoints, monitoring intermediate results, etc.), history tracking, and graceful handling of run-time errors. This follows in part from the fact that in many cases compositions are executed in a distributed environment using middleware that is not geared towards interactive use and exploration by technically naive users.

This gap between the needs of end users and todays technology has two adverse consequences: (i) *The cost of producing effective compositions is high* because end users must become experts in implementation details not relevant to their primary task. (ii) *The quality is low* because compositions tend to be brittle and in many cases fail to meet their extra-functional requirements. Also, compositions are difficult to reuse, modify, and maintain, leading to gratuitous reinvention and errors.

2   Research Approach

My approach to address this problem has been to view end user composition activity as engaging in a high-level architectural design within a domain-specific style and to represent those end user architectures explicitly. Figure 1 illustrates the overall organization of end user composition tools and the placement of an architectural layer.

Part (a) of the figure shows the current state of affairs: users must translate their tasks into the computational model of the execution platform, and become familiar with the

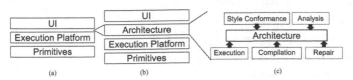

Fig. 1. End-user Architecting Approach

low-level details of that platform and primitive computational elements (applications, services, files, etc.) — leading to problems outlined in Section 1. Part (b) illustrates the new approach. Here, end-user architectures are explicitly represented as architectural models defined in a domain-specific architectural style. These models and the supporting infrastructure can then support a host of auxiliary services, including checking for style conformance, quality attribute analysis, compilation into efficient deployments, execution and debugging mechanisms, and automated repair — as shown in part (c).

By decomposing the problem in this way we identify a new field of concern, which we term *end-user architecting* [3]. Similar to end-user programming [4], it recognizes upfront that the key issue is bridging the gap between available computational resources and the skill set of the users who must harness them — users who typically have low programming skills. But unlike end-user programming, it seeks to find higher-level abstractions that leverage the considerable advances in software architecture languages, methods, and tools to support component composition, analysis and execution.

While we investigated the potential of this approach across various domains — and specially the ones that already had successful end user composition platforms like Taverna and Wings in e-sciences — we found effective ecosystems consisting of domain-experts, component developers, platform developers, and end users at play. While richer compositions environments manage this synchronization quite well (although, at a great cost), several impoverished composition environments enforce end users to perform all these roles by themselves. The end user architecting approach address the problems of such end users, and the other developers in the ecosystem.

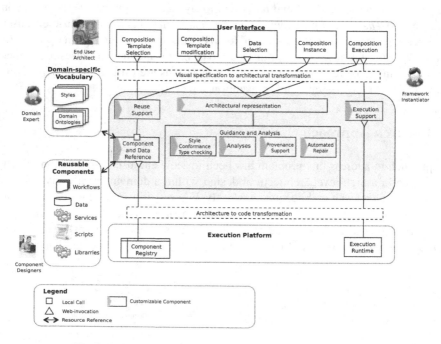

Fig. 2. Building Blocks of End User Architecting Framework

To allow an easier use of this approach, we have designed a customizable framework that can be instantiated across a large number of domains. Figure 2 shows the high-level building blocks of the framework and the larger ecosystem of developers that it helps. For preliminary investigations, we have instantiated our framework in three domains: dynamic network analysis, brain imaging, and geospatial analysis [3]. Across these domains, the end users are technically naive users (such as analysts and neuroscientists) who write compositions that are variations of dataflows and pub-sub.

Our hypothesis is that the End User Architecting framework factors out the commonalities across different classes of composition environments and computation models. Undoubtedly, some upfront cost is required to develop the composition components, the architecture styles, analyses, templates, etc. However, components, styles, templates, and analyses are reusable artifacts; thus, building libraries of them will amortize cost and reduce End User Architecting efforts for future projects.

3   Concluding Remarks and Future Research

My current research focus is to validate the End User Architecting approach with respect to i) generality, ii) quality of compositions, and iii) reduced cost of for platform development. Apart from the three case studies mentioned in [3], I am conducting studies to determine the feasibility of applying the end user architecting approach to a larger set of domains. Examples include astronomy, bioinformatics, digital music production and other scientific computing and arts related domains where end user architecting could potentially be a good fit. Additionally, I plan to conduct usability studies to evaluate the usability and extensibility of the framework with the entire ecosystem of users in consideration.

If successful, this research will have many contributions to the field of *end user software engineering*. End user Architecting could be an effective technique for dramatically reducing the time, cost and difficulty of building a significant class of end user composition environments. This will be supported by a reusable framework that would provide interfaces, libraries, control structures and the necessary plug-in points for developing composition environments, as well as analyses that will improve end user composition experience.

Additionally, this research will also contribute to the field of *software architecture* through extensions to architecture description languages to support export and reuse of architectural specifications through generalized APIs, prior compositions, and access to repositories. The generic and reusable analytic capabilities that I am developing as a part of this research will be another significant contribution to this field.

Acknowledgements. I thank my advisor, Prof. David Garlan, for his continuing guidance and support. I also thank Bradley Schmerl, Perla Velasco Elizondo, and Ivan Ruchkin who have closely collaborated on this research. This material is based upon work funded by the Department of Defense under Contract No. FA8721-05-C-0003 with Carnegie Mellon University and Software Engineering Institute. Further support for this work came from Office of Naval Research grant ONR-N000140811223 and the Center for Computational Analysis of Social and Organizational Systems (CASOS).

References

1. Casati, F.: How end-user development will save composition technologies from their continuing failures. In: Costabile, M.F., Dittrich, Y., Fischer, G., Piccinno, A. (eds.) IS-EUD 2011. LNCS, vol. 6654, pp. 4–6. Springer, Heidelberg (2011)
2. Dwivedi, V., Velasco-Elizondo, P., Fernandes, J.M., Garlan, D., Schmerl, B.: An architectural approach to end user orchestrations. In: Crnkovic, I., Gruhn, V., Book, M. (eds.) ECSA 2011. LNCS, vol. 6903, pp. 370–378. Springer, Heidelberg (2011)
3. Garlan, D., Dwivedi, V., Ruchkin, I., Schmerl, B.: Foundations and tools for end-user architecting. In: Calinescu, R., Garlan, D. (eds.) Monterey Workshop 2012. LNCS, vol. 7539, pp. 157–182. Springer, Heidelberg (2012)
4. Nardi, B.A.: A small matter of programming: perspectives on end user computing. MIT Press (1993)

TagTrainer: A Meta-design Approach to Interactive Rehabilitation Technology

Daniel Tetteroo

User Centred Engineering Group, Department of Industrial Design,
Eindhoven University of Technology,
Den Dolech 2, 5612 AZ Eindhoven, The Netherlands
d.tetteroo@tue.nl

Abstract. Together with the rising demand for healthcare, the need for assisting technology within the field of rehabilitation is increasing. However, this technology needs to be flexible and adjustable to address the variability and context dependency of therapy in daily practice. Current technology is hardly adjustable and therefore often fails in regular therapy situations. This research applies the principles of End-User Development and cultures of participation to create a socio-technical environment in which technology providers, care providers and patients are enabled to adjust technology to the needs of rehabilitation therapy.

Keywords: rehabilitation technology, tangible interaction, end-user development, cultures of participation.

1 Introduction

With an ageing population, the demand for extended and improved healthcare is a worldwide emerging trend. Amongst the consequences of an ageing population is the rising number of patients that suffer from age-related diseases such as stroke [11]. Stroke survivors often suffer from arm-hand impairments that can only be treated by long and intense rehabilitation therapy. Therefore, a sector that is particularly influenced by this trend is that of rehabilitation.

Smart use of new technologies can aid the healthcare sector to better cope with the increasing demands. However, these technologies need to be adjustable to the needs of individual patients, in order to offer an effective solution [2,10]. This is where End-User Development [8] and cultures of participation [4] can play an important role, since they enable domain specialists (such as rehabilitation therapists) to appropriate technology to the needs of their patients.

This research therefore, is situated around the central question: "How can healthcare specialists, more specifically rehabilitation therapists, be empowered to appropriate new technology to the needs of their patients?".

2 Theoretical Background

This research resides on the cross-section of a number of topics: rehabilitation technology, tangible interaction, EUD and cultures of participation. This section

Y. Dittrich et al. (Eds.): IS-EUD 2013, LNCS 7897, pp. 289–292, 2013.

defines the scope of the project by identifying the relations that exist between these topics.

Although there have been previous attempts on integrating tangible technology in the domain of rehabilitation, research has shown the importance of extendibility such that the technology can provide patients with challenging therapy for a prolonged period of time [10]. Many technologies that have been designed specifically for rehabilitation offer a limited range of exercises and therefore have limited use in daily therapy. On the other hand, many platforms exist (such as Nintendo's Wii) that offer large variability, but fail to adequately address the issues that play a role in rehabilitation therapy.

A previous project by Carmien and Fischer, showed that persons with disabilities often represent a "universe of one" and that EUD and meta-design can help to improve the lives of these persons [2]. In a similar fashion, EUD and cultures of participation could be applied to create a socio-technical environment for rehabilitation therapy. Patients could benefit from technology assisted therapy, while not being subjected to the "one-size-fits-all" philosophy with which current technology is often designed.

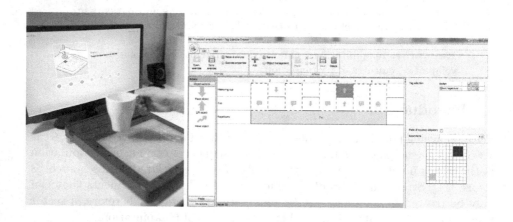

Fig. 1. The TagTrainer platform (left), and the Tag Exercise Creator software (right)

The basis for *this* research is formed by the TagTrainer: an extensible tangible platform for rehabilitation training (see Figure 1). The platform consists of the TagTile board, an interactive board that can locate and identify RFID-tagged objects and provide visual and auditory feedback, and software that allows the modification and creation of therapy exercises in an EUD approach.

3   Research

The first part of this research consisted of the evaluation [7], re-design and implementation of the prototype TagTrainer platform, with the Tag Exercise

Creator (see Figure 1) as an EUD tool that allows therapists to modify and create exercises for rehabilitation therapy.

As has been shown before, the matter of enabling end-users to create and modify their tools is more than just a technical endeavour [3]. Although it is essential that end-users have appropriate tools to perform these tasks, matters of motivation, collaboration and organization are at least equally important. Therefore, the remaining part of the research focuses less on the development of appropriate EUD-software, and more on the sociological, organizational and motivational aspects that play a role in the process of creating cultures of participation.

Throughout the research project, Action-Research (AR) [1] is being applied as a research methodology. AR involves both action and research within the same process and aims at generating knowledge by improving practice, and improving practice by the application of knowledge. This methodology perfectly fits the meta-design paradigm, since it leaves room for use-time adaptations, emergence and co-creation [5]. Within the AR-approach, study tools such as semi-structured interviews with therapists, observations on the creative process and collaborative efforts, as well as log-data collection from system usage are used to gather a rich view on the process of integrating the TagTrainer system as part of regular therapy.

4   Results and Future Steps

As a first step in this project, a software tool (the Tag Exercise Creator, or TEC) was developed that allows therapists to create and modify exercises for the TagTrainer system. This EUD tool was designed on the basis of the results of a usability study on an earlier prototype [7] and research on the implementation of assisting technology in the domain of stroke rehabilitation [6].

In a next step, the TagTrainer system was implemented as part of daily therapy within a rehabilitation clinic [9]. During the three-week implementation process, the therapists were observed on the way they used the system as part of daily therapy. Furthermore, data about system usage, usefulness in therapy and factors that influenced EUD and sharing processes were recorded. The results from this evaluation were used to prepare a new, larger scale study in which multiple clinics are involved over a longer period of several months per clinic.

It is expected that through the implementation of the TagTrainer in additional clinics, a foundation will be formed for a culture of participation from which an intra-organizational community of therapists, patients and other stakeholders can benefit. Future research should investigate the issues that play a role in the growth, development and sustainability of such a community.

5   Expected Contributions

The expected contributions of this research are a better understanding about:

1. Issues concerning the implementation of EUD tools in the healthcare context
2. How cultures of participation might develop in intra-organizational contexts
3. The feasibility of EUD in tangible, interactive systems

Finally, it is expected that the developed rehabilitation technology will increase patients' motivation and performance, thus improving the overall quality of arm-hand rehabilitation.

Acknowledgements. The author acknowledges the support of the Innovation-Oriented Research Programme 'Integral Product Creation and Realization (IOP IPCR)' of the Netherlands Ministry of Economic Affairs, Agriculture and Innovation.

References

1. Anderson, G.L., Herr, K.: The Action Research Dissertation: A Guide for Students and Faculty. SAGE (January 2005)
2. Carmien, S.P., Fischer, G.: Design, adoption, and assessment of a socio-technical environment supporting independence for persons with cognitive disabilities. In: Proc. CHI 2008, pp. 597–606. ACM, New York (2008)
3. Fischer, G.: Meta-design: Expanding boundaries and redistributing control in design. In: Baranauskas, C., Abascal, J., Barbosa, S.D.J. (eds.) INTERACT 2007. LNCS, vol. 4662, pp. 193–206. Springer, Heidelberg (2007)
4. Fischer, G.: End user development and meta-design: Foundations for cultures of participation. J. Organizational and End User Computing 22(1), 52–82 (2010)
5. Fischer, G., Giaccardi, E.: Meta-design: A framework for the future of end-user development. In: Lieberman, H., Patern, F., Wulf, V. (eds.) End User Development, vol. 9, pp. 427–457. Springer, Netherlands (2006)
6. Hochstenbach-Waelen, A., Seelen, H.A.M.: Embracing change: practical and theoretical considerations for successful implementation of technology assisting upper limb training in stroke. J. Neuroeng. Rehabil. 9, 52 (2012), PMID: 22856548
7. Hochstenbach-Waelen, A., Timmermans, A., Seelen, H.A.M., Tetteroo, D., Markopoulos, P.: Tag-exercise creator: towards end-user development for tangible interaction in rehabilitation training. In: Proc. EICS 2012, pp. 293–298 (2012)
8. Lieberman, H., Paterno, F., Klann, M., Wulf, V.: End-user development: An emerging paradigm. In: End User Development, vol. 9, pp. 1–8. Springer (2006)
9. Tetteroo, D., Timmermans, A.A.A., Seelen, H.A.M., Markopoulos, P.: TagTrainer: Supporting exercise variability and tailoring in technology supported upper limb training (submitted for publication, 2013)
10. Timmermans, A.A.A., Seelen, H.A.M., Geers, R.P.J., Saini, P.K., Winter, S., te Vrugt, J., Kingma, H.: Sensor-based arm skill training in chronic stroke patients: results on treatment outcome, patient motivation, and system usability. IEEE Trans. Neural Syst. Rehabil. Eng. 18(3), 284–292 (2010), PMID: 20388603
11. Truelsen, T., Piechowski-Jozwiak, B., Bonita, R., Mathers, C., Bogousslavsky, J., Boysen, G.: Stroke incidence and prevalence in Europe: a review of available data. European Journal of Neurology 13, 581–598 (2006)

Socio-technical Systems That Foster and Support Mindfulness Can Benefit from End-User Control Mechanisms

Jason Zietz

University of Colorado Boulder, Boulder, Colorado
jason.zietz@colorado.edu

Abstract. Human beings often make decisions without fully realizing the factors that influence their choices. A woman buys the same type of car that most of her neighbors drive. A man at a salad bar loads up on the croutons that are in the front row of items instead of olives that are in the middle row. While these mindless decisions aren't always deleterious, they may not be what a person most desires or what is best for them. Deciding mindfully, however, may provide a person the opportunity to be fully aware of their choices and select the best outcome based on their needs. Socio-technical systems can be designed to support mindful decision making, and these systems can benefit from the incorporation of end-user controls. End-user controls can provide users with opportunities to analyze new information and create new categories, two useful techniques in fostering mindful behaviors and decisions. This paper discusses how end-user controls that support mindful decision making will be added to EMPIRE, a socio-technical system designed to help consumers reduce their electricity consumption.

Keywords: mindfulness, end-user design, socio-technical systems.

1 Introduction and Theoretical Background

The ability to manipulate peoples' behaviors over short periods of time has been demonstrated in numerous tasks, including menu choice [1], food intake regulation [2], and salad bar item selection [3]. The interventional strategies used to elicit the behavior change have not been demonstrated to affect people's choices after they were removed, however. Social proof [4], social norms [5], and competitions [6] have been shown to influence people's behaviors, but their impacts have only been observed when present; their effects after removal have not been rigorously examined. Achieving behavior change over long durations is generally the goal of behavior modification programs, but it is one that is often difficult to achieve. One method of establishing long-term behavior change may be to encourage individuals to approach their behavior modification endeavors mindfully.

Mindfulness has been described as a purposeful, nonjudgmental way of paying attention in the present moment [7]. Mindfulness is typically seen in therapeutic

Y. Dittrich et al. (Eds.): IS-EUD 2013, LNCS 7897, pp. 293–297, 2013.

environments, but it also has the potential to assist people in their efforts to stop undesirable choices [8]. It can allow people to experience greater control over and richer options within their decisions [9] Two methods that can be used to foster mindful decision making are the creation of new categories and the analysis of automatic behaviors.

We use categories to help us better interact with the world around us. Dogs and cats are domestic animals so we can pet them without (much) fear of being attacked. While lions and tigers are cats, they are not domesticated, thus, petting them would likely result in injury. Categorization can keep us out of danger, but it can also foster a sense of myopia. For example, people might categorize their electricity usage as something they have little control over and pay for once a month, like rent or trash removal. When a person creates a new category such as "utilities I can influence" and assigns electricity to it, they are now free to explore ways to reduce their electricity. Making new categories helps us to achieve mindfulness by paying attention to the situation and context we are in [9].

Similarly, being willing to evaluate and accept new information is another way to be mindful [9]. Over time, we may create wasteful habits such as leaving a television on when we're not watching it. We might do this because we feel uncomfortable without some background noise or we simply don't think to turn the television off. Examining the occurrence of mindless behaviors and why we do them allows us to observe our actions mindfully.

I seek to address the following questions with my research: (1) How do we design socio-technical systems that facilitate mindful decision making? and, (2) How and under what conditions do user controls affect mindful decision making? My approach to answering these questions follows.

2   Research Approach

My research entails the continued development of the system EMPIRE (Empowering People in Reducing Energy Consumption), a socio-technical system designed to provide consumers access to their home electricity usage as a means to reduce their energy consumption [10]. While EMPIRE is currently accessible through a web browser, my work will include the addition of a native mobile application that will exploit the strengths of mobile devices to support mindful behaviors, including the ability to always be on and in-hand, utilize location awareness capabilities, and access data regardless of geographic location.

Controls will be provided that will allow end users to tailor the presentation of their electricity usage in such a way that it becomes more meaningful to them. Specifically, users will be able to control the content of the electricity data displayed, the frequency in which it is displayed, and the mode in which the content is provided to them, supporting individual awareness and attention needs.

Electricity usage is typically reported in kilowatt-hours, a unit of measurement that means very little to most people. EMPIRE will allow users to modify the content of their data by providing alternative representations of electricity usage, namely coal, carbon dioxide, and US dollars, giving them the opportunity to view their electricity consumption in a more personally meaningful representation. Additionally, these representations provide users with new information about their electricity usage which will allow them to begin to think about energy consumption more mindfully.

EMPIRE will provide users with a summary report of their electricity usage on an hourly, daily, weekly, or monthly basis, with users deciding how frequently they receive these reports. These reports will give users information that prompts introspection in order to guide users to consider the implications of their consumption. For example, one prompt might read: "A cable box consumes electricity even when you're not watching television. Turning your cable box off before you go to bed can save approximately 300 pounds of coal from being burned a year. Do you have any devices you can turn off when you're not using them?" Prompts such as these help consumers to create new categories for their electricity-consuming devices (e.g., devices that can be turned off at night), further allowing them to become more mindful of their electricity use.

Users will be able to further customize their experience through the use of alerts. Alerts will be used to notify users when events that meet specific criteria based on their electricity usage occur and will be created via a flexible "fill-in-the-blank" form. Alerts will be able to notify users when their electricity spikes, remind them to switch off power draining devices before they go to sleep, and inform them when their daily usage exceeds a certain level, among other events. Users will be able to choose to receive these alerts via email, SMS text message, or native notification within their mobile device. Furthermore, EMPIRE will provide access to an alert repository, where users can view, copy, and modify alerts created by other users as well as share their own. Users will be able to specify where geographically they would like to receive alerts, such as only in their homes or within a certain distance of it. This feature is important because some alerts will be actionable only within a certain context, namely within proximity of an individual's home. This feature will leverage GPS functionality of mobile devices as well as location-based services where appropriate. Users will be able to leverage what they have learned through the alternative representations and introspective prompting to create useful alerts and, in the process, reinforce the mindfulness these system features have fostered.

3   Results

In a series of studies, I examined how representations of electricity usage affect individuals' willingness to commit to pro-environmental actions. In the first study, I compared subjects' emotional responses to different representations of electricity consumption, namely kilowatt-hours (control), coal, carbon dioxide, and US dollars. Subjects in the control group were given a textual definition, while subjects in the three experimental groups were shown an image of an alternative representation of energy consumption (coal, carbon dioxide, or US dollars) along with a description of the pictured representation. Subjects were then asked to rate their emotive state utilizing Ekman's six basic emotions (anger, sadness, happiness, fear, surprise, and disgust) [11] on a 6-point scale (0-5) for each emotion. This first question represented an *unframed* context as the experimental representations were presented without any specific information regarding electricity use. For the second question, the *framed* context, subjects read a statement detailing how much of their respective representation of electricity usage was needed to provide electricity to an average US household each month. Subjects were then asked to rate their emotive state as before.

In the second study, subjects were randomly assigned to groups as described above and provided with the statement from the framed context described above for their respective representation. Instead of asking about the subjects' emotional responses, however, I asked how likely they would be (on a scale from 0-5) to reduce their electricity usage by either 5% or 15%.

Given the perspective that emotions influence motivations for action [12], my hypothesis was that the representations that yielded the largest shifts in reported emotional reactions would be the most likely to motivate individuals to want to reduce their electricity usage. The results from the first study demonstrated that coal and US dollars elicited the greatest emotional shifts. The results of the second study showed that while there wasn't a significant difference between the representations' impact on subjects' likelihood to reduce their electricity use 5%, subjects were more likely to state that they would try to reduce their electricity by 15% after they saw coal and US dollars than if they saw kilowatt-hours and carbon dioxide.

While these results support my hypothesis and allow us to draw some conclusions regarding the effectiveness of certain representations in encouraging pro-environmental behaviors, it would be short-sighted to design a system that only uses coal or US dollars as electricity usage representations. Instead, we can use these results to suggest representations that might be most motivating but still allow end users to decide for themselves which representations are most meaningful to them in their endeavors to commit pro-environmental behaviors.

4   Conclusion

Socio-technical systems that foster mindfulness can benefit from the incorporation of features that support end-user control. Providing users with the ability to customize their experience can help them create new categories as well as analyze automatic behaviors, two methods useful in cultivating mindfulness. The continued development of EMPIRE as described above and subsequent evaluation of its use will help us to better understand how and under what conditions socio-technical systems can benefit mindful decision making.

References

1. Dayan, E., Bar-Hillel, M.: Nudge to nobesity II: Menu positions influence food orders. Judgment and Decision Making 6(4), 333–342 (2011)
2. Geier, A., Wansink, B., Rozin, P.: Red Potato Chips: Segmentation Cues Can Substantially Decrease Food Intake. Health Psychology (2012) (Advance online publication)
3. Rozin, P., Scott, S., Dingley, M., Urbanek, J.K., Jiang, H., Kaltenbach, M.: Nudge to nobesity I: Minor changes in accessibility decrease food intake. Judgment and Decision Making 6(4), 323–332 (2011)

4. Cialdini, R.B.: Influence: Science and Practice, 5th edn. Prentice Hall, New Jersey (2008)
5. Schultz, P.W., et al.: The constructive, destructive, and reconstructive power of social norms. Psychological Science: A Journal of the American Psychological Society/APS 18(5), 429–434 (2007)
6. Geelen, D., et al.: Exploring the use of a game to stimulate energy saving in households. Journal of Design Research 10(1), 102–120 (2012)
7. Kabat-Zinn, J.: Wherever you go, there you are: Mindfulness meditation in everyday life. Hyperion (1995)
8. Johnson, E., Weber, E.: Mindful judgment and decision making. Annual Review of Psychology 60, 53 (2009)
9. Langer, E.J.: Mindfulness. Addison-Wesley/Addison Wesley Longman (1989)
10. Dick, H., et al.: Empowering users to become designers: using meta-design environments to enable and motivate sustainable energy decisions. In: Proceedings of the 12th Participatory Design Conference: Exploratory Papers, Workshop Descriptions, Industry Cases, vol. 2, pp. 49–52. ACM, Roskilde (2012)
11. Ekman, P., Friesen, W.: Constants across cultures in the face and emotion. Journal of Personality and Social Psychology 17(2), 124–129 (1971)
12. Frijda, N.: Emotions and Action. In: Manstead, A., Frijda, N., Fischer, A. (eds.) Feelings and Emotions: The Amsterdam Symposium. Studies in Emotion and Social Interaction. Cambridge University Press (2004)

Workshop on EUD for Supporting Sustainability in Maker Communities

Alexander Boden[1], Gabriela Avram[2], Irene Posch[3],
Volkmar Pipek[1], and Geraldine Fitzpatrick[3]

[1] University of Siegen, Germany
{alexander.boden,volkmar.pipek}@uni-siegen.de
[2] University of Limerick, Ireland
gabriela.avram@ul.ie
[3]TU Vienna, Austria
geraldine.fitzpatrick@tuwien.ac.at, ireneposch@gmail.com

Abstract. Recently, there has been a proliferation of Do-It-Yourself (DIY) communities that can be generally included in the larger all-encompassing maker movement: Hackerspaces, FabLabs, Transition Town groups etc. Made possible by the new horizons opened by digital fabrication and the Internet, the maker movement has a great potential to foster sustainable living by supporting innovation in this field, facilitating its appropriation and propagating its practical use. However, technology-driven maker communities are often perceived as places for tech-savvy people and have difficulties to attract wider audiences. In this workshop, we would like to discuss how can EUD concepts support sustainability in maker communities by ensuring wider scale access to digital fabrication, supporting user innovation and leveraging knowledge sharing across communities.

Keywords: maker communities, digital fabrication, end user development, prosumption, culture of participation, sustainability.

1   Description

Doing things yourself, on your own initiative with your own hands and head involved is probably one of the oldest and most natural activities of human nature. Parallel to increasing technological advances, a culture of making things yourself—not just out of pure necessity, but also for your own joy and fulfilment—has developed and gained momentum starting in the second half of the 20th century until today. Recent surveys from diverse countries around the world show that consumers spend a significant portion of time and money to create and modify consumer products for their own use. They demonstrate that do-it-yourself (DIY) is not just a marginal phenomenon, but it is also of increasing economic and societal value. Users, as being closest to the products they use and knowing best the needs and expectations associated with them, play an important role for advances and innovation, especially in fields generally considered niches, and thus not pursued by big industries.

Y. Dittrich et al. (Eds.): IS-EUD 2013, LNCS 7897, pp. 298–303, 2013.
© Springer-Verlag Berlin Heidelberg 2013

In contrast to homemade production—which is rather focused on economic aspects such as cost saving (in the sense of a "make or buy decision")—DIY is about meeting individual needs. Making in the new sense can be seen as an empowering experience that is supported by new models of communication in communities, making it easier (and socially recognized) to share self-made creations and related innovation. This trend is very much connected to the communities of hobbyists and crafters that have spawned the home computer industry. As the proliferation of digital means of construction have enabled end user production and the appropriation of technologies formerly reserved to specialized companies, the DIY movement has increased potential for innovation. Once they will become available to the general public, digital fabrication technologies are predicted to have an influence comparable to that of the introduction of personal computers.

The maker movement has a great potential to foster sustainable living by supporting related innovations, fostering their appropriation and propagating their practical use. Often though, technology-driven maker communities associated with FabLabs or Hackerspaces are perceived as places for people who are knowledgeable about technology and have difficulties to maintain an open dialogue with the society at large. Hence, attracting wider categories of public, as well as sharing innovations created by users are still seen as challenges.

End User Development (EUD) as research field focuses on methods, techniques, and tools that allow non-professionals to create, modify and extend technologies. Tools for EUD include, for example, visual programming environments, mash-up editors and service orchestration tools. EUD concepts can play a big role in supporting sustainability in maker communities by facilitating sustainable access to digital fabrication, in order to support user innovation and leverage knowledge sharing across communities. In this respect, we understand sustainability from multiple angles:

- disseminating sustainable behaviour and lifestyles by supporting the diffusion of related innovations from the maker culture to the society at large;
- improving innovation sustainability by supporting participation and knowledge exchange across diverse communities and backgrounds;
- supporting diverse communities across the population to embrace emerging digital technologies.

In particular, we believe that EUD research could bring a contribution at several different levels:

- At a **technical level**, EUD concepts can help to support the appropriation of DIY by making it easier for non-professionals to create, modify or extend digital and material artefacts in DIY projects.
- At a **social level**, EUD approaches can contribute to popularize DIY with the help of social media in order to make local DIY initiatives more visible, provide new opportunities for lurking and legitimate peripheral participation, and support knowledge exchange and appropriation of related innovations, technologies and ideas.

- At an **empirical level**, EUD oriented ethnographic studies can contribute to the understanding and analysis of DIY/maker communities practices in minute detail, in order to get a better understanding of their practical needs and opportunities for innovation.

During the workshop, we intend to discuss examples of DIY activities that are of interest in the context of sustainability and End User Development. Related questions include, but are not limited to:

- What are good examples of EUD and DIY tools that support sustainable innovation or could be adapted in this respect?
- How can EUD principles be leveraged to include a more diverse user group, particularly across generations, cultural backgrounds and among people with different levels of technical expertise?
- In the context of projects that address individual needs, how could more citizens become aware and be attracted to use digital fabrication technologies? What are the tools and infrastructure needed to achieve this?
- How can domestic activities constitute a trigger for establishing a sustainable use of personal fabrication technologies? What potential lays in attracting new user groups in order to reach inclusive participation and foster a broad discussion and evaluation of challenges and opportunities?
- How can traditional crafts be integrated in the context of maker communities? How can knowledge about crafts and traditional techniques be included, given that most people possessing this type of knowledge are not amongst the usual users of digital technologies?
- What tools are needed to anchor digital fabrication as a widely accepted possible extension of current fabrication and making routines?
- What are the new production and consumption patterns developed through sharing and collaboration by diverse groups of makers on a local and global scale? How can these be extended to the context of repairing, extending the life cycle of existing products, recycling and upcycling?
- How can practitioners be supported in documenting their work in order to allow knowledge sharing and diffusion of innovation? How could creative forms of documenting be established to better fit the maker culture?

More information on the workshop can be found on our website at http://eudforsustainability.wineme.fb5.uni-siegen.de/

2   Workshop Presentations

Hacking Sustainability: Broadening Participation through Green Hackathons.
Jorge L. Zapico, Daniel Pargman, Hannes Ebner, Elina Eriksson (Media Technology and Interaction Design – MID, KTH Royal Institute of Technology, SE100 44 Stockholm, Sweden).

Abstract. Green Hackathon is an international series of coding events with sustainability purpose. Developers, researchers, environmental practitioners, and anyone interested, work for a limited and focused amount of time to create innovative software solutions for sustainability. These events have explicitly invited broad spectra of expertises besides technical ones. This article presents the experiences and tensions of including these end users in a mostly technical oriented event, and discusses how end-user development could be used for a more reflective practice empowering broad participation and interdisciplinary collaboration in these events.

Generative Design Materials in DIY Digital Art Creation. Nicolai Brodersen Hansen, Kim Halskov (PIT & CAVI, Department of Aesthetics and Communication, Aarhus University, Denmark).

Abstract. We intend to study the interplay between software tools and artefacts and creativity. We do this through a case study of a community of DIY digital art creation among hobbyists. Specifically we investigate how they, the so called "demo-sceners" collaborate through the use of different design materials to create digital art and how they in that process utilize their different skills, and outline how we intend to study and present their work process at the workshop at IS-EUD.

End-User-Development for Smart Homes: Relevance and Challenges. Rémy Dautriche, Camille Lenoir, Alexandre Demeure (PRIMA, INRIA, LIG, Universités de Grenoble, France), and Joëlle Coutaz (IIHM, LIG, Universités de Grenoble, France).

Abstract. Ubiquitous computing is now mature enough to unleash the potential of Smart Homes. The obstacle is no more about hardware concerns but lies in how inhabitants can build, configure and control their Smart Home. In this paper, we defend the idea that End-User-Development (EUD), which considers inhabitants as makers rather than mere consumers, is an effective approach for tackling this obstacle. We reflect on the lifecycle of devices and services to dis-cuss challenges that EUD system will have to address in the Smart Home con-text: installation and maintenance, designation, control, development (including programming and testing), and sharing.

EUD@Smart Homes - Smart Refurbishment of Rented Apartments to Improve Energy Efficiency. Timo Jakobi, Gunnar Stevens (University of Siegen, Human Computer Interaction, Siegen, Germany), Tobias Schwartz (Fraunhofer FIT, Sankt Augustin, Germany).

Abstract. The smart home of the future is typically researched in lab settings or apartments that have been built from scratch. However, comparing the lifecycle of buildings and information technology, it is evident that modernization strategies and technologies are needed to empower residents to modify and extend their homes to make it smarter. In this paper, we describe a case study about the deployment, adaption to and adoption of tailorable home energy management systems in 7 private households. Based on this experience, we want to discuss how hardware and software technologies should be designed so that people could build their own smart home with a high usability and user experience.

If We Build It, Who Will Come? Considering the Who, What and Why of Web EUD. Mary Beth Rosson (Center for Human-Computer Interaction/College of Information Sciences and Technology, The Pennsylvania State University, University Park, Pennsylvania 16802 USA).

Abstract. The increased access to online information, services and tools raises many opportunities for everyday users to develop novel computational products. However very few end users take the time to investigate and acquire skills in end-user development (EUD), whether on the Web or elsewhere. In this brief paper, the author draws from a series of inter-related projects to consider what it is that prompts a non-programmer to invest time in novel technologies such as web development. Building upon previous discussions of the Production Paradox (Carroll & Rosson, 1987) and the Attention Investment Model (Blackwell, 2002), the author characterizes a space of causal factors that include the activity situation, a person's individual characteristics, and the resources that are apparent to the user. Working within this framework, the author summarizes findings from a series of related studies of Web EUD. The paper argues that if we hope to engage a large and diverse population of everyday users in the opportunities inherent in EUD, we must first understand a diverse landscape of activity contexts, and use minimalist design techniques to both attract users' interest and support them in their Web EUD learning processes.

Sustainable DIY Technologies in the Service of Cultural Heritage Professionals. Laura Maye (Interaction Design Centre, University of Limerick, Ireland).

Abstract. The paper presents a research project that aims to demonstrate how DIY technologies can be used in the design and development of cultural heritage interactive artefacts. Current digital interactive exhibits are usually created by technology experts, with limited involvement of cultural heritage professionals. Because of the high levels of technical knowledge required, it is almost impossible for curators to create, re-configure or bring up-to-date such artefacts. Many interactive exhibits end up only being used for demonstration purposes or punctual events and then never again. However, DIY technologies are increasingly becoming easier for amateur and novice users to use. Furthermore, developments in 3D printing and digital fabrication have made it possible to print embedded digital circuitry and recycle used materials. For these reasons, it should become possible for curators to create and adapt their own exhibits with embedded digital materials. The aim of this research project (still in its early stages) is to analyse how interactive exhibits can be created and adapted easily by curators, using sustainable technologies.

3   Workshop Plan

The one day workshop will bring together a maximum of 20 participants. Our intended audience primarily consists of researchers who are actively engaged in studies of EUD in DIY contexts, but also of DIY enthusiasts and members of maker communities. We are encouraging a mix of practitioners, graduate students, new faculty and established researchers to participate.

The accepted papers will be made available to the participants in advance and discussants will be assigned to each paper. The morning session will include an introduction to the workshop objectives, followed by a working session where the discussions will be based on the material provided by the participants. In the afternoon, we will focus on the broad picture resulted, highlighting strengths and limitations of the material presented. We will close the day with a session dedicated to outlining a list of issues that need to be addressed by future research in the area.

4   Organizers

Alexander Boden has a background in Cultural Anthropology and has received his PhD in Information Systems working at the intersection of HCI/CSCW and Software Engineering. He is currently working as a post doc researcher at the University of Siegen and is interested in topics such as supporting the appropriation of digital fabrication technologies by non-professionals, and designing support systems for distributed and co-located communities.

Gabriela Avram is lecturer in Digital Media and Interaction Design and senior researcher at the Interaction Design Centre at the University of Limerick in Ireland. Building on a CSCW and Knowledge Management background, her research currently focuses on mobile and local uses of Social Media, urban communities and facilitating technology adoption. She has an active involvement in the hackerspaces community in Ireland, as well as in urban gardening and biodiversity groups.

Irene Posch is a lecturer and researcher with a background in Computer Science and Media, and active member of the FabLab community. She previously worked on making technology accessible in interactive experiences and exhibitions. Her current research focus lies on the integration of current technological development into the fields of art and craft as well as DIY culture and how this can be achieved in an aesthetic and personal fulfilling way.

Volkmar Pipek is a Professor with the Institute for Information Systems at the University of Siegen, Germany, and chairs the board of trustees of the International Institute for Socio-Informatics (IISI). His research focuses on arrangement and acquirement of cooperative software systems in organisations, questions about communication based knowledge management as well as support of communities.

Geraldine Fitzpatrick heads the Institute for Design and Assessment of Technology at the TU Vienna. Her research focuses on the intersection of social and computer sciences to support social interaction/collaboration, with a particular interest in the potential for new and emerging technologies such as mobile, wireless and sensor-based technologies to support social and community engagement, motivation and behaviour change.

Cultures of Participation in the Digital Age: Empowering End Users to Improve Their Quality of Life

David Díez[1], Anders I. Mørch[2], Antonio Piccinno[3], and Stefano Valtolina[4]

[1] Universidad Carlos III de Madrid, Spain
ddiez@inf.uc3m.es
[2] University of Oslo, Norway
anders.morch@intermedia.uio.no
[3] Università degli Studi di Bari, Italy
antonio.piccinno@uniba.it
[4] Università degli Studi di Milano, Italy
valtolin@dico.unimi.it

Abstract. The International Workshop on Cultures of Participation in the Digital Age - Empowering End Users to Improve their Quality of Life (CoPDA) focuses on how ICT can have an impact on "quality of life", promoting new ways of design that allow us to face these challenges.. The workshop brings together contributions from researchers from a diverse range of interdisciplinary fields. The aim is to establish a community of researchers and practitioners and facilitate the production of a coherent body of work related to this area.

Keywords: cultures of participation, digital living, end-user development, meta-design, socio-technical systems.

1   Introduction

With the emergence of affordable computers and user interfaces that are increasingly becoming more usable, useful, and engaging, computing has reached well beyond its experimental days in engineering laboratories and into the homes and workplaces of ordinary people (non professional computer users). New concerns and new concepts come to the fore: digital literacy, digital divide, and digital living to name a few, it is difficult to frame all the fundamental challenges taking place in society (e.g.: education and learning, health, energy sustainability) without taking into account information and communication technology (ICT). Moreover, in this digital age we should think not only about efficiency and productivity, but also about how ICT can have an impact on the "quality of life:", promoting new ways of designing and using computers that allow us to face these challenges.

Cultures of participation (CP) is a key concept for understanding the transition, which means to provide end-users with the means to actively participate in problems that are personally meaningfully to them. An overall aim of CP is to apply collective knowledge to address major problems facing our societies today. Although CP is not a novelty at this point, its maturity is still far away, implying more research is needed. Examples of

Y. Dittrich et al. (Eds.): IS-EUD 2013, LNCS 7897, pp. 304–309, 2013.

successful cultures of participation are OSS development and Wiki-based environments. But even these systems have shortcomings, such as accumulation of irrelevant information, lack of one coherent voice, and under/over consideration of some aspects of a problem to be solved (e.g., usability aspects in free software). Therefore, a fundamental challenge for CPs should be to conceptualize and create socio-technical environments that not only support multiple stakeholders but also promise quality solutions and contributions oriented toward achieving common goals.

The purpose of the workshop is to explore conceptual, methodological, and technological aspects of cultures of participation in their capacity to impact the quality of life in the digital age. The following questions will be explored (but not limited to):

Conceptual

- How and to what extent can cultures of participation affect, positively or negatively, end users' quality of life?
- What are the strengths and weaknesses of cultures of participation for fostering collaborative problem-solving activities?
- What does it mean to do EUD in large community and mass collaboration?

Methodological

- What are the methods to employ to study the activities of cultures of participation?
- How to support different levels of participation (e.g. interested outsiders, collaborators, partial contributors, full contributors, meta-designers, etc.)?
- How to assess individual contributions in terms of contributing to a common goal?

Technological

- In what ways can EUD tools can support cultures of participation?
- What types of interactive environments can stimulate participation?
- What kind of technological platforms can support large community and mass collaboration EUD?

The workshop brings together researchers from a diverse range of interdisciplinary fields, such as human-computer interaction, software engineering, artificial intelligence, computer supported cooperative work and cognitive psychology. To facilitate cross-fertilization between of latest research in the above areas, the workshop has invited research posters in addition to academic papers.

2   Organization

Perspective participants were invited to submit an extended abstract and/or position paper up to 500 words. The submissions were peer-reviewed for their innovation, relevance to the workshop topics and their potential to generate interesting discussions. Accepted position papers will be posted on the workshop website and the most interesting proposals will be invited to submit full papers to a special issue of an international journal.

3   Organizers' Background

David Díez is Assistant Professor at the Computer Science and Engineering Department of Universidad Carlos III de Madrid. David Díez holds an MSc in Computer Science and Technology (2007) and a PhD Thesis in Computer Science (2009) from the Universidad Carlos III of Madrid. From 1998 to 2005, he worked as software engineering and project manager for different multinationals companies. Currently, he is member of the DEI –Interactive Systems research group. David's research interests are related to socio-technical systems design (STSD).

Anders Mørch is professor at InterMedia, University of Oslo, Norway. He received his PhD in informatics from the University of Oslo and an M.S. in computer science from the University of Colorado, Boulder. He developed educational software at NYNEX Science and Technology Center, New York. His research interests are technology-enhanced learning and social media, collaboration and learning in virtual worlds, end-user tailoring and evolutionary application development. Contact him at http://www.uv.uio.no/intermedia/english/people/aca/andersm/

Antonio Piccinno is Assistant Professor at the Computer Science Department of University of Bari "Aldo Moro". He is member of the Interaction, Visualization, Usability & UX (IVU) Lab. Since July 2001, after he got his laurea degree in Computer Science, he has been working at the Department of Computer Science of University of Bari, with different positions: research collaborator, fixed term researcher, lecturer, and finally as assistant professor. In March 2005 he got the PhD in Computer Science at the University of Bari. Antonio Piccinno's research interests are in Human-Computer Interaction, particularly on End-User Development, Visual Interactive Systems, Theory of Visual Languages, Adaptive Interfaces, Component-Based Software Development, Multimodal and Multimedia Interaction.

Stefano Valtolina is Assistant Professor at the Computer Science (DI) Department of Università degli Studi di Milano. He obtained his PhD in 'Informatics' from Università degli Studi di Milano and an MSc in Computer Science from the same university. His research interests include: Human-Computer Interaction (HCI), Creative Design, as well as studies in semantic, social and cultural aspects of information technologies with an emphasis on the application of this knowledge to interaction design. Stefano Valtolina's research activity is directed toward the study of aspects of Human Computer Interaction and Database Management investigating methods, interactive systems, and tools for Knowledge Management and Fruition.

4   Program Committee

Ignacio Aedo (Universidad Carlos III de Madrid, Spain)
Barbara Rita Barricelli (University of West London, UK)
Maria Francesca Costabile (Università degli Studi di Bari, Italy)
Paloma Diaz (Universidad Carlos III de Madrid, Spain)

Gerhard Fischer (University of Colorado at Boulder, USA)
Daniela Fogli (Università degli Studi di Brescia, Italy)
Elisa Giaccardi (Delft University of Technology, Netherlands)
Thomas Herrmann (Ruhr-University of Bochum, Germany)
Monica Maceli (Drexel University, USA)
Maristella Matera (Politecnico di Milano, Italy)
Volker Wulf (University of Siegen, Germany)

5   Accepted Papers

The full versions of the position papers accepted to the workshop are available to download as PDFs at http://homes.di.unimi.it/cslab/copda. The abstracts of the papers are summarized here:

Is More More or is Less More: Exploring Frames of Reference for Quality of Life in the Digital Age, by Gerhard Fischer from the University of Colorado at Boulder USA. The paper raises questions regarding how technology can and should support quality of life. He poses a dilemma between the increasing tendency of technology and our society to promote am ever increasing utilitarian lifestyle, always aiming for more (more publications, more apps, more Facebook friends, etc.), and on the other a society in which technology shields is from unwanted information and helps us to focus our lives on our interests, passions and dreams.

Using Participatory Observation in End-User Development Research: A Study of Knowledge Seeking and Contribution in an EUD Support Community. by Henri Korvela from Åbo Akademi, Finland. This paper proposes participatory observation as a method to study EUD in large communities. With this method the researcher is a full member of the community and therefore also has full access to information in the environments and can explain findings with first hand insight. There are both benefits and drawbacks associated with this approach, which will be discussed. It is argued benefits will outweigh shortcomings when a study is carefully designed.

HCI Research in Group Recommenders for Lifestyle Change, by Julian Koschwitz and Francesco Ricci from Free University of Bozen-Bolzano, Italy. Group recommender systems (GRS) aim at recommending the right items to a group of people in order to satisfy them as a whole, on the basis of individual preferences. In this paper, the authors aim at discussing the main aspects of the interaction design of a GRS such as a living space and a family home, which recommends activities and items for a healthy lifestyle. The authors considered an application that collects preferences from the group members in order to provide recommendations for shared activities, social entertainment as well as food.

Open Design and Medical Products: Irreconcilable Differences, or Natural Bedfellows? By Matt Dexter, Sheffield Hallam University, United Kingdom. This position paper highlights the complex nature of involving a community of people with Cystic Fibrosis during the design and development of medical products through open design strategies. Specifically the author describes, through a real test, important aspects of the open design such as: the role of the community of practitioners, the space in which they meet and the vehicle by which ideas are disseminated.

Learning from the Learners: MOOCs and Cultures of Participation, by Monica Maceli, Drexel University, USA. The author outlines as MOOCs (Massive Open Online Courses) provide conceptual challenges in designing the large-scale and experimental models of social education. Due to the character of such courses and the large number of students involved, their success relies on meta-design of social-technical systems based on cornerstone concepts such as: cultures of participation, mutual learning emergent behavior and reflection strategies.

A trajectory from tools to sustainable learning and community awareness, by John Carroll, The Pennsylvania State University, USA. More than 20 years of works has allowed the author to have a broad view of large-scale deliberation and ideation. From user interfaces toolkits to discussion forum tools, passing through the study of community awareness, ,the author highlight the existence of needs and opportunities for end-user tool development. Particularly, for technological platforms that support communities activities.

Towards "non-disposable" software architectures for participation, by Aurélien Bénel, Pascal Salembier, and Jean-Pierrer Cahier, Université de Technologie Troyes, France. Based on the knowledge acquired through the performance of different empirical studies in a wide span of both professionals and non-professional settings, author propose a software platform oriented to capitalize the experience gained on each design project. The paper presents a set of lessons related to the elicitation process and the semiotic nature of "topics".

Methods for Researching Cultures of Participation: The Role of Social Network Analysis and the Mixed Methods Approach, by Renate Andersen and Anders Mørch, University of Oslo, Norway. This paper argues for a "mixed methods approach" in empirical research of cultures of participation. They suggest combining (quantitative) social network analysis with (qualitative) interaction analysis in order for the former to provide a rationale for data selection of the latter. When the aim is to understand large groups (>100), selecting a small sample (<10), need to be combined with scientific techniques to argue for data reduction without loss of validity.

Digital Cultural Heritage and Living Labs, by Stefano Valtolina[1], Barbara Rita Barricelli[2], Michele Sciarabba[1,] [1]Università degli Studi di Milano, Italy and[2]University of West London, UK. This position paper aims to highlight the importance of a strict collaboration among public administrations, enterprises and citizens for preserving and promoting Cultural Heritage. The authors claim that information systems can no longer used only for archival and management purposes but for supporting collaborative and distributed participation in a continuous research process for fostering cultural and historical awareness in current and future generations of citizens. In this way the citizens can be actively involved as experts of the history and the culture of the places they grew up in and where they live.

Toward A Successful Culture of Participation in Emergency Management, by David Díez, Paloma Díaz, and Ignacio Aedo, Universidad Carlos III de Madrid, Spain. Emergency Management has gradually been evolving from a top-down model, focused on professionals and governmental organizations, to a network context, oriented to involve citizens and community members. Supporting this new reality requires exploring different technological artifacts that promotes the effective collaboration between citizens and official agencies. Crowdsourcing models, meta-design guidelines, co-design techniques, Web-bases platforms, and new interactive technologies are necessary mechanism to transform emergency management increasing the involvement of citizens.

Fostering Cultures of Participation through Composition of Service-Based Interactive Spaces, by Carmelo Ardito[1], Maria Francesca Costabile[1], Giuseppe Desolda[1], Rosa Lanzilotti[1], Maristella Matera[2], Antonio Piccinno[1], Matteo Picozzi[2,] [1]Università di Bari, Italy· [2]Politecnico di Milano, Italy. The paper presents an ongoing research aimed at investigating models, paradigms and technologies for supporting the lightweight construction of Personal Information Spaces (PISs) by users who are not professional developers. PISs are interactive work-spaces where people can manipulate the retrieved content to tailor it to their own personal needs and possibly create new content and services to be also shared with others. The proposed platform allows end users to retrieve contents from heterogeneous sources and use them to compose their PISs with the means to integrate data, services and tools, playing an active role in solving their every-day problems.

Supporting User-Designers Collaboration in Open-Source Software Projects, by Fabiana Pedreira Simões, Simone Diniz Junqueira Barbosa. Informatics Department, PUC-Rio. Based on the knowledge acquired in studying Open Source Software (OSS) projects, the authors explain the opportunity provided by OSS development practices at anyone, user or contributor, to report HCI-related bugs more efficiently. In fact, involving end-users through user-reported HCI incidents in OSS development is one potential approach to overcome HCI problems in OSS projects through which users can make useful contributions without major commitments of effort and learning.

Acknowledgment. We would like to thank the organizers of the IS-EUD 2013 conference, for giving us the opportunity to organize our workshop. We would also like to acknowledge the help and professional attitude of the Program Committee members for their reviews within a short deadline.

Author Index